The Entrepreneurial Personality

Is there such a thing as an 'entrepreneurial personality'? What makes someone an entrepreneur is a question that has intrigued the lay person and the scholar for many years, but can such a personality be identified or is it simply a socially constructed phenomenon? Elizabeth Chell pursues an alternative line of argument: to show that the entrepreneurial personality is, on the one hand, socially constructed, but on the other hand, presents consistency in behaviours, skills and competencies.

This second edition of the highly acclaimed *The Entrepreneurial Personality* revisits the topic and updates the evidence from a multi-disciplinary perspective. The book carefully weaves together the arguments and views from economists, sociologists and psychologists in order to develop a strong conceptual foundation. It discusses the inferences that these experts have made about the nature of entrepreneurs and the entrepreneurial process, and explores whether such evidence has enabled psychometricians to develop robust instruments for assessing the characteristics of entrepreneurs. The evidence for a range of purported traits is reviewed and the models and research designs of interested social scientists are explained and evaluated. Throughout, Chell laces her argument richly with a set of cases derived from primary and secondary sources.

This book presents a timely set of views on the entrepreneurial personality, and will be of great interest to academics in the fields of entrepreneurship, economics, management, applied psychology and sociology. This accessible text will also appeal to the interested general reader, as well as practitioners and consultants dealing with entrepreneurs in the field.

Elizabeth Chell has held chairs at the universities of Newcastle, UMIST/ University of Manchester and Southampton. She is a Fellow of the Royal Society for the Arts (RSA) and the British Academy of Management.

The Entrepreneurial Personality

A Social Construction

Second edition

Elizabeth Chell

Routledge
Taylor & Francis Group

LONDON AND NEW YORK

First published 2008 by Routledge
2 Park Square, Milton Park, Abingdon, Oxon, OX14 4RN

Simultaneously published in the USA and Canada
by Routledge
711 Third Avenue, New York, NY 10017
First issued in paperback 2013
*Routledge is an imprint of the Taylor & Francis Group,
an Informa business*

© 2008 Psychology Press

Typeset in Sabon by
RefineCatch Limited, Bungay, Suffolk

British Library Cataloguing in Publication Data
A catalogue record for this book is available from the British Library

Library of Congress Cataloging-in-Publication Data
Chell, Elizabeth.
    The entrepreneurial personality : a social construction /
Elizabeth Chell.—2nd ed.
        p. cm.
    Includes bibliographical references.
    ISBN 978-0-415-32809-8 (hardcover)
    ISBN 978-0-415-64750-2 (paperback)
    1. Entrepreneurship—Case studies.   2. Small business—Case studies.
I. Title.
    HB615.C62 2008
    658.4′21019–dc22   2007046127

ISBN 978–0–415–32809–8
ISBN 978-0-415-64750-2

Contents

List of tables   vii
List of figures   viii
Acknowledgements   ix

1   Who is an entrepreneur?   1

2   The economists' view of the entrepreneur   17

3   The socio-economic environment   51

4   The search for entrepreneurial traits: 'The Big Three'   81

5   New entrepreneurial traits   111

6   Interactionism and cognitive approaches to personality   142

7   Paradigms, methodology and the construction of the entrepreneurial personality   174

8   The heterogeneity of entrepreneurs: cases and colour   210

9   The entrepreneurial personality: the state of the art   244

Bibliography   269

Index   293

Tables

1.1	Disciplinary approaches to entrepreneurship compared	6
2.1	Timeline of economists in relation to developments in entrepreneurship	38
2.2	Roles identified for the entrepreneur by economists	47
4.1	Trait theory of entrepreneurship: summary of findings	107–109
5.1	The 'Big Five' based on Costa and McCrae's (1992) model of personality structure	123
6.1	Cognitive-affective units	149
6.2	A summary comparison between the CAPS and trait approaches	151
6.3	Potential heuristics and biases of entrepreneurs	159
6.4	Components of creative performance	167
6.5	Components of investment theory	169
7.1	Summary of key differences between nomothetic and ideographic assumptions of social science paradigms	177
7.2	Local/emergent versus elite/a priori approaches	183
7.3	The positioning of personality theories in respect of assumptions of social science	199
7.4	A comparison between social constructionist, social cognitive and trait approaches to understanding personality	201–202
8.1	Summary of practical criteria for judging the existence of entrepreneurial behaviour	211
8.2	Analysis of case study material using 'expert terms' derived from interdisciplinary review	215
9.1	Entrepreneur–opportunity interchange characteristics summarised	256

Figures

1.1 The entrepreneur and entrepreneurial process within the
    socio-economic environment   7
1.2 Organisation of the book   11
3.1 A social constructionist view of the socio-economic and
    political environment   58
6.1 Person and situation influences that shape entrepreneurial
    behaviour   147
6.2 Factors triggering entrepreneurial potential   155
6.3 Thinking outside the box   168
6.4 Solution to the problem in Figure 6.3   173
7.1 Dimensions of contrasting social science approaches to
    investigation   178
7.2 The four paradigms   180
7.3 Assumptions made in social science inquiry   181
9.1 The individual–opportunity interchange   253

Acknowledgements

I read recently of literary works that it is vogue to acknowledge just about everyone, including the lady who serves one reviving cups of cappuccino at the local café! Well, one can think of many 'life savers', but what I would not want to do is write a list that appeared in any sense disingenuous. The first edition of this book was published by Routledge in 1991 and so my acknowledgements go further back than the work that has gone into this second edition. There were, I would say, several significant events that led to the earlier edition: first my move to Salford University in 1979, where I met Jean Haworth and joined her in a small business research project, which resulted in my meeting James Curran and John Stanworth at one of the first UK-based Small Business Research Conferences. This started my professional interest in small firms; the annual conferences became the Institute for Small Business Affairs (ISBA), of which I was a founding member. In 1984, I attended one such conference based at Nottingham Trent, where a person, who shall be nameless, gave a poor account of the 'entrepreneurial personality'. Being young I was outraged and quit the conference. I spent the next day in the kitchen of the friends I was staying with and drafted out the paper 'The entrepreneurial personality: a few ghosts laid to rest?' published in 1985 in the *International Small Business Journal*. I therefore record a wholehearted vote of thanks to Jean, James, John and an unnamed individual for giving such impetus to my early career.

I should also like to thank anonymous referees who supported my application for research monies from the Economic and Social Research Council and the Nuffield Foundation, which enabled Jean Haworth and I to conduct the original interviews that formed the basis of the empirical work of the first edition of this book. I also thank Sally Brearley, Jean's one time research associate, who stimulated the thought of using neural networks methodology in the original edition of this book. Her help in this aspect of the book is much appreciated. Once I took my first chair at the University of Newcastle, UK, I expanded my knowledge of entrepreneurship and became involved in a number of projects. Several staff, research associates and doctoral students helped to stimulate my thinking, including Norman Jackson, Geoff Robson (who sadly died in a road accident), Ian Forster, Jane

Wheelock, Susan Baines, Luke Pittaway and Paul Tracey. Elsewhere, I should thank Helga Drummond, John Hayes, Christopher Allinson, Ray Oakey, Peter McKiernan, David Storey, Robert Blackburn, Rod Martin, Bengt Johannisson, Gerald Sweeney, Clive Woodcock (now sadly deceased), Mark Casson and many others for their unstinting support – in particular colleagues of the British Academy of Management, where I set up and ran a special interest group in Entrepreneurship for many years. Whilst at Southampton University, I would particularly like to thank Denise Baden for the library work she carried out that underpinned Chapters 4 and 5; it resulted in several piles of papers that I was subsequently to read! I would also like to thank Katerina Nicolopoulou, Mine Karatas-Ozkan and Juliet Cox for supporting other research endeavours that we were engaged in at this busy time. My lack of expertise in producing figures electronically means that I am indebted to Huang Qingan for carrying out this task for me with such diligence and care. As ever, it is invidious to name names, particularly as there is always the dreadful thought that one may have left someone out; I hope not, but there are certainly others who have had an impact on my career in one way or another!

The two most enjoyable aspects of my career have been without doubt meeting and talking to small business people and entrepreneurs, and writing. I would therefore like to express my gratitude to those many unnamed people who have helped to shape my thinking about small business behaviour and the entrepreneurial process. In particular, I would like to thank: Henri Strzelecki of Henri-Lloyd Ltd for giving permission to reprint an abbreviated version of the case published in the 1991 edition; Roger McKechnie for the insightful interview giving rise to the case study of Derwent Valley Foods and the Phileas Fogg brand; Simon Woodroffe for permission to publish an account of the early days of Yo! Sushi; and three anonymised small business owners who gave generously of their time to recount the various difficulties they experienced when establishing their business venture.

I should not forget the staff at Psychology Press, especially Sarah Gibson, Lucy Kennedy and Tara Stebnicky, for their considerable patience in waiting for this book to emerge. My gratitude is also extended to four reviewers used by Psychology Press – Brian Loasby, Andrew Burke and two anonymous reviewers all with different disciplinary perspectives – for their perceptive comments on the original draft manuscript. The revised draft was much improved as a consequence and any errors are mine entirely. Finally, thanks also to the University of Southampton for the eight months of research leave that enabled me to concentrate much of my time on completing the manuscript for this book.

Unlike the relatively young academic that I was in 1984, I am now wise enough to know that one never writes the definitive article or book, but I do hope that this volume will be of benefit to students of entrepreneurship wherever they are and generate many doctoral theses. It should be of interest to a wide range of people who may be approaching the subject from a particular disciplinary or business perspective – not only economics, sociology or psychology, but also management more broadly. When I commenced my career entrepreneurship was not on the curriculum; now I look forward to the further development of entrepreneurship theory and understanding, to which I hope I have made a contribution.

1   Who is an entrepreneur?

Introduction

Over the past decade entrepreneurship has been a 'hot topic'; the ability to 'get rich quick' fuelled the motivation of individuals, while at the corporate level the label 'fat cats' was attributed to Chief Executive Officers (CEOs) and heads of multinational corporations (MNCs). Moreover, governments exercised by national competitiveness, productivity and the state of the national economy saw entrepreneurship and innovation as a means to grow the national assets, increase the wealth of its citizens and enhance performance that would translate into the ability to wield political influence on the world stage. But entrepreneurship was not to be confined to the private sector; on the contrary, it was believed that a range of public sector services could become more entrepreneurial and thereby more efficient and effective. In this book we are concerned principally with private sector entrepreneurship and, in particular, nascent entrepreneurship. But we believe that the basic model of the entrepreneur and entrepreneurial process can be applied wherever the recognition and pursuit of opportunity for the purpose of value creation occurs. This may be in an established enterprise, a corporate business, a social enterprise or an innovative spin-out from the public sector. But, it is important to acknowledge the importance of the socio-political and economic context in which entrepreneurship is being exercised; this will be demonstrated theoretically and through case studies in subsequent chapters.

Definitions

The question 'who is an entrepreneur?' refers to an earlier controversy, with which the *cognoscenti* will be only too familiar (Carland *et al.*, 1988a; Gartner, 1989). My starting premise will be that 'who is an entrepreneur?' is not the only question, but it is nonetheless a legitimate question. It is a legitimate question because it is people who explore opportunities for the development of innovations, found businesses and do so from the recognition of a socio-economic problem, which they endeavour to resolve through the identification of creative solutions. In this book therefore the focus is on the individual *and* the process, because individuals are the source of action, and actions do not take place in a vacuum but in a context that in this case I delineate as being primarily socio-economic.

The earlier definitions of 'entrepreneur' and 'entrepreneurship' reflect the state of understanding at the time: the lack of theoretical underpinnings, of robust research evidence or of a depth of understanding. For example, Livesay (1982: 13) described it as 'an artistic activity'; the much quoted Kilby (1971: 1) likened the entrepreneur to a 'Heffalump' – a fictitious animal created by A. A. Milne in his famous children's book, *Winnie-the-Pooh*. Thus, if the entrepreneur is so elusive then it might be better to follow the advice of Harwood (1982: 92), who suggests 'Know them instead by the environmental variables that mould their behaviour and determine their range!' Others have suggested that entrepreneurship performs an economic function and that the term 'entrepreneur' defines an ideal type, thus senior business personnel in the private sector and staff in public sector jobs or operating non-market activities could exercise entrepreneurship (Cochran, 1969: 90; Schultz, 1975, 1980). Moreover, entrepreneurship is required to transform large corporations, through both radical and incremental innovations (Schon, 1965; Rothwell, 1975; Rothwell and Zegfeld, 1982; Kanter, 1983).

Most theorists do not hold out much hope of achieving agreement on definitions of entrepreneurship or the entrepreneur. However, they do agree on the importance of defining one's terms. For that reason I shall commence with the following definitions and make a series of observations:

1   Entrepreneurship is the *relentless* pursuit of opportunity without regard to resources currently controlled (Stevenson and Sahlman, 1989: 104).
2   Entrepreneurship is a process by which individuals – either on their own or inside organisations – pursue opportunities without regard to the resources currently controlled (Stevenson and Jarillo, 1990: 23).
3   Entrepreneurship is the process by which individuals pursue opportunities without regard to *alienable* resources they currently control (Hart *et al.*, 1995).
4   'One cannot and should not pursue opportunities without regard to available resources . . . the entrepreneur must take into consideration available resources as early as possible. [Further] . . . resources as well as opportunities do not have "objective" character. [Contrary to Stevenson] entrepreneurship is the ability to recognise opportunity while simultaneously figuring out whether there exists a possibility to tap the necessary resources to exploit it. . . . [Moreover] it is through pre-existing credit [financial, social or intellectual capital] that entrepreneurs are given access to resources . . . to exploit the opportunities they have recognised' (Kwiatkowski, 2004).
5   Entrepreneurship is the process of recognising and pursuing opportunities *with* regard to the alienable *and inalienable* resources currently controlled with a view to value creation (Chell, 2007a: 18).

The nature of entrepreneurship is such that no business venturer (of whatever complexion) has complete control over resources.[1] The exercise would otherwise be trivial. Moreover, resources should not be seen solely in economic terms, but as pre-existing states that may include human and social capital. Further, to behave entrepreneurially is to engage in a process that creates value. Both of these statements enable us to deal in a definition that encompasses the heterogeneity of entrepreneurs and entrepreneurial behaviour: it takes the practices to their lowest common denominator. It enables us to include social and not-for-profit enterprises, because we can argue that the value created is mixed and perceived differentially by various stakeholders. The fact that an enterprise increases employment in an area is viewed favourably by government bodies; the creation of some wealth enables a social enterprise to become sustainable; the production of goods such as food, health products and services, medical equipment, etc. is of considerable social worth despite the fact that the enterprise also produces wealth. The above definition also enables us to move away from 'business founding' as being the exemplary behaviour associated with the core of entrepreneurship (as stated by Gartner, 1989, and others). Business founding is too exclusive; it excludes, for example, social and community enterprise and corporate entrepreneurship.

The fifth definition also drops the term 'relentlessly' on the grounds that, whilst it could be interpreted as meaning 'persistently', there is also the connotation of mindlessness. We believe that entrepreneurs are very minded when they pursue opportunities; they test the opportunity and will in fact drop it if they come to believe that it is of less value than they originally thought (Chell *et al.*, 1991). Entrepreneurs are also well networked (Birley, 1985; Aldrich and Zimmer, 1986; Johannisson, 1987, 1995; Dubini and Aldrich, 1991; Chell and Baines, 2000); from this they glean social capital and the facility enabling them to develop an idea into an opportunity. However, all five definitions focus on the *process* of entrepreneurship; Stevenson argues that this is appropriate as it positions entrepreneurship within management. However, it leaves open the question: 'Am I the right person to engage in this process?'

Different approaches to entrepreneurship

It is facile to say that there are different approaches to entrepreneurship based on the disciplinary root from which the approach has emanated. Within the disciplines of economics, sociology and psychology there are different approaches, some of which have emerged as entrepreneurship, innovation, management or business. Some literature streams generated from particular disciplinary bases have little in common other than the umbrella term 'entrepreneurship', 'innovation' or a related term, and there is unhelpfully little cross-referencing. In this volume I have specifically pursued an interdisciplinary approach, drawing on the base social science disciplines, pulling ideas together where it is possible to create a synthesis, critiquing what I believe to be inadequate and generating what I hope will be cogent and coherent theory and insights into the nature of entrepreneurs and the entrepreneurial process.

People live out their lives within a social environment, which means, broadly speaking, that their actions and behaviours are interconnected through a socially constructed framework of social norms, rules and responsibilities that are further constrained within economic, political and legal systems of rules and regulation. The social constructionist approach seeks to understand in a holistic way how people behave in particular circumstances and to glean insights into their behaviour. This approach contrasts markedly with economic and psychological approaches, in particular trait psychology. A cogent reason for adopting this approach is as a basis for critiquing positivist approaches to understanding a phenomenon, in this case entrepreneurial behaviour. Social constructionism emphasises the subjective, phenomenal experiences of each person, based on the truism that one can never experience another person's sensations or the contents of their mind. Hence, in that sense each person's experience of an event is unique. Thus, through communication we learn what another person is sensing and perceiving relatively (Hayek, 1952). Thus, when we talk about other persons, we must base our judgement on the outward manifestations of their persona, which is based on perception and interpretation. Psychologists infer dispositional tendencies based on the categorisation of behaviours that appear similar to, and different from, other types of behaviour. Again, there is no absolute; differences and similarities are relative.

Economists are concerned with decisions that are relevant to resource allocation, which lead to particular economic outcomes, such as the performance of firms, industries and countries. Generally, economists have not been concerned with individual entrepreneurs. However, that has not prevented certain economists from inferring and attributing specific personality characteristics to them (e.g. Schumpeter, 1934; Casson, 1982).

The focus by psychologists on 'individual differences' has necessitated that they identify and measure 'traits': that is, psychological descriptors that are assumed to be part of the psychological make-up of individuals that *cause* them to be disposed to behave in particular ways. The assumption of causation enables psychologists to predict the likelihood of certain kinds of behavioural outcomes. Whilst this traditional approach to individual difference research predominates in psychology, it has not gone unchallenged (Mischel, 1968, 1973) and the implications are elaborated for understanding the entrepreneur (Chell, 1985a). Further, social constructionists have questioned what they term 'this "essentialist" approach' (Burr, 1995). To identify the essence of something is to distil that which is a necessary component without which the 'thing' would cease to be that particular class of thing. Applying this concept to personality suggests that each person's personality comprises such essential components; one problem is that this is a very static view that does not permit change or development. Moreover, any 'essence' must be inferred; it cannot be viewed and as such is a theoretical construct. Further, taking the observer's perspective, it is clear that if people are to understand each other then an interpretation must be placed on their behaviour. Psychologists take this a step further by means of classification. The classification of behaviour into trait terms assumes interpretation and analysis but it merely permits the prediction of probable behaviours linked to the trait term from a sample taken randomly from a given population. It does *not* allow the prediction of a specific behaviour by a particular person who is deemed, through analysis, to have that particular trait on a particular occasion. The traditional trait view went further and attempted to assert a chemical basis to the trait. An attempt has been made to resurrect this view by psychologists who hold that people are 'hard-wired' (Nicholson, 1998). This retreads a philosophical, but not less real, problem created when psychologists attempt to claim *correspondence* between psychological traits that classify observed and interpreted physical behaviour and an underlying neural, genetic or chemical order (Hayek, 1952). However, in a later article, Nicholson argues that such linkage would be simplistic (Nicholson, 2005a: 400–401). Table 1.1 summarises some of the key differences between these approaches, which will be pursued in greater depth in subsequent chapters.

Interdisciplinarity

Economists have for decades developed entrepreneurship theory and deduced from theory the personality and/or behavioural characteristics (Schumpeter, 1934; Penrose, 1959; Casson, 1982; Witt, 1998, 1999). However, economists tend not to develop entrepreneurship theory by melding together several relevant literature streams. There are, arguably, other theoretical perspectives that do so, for example population ecology, which includes organisation theory, strategy and transaction cost economics (Brittain and Freeman, 1980) and organisational births and deaths, strategic issues concerned with survival and adaptation, competition and technological innovation (Carroll and Delacroix, 1982; Tushman and Anderson, 1986). Human capital theory identifies human capital (such as experience, expertise/ability, learning and training, knowledge and skills) as just one type of resource that affects firm or venture performance, along with financial, physical, technological/technical, social and organisational capitals (Davidsson, 2004). This theory moves away from the idea of explaining enterprise performance through the performance of one individual and attempts to encapsulate all human and other capitals within the organisation that are deemed relevant to performance outcomes. Socio-cultural theories also are interdisciplinary as they focus on organisational, sociological, ideological and economic issues that affect enterprise performance (Weber, 1930; Cochran, 1965; Alexander, 1967; see Low and MacMillan, 1988). Hence, within the interdisciplinary approach a particular theoretical perspective is assumed. In this

Table 1.1 Disciplinary approaches to entrepreneurship compared

Economics	Sociology	Psychology
Equilibrium theory assumes a model of economic behaviour in which decisions are made to allocate resources in such a way as to ensure that the supply of a product or service meets demand.	*Structuration theory* assumes that behaviour is influenced (or determined) through social rules, norms and responsibilities, which give meaning, legitimacy and power to the agent. However, such behaviour is constrained at each level in the socio-economic system through economic, political and legal rules and regulation.	*Trait psychology* assumes that there is an 'internal' structure to personality. This structure can be boiled down to five broad traits. The mix and strength of these determine the overall persona.
Where perfect information is assumed, there is no function for the entrepreneur to perform.		*Specific traits* are also identified that measure particular attributes of the person. At this level, attempts have been made to identify traits that typify the entrepreneur.
Imperfect information distribution allows the *alert* individual (entrepreneur) to use that information in order to realise an opportunity that others are unaware of.	The entrepreneur must work within this system; as such, behaviour emerges from an interplay of agentic-structure interaction/interpretation.	Trait psychology assumes that a trait is a relatively stable and enduring characteristic that will strongly influence behaviour. It should therefore be possible, if the correct trait is identified, to predict the behaviour of a sample of entrepreneurs. Trait psychology cannot predict behaviour in particular instances, but can predict the likelihood of a behaviour, given the trait. Alternatives to traits are person constructs, skills, strategies and plans.
Radical innovation theory, however, assumes the creation of a new product or service that creates disequilibrium.	*Social constructionism* assumes that each agentic decision-maker is unique and that a holistic view should be taken of behaviour and context. Social constructionists critique positivism and trait theory as being 'essentialist'.	

volume we adopt a social constructionist approach to theorising about the entrepreneur and entrepreneurial process (see Figure 1.1). By taking an interdisciplinary approach, greater depth and breadth of theory can be developed (Shane, 2003).

The entrepreneur and the entrepreneurial process

Two key questions are at the heart of this book:

1   Does it make sense to suggest that a profile of person characteristics could be identified that would make it more likely that the incumbent would become an entrepreneur?

2   Are there personality profiles that make it more likely that the incumbent would be able to identify entrepreneurial opportunities more often and more successfully that would lead to innovative outcomes (and not simply business founding)?

Figure 1.1 presents a general model of the entrepreneur and entrepreneurial process embedded within the socio-economic environment, comprising a system of rules that regulate, control and variously influence the agent's behaviour. In Chapter 3, how this socio-economic system works at the macro-, meso- and micro-levels will be explicated further. The link between environment and agent is information that is perceived, ignored, absorbed and interpreted by agents going about their business. The agent or person comprises a history (suggested but as yet unspecified), human capital and generic person constructs (which psychologists would normally refer to as traits, as discussed further in Chapters 4 and 5). The model suggests that socio-economic situations are construed by the agent qua entrepreneur assuming an entrepreneurial function as problems and/or opportunities; the process involves recognition, development and exploitation undergone with a view to creating value. The process has temporal and spatial aspects to it and will involve various action and operational strategies and decisions taken in an attempt to achieve desired ends. These (entrepreneurial) outcomes

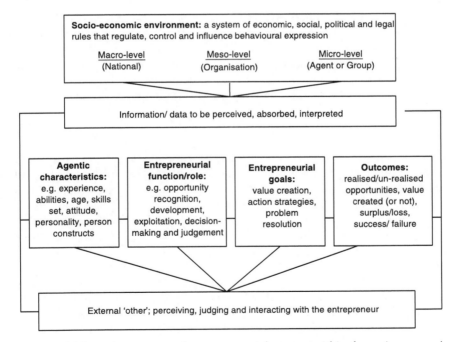

Figure 1.1 The entrepreneur and entrepreneurial process within the socio-economic environment.

include realised (or unrealised) opportunities, value creation (or not), the generation of a surplus or loss (wealth or debt) and success or failure (Chapter 8 presents case studies that exemplify this process). The process and outcomes that are produced are evaluated by other parties; these people are likely to be significant others who are supportive of the venture or even threatened by it, as in the case of competitors. They will judge whether the results are a success or failure, although entrepreneurs may also put themselves in positions whereby they can influence such judgements. The feedback loops in the model represent the potential for learning and adjustments to further activity.

Links between the entrepreneurial process and outcomes

The above discussion highlights a further issue: the problem of tying entrepreneurial behaviour exclusively to venture creation – entrepreneurs may be arbitrageurs, license technology and collect royalties, loan property and collect rent. The founding of a firm, which is what Gartner alternatively means by venture creation, is neither necessary nor sufficient (Gartner *et al.*, 1992), though from an economic perspective it is important to clarify under what conditions an individual might organise resources within the administrative wrapper of a firm (Penrose, 1959; Witt, 1998; Casson, 2005). However, the problem of linking entrepreneurship exclusively to business founding can be avoided (as I have argued above) by focusing on value creation – where value may refer to wealth, profit, rent or social value (social housing, medical advances, community enterprises), and so forth. It is clear from this brief overview that to understand the link between process and outcomes, theoretical perspectives from economics and business are important. I have therefore provided a foundation to this understanding in Chapter 2.

Typologies

Entrepreneurship researchers have tended to view entrepreneurs and small business owners as heterogeneous. This has lent support to the supposition of social constructionists, that no two entrepreneurs and their circumstances are alike. On the other hand, it has also led to the idea that one might devise a classification of different types of entrepreneur (Hoy and Carland, 1983; Timmons *et al.*, 1985; Haworth, 1988; Chell *et al.*, 1991). However, there is still room for debate as to how one might go about this task, and how one might distinguish between entrepreneurial 'types' and bureaucrats or indeed managers within corporations as opposed to small firms. The early work of Smith (1967) distinguished between 'craftsmen' and 'opportunists'. Hornaday (1990), in contrast, suggested that 'craftsmen' practise a trade – and in our terms they are self-employed and are likely to comprise the petite bourgeoisie (Bechhofer and Elliott, 1981; see also Casson, 2005, on this point) – and could be distinguished from 'entrepreneurs' who pursued wealth creation and 'professional managers' who built organisations. This approach to typographical research was pursued further by Woo *et al.* (1991) and Miner *et al.* (1992). In this vein, Chell *et al.* (1991) distinguished between caretakers, professional managers, quasi-entrepreneurs and entrepreneurs on the basis of a set of explicit entrepreneurial behaviours. This study also separated out behaviours (which fit the criteria of entrepreneurship) and entrepreneurial performance, recognising that entrepreneurs do indeed occasionally fail to realise their goals. We also considered a longitudinal element to the behaviour over the course of part of their life cycle in which it appeared that some entrepreneurs ceased to behave entrepreneurially. This is consistent with Schumpeter's view that entrepreneurs are only such when they are engaged in entrepreneurial acts, otherwise they become managers of their enterprise (Schumpeter, 1934). It also supports the view that entrepreneurial behaviours may be learnt and perhaps unlearnt during the life course.

Other classifications include: nascent entrepreneurs (Aldrich, 1999: 77), where the individual is demonstrably giving 'serious thought to the new business'; 'novice entrepreneurs', defined as 'those individuals with no prior experience of founding a business'; 'habitual entrepreneurs', defined as those 'founders [that] had established at least one other business prior to the start-up of the current new independent venture' (Birley and Westhead, 1993: 40); serial entrepreneurs who found, disengage and establish a further business; and portfolio entrepreneurs who retain the businesses that they found, inherit or purchase. Westhead and Wright (1998, 1999) have identified differing characteristics and motivations of novice, serial and portfolio entrepreneurs. In a more recent study, Westhead *et al.* (2005) have shown some further differences between these three types based on analysis of their stock of experience, information search behaviour and opportunity recognition. Whilst the research is preliminary, it showed some interesting differences in the expression of entrepreneurial behaviour between the three types.

Jenkins and Johnson (1997) took a somewhat different approach to the above; distinguishing between entrepreneurs and non-entrepreneurs, entrepreneurial intentions and outcomes, they made voluntaristic (as opposed to deterministic) assumptions and intentional behaviour a central part of their analysis. They then examined the relationship between intentions and outcomes. Thus, based on the work of Carland *et al.* (1984), they suggest that:

> [E]ntrepreneurial intentions are inferred where the owner-manager has an explicit desire to increase ... performance of the business; entrepreneurial outcomes are inferred where the entrepreneurial venture has achieved consistent growth in sales and profit ... over a five year period. Non-entrepreneurial intentions are inferred where the owner-manager has an explicit desire to stabilise the ... performance of the business.

Non-entrepreneurial outcomes are inferred where the business venture is stable . . . over a five year period.

(Jenkins and Johnson, 1997: 897)

This enabled the researchers to divide the sample of owner-managers (OMs) into four types according to their intentions and outcomes: those with entrepreneurial intentions but non-entrepreneurial outcomes were termed 'unrealised entrepreneurs'; those exhibiting entrepreneurial intentions and entrepreneurial outcomes were labelled 'realised entrepreneurs'; OMs revealing their non-entrepreneurial intentions and non-entrepreneurial outcomes were termed 'realised non-entrepreneurs'; and OMs with non-entrepreneurial intentions who demonstrated entrepreneurial outcomes were labelled 'emergent entrepreneurs' (ibid.: 898). These authors point out that the literature tends to assume that entrepreneurial strategies are realised rather than unrealised or emergent.[2] One point of contrast between these types was found to be that while 'unrealised entrepreneurs' had a coherent strategy ('talked the talk'), emergent entrepreneurs focused on internal operations such as efficiency and, while they had no real entrepreneurial aspirations, their efficiency made them successful. 'Realised entrepreneurs', on the other hand, focus on both a coherent strategy *and* internal aspects of business operations. 'Realised non-entrepreneurs' focus on personal outcomes but focus on both internal and external issues, whereas 'realised entrepreneurs' emphasise organisational outcomes. This study underscores the importance of considering entrepreneurial thinking and its relationship with entrepreneurial performance over time.

This analysis enables us to highlight further issues that have dogged the development of entrepreneurship theory for twenty years or more. First, there are those scholars who focus on intention (Carland *et al.*, 1984; Bird, 1988) and those who focus on what they perceive as a fundamental entrepreneurial behaviour – venture creation (Gartner, 1989). The controversy that erupted between Gartner and Carland *et al.* (1988b) centred on the dismissal by the former of the trait approach (and anything psychological). Certainly, it is true that in the 1980s decade the trait approach had made little apparent progress in either explaining or predicting entrepreneurial behaviour as numerous critics argued (Wortman, 1986; Low and MacMillan, 1988). However, this is *not* a sufficient reason for dismissing the role that psychology could play in theory development and explanation (Baum *et al.*, 2007). The trait view of personality is only one (albeit dominant) theory of personality, but there are other theoretical perspectives that: enable us to identify aspects of *character* that may play their part (Mischel, 1968, 1973); link character to context and their interaction (Chell, 1985a, 1985b; Chell *et al.*, 1991); link process to outcomes (Rausch *et al.*, 2005); and seek to relate cognition/cognitive style to entrepreneurial processes and outcomes (Allinson *et al.*, 2000; Alvarez and Busenitz, 2001; Sadler-Smith and Shefy, 2004).

Organisation of the book

Figure 1.2 presents the organisation of the book and its chapters and the links between them. This precise order and sequence does not have to be adhered to, but I would recommend that readers do start with Chapter 1. Some readers may wish to read Chapter 8 next before reading the theoretical chapters, and then reread Chapter 8 before moving on to the final chapter, which summarises and draws together the various threads. Below I present a brief overview of each chapter's contents, outlining some of the linkages between it and other chapters and the questions that they address.

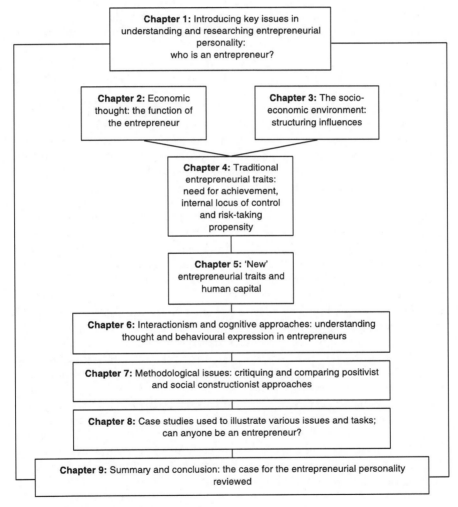

Figure 1.2 Organisation of the book.

In Chapter 2, I commence with a historical perspective on various economic approaches to entrepreneurship and the entrepreneur. In going through the different schools of thought, the points of contrast are drawn, as indeed is a brief history of ideas. This spans the three centuries through the identification of some key figures whose contributions to entrepreneurship theory have been considerable. I show how these economists have influenced theory development and how they have also contributed to an understanding of the psychology of the entrepreneur. Some of the crucial questions that this chapter addresses in respect of the role and function of the entrepreneur in an economy are:

- Can entrepreneurship be characterised as simple arbitrage: that is, buying cheap and selling dear? If not, under what conditions should an entrepreneur create a firm? Is it primarily a device for the organisation of resources?
- Where demand and supply are out of equilibrium, is the role of entrepreneur to allocate resources in order to bring about a state of equilibrium?
- Where there is no extant market (because the particular good has not been created) but there is a (potential) recognised need, is the role of entrepreneur to recognise and supply that need? Hence, is the behaviour characteristic of an entrepreneur to recognise such needs and develop them as opportunities or to cause conditions of disequilibrium by producing something entirely novel?

Chapter 3 focuses on the 'socio-economic environment' in which entrepreneurs make decisions, and seeks to understand how the theory of entrepreneur–environment interaction may be developed. In this chapter I draw on Giddens' structuration theory. I also consider the levels of interaction from macro-, meso- to micro-level; this comprises the impact of institutions and their practices on behaviour at the levels of the firm and the agent. I raise some of the issues that structuration theory implies and apply it to an understanding of entrepreneurship. At the meso-level I focus particularly on the firm and industry and seek to understand how, on the one hand, the socio-cultural environment shapes entrepreneurial behaviour, and, on the other hand, how competitive forces are taken to be a major influence in contemporary approaches to the theory of the firm and inherent entrepreneurial behaviour. Finally, I consider the micro-level socio-economic influences and return to structuration theory to consider further how the process of opportunity recognition, development and exploitation might be explained. There is a clear link between this chapter and Chapter 2 in that economic theory informs the institutional framework of financial, fiscal and generally economic rules and regulation that shapes the environment in which entrepreneurs function. Further, Chapter 3 explains the socio-economic process by which entrepreneurial behaviour is shaped and influenced at the various levels of an economy. Some questions that are addressed include:

- Is the role of entrepreneur purely economic or could it be described more accurately as a social role?
- Do institutional structures within society determine the rules and also what resources are available, and thus shape the role of entrepreneur? Hence, could anyone be an entrepreneur provided that they learned the rules and were able to gain access to appropriate resources?
- What role does the entrepreneur qua agent play within the socio-economy? Does s/he form embedded links within appropriate institutional structures to enable him/her to leverage resource and garner support for his/her vision or plan? Or, does s/he learn the 'scripts' (how to 'play the game') and iteratively engage with various aspects of the socio-economy in the formation and realisation of an opportunity?

Although Giddens' work has been extremely influential, the theory of agency is arguably underdeveloped. It is as if the institutional framework within which agents operate is overwhelmingly powerful in giving the rules, dictating the constraints and facilitating the conditions within which behaviour is socially and situationally determined. However, agents are theorised to have freedom to make choices. Beyond that, *how* the agent behaves and what this means for social interaction, social mores, social development and, in general, society is under-theorised. This leaves a gap in our understanding: what does it mean to be that agent, to be faced with those choices and to have the responsibility of taking one decision rather than another? Translated into entrepreneurship theory: is there sufficient evidence from psychology to contribute to our knowledge of agentic behaviour? This provides the link to Chapters 4 and 5. Thus, in Chapter 4 we commence this sifting procedure. Three personality traits are considered that have dominated thinking about the nature of entrepreneurs: the 'need for achievement', 'internal locus of control' and 'propensity to take risks'. A fundamental issue for such work is its predictive capability; only by assessing nascent entrepreneurs (as opposed to established entrepreneurs) using these measures can we test whether such individuals have a greater propensity to engage in entrepreneurial acts such as opportunity recognition, formation and exploitation. Research design is often problematic, leading to conflicting results. The key question that this chapter addresses is:

- Is there any robust evidence to suggest that the traits of need for achievement (NAch), internal locus of control (LOC) and risk-taking propensity (Risk) are fundamental to the entrepreneurial persona?

In Chapter 5, I discuss initially the low confidence in personality theory that characterised the 1970s and 1980s (recounted in Chell *et al.*, 1991) and formed the basis of deep scepticism in respect of an entrepreneurial persona, although other ways of reconceptualising personality were being considered – work that was spearheaded by Mischel (1968, 1973), Hampson (1984, 1988) and others. Thus, in Chapters 5 and 6 this debate is addressed. In Chapter 5, specifically, I consider evidence for alternative traits to NAch, LOC and Risk. Now, researchers were testing for the possibility of a trait profile, as opposed to a single trait that would differentiate between entre-preneurs and non-entrepreneurs. New measures specific to the entrepreneur had been developed, in addition to extant general measures such as the Myers Briggs Type Indicator (MBTI). Encouragingly, some researchers have based their measures around developed theory, for example the proactive personality scale – proactivity and the taking of initiative is considered to be a key trait. Other key traits for which there would appear to be a strong theoretical rationale are 'opportunity recognition', 'self-efficacy', 'social competence' and 'intuition'. There is also evidence that some researchers felt the need to include other human capital variables, such as skills, abilities and attitudes. Key questions that this chapter addresses are:

- Is there evidence of an entrepreneurial profile?
- How robust is that evidence?
- Should more consideration be given to other human capital variables?

In Chapter 6, I return to the debate that promoted alternative methodolo-gies over that of the traditional trait approach. This enables us to recon-sider 'interactionism' and the so-called 'person–situation' debate. I revisit Mischel's work: the 'cognitive social learning person variables', the part played by situation in shaping behaviour and the argument that the focus should be on the person and not personality. Mischel's later work includes the CAPS (cognitive-affective-personality-system) model, which aims to identify a person's unique signature (behaviour in specifiable situations) that includes a combination of how they think and feel. Clearly this is complex work, but it serves to remind us of the often forgotten affective states that underpin behavioural expression. The next section of this chapter is devoted to an exposition of cognitive research, specifically as applied to entrepreneurial behaviour. It includes a consideration of cognitive heuristics, schema and biases that affect judgement and decision-making. The work has focused on entrepreneurial potential and the intention to act entrepreneur-ially, factors that influence the individual's belief that they can pursue an entrepreneurial course of action successfully and the rules of thumb used to help in decision-making. Further work examines counter-factual thinking, regret, commitment to decisions and risk perceptions. Another approach seeks to understand three aspects of the initial venturing decision: knowl-edge in respect of the venture's feasibility, propensity to act and various abilities to start the venture. Finally, other studies focus on why some people are able to recognise opportunities (whilst others cannot) and how they do so. Trial and error, counter-factual thinking and veridical perception are just some of the dimensions of cognitive capability identified by these researchers. Here is a rich seam of possibilities, but as yet it leaves several questions unanswered. The work in this chapter relates to some key behavioural aspects of the economic function of the entrepreneur explained in Chapter 1. It also serves to critique the trait approach and to consider the robustness of alternatives; in these respects it builds on the preceding two chapters. Further, it provides a bridge to Chapter 7, where cognitive constructivism is explained. The questions addressed in Chapter 6 include:

- How might entrepreneurial behaviour be theorised to include both person and situation (environment) aspects?
- What psychological theories exist that can contribute to our understanding of situated behaviour? At a lay level we understand that feelings matter, but how might they be accounted for in theories of entrepreneurial behaviour?
- Given that entrepreneurs must make judgemental decisions (see Chapter 2), how might we theorise about the thinking or cognitive aspects of entrepreneurial behaviour?

Having examined various theoretical approaches to entrepreneurship, drawing on different disciplines and their methodologies, I take a step back in Chapter 7 to examine the assumptions inherent in these paradigmatic positions. This enables us to consider how we come to know what we believe we know from, on the one hand, a positivist or realist perspective to, on the other hand, an interpretive or constructionist position. This chapter raises a number of fundamental questions within these spectra:

- How do we construct our reality?
- What is going on with and through the use of language?
- Is it also the case that we construct our notions of personality, and if so how might this work?

Finally I compare and contrast social constructionist, social cognitive and trait approaches to personality. This enables me to consider some of the interdisciplinary issues and also what is helpful in explaining behaviour, in particular as applied to the entrepreneurial personality and entrepreneurial process. This chapter identifies that there is more work to be done and many fruitful lines for further enquiry.

Chapter 8 adopts constructionism as a basis for considering the form of life known as entrepreneurship. Using the expert conclusions derived from research discussed in the preceding chapters, a set of behavioural descriptors is presented and applied to nine individuals who have founded business enterprises in differing industrial sectors and times during the twentieth century. Many of these cases are available in the public domain. A qualitative method of analysis is described in such a way that others may replicate it. The results distinguish between prototypical cases of superior entrepreneurial performance and non-entrepreneurs who fail to demonstrate the skills and behaviours appropriate to what is recognised as entrepreneurial.

Chapter 9 gathers and summarises the threads of argument and the key issues that have been identified in the preceding chapters. Here I revisit the interdisciplinary approach and look at possible ways of integration in order to produce a coherent model of the entrepreneurial process and the part played by the entrepreneur within it. In building this framework, from social constructionist, cognitive constructivist and trait theoretical perspectives, important issues concerning the entrepreneurial personality fall into place. Areas for further research and development, including methodology and multi-level analytical work, are discussed, including the important link between entrepreneurial and enterprise performance, types of entrepreneur and levels of entrepreneurial performance. Some practical and policy issues are highlighted, particularly education and training for entrepreneurship. Finally, I conclude that the book has contributed theoretically, methodologically and practically to the question 'who is an entrepreneur?' It has also demonstrated that, whilst anyone may engage in the process, not everyone can be an entrepreneur.

Notes

1 Here, I am excluding arbitrage.
2 With the exception of the Chell *et al.* (1991) study.

2 The economists' view of the entrepreneur

In the distant past, economists have not concerned themselves with entrepreneurship per se – with some notable exceptions. Such exceptions will be the focus of this chapter, as we attempt to bring a historical overview of the contribution of economic thought to the study of entrepreneurship to the present day. Essentially, economists are not concerned with personality or psychological aspects of entrepreneurship, although many in the ensuing pages do make allusions to the entrepreneur's personality and indeed their theoretical position may assume the attribution of particular qualities (Schumpeter, 1934; Casson, 1982, 2000; Kirzner, 1982a). They are concerned primarily with the role or function that an entrepreneur might play in an economy. Such a function has been interpreted in different ways according to whether the particular economist had in mind a dynamic or static view of the economy and whether the entrepreneur was perceived as a force of change. The historical context in which they were writing is important insofar as it is indicative of the issues that were preoccupying them at the time. There are several schools of thought that have emerged and I have chosen to label them according to country of origin. The earliest and most apt statement on the economic function of the entrepreneur came from France. Until the turn of the twentieth century, the British contributed little; at best they ignored the entrepreneur and at worst they confused his role with that of the capitalist. The German and Austrian schools added to the debate, with the Austrian school holding sway on present-day thinking, whilst the American school, developed after the Civil War, has made a sustained contribution to our understanding of entrepreneurship, arising from the seminal work of some notable 'émigrés' – Schumpeter being arguably the most well known. Given somewhat limited opportunities for the interchange of ideas, these schools developed their own characteristic approaches.

This chapter falls into two parts: a historical overview and a presentation of contemporary influences on economic thought. Within the historical perspective, there is no pretence at comprehensive coverage. At best, such fragments, as have been gleaned here, give clues to the variety of views held by economists over the centuries – views on the nature, but more particularly the function, of the entrepreneur in economic activity. The chapter concludes with an examination of contemporary economic thought. It reveals how current economic thought now recognises the importance of the role of the entrepreneur and the modifications in theory required to accommodate that. Further, there is continued interest in the psychology of the entrepreneur insofar as economists throughout the twentieth century have deduced psychological characteristics of entrepreneurs. This opens up the possibility of a combined approach, whether it is through psychological economics or economic psychology.

Historical perspective

The French school

It is generally accepted that the first economist to recognise the role of the entrepreneur was an Irishman, Richard Cantillon (1680–1734), who lived most of his life in France and died under mysterious circumstances in London.[1] He is claimed to be an important figure in the Physiocrats school of economics and a precursor of the Austrian school of economic thought (see below). In his *Essai* published posthumously in 1755, he described an early market economy, in which he distinguished between the role of land-owner, entrepreneur and hirelings. Indeed, this tendency to so identify the *dramatis personae* is one of the hallmarks of the classical economists. He suggested that the entrepreneur engages in exchanges for profit and that he is someone who exercises business judgement in the face of uncertainty – a fundamental feature of entrepreneurial behaviour that is evident in current literature (see, for example, Casson, 1995: 80).

Cantillon's entrepreneur is an arbitrageur or 'middleman' who operates in conditions of imperfect information. The supply of a good is known to the arbitrageur, as is the price that must be paid for it. It is then sold on in a market in which the arbitrageur must interpret demand correctly if s/he is to make a profit. The profit is the reward for bearing the risk associated with uncertain conditions. Hence, entrepreneurs are people who must interpret market forces, and *successful* entrepreneurs are those individuals who are able to make better judgements (forecasts) about the market. The market system is in disequilibrium due to incomplete information and society is characterised as disordered, less predictable and less stable than is the case for other classical economists (Pittaway, 2000).

Cantillon's analysis raises several issues, the resolution of which is critical to a contemporary understanding of the role of the entrepreneur. These issues are: the nature of risk and uncertainty facing the entrepreneur qua decision-maker; the respective roles of capitalist and entrepreneur in an economy; and the innovative function of the entrepreneur. Cantillon's position on these three critical issues was clear. The uncertainty facing the entrepreneur is of the 'unknowable' kind, by which it is presumed that the entrepreneur cannot calculate the risk with which s/he is faced in making a decision. Even if the entrepreneur were penniless, s/he does indeed risk something and that is the opportunity cost of pursuing an entrepreneurial venture rather than a safe occupation. The roles of capitalist and entrepreneur are separate. The role of Cantillon's entrepreneur is to be aware of the level of demand and supply, but s/he is not expected to create a demand and in that sense s/he is *not* an innovator.

Successive French economists developed further the concept of the entrepreneur. For example, Nicolas Baudeau (1730–1792) born in Amboise, a theologian and economist, undertook the first review of economists in France. He injected a sense of the entrepreneur as innovator. His idea was that of a person, possibly a farmer, but certainly in agriculture, who invents and applies new techniques to increase the harvest, may reduce his costs and thereby raise his profit (this notion was typical of the so-called 'Physiocrats'[2] at about this time). Certain qualities are needed in order to achieve this; these he identified as ability and intelligence. Through such characteristics, the entrepreneur is able to exert a degree of control over some economic events. Such analyses suggested that entrepreneurship was, by and large, concerned with the management and coordination of business activities.

Anne Robert Jaques Turgot, Baron de l'Aulhne (1727–1781), was arguably the leading French economist of his day, whose ideas surpassed those of the Physiocrats. He had a number of 'disciples' that included Abbé Morellet and the Marquis de Condorcet. He is also said to have had a deep influence on Adam Smith, who was living in France in the 1770s and with whom he was a close friend. Turgot, a contemporary of Baudeau's, elaborated upon the distinction between capitalist and entrepreneur and derived his observations from actual situations. This contrasted with another of his contemporaries – Francois Quesnay – whose economic philosophy was derived from abstract reasoning and the construction of models that were inconsistent with what was actually happening. The gist of Turgot's idea was that it is the capitalist who has the choice of how he invests his money. If the money is invested in land then he is a capitalist and a landowner. Whilst the capitalist, who is an entrepreneur, has the function of managing and developing a business, the entrepreneur in this scheme of things is thus distinguished by his labour (Barreto, 1989).

Jean-Baptiste Say (1767–1832) was born in Lyons to a family of textile merchants of Huguenot extraction. He was an ardent republican and served as a volunteer in 1792 to repulse the allied armies from France. His involvement with *laissez faire* economists, his journal editorship and his published work led to his pre-eminence and he was nominated to the Tribunate in 1779. It was in 1803 that he published his most famous work, *Treatise on Political Economy*, in which he outlined his infamous 'Law of Markets', which was restated by John Stuart Mill as 'supply creates its own demand'. However, the Treatise was proscribed by Napoleon and, disgusted, Say moved to Pas-de-Calais, where he set up a cotton factory and became exceedingly wealthy. However, he maintained his academic connections and in 1831 he was awarded the first chair in economics at Collège de France.

Say helped to popularise Cantillon's theory, but unlike Cantillon, according to Hébert and Link (1988), Say considered entrepreneurial activity as being virtually synonymous with management:

> [The entrepreneur] is called upon to estimate, with tolerable accuracy, the importance of the specific product, the probable amount of the demand, and the means of its production: at one time he must employ a great number of hands; at another, buy or order the raw material, collect labourers, find consumers, and give at all times a rigid attention to order and economy; in a word, he must possess the art of superintendence and administration.
>
> (Say, 1845, quoted in Hébert and Link, 1988: 38)

However, this may misrepresent Say's position. For example, Schumpeter (1961) suggests that Say was the first to afford the entrepreneur a definite position in the economic process. This was to recognise that the role of the entrepreneur is to 'combine the factors of production into a producing organism' (Schumpeter, 1961: 555). But he did not think that Say's formulation went far enough. It is one thing to combine the factors of production in a firm by taking, as it were, a 'formula approach' (a coordinator) and quite another to reorganise such factors in an entirely novel way. Thus, according to Schumpeter, it would appear that the problem with Say's formulation is that it detracts attention from a key role of the entrepreneur as a force of change in a dynamic economy.

Say (1821) also suggested that the entrepreneur is at the heart of the production system, acting as an intermediary between production agents. He distinguished between: scientific knowledge of the product; entrepreneurial industry – the application of knowledge to useful purpose; and productive industry – the manufacture of the item by manual labour. As was the case for Cantillon, the actions taken involve operating in uncertain conditions, that is, an uncertain market, which required the entrepreneur to exercise judgement. Profit is the reward for bearing risk when the judgement and market sense are correct. Hence, the qualities of the entrepreneur that are needed, according to Say's analysis, are sound judgement, good market sense and the ability to understand how to meet market needs. Say's entrepreneur operated within an equilibrium process; his judgement is confined within that process and does not extend beyond it to the discovery of new processes. His or her income is not so much profit, but wages as a payment for the scarcity of his or her labour (Hébert and Link, 1988: 31).

The British school

The development of the concept of 'entrepreneur' by the French economists progressed in a variety of directions in a less than strict evolutionary sense. The entrepreneur as such did not feature prominently in the writings of the British economists during the early eighteenth century. The British school was led by the most eminent economist Adam Smith (1723–1790), a Scot born in Kirkcaldy, who attended Oxford University on a scholarship at the age of 17. In 1751 at the age of 28 he became Professor of Logic at Glasgow University and the following year took the chair in moral philosophy. He was a quiet solitary individual, a bachelor who for the most part lived with his mother. However, he did spend two years in Paris, where he met the French Physiocrats and several luminaries of the day. In 1776, his seminal work, *An Inquiry into the Nature and Causes of the Wealth of Nations*, was published. For the first time, here was a treatise that did not deal with the class structure or espouse the interests of a particular class; Smith was concerned with the wealth of all, that is, the goods that all people consume. This was a radical philosophy no longer concerned with the wealth of kings, merchants or guilds. Central to this work was his explanation of how self-interest was a driver of the economy and that the market where people 'truck, barter and exchange' is at its heart.

However, as regards entrepreneurship, the function of entrepreneur was conflated with that of the capitalist; profits were regarded solely as a reward for risking capital. The logic of Smith's argument is clear when it is understood that he was concerned to identify the motives and conditions for the creation of wealth; one such motive being *self-interest*[3] within the context of free trade, competition and choice. Smith's answer to the question 'why should a person employ others if no personal benefit is to accrue for so doing?' was unequivocal. Not only might the manufacturer expect to make a profit from his undertaking, but the profit might be expected to bear some relation to the extent of his investment:

> He could have no interest to employ them, unless he expected from the sale of their work something more than what was sufficient to replace his stock to him; and he could have no interest to employ a great stock rather than a small one, unless his profits were to bear some proportion to the extent of his stock.
>
> (Smith, 1976: 42)

The profits, which accrue to the entrepreneur ('undertaker' or 'projector' as they were then called), are not a form of wage arising from the execution of directorial duties; they are a consequence of the level of investment made. In this way, Smith equated the function of the entrepreneur with that of the capitalist. However, there is a lack of clarity about Smith's treatment of the entrepreneur; according to Hébert and Link (1988: 37), he viewed the entrepreneur as either a 'menace or a boon', thus leaving the concept rather muddled!

Amongst the many people whom Adam Smith's work influenced was David Ricardo (1772–1823), born in London of a Portuguese Jewish family. At 14 he joined his father in the London Stock Exchange, where he learnt about the workings of such financial institutions. He wrote his first economics article aged 37 and became a highly influential classical economist. As a businessman he amassed a considerable fortune and at the age of 41 he retired, bought the estate of Gatcombe Park and set himself up as a country gentleman. He took a seat in Parliament in 1819, where he served until his death in 1823.

Apart from Adam Smith's influence, Ricardo was a contemporary and friend of Jeremy Bentham and Thomas Robert Malthus; he was also cognisant of the work of Say and Destutt de Tracy. However, to all intents and purposes Ricardo and his followers ignored the French tradition. Ricardo expounded the basics of the capitalist system, describing the effect of market forces on the movement of capital. The role of manufacturer is to invest his capital in the business according to demand for his products. If demand falls off then he may 'dismiss some of his workmen and cease to borrow from the bankers and moneyed men. The reverse will be the case where demand increases' (Ricardo, 1962: 49). In this passage the role of the capitalist is fundamental to the workings of the economy. The manufacturer is a capitalist insofar as he invests in his own business, over and above which his role is one of superintendence. The role of entrepreneur was effectively 'squeezed out' of such an analysis.

Jeremy Bentham (1748–1832) was, until relatively recently, underestimated for his economic writings (Stark, 1952) and is perhaps better known for his moral philosophy and influence on followers such as John Stuart Mill. He was born in London of a family whose members were dominated by the legal profession. Perhaps not surprisingly, after graduation from Queen's College, Oxford, in 1764 he went on to study law at Lincoln's Inn. He focused thereafter on issues of legal reform. During his lifetime, there were major social, economic and political upheavals as a consequence of the Industrial Revolution and the political situation in France and America. On his death, in London, he left a large estate that was used to finance the establishment of University College London, where his embalmed body resides in a chair in a corridor of the main building.

Bentham's source of inspiration was Adam Smith's *The Wealth of Nations* (1976), but like his contemporaries he did not tackle the issue of the nature of the entrepreneur. However, he did single out the role of talented individuals, whose imagination and inventiveness have been responsible for the progress of nations. He believed that innovation is the driving force behind the development of humankind and as such he saw the 'projector' or entrepreneur as an innovator. 'Projectors' depart from routine, discover new markets, find new sources of supply, improve existing products and lower the costs of production. Hébert and Link (1988: 43–44) point out that Bentham's view appeared to have a close affinity with that of Schumpeter, as indeed he identified four out of five 'new combinations' (see later section). Further, Bentham departed from Smith's view of the 'projector' and economic development quite starkly. Whereas Bentham saw the 'projector as an exceptional individual, Smith saw him as a 'common type'.

Bentham's most famous work, *Defence of Usury* (1787), argued how interest rate ceilings would discriminate against entrepreneurs taking risks in funding new projects. Usury laws tend to limit the amount of capital lent, keep away foreign money and cannot discriminate between good and bad projects. His theory of production was expounded more with an eye to the role of government. He singled out three key factors that impact upon production. These factors comprised: inclination (the will to produce wealth); the knowledge of how to produce it (in particular technical skill); and power over external things, especially capital and capital goods. He concluded that the Government could do little through legislation to affect inclination and knowledge, nor could it do anything about the scarcity of capital. He advocated a *laissez faire* approach.

A picture of the nineteenth-century mill owner as the Industrial Revolution spread throughout England can be detected in the writings of John Stuart Mill (1806–1873), although his major works covered political, social and moral agendas. He was arguably the greatest nineteenth-century British philosopher. His father, James, was a Scot, friend of Jeremy Bentham and intellectual leader of the British Radical party. It was not until their deaths that J. S. Mill expanded his work and developed the 'Philosophic Radicals'. In Book 1 of his *Principles of Political Economy*, J. S. Mill gave the impression of the entrepreneur as a passive capitalist:

> A manufacturer, for example, has one part of his capital in the form of buildings, fitted and destined for carrying on his branch of manufacture. Another part in the form of machinery. A third consists, if he be a spinner, of raw cotton, flax or wool ... Each capitalist has money, which he pays to his workpeople, and so enables them to supply themselves; he has also finished goods in his warehouses, by the sale of which he obtains more money, to employ in the same manner, as well as to replenish his stock of raw materials, to keep buildings and machinery in repair, and to replace them when worn out. His money and finished goods, however, are not wholly capital ... he employs part of the one, and of the proceeds of the other, in supplying his personal consumption and that of his family.
>
> (Mill, 1965: 55–56)

One of the concerns of the time, due to the rapid rise in the population, was how to achieve an increase in productivity. Mill (1965) identified the necessary attributes as being the greater energy of labour, superior skill, knowledge, intelligence and trustworthiness. Not everyone, according to Mill, was fitted to direct an industrial enterprise because they lacked the intelligence, but he thought that this could be improved by education.

Why was the British classical school of economics so limited in its contribution to entrepreneurship and so different to that of the French classical economists? Pittaway (2000: 37–38) suggests three reasons why the British school did not distinguish between the capitalist and the entrepreneur. First, 'entrepreneur' is a French word that has no real English equivalent; second, French law distinguished between the ownership of capital and the ownership of business; and third, the French approach was micro-economic, whilst the British conducted a macro-economic analysis. However, other reasons appear to be a preference for deterministic economic models, using mathematical techniques available at the time. This tendency was apparent in the neo-classical model where comparative static equilibrium models prevailed.

The British neo-classical approach took a micro-economic lens to the later development of economic thought. However, the unit of analysis was at the level of the firm (not the entrepreneur or business owner) and theories were based on attaining equilibrium between supply and demand, production and consumption. Thus, equilibrium models are concerned with changes in demand and supply of a good, with consequent price implications. To take a contemporary example, the supply of a new product, such as the mobile phone, initially was produced to meet a relatively low demand, as the high price of the new technology deterred consumers. When the demand for mobile phones increased substantially, the supply of this commodity was raised to meet the new demand. As more phones flooded the market, different suppliers competed, the price dropped and a new equilibrium between supply and demand was reached. The model is quite mechanistic; changes in the price of goods and output are not a matter of judgement. They can be predicted by the model. In this analysis entrepreneurship is irrelevant (Storey, 1982).

Neo-classical economic models assume that everyone has free access to all the information they require about demand and supply conditions and thus trivialises decision-taking. Typical neo-classical economists are Leon Walras, Alfred Marshall, J. B. Clark, M. Dobb and C. Tuttle. Barreto (1989) criticised these economists for allowing the entrepreneurial function to disappear. He suggests several reasons why this occurred: (a) the rise of the theory of the firm; (b) the production function within the firm assumed *rational choice* and *perfect information*, thus denying the very conditions in which entrepreneurial behaviour occurs; and (c) a mechanistic philosophy of the real world was assumed in which everything was assumed to have a cause and thereby to be possible of prediction. These very notions are challenged by economists such as G. L. S. Shackle (1979) – see below.

At the turn of the nineteenth century, the 'discovery process' that typified classical political economy gave way to the deterministic models of neo-classical writers – professional economists who applied mathematical reasoning to the development of their economic models. Alfred Marshall, who spanned the nineteenth and early twentieth centuries, was on the cusp of these changes. Alfred Marshall (1842–1924) was born in London and was a dominant figure in British economics. As a boy, Marshall was destined to join the clergy, but on entering St John's College, Cambridge, his capability in mathematics set the seal on his academic future and in 1868 he became a college lecturer in moral science; and in 1885 he took a chair in political economy at Cambridge, after appointments at Bristol and Oxford. Marshall not only injected mathematical rigour into micro-economic analysis, but also gave us many of the fundamental concepts of micro-economics, such as supply, demand, equilibrium, consumer surplus, price elasticity of demand, and so forth.

It is difficult to assess the extent to which Alfred Marshall was influenced by Charles Darwin's theory of evolution. He was concerned to make the discipline dynamic and not based around static models. As such, he espoused the language of evolutionary theory; in particular, his references to the survival of the fittest were pointedly applied to the rise and decline of businesses (see, for example, Marshall, 1920: 495). He identified two types of business owner: those who will open out new and improved methods of business and who are unable to avoid taking risks; and those who 'follow beaten tracks' and are given 'wages of superintendence'. To Marshall, business development requires more than mere superintendence of labour; it requires a thorough knowledge of the trade:

> He must have the power of forecasting . . . of seeing where there is an opportunity for supplying a new commodity that will meet a real want or improving the plan of producing an old commodity. He must be able to judge cautiously and undertake risks boldly; and he must . . . understand the materials and machinery used in his trade. [In addition, he must be] a natural leader of men.
>
> (Marshall, 1920: 248)

Marshall's undertaker is both alert and an effective manager:

> . . . the alert businessman strives so to modify his arrangements as to obtain better results with a given expenditure, or equal results with a less expenditure . . . He pushes the investment of capital in his business in each of several directions until what appears in his judgement to be the outer limit, or margin, of profitableness is reached; that is, until there seems to him no good reason for thinking that the gains resulting from any further investment in that particular direction would compensate him for his outlay.
>
> (ibid.: 295, 298–299)

Business ability is not a scarce resource insofar as everyone has a natural aptitude for it in the conduct of his or her life; it is non-specialised (unlike technical ability and skill) and is identified with the qualities of 'judgment, promptness, resource, carefulness and steadfastness of purpose' (ibid.: 503). Further, it would appear that Marshall was beginning to drive a wedge between the notion of capitalist and entrepreneur. In a revealing footnote he quotes Walker:

> [It is] no longer true that a man becomes an employer because he is a capitalist. Men command capital because they have the qualifications to profitably employ labour.
>
> (ibid.: 503)

He considered that the job of managing a profitable enterprise comprises two important elements: the mental strain in organising and devising new methods, and great anxiety and risk. Profits are the payment for such services and not merely for the job of superintending the business.

Marshall appears to regard the abilities of the successful businessman to be rare. Somewhat graphically, he states that:

> . . . it would be as wasteful if society were to give their work to inferior people who would undertake to do it more cheaply, as it would be to give a valuable diamond to be cut by a low waged but unskilled cutter.
>
> (ibid.: 553)

Marshall developed the concept of 'entrepreneur' relative to the usage of his predecessors, the classical economists, insofar as he thought of entrepreneurs as businessmen who emerged through the evolutionary process of survival of the fittest. However, he was more concerned with efficiency and, as such, organisation was identified as a fourth factor of production (B. Loasby, private communication). Whilst his entrepreneurs were innovative in the sense of devising new methods to reduce costs and therefore produce goods more efficiently, it was left to Schumpeter to develop this notion in a fuller sense. Loasby (1991: 16) is less kind to Marshall. He points out that Marshall 'associated (economic) development with evolution and co-ordination with equilibrium, and attempted to incorporate both equilibrium and evolution within a single body of analysis; but he failed'. Marshall's successors, Pigou and his most brilliant student Keynes, added little to the notion of entrepreneur.

The German school

How is the entrepreneur to be compensated for his activity? This was an issue addressed by the German school. The thinking here was predicated on the premise that if entrepreneurial talent is a scarce resource then profit could be regarded as a special kind of payment. In theory, Johann von

Thunen (1785–1850) distinguished between the return to the entrepreneur from that of the capitalist by emphasising a residual, which is the return to entrepreneurial risk – the risk that is uninsurable. He distinguished between the entrepreneur and manager of an undertaking by suggesting that it is the entrepreneur who takes the problems of the firm home with him. He is the one who has sleepless nights. For Thunen the entrepreneur is both a risk-taker and an innovator. The return thus comprises the gain or loss associated with an uninsurable risk and entrepreneurial ingenuity qua problem solver and innovator.

The issue of risk was extended by refinements suggested by Mangoldt (1824–1858). He put forward the now familiar distinction between producing goods to order or for the market so that he could illuminate the relationship between the nature of production and degree of risk. Thus, where a firm produces goods to order it reduces the risk entailed, whereas producing for the market is more speculative, given the twin market conditions of uncertain demand and unknown price. He also suggested that the longer the time to final sale, the greater the uncertainty; and, conversely, the shorter the time the less the uncertainty and, by definition, the less entrepreneurial.

Such a distinction may serve to differentiate types of entrepreneur: the former is the innovator or inventor, the development of whose product requires a long time scale; the latter is the 'opportunistic entrepreneur' who becomes aware of a change in taste and capitalises on that foreseen opportunity. He is nevertheless entrepreneurial in that he has to estimate likely demand, whereas the innovator or inventor must create a demand.

The German school[4] emerged in the nineteenth century led by Roscher (1817–1894), Hildebrand (1812–1878) and Knies (1821–1898). It was distinctly different to the classical school of Ricardo and Mill and identified more with the English historical school, which suggested that economic 'laws' are contingent upon their historical, social and institutional context; the method involved looking at economic life with the eye of a historian and sociologist. The German school tenets were challenged by the Austrian school, led by Carl Menger, although the historicists retained control of German economics chairs and extended their influence into America through the early American institutionalists.

The Austrian school

The Austrian school had a considerable influence on the development of the concept of entrepreneur, its originator being Carl Menger[5] (1840–1921).[6] According to Menger, entrepreneurial activity includes obtaining information about the economic situation. This is because it is the individual's awareness and understanding of the situation that give rise to economic change. The entrepreneur must make various calculations in order to ensure efficiency of the production process. There must be an act of will to bring about the transformation of higher order goods (e.g. wheat) into lower order goods (e.g. flour), for which there is a market demand and there must be supervision of the production plan. Throughout this process the entrepreneur faces uncertainty with regard to the quantity and quality of the final goods s/he can produce. Despite this very clear acknowledgement of the part played by uncertainty, Menger asserted that risk-bearing cannot be an essential function of the entrepreneur. In this regard he foreshadowed Schumpeter. However, Schumpeter stood Menger on his head, as Menger saw economic progress leading to entrepreneurship, whereas for Schumpeter it was the other way round: entrepreneurial activity led to economic development (Hébert and Link, 1988: 63).

Menger was also one of the precursors of the subjectivist theory of value of the early 1870s (Lachmann, 1990: 4). Along with Jevons and Walras, he published works on the marginalist theory of value, which revolutionised the way economists viewed value and price theory. Value now was seen to consist of the relationship between the active, evaluating mind and the object being valued. Moreover, different people would assign different values to the same object. This work, which became known as the theory of marginal utility, was profoundly influential in Europe and inspired the later works of Von Mises and Hayek.

Menger's contemporary, Leon Walras (1834–1910), is generally recognised as the founder of general equilibrium theory. His theory, however, was static, based on an elegantly constructed set of mathematical equations to represent the economic system and interdependence of its parts. He identified four factors of production: labour, landowner, capitalist and entrepreneur. The capitalist and entrepreneur, he suggested, have separate roles, with coordination and supervision being excluded from that of entrepreneur, as this is simply routine management rewarded by wages. Rather, the entrepreneur has an equilibrating role in an economy motivated by profitable opportunities, as s/he identifies them. However, in his static general equilibrium model, Walras introduced the concept of the 'zero-profit entrepreneur', thus eliminating the function in theory, although he clearly recognised the importance of the entrepreneur in practice.

Ludwig Von Mises (1881–1972) is identified with the 'Austrian revival'. Defining economics as the *study of human action*, he put forward the view that human action influences, and is influenced by, *the future* (Mises, 1949). Furthermore, he took subjectivism to a second stage by positing a means–end decision nexus, in which a person could continuously ponder their choice of means to attain a (given) end. This is a precursor of Shackle's subjectivist thought (see below). Ends lie in the future and it is necessary from time to time to consider whether particular ends are worth pursuing. Hence, economic decisions, like any other decisions, involve *making choices* and, in addition, *coping with future uncertainties*. However, his concept of 'entrepreneur' is all-embracing.

Indeed, Von Mises felt that Schumpeter had confused entrepreneurial activity with technological innovation.[7] The entrepreneur is a decision-taker; making decisions concerning innovative practices is only a part of his sphere of activity. Further, he contended that the profitability (or otherwise) of the enterprise was a consequence of such entrepreneurial acts; it was nothing to do with capitalism. His position on the issue of uncertainty was no different to that of Knight (see the next section). He was also a strong influence on the work of Kirzner.

During the twentieth century some key figures argued for the importance of entrepreneurship as a cornerstone of economic growth (Baumol, 1968), against a tide of economists who pursued the logic of an equilibrium system in which there was no place for the entrepreneur. Some were particularly controversial, for example Hayek (1899–1992). Friedrich August von Hayek was a central figure in twentieth-century economics. He was born in Vienna and served as an artillery officer in World War I, after which he took doctorates in law and economics from the University of Vienna. He spent a year in New York in 1923, and in 1927 he became the first Director of the Austrian Institute for Business Cycle Research. He lectured at the London School of Economics in 1931, where he subsequently accepted the Tooke Chair. In 1950 he moved to the USA (the University of Chicago) and in 1962 returned to Europe, taking appointments at the universities of Freiberg and subsequently Salzburg. He was honoured with the 1974 Nobel Laureate in Economics.

Hayek (1937) asked whether economics could say anything about the real world and criticised equilibrium theory as a system of pure logic. He asserted that the assumptions in an equilibrium system are unrealistic. It assumes: (a) the simultaneous and independent action of economic agents; (b) that those actions arise in the same external circumstances; (c) that there is compatibility between individual agents' plans; (d) a confusion between facts of the situation (which could be verified) and subjective choice, i.e. plans based on a subjective inference; and (e) correct foresight – in order to achieve equilibrium, suppliers must be able to *accurately* predict demand. This was a problem of coordination and the occurrence of coordination failures in market economics. For example, builders (of houses) must know the plans of purchasers in advance of formulating their own plans. However, people only ever have partial knowledge and in practice the cost of obtaining information that would enable such a system to reach equilibrium would be prohibitively costly (Casson, 1982). There is thus a need to distinguish between theory and empirical reality, and to shift the focus. Also, in practice, suppliers and consumers must make adjustments. Hayek was concerned with the circumstances that would result in such coordination failures, not entrepreneurship. It is one thing to achieve coordination at a single point in time and quite another to do so over a time period. It is clear that this is a fundamental problem for the entrepreneur: of making decisions now in anticipation of decisions made by others – producers and consumers – in the future. Hayek argued that it is this time element that exacerbates investment decisions and leads to cumulative errors of judgement. At the time of decision, the error of judgement would be unknown, leading to a temporary 'boom'; however, once the mistake was realised adjustments would be made, leading to economic 'bust'. Hayek made many other contributions to theory; importantly, as with Menger and Mises, he shifted attention from objects of value to subjects that do the valuing. He was thus a 'subjectivist' and also a 'methodological individualist' because he believed that spontaneous economic order was a consequence of individual actions. His criticisms of equilibrium theory, however, were not only strident but they were also pursued by others.

Importantly, equilibrium theory can tell us nothing about changes in information and knowledge that have no theoretical correspondence or significance. Schumpeter's answer was to suggest radical innovations that rupture the established pattern of equilibrium, whereas Kirzner (1982b) separated the market process from the analysis of equilibrium and suggests that the entrepreneur is the person who is alert to gaps in this market process, and may act on the opportunities that they perceive have been overlooked by others. Loasby (1983) argues for a relaxation of the 'perfect knowledge' assumption, which would mean that different firms (managers or entrepreneurs) are likely to have different perceptions of situations and this would enable a better understanding of their behaviour. He argues that people behave like scientists; they have an implicit theory by which they interpret events and make predictions. Furthermore, entrepreneurs learn heuristically such that experience enables them to develop frameworks by which they make good interpretations, thus avoiding mistakes and the potential collapse of the nascent enterprise.

The American school

The American school began to emerge after the Civil War of 1861–1865, led by early proponents Amasa Walker and his son General Francis A. Walker. Amasa Walker (1799–1875), a representative to the United States Congress, was born in East Woodstock, Connecticut, moved to Massachusetts and entered commercial life and mercantile pursuits for a further fifteen years (Mick, 1940). In 1842 he took a lectureship in political economy at Oberlin College, Ohio, before entering politics and serving in various capacities until 1853. He then lectured at Harvard for a further seven years before re-entering politics in 1860. His son, Francis A. Walker (1840–1897) was born in Boston and graduated from Amherst College in 1860, where he studied law. He fought in the Civil War and rose to brevetted Brigadier General at the age of 24. He held a number of prestigious posts during his career, including Chief of the Government Bureau of Statistics, Director of the US Census at the age of 30, Professor of Political Economy at Yale (from 1872–1880), First President of the American Economic Association and, from 1881 to his death, President of the Massachusetts Institute of Technology.

Amasa Walker disassociated from what he viewed as confusion by the English economists. He recognised the role of the entrepreneur as a creator of wealth and, as such, it should be distinguished from that of the capitalist. His son followed this lead and suggested that the successful conduct of business requires exceptional abilities and opportunities. Successful entrepreneurs have the *power of foresight*, a facility for organisation and administration, unusual energy and leadership qualities, which are generally in short supply. Interestingly he distinguished between *four types of entrepreneur*: the rarely gifted person, those with high ordered talent, those who do reasonably well in business and the ne'er do wells. The characteristics he identified with each type are also of interest. The rarely gifted person has the power of foresight, is firm and resolute even in the face of disaster and is able to motivate and lead others. Persons with a high ordered talent have a natural mastery; they are wise, prompt and resolute. Those who do reasonably well in business tend to do so through diligence rather than flair or genius, whereas the ne'er do wells have perhaps misidentified their vocation and, consequently, they suffer mixed fortunes. This classification conjures up a variety of images of the personality characteristics of business owners and entrepreneurs.

Walker believed that profit is the return to the entrepreneur for his skill, ability or talent. This represented just one view of profit. A theory of profit, as Knight later pointed out, is fundamental to understanding risk and uncertainty (Knight, 1921). In stark contrast, John Bates Clark (1847–1938) put forward the notion of the profitless 'static state'. Clark was born and brought up in Providence, Rhode Island, and graduated from Amherst College, Massachusetts, at the age of 25. He then attended the University of Zurich and the University of Heidelberg (1872–1875), where he studied under Karl Knies of the German historical school, discussed above. Unsurprisingly, Clark's early writings reflect this German socialist background and showed him to be a critic of capitalism. However, he later became a leading supporter of the capitalist system and an opponent of the institutionalist school. On return to the USA he taught at various colleges, including his alma mater, and in 1895 he took a post at Columbia University.

Clark's theory assumed a static state, which itself was assumed to be the 'natural' state of things. The static state is free of all disturbances that progress causes. To realise the static state, five kinds of generic change have to be eliminated: population increase; capital increase; improving methods of production; change in the forms of industrial establishments; and the increase in wants of consumers. In this theoretical state of affairs the cost and selling price are always equal. There can be no profits beyond wages for the routine work of supervision. The prices of these goods are their 'natural price', that is, their 'static price'. Clark argued that profits must arise from a dynamic state. However, these profits are temporary, as the forces of competition are always at work to reduce them (Clark, 1907: 129ff). Static state theory has been criticised on two grounds: firstly, the idea that the static state is the 'natural' state; and, secondly, that it is change per se that is the cause of profit.

This relationship between profit and the assumption of risk was pursued by a contemporary of Clark – F. B. Hawley (1843–1929). In Hawley's distributive theory, profit is the reward to the entrepreneur for assuming risk. If there was no such inducement there would be no reason for the entrepreneur to embark on risky ventures. Hawley, however, did not distinguish between insurable and non-insurable risk. It was Knight who later attempted to reconcile these two theories on the grounds that uncertainty is fundamental to understanding profit, profit is bound up with economic change (because change is a condition of uncertainty) and profit is a result of risk, which cannot be measured.

Frank Hyneman Knight (1885–1972), founder of the Chicago School of Economics, was an important economist of the early twentieth century. Said to be eclectic, a deep thinker and at times belligerent, Knight is best known for his distinction between risk and uncertainty. Moreover, he contributed to the understanding of entrepreneurship in several ways. Knight (1921) argues that if a change is predictable the result will be neither loss nor profit. Only if the change and its consequences are unforeseen will there be a possibility of profit arising from that change. From this it may be concluded that it is *not* change per se but uncertainty that causes profit:

> Without change of some sort there would, it is true, be no profits, for if everything moved along in an absolutely uniform way, the future would be completely foreknown in the present and competition would certainly adjust things to the ideal state where all prices would equal costs.
>
> (Knight, 1921: 37)

The issues of risk and market uncertainty received considerable prominence at the turn of the century. Whilst for some (e.g. Hawley) a business transaction is carried out in conditions of uncertainty *à la* Cantillon, for others (e.g. Clark, Davenport and later Schumpeter) risk-bearing was not an entrepreneurial activity. Knight's objective, however, was to define the limits of the model of perfect competition. This lay the foundations not only to a critique of that model, but as a fore-runner to a system that reflected the reality of decision-taking in conditions of partial knowledge and information, in contrast to equilibrium systems that represented theoretical ideals. In his more elaborate theory of risk and uncertainty, he distinguished between changes in circumstances that are foreseeable (i.e. predictable) and the risks associated with them that are calculable (based on statistical probability), and changes that cannot be predicted. The former risks are insurable, whereas the latter are uninsurable. Thus risk is associated with future unknown outcomes, but whose probability distributions (i.e. the likelihood that any one outcome would occur) are known. Uncertain outcomes, he argued, occur randomly and there are no associated probabilities (i.e. decision rules) that would help the decision-maker.

His theory of profit related to non-insurable uncertainty to rapid economic change. This type of uncertainty and risk – uninsurable uncertainty – he suggests is associated with rapid economic change and entrepreneurial decision-making capability. He argued that in situations of risk it was possible for the entrepreneur in effect to assign a probability estimate to the likely occurrence of an event. In practice this would depend on the entrepreneur's judgement, whereas in cases of true uncertainty no such assignment can be made – the situation is unique. In such cases, all that can be done is to make a judgement – a best guess – based on experience. There is no sense in which the individual can calculate the probability that s/he is wrong. Hence, it is the entrepreneurs who are able to identify the risks and bear the uncertainty for which they receive an uncertain return.

A refinement of Knight's distinction suggests that there are three states of risk/uncertainty: risk in the sense of a probability distribution of possible outcomes that are calculable and known; uncertainty where the possible outcomes are capable of being listed but the probability distribution is unknown; and radical uncertainty where the possible outcomes are unknown and are not capable of being listed (Hébert and Link, 1988). However, Knight's distinction between a probable outcome and an uncertain outcome has been questioned on the grounds that from the stance of the entrepreneur the probable outcome is ultimately a subjective probability. On the other hand, it has also been argued that the entrepreneur's position where s/he is considering future outcomes is at best a subjective judgement in which possibilities are being weighed up; there can be no objective probabilities assigned to them (Shackle, 1979). The assignment of 'subjective probabilities' is indicative theoretically of rational choice; this view was criticised by Shackle on the grounds that such 'rationality' was grossly unreasonable (B. Loasby, private communication). Whilst the entrepreneur may have more *confidence* in his judgement in such cases, it does not obviate the fact that he is still operating in conditions of uncertainty. Furthermore, the judgement may, in practice, be based on no more than a whim or gut reaction.

Knight's theory of uncertainty helps to establish the boundary between the manager and the entrepreneur: a manager becomes an entrepreneur when the exercise of his/her judgement is liable to error and s/he assumes the responsibility for its correctness. Whilst s/he is prepared to take risks in an uncertain world, s/he is nonetheless a calculated risk-taker. Thus, Knight suggests that the characteristics possessed by individuals who are able to direct others in conditions of uncertainty are: knowledge and judgement, foresight, superior managerial ability and confidence in their judgement. Entrepreneurial income comprises two parts: a wage or rent element for his/her abilities and payment for uncertainty bearing. In other words, Knight's entrepreneur is able to make informed judgements and take decisions, having calculated the risk and borne the uncertainty concerning a business opportunity. The reward for doing so *successfully* is profit. Others who do not wish to take such risks settle for relatively secure employment.

Entrepreneurship as an endogenous force

All the theories of entrepreneurship outlined to this point assumed an entrepreneur who responded to an outside force that impacted upon the market system. Joseph Alois Schumpeter[8] (1883–1950), in contrast, suggested that the entrepreneur is a dynamic, proactive force – an endogenous factor. Indeed, arguably, Schumpeter's greatest recognised contribution is to the theory of entrepreneurship, for as an economist, like his contemporary Frank Knight, he was difficult to classify into a school of thought. Joseph Schumpeter was born of Austrian parents, studied economics and law at the University of Vienna, published his first book (*Theory of Economic Development*) at the age of 28 and in 1911 took the chair in economics at the University of Graz. He served as Minister of Finance in 1919, left Graz in 1921 and became president of a small banking house until 1924. In 1925 he moved to Bonn where he was professor until 1932. With the rise of Hitler, he left Europe and emigrated to America, where he accepted a permanent position at Harvard until his retirement in 1949.

Schumpeter (1934, 1943) is the architect of a theory of economic development in which the entrepreneur is central; the entrepreneur's role is to disturb the economic status quo through innovations. In this theoretical framework, the question is how capitalism creates and destroys existing structures. Schumpeter's answer is that economic development is a process defined by the carrying out of new combinations of factors of production. The entrepreneur innovates and thereby creates these 'new combinations'. Innovations may be of various sorts according to Schumpeter. They may result from: the creation of a new product or alteration in its quality; the development of a new method of production; the opening of a new market; the capture of a new source of supply; or a new organization of industry.

> Everyone is an entrepreneur only when he actually 'carries out new combinations,' and loses that character as soon as he has built up his business, when he settles down to running it as other people run their businesses.
>
> (Schumpeter, 1934: 78)

This kind of innovation assumes a depth of understanding of an industry, including technological and product market knowledge, and also leadership ability. The entrepreneur is the special person who can bring about such events. S/he is an innovator and a catalyst of *change* through the introduction of new technological products or processes. This contrasts with routine management and thus, for Schumpeter, not all business men or women are entrepreneurs. Typically an entrepreneur is the founder of a new firm rather than the manager employed by an established firm (Casson, 1982). More-over, the innovator is only an entrepreneur whilst engaged in the change or creative destruction process. As soon as production becomes routine s/he ceases to be an entrepreneur. The motive is one of profit.

Thus, in a stable economic environment, the entrepreneur identifies a possible innovation and estimates its advantage (i.e. likely profit). This opportunity is not open to others as they cannot anticipate the entrepreneur's vision. The launch of the new venture will come as a shock because the new possibilities that have been created present a threat to the viability of existing business. The greater the innovation and the greater the competitive advantage, the more likely it is that the innovation will devalue the extant industry's products and processes (i.e. the old combinations). Hence, this kind of entrepreneurship creates as it destroys, and destroys as it creates – thus it commences a cycle of creative destruction.

This cycle may be characterised like this. Having launched an innovation that is, for example, patent protected, the new business will enjoy a monopoly position for sufficient time to enable it to establish market share and make a profit. In contrast, the old industry producers lose market share as customers switch allegiance. Many of these firms will become non-viable. In order to survive, some firms will be stimulated to compete and create a new range of products or processes. Moreover, after a period of time, imitators will produce similar products that compete with the innovation. Thus, the pioneering enterprise plus imitators will create a boom. The demise of displaced firms plus the recognition of excess credit precipitate a recession in which entrepreneurs will have no secure basis for calculating the prospects for their new ideas; the slump provides stability in which such calculation is again possible. Thus, the recession will be overcome and the economy will stabilise around a new equilibrium. New ventures are again launched, starting the next cycle as such new disruptive innovations are released on to the market. An example of this type of innovation is the Dyson cyclone household cleaner.

Schumpeter's position was that entrepreneurial profits may be separated from the earnings of management. Profit is a residual, a surplus – a surplus that arises solely due to the economic development process described above, in which the innovative act of the entrepreneur is central. The size of the surplus is directly attributable to the entrepreneur's productivity. This productivity concerns the ability to create something so novel that it leaves existing industry standing and, whilst that industry is regrouping, market share is established. The successful innovation makes a surplus and as such the innovator (the entrepreneur) reaps his/her reward. In this way, Schumpeter arrived at the conclusion that profit is not a return to risk. Risk falls on the capitalist not the entrepreneur qua entrepreneur. However, Schumpeter ignores all forms of risk other than financial; he does not, for example, contemplate possible risk to reputation. Indeed, if we distinguish between risk and uncertainty (as did Knight), Schumpeter's entrepreneur carries out innovations under conditions of uncertainty (and absence of predictability); insofar as s/he invests time, effort and/or funds in the new venture s/he takes a risk, but this risk is not calculable. If s/he is wrong and the venture fails, the consequence is a loss of face and the opportunity cost of investing time and effort. If s/he succeeds, the reward (a profitable enterprise) is for her/his correct entrepreneurial judgement in the face of uncertainty.

Schumpeter's theory provides a useful concept of the entrepreneur as a catalyst of economic development that stands up well in the contemporary economic environment. His theory is to some degree inimical to conventional economic theory that requires a basis for prediction. However, in conditions of creative destruction, is it the case that there is Knightian uncertainty? Probably; Schumpeter's entrepreneurs operate in a dynamic world where knowledge is bounded, the future is unknown and uncertain and the entrepreneur must base his/her judgement on his/her best guess. At the point where an entrepreneurial decision is being made, Schumpeter's entrepreneurs appear to think and act intuitively. This is because creative destruction requires exceptional individuals with cognitive abilities that operate against fixed habits of thinking and routine behaviours. They have 'the ability to see an opportunity from a situation of limited knowledge' (Pittaway, 2000: 58). Furthermore, Schumpeter argues, they have the determination to succeed despite all personal and institutional obstacles. Hence, this analysis reminds us again that entrepreneurship is not only a role played out in an economy, but a way of thinking and feeling and the ability to make decisions in conditions of uncertainty.

Human capital theory

T. W. Schultz (1902–1998), like Knight, was a member of the Chicago School of Economics and is perhaps best remembered for his economics of agriculture and of the poor. He pioneered human capital theory, and underscored the fact that people are not capital goods or commodities. He criticised, and attempted to broaden, the concept of entrepreneurship, by suggesting that, in a dynamic economy, entrepreneurial behaviour may be manifested by people other than those in business. Such behaviour is a function of the demand, supply and value of their services. Hence entrepreneurial behaviour may be considered to be another form of capital. At any point in a person's life cycle s/he may, due to changes in economic circumstances, *become* entrepreneurial (Schultz, 1980). Entrepreneurial ability is the 'ability to reallocate their services in response to changes in the value of the work they do' (ibid.: 441). In this sense some educational activities can be considered to be entrepreneurial. It is the supply of entrepreneurial ability that is of economic value but has received scant consideration in the economic literature. Given that what they do has economic value, this value accrues to them as rent. Further, Schultz argues strongly that risk-bearing is not a unique attribute of the entrepreneur. Even in a static economy there is risk, but there are no entrepreneurs. He concludes that the bearing of risk does not distinguish between people who are entrepreneurs and those who are not. In essence, the entrepreneurial reward is solely for their ability and not as a consequence of their taking risks.

He argued that people (not simply businessmen) from all walks of life may face disequilibria and as such the essence of entrepreneurship is having the ability to deal with such conditions. He provided evidence to support his view that education developed an individual's ability to perceive and react to disequilibria. For example, in farming the entrepreneur can, through education, increase his/her understanding of new agricultural techniques and so gain a competitive advantage. The decision to reallocate resources rests on current information and expectations based on that information. This implies a need to keep constantly up to date. The more able the entrepreneur, the more efficient s/he is likely to be in acquiring and acting upon information. However, Schultz also believed that entrepreneurial ability is a scarce resource and that the market for it adheres to normal supply and demand functions. Thus, where there is a particular demand, entrepreneurs will reallocate their resources and thereby bring that aspect of the economy back to equilibrium. Doing so involves risk and has value, for which the rent accrued forms the reward. For Schultz, human capital was principally in the form of education and experience.

Human capital issues continue to be researched (Reynolds, 1997; Burke *et al.*, 2000; Delmar and Davidsson, 2000; Minniti *et al.*, 2005), as exemplified in the various annual Global Enterprise Monitors (GEM reports). This type of research is useful for identifying trends of large cohorts, but it can be undiscriminating, for example focusing on the self-employed (Burke *et al.*, 2000), which may include lifestyle and growth businesses, and on nascent entrepreneurs where there is an intention to found a business (GEM studies). Davidsson and Honig (2003) were able to show that both human and social capital factors differentiated between a cohort of nascent entrepreneurs and a control group. This reinforces Schultz's view that the quality of human capital in respect of education and experience is an important factor in business venturing.

Summary of historical actors

By way of an overview of the historical perspective, Table 2.1 presents a timeline of some of the key economists from Richard Cantillon to the present day.

Contemporary influences and some radical thoughts

Subjectivism and the role of imagination

George Leonard Sharman Shackle (1903–1992)[9] was viewed as a controversial figure because he developed a radical subjectivist approach in

Table 2.1 Timeline of economists in relation to developments in entrepreneurship

---

- Richard Cantillon (1680–1734), *Essai* (1755) represents a watershed in entrepreneurial theory, emphasising the role of entrepreneur in a market economy
- Adam Smith (1723–1790), *The Wealth of Nations* (1776) deals with the wealth of all rather than simply the king, the landed gentry, merchants or guilds
- A. R. J. Turgot (1727–1781) and Nicholas Baudeau (1730–1792), French Physiocrats
- Jeremy Bentham (1748–1832), British moral and political philosopher at the time of the Industrial Revolution; *Defence of Usury* (1787)
- Jean-Baptiste Say (1767–1832) *Treatise on Political Economy* (1803)
- David Ricardo (1772–1823), friend to James Mill, father of J. S. Mill, contemporary of T. R. Malthus; classical economist influenced by Adam Smith
- Johann von Thunen (1785–1850), German school
- Amasa Walker (1799–1875), American school, father of Francis A. Walker
- John Stuart Mill (1806–1873) *Principles of Political Economy* (1965)
- Hans Karl Friedrich von Mangoldt (1824–1868), German school; between classical and neo-classical economics, using supply and demand curves to explain price
- Leon Walras (1834–1910), French school; formulator of a static mathematical equilibrium economic system in *Elements of Pure Economics* (1874)
- Carl Menger (1840–1921), founder of Austrian school; subjectivist theory of value
- Francis A. Walker (1840–1897), American school; towards neo-classicist; fought in the American Civil War (1861–1865)
- Alfred Marshall (1842–1924), dominant British economist; *Principles of Economics* (1890); price and output determined by supply and demand
- John Bates Clark (1847–1938), American neo-classical economist
- Ludwig von Mises (1881–1972), Austrian school; *Human Action: A Treatise on Economics* (1949); strong influence on his student Israel Kirzner
- Joseph A. Schumpeter (1883–1950) *The Theory of Economic Development* (1921)
- Frank H. Knight (1885–1972); founder of the Chicago School; *Risk, Uncertainty and Profit* (1921) – distinguishes between insurable risk and uninsurable uncertainty
- George I. S. Shackle (1903–1992), subjectivist; *Epistemics and Economics* (1972); *Imagination and the Nature of Choice* (1979)
- Israel M. Kirzner (1930–), Austrian school; alertness to and discovery of opportunities; market process; *Competition and Entrepreneurship* (1973); *Discovery and the Capitalist Process* (1985)
- Mark C. Casson (1945–), British; *The Entrepreneur – An Economic Theory* (1982) – importance of judgemental decision-making

---

economics. Born in Cambridge, UK, he took a degree at the University of London after several years' employment as a bank clerk and then a teacher. He commenced a doctorate at the London School of Economics under the supervision of Friedrich Hayek, but later switched to an interpretation of Keynes' *General Theory*, obtaining his doctorate in 1937. At the outbreak of World War II in 1939, he was appointed to S-Branch, Sir Winston Churchill's inner office of economists. He subsequently spent short spells in the Cabinet Office and at the University of Leeds before taking the chair in economics at the University of Liverpool – a post he held until his retirement in 1969. He continued to publish well into his retirement. In a revealing interview[10] he discusses the influence of Keynes and others on his thinking. He explains, for example: the contradiction between the then assumption of 'perfect knowledge' and the 1930s Depression; the need for economics to take into account 'shocks'; his theory of choice and indeterminacy; and his insistence that economics should not be viewed like a science such as physics.

Shackle's concern is with the psychic act of decision-making in conditions of bounded uncertainty. He theorises that an entrepreneur, like an artist, is an 'originator'. Shackle's position rests on a philosophical argument about the nature of humankind and free will as fundamental to the human condition ('predicament'). Free will, contrasted with determinism, is manifested in our ability to choose between courses of action. Thought, argues Shackle (1979), is our intuition of time and occurs in the present, but we can have thoughts about possible future actions; these are imagined possibilities that we can choose amongst. The choices or the options that we imagine are not predetermined; rather, the position of choice is 'the beginning' – the 'uncaused cause'. Choice as a human action is emotionally charged; as we value some courses of action more than others, this invokes feelings such as excitement, inspiration or danger. Ultimately these envisaged possibilities are acts of the imagination and they are subjective. Once chosen, the course of action commits the individual to associated sequels of activity, which may commit resources and the means by which the course of action may be pursued. If, for example, the proposed action is an investment, then valuation of the *imagined* sequence will, according to Shackle, occur; this will involve conjecture or speculation about the *value to come* from that particular choice and sequence. All markets are in that sense matters of speculation. Further, the value of the item is considered in relation to its potential to serve the person's ends.

A business person or entrepreneur needs imagination in order to make decisions. 'Enterprise' is the choice of course of action, the commitment to resources and the system that is devised in its pursuit. However, at the point of choice, the future is yet to come and there is a period of 'unknowing'. In that sense the individual takes a gamble based on their imagination: the imagined sequence of possible events yet to come. At that point, the individual cannot attach a probability to their choice working out; all they can say is that they believe that it will. Thus, those favoured *possibilities* are characterised by an absence of disbelief, with disbelief representing an obstacle to the pursuit of a particular course of action.

In considering rival skeins (possibilities), individuals make their choice on the basis of implicit criteria: desirability, disbelief and interest. In effect, they ask themselves: do I want to do this, do I believe that I can, how arresting/interesting is this course of action (to me) and will it make a difference?

There is no scale of measurement in the person's head enabling him/her to make the decision; rather, the person adjudges the possible course, using such implicit criteria. Even though individuals may draw on some information or experience to aid their decision, this does not obviate the fact that: (a) the possibilities are just that and are, at this point, figments of the imagination; and (b) the information must be interpreted. Moreover, Shackle argues, in these circumstances individuals cannot calculate the risk because they are dealing with possibilities, not probabilities; the speculation is in the future, not the past, and any calculation of probability would require data, which for these purposes do not exist.

Hence the individual is conscious that there are rival possibilities, and that to make a choice is to commit resource to that decision. But s/he cannot know the right course of action to take, because humankind is limited in both power and knowledge. The resources s/he has to commit are limited. Hence the gamble taken is based on the imagination, the imagined possibilities. The enterprise is thus uncertain and all the individual can attempt to do is exploit it. The only thing that is knowable to the individual is his/her state of mind and it is on that that the choice is made. This is why ultimately the choice (and the economics of choice), according to Shackle, is *subjective*.

Hence, the market or economic situation facing the entrepreneur is unique and uncertain as a context for making decisions. The entrepreneur can but ponder the potential of the situation and resources at his/her disposal and take a punt, that is, gamble on his/her imagination. This is inimical to the way economic thought has progressed and, in particular, to the assumptions that underpin it. However, it surely resonates with Knight's (1921) idea of radical uncertainty, discussed above. On the whole, however, as Pittaway's analysis has shown, economists have ignored the unknown and the unknowable and the significance of time. Shackle's thesis stands accepted economic thought on its head; it suggests that knowledge per se is insufficient to make economic decisions, because human intelligence is finite and people do not possess the faculty of knowing the future. Here, not only knowledge but also personality, desires, ambitions and priorities have a part to play in shaping the decision. Hence action is required in the here and now to try to ensure that the most desired imagined sequence of choices is achieved. Shackle terms this behaviour 'enterprise' and views it as the effective outcome of any choice that depends upon the individual's goals and aspirations. Thus, anyone can be enterprising if they use their imagination to deal with uncertainty. Decisions are wholly subjective and people deal in possibilities not probabilities when making decisions.

Lachmann (1990) positions Shackle in the 'history of subjectivist thought'; he went beyond classical economics, in which the key components were the market, the object, wealth creation and the principal actors, producers and merchants. With the development of a subjective theory of value the consumer could no longer be ignored. Indeed, Shackle went beyond the idea of 'preferences' to that of expectations. Shackle also drew on economic history and case study rather than general theory. Whilst he did not believe it possible to predict the future, he did believe that it was possible to explain the present based on one's interpretation of the past. Perlman (1990) identifies how various economists before Shackle assumed implicitly the role of imagination, as indeed does Kregel (1990: 89). Shackle's entrepreneur was not only imaginative, but also a subtle thinker; he recognised the importance of keeping his/her rivals in ignorance and that profit rested on different valuations of a good by different individuals. He believed that 'speculative markets are balanced on a precipice of diversity of opinion and are inherently changeable' (Kregel, 1990: 92). Indeed, Shackle's position contrasted markedly with general equilibrium theory, which assumed 'rational economic man' as the model of decision-making behaviour. Rational economic man not only was capable of taking decisions in an objective, mechanical way but he was devoid of imagination. Further, in a very entertaining paper, Wiseman and Littlechild (1990) eschew the orthodox neo-classical model of decision-taking, in which both choices and outcomes are assumed to be known, for a subjectivist approach, after Shackle. In the latter, the alternatives and the outcomes are not given, outcomes may differ from what was expected and the decision-taker may feel that it is worthwhile to collect information. To illustrate this approach they analyse the decision-making behaviour of Robinson Crusoe and, moreover, point to a variety of economic principles. It will be recalled that Crusoe found himself alone, shipwrecked and washed up on the shores of an island, and in a situation so beyond the bounds of his experience he was forced to use his imagination, his judgement, make choices and prioritise his time and effort in order to eke out a subsistence living. However, he was able to produce capital goods (tools), increase his productivity (i.e. use of his work time) and enhance his future consumption prospects thereby!

Alertness to opportunities

Israel Meir Kirzner (born 1930)[11] followed a different tack; he is a leading economist in the Austrian school. Son of a well-known rabbi, he was born in London but lived in Cape Town, where he attended university from 1947 to 1948, before moving to the USA. He took a BA, *summa cum laude*, from Brooklyn College in 1954, an MBA in 1955 and a PhD from New York University in 1957, where he studied under Ludwig von Mises. He retired in 1995 and is emeritus professor of economics at New York University and an authority on von Mises. He is also a rabbi and Orthodox Judaism expert.

Kirzner's main contribution that will concern us is his entrepreneurial theory of the market process, in which the entrepreneur through 'alertness to profit opportunities' makes an adjustment in the market, bringing it back towards equilibrium. The psychological aspect of such a definition is that it is based on individual differences in perception. Using Kirzner's own example, an entrepreneur is the person who, seeing a $10 bill on the ground, will quickly grab it, being alert to the profit opportunities that it holds, whereas the non-entrepreneur would be slower to react. Initially, Kirzner's entrepreneur was an arbitrageur for whom there was no need for acts of creative imagination in the face of uncertainty; rather, the arbitrageur's behaviour is more a case of adjusting prices and costs in the light of experience. This, of course raises some interesting issues. The arbitrageur knows what s/he has paid for a good (a stock of cheap swatches, for example), and intends to sell them on at a future time and different spatial zone. As with 'Del Boy',[12] he may win some or lose some. However, alertness to opportunities and the entrepreneurial act is more subtle, as Kirzner later acknowledged. For example, two people stand in a derelict site, one person sees a heap of rubble and the other a multi-million-pound shopping mall – here the role of imagination is crucial.

Kirzner, in contrast to Schumpeter, assumes that the economic system operates as a market that moves towards equilibrium. Entrepreneurial decisions are the driving force and human agency, which may be irrational, comprises subjective preferences. Thus, human action is guided by choices and decisions, but also the propensity to be alert to opportunities, which is the entrepreneurial element in decision-taking. Kirzner explains the value of entrepreneurship as a 'corrective' to unexploited profit opportunities arising from the misallocation of resources, which result in 'social waste'. Such a misallocation, he argues, arises from imperfect knowledge, but this knowledge has to do with awareness rather than the gathering of information, which indicates a subtle difference between his position and that of Schultz.

Entrepreneurial profit opportunities exist where people do not know what they do not know, and do not know that they do not know it. The entrepreneurial function is to notice what people have overlooked (Kirzner, 1982a: 273).

Alertness is required in order to know which goals to pursue and to pursue them efficiently. The acquisition of market information provides for alertness to opportunities. The entrepreneur is able to correctly interpret the market and consider new possibilities (i.e. opportunities). Hence, entrepreneurial behaviour comprises both the cognitive component (the perception and interpretation of market information) and the motivational element (alertness), which result in a sequence of decisions and actions. Moreover, due to people having imperfect knowledge, the pure entrepreneurial role may be thought of as 'alertness to hitherto unnoticed opportunities'. Hence, an entrepreneur is someone who has the ability to predict successfully changes in market conditions. All people are entrepreneurs in this sense because, theoretically, they are able to act on their anticipation of future market conditions, but it is the entrepreneur who identifies opportunities as yet unnoticed.

In contrast to Shackle's position, for Kirzner entrepreneurs pursue opportunities that actually exist and successful entrepreneurship is the ability to be aware of them. For example, Kirzner's entrepreneur might create a new flavour of ice-cream (say, bran and prune). For Shackle, such opportunities exist in the imagination and successful entrepreneurship is the ability to create one's imagined future (e.g. conceiving of combined leisure facilities and shopping malls). For Schumpeter, the act of creative destruction plunges the entrepreneur-innovator into a wholly uncertain future where, at the point of decision and exploration, opportunities are created and, as concepts initially, they have no external reality.

The soundness of entrepreneurial judgement

Mark C. Casson (1945–) was educated at Manchester Grammar School, the University of Bristol and Churchill College, Cambridge. He joined the University of Reading as a lecturer in economics in 1969, taking the chair of economics in 1981, where he has pursued his particular interest in entrepreneurship. He too recognises the importance of rejecting the economists' simplifying assumption of perfect knowledge[13] and replacing it with a definition of the entrepreneur as a 'judgemental decision-maker'. Casson (1982) also draws upon psychological concepts in his account of what constitutes entrepreneurial behaviour. Indeed, he considers the integration of the functional and the indicative approaches to be a primary purpose of his work. The indicative or inductive approach tends to be adopted by economic historians and provides a *description* of the entrepreneur's position in society, what s/he does and what characteristics s/he has. Economists generally are positioned as functionalists, identifying the function or role performed by an entrepreneur in an economy. The functional approach is concerned with prediction and is associated with positivism (see Burrell and Morgan, 1979: 3; and Chapter 7 of this volume).

Casson's view is that an entrepreneur is someone who *specialises* in taking judgemental decisions about the *coordination* of scarce resources (ibid.: 23). The notion of the judgemental decision is central. It is a decision 'where different individuals, sharing the same objectives and acting under similar circumstances, would make different decisions' (ibid.: 24). They would make different decisions because they have 'different perceptions of the situation' as a result of different information or interpretation. The entrepreneur is therefore a person whose judgement differs from that of others. His reward arises from his backing his judgement and being right. However, does Casson's concept of 'specialisation in judgemental decision-making' allow the entrepreneur to make a mistake? Casson (2005: 331) appears to recognise this problem when he states that entrepreneurs may differ as to whether they exercise good or bad judgement and as such it is linked to success – the measure of which is sustainability of the enterprise. However, as we cannot distinguish between these individuals except *ex post facto*, we are left with the presumption that anyone could be an entrepreneur and, with practice, they might become successful at it. But, Casson (2005: 330) also states that entrepreneurs make judgements on the basis of both public and private information. Is it not the holding of private information or, indeed, perceptions that is the distinguishing feature? These private thoughts, which he must keep to him/herself (cf. Shackle, 1979), are the link to risk and uncertainty, because the entrepreneur cannot be certain that s/he is right; the risk is backing her judgement that s/he is right (Casson, 2005: 330).

The term 'coordination' is defined by Casson (1982) as the 'beneficial reallocation of resources': a dynamic concept intended to capture the entrepreneur as an agent of change. This assumption that coordination is 'beneficial' is defined specifically to imbue the concern of the entrepreneur with improving the allocation of resources; it does not mean that s/he is altruistic or pro-social; on the contrary, Casson assumes s/he acts out of self-interest. Hence, whilst it is accepted that the entrepreneur chooses to reallocate resources, allowance must be made for the fact that on occasions s/he fails to do this beneficially, otherwise 'success' is implicit in his definition of 'entrepreneur'.

A further adjunct to the theory is the exposition of the qualities associated with the entrepreneur. As an active decision-maker, the entrepreneur is likely to be faced with either new knowledge (e.g. scientific discovery) or new information that requires simple updating. Entrepreneurs are, Casson argues, active planners; they may be viewed as people who instigate change or react to it. The psychological literature, on the whole, suggests that entrepreneurs are proactive (see Chapter 5 of this volume). Decision-making involves the use of mental resources (in particular), which have a positive opportunity cost. Some aspects of the decision-problem-solving situation may be delegated, bearing in mind that there is a risk of default.[14]

Casson (1982) argues that the successful entrepreneur must generally be proficient in all aspects of decision-making (unless he is to delegate). The qualities of *imagination* and *foresight* are scarce and so the possession of them confers an advantage. Further, *self-knowledge* and *communication* skills are also essential qualities for effective decision-making, according to Casson (2000: 31). He discusses all these skills in terms of whether they are innate, scarce, difficult to screen for and/or likely to be enhanced through experience or training. This particular analysis is an example of psychological economics and its accuracy is an empirical question. Casson (2005), however, in deducing the likely attributes of the entrepreneur in contrast to his earlier work, has dropped the idea of imagination and foresight. Rather, he emphasises that, given the subjectivity of risk perceptions, the entrepreneur is more likely to have a lower aversion to risk and is more likely to be confident about his/her judgement and optimistic about the likely success of his/her proposed project. Moreover, following Witt (1998) he suggests that an entrepreneur's optimism has a functional purpose in that it influences other people's judgements about the likely success of the enterprise; there is thus a 'strategic value in self promotion' (Casson, 2005: 342) as s/he, like other entrepreneurs, makes considerable efforts to enhance her/his personal image.

Drawing the threads together

By taking a historical purview of economic theory, it has been possible to identify various landmarks in economic thought, starting with Cantillon, who was the first person to focus on the role of entrepreneur in an economy. Other notable landmarks include such classical economists as Adam Smith, whose work, *The Wealth of Nations* (1776), represented a further watershed as it moved economics from a narrow consideration of the treasury (the king's wealth and that of the aristocracy) to the modern interpretation (all national wealth created by each and every person). In the eighteenth century there was a tendency, particularly in the British school, to conflate the role of capitalist and entrepreneur, and to think of the entrepreneur as a manager or superintendent; this tendency spilled over into the early nineteenth century, as evident in work such as that of J. S. Mill. Alfred Marshall at the turn of the nineteenth century appeared to straddle classical and neo-classical economic thought.

The development of mathematical models, in particular the static equilibrium economic system of Leon Walras in 1870, could be said to represent a bridge from the classical system to that which was to dominate economics to the present day. A crucial problem with equilibrium theory is that it expunges uncertainty, because it is not possible to calculate a solution without the ability to include calculable elements, such as probable levels of risk; no levels of probability can be attributed in conditions of uncertainty. Furthermore, neo-classical economics centred theoretical thought on *comparative statics*, and models that were deterministic and governed by equilibrium assumptions. The essential assumption was that all other things would remain equal or the same unless some external event occurred to disturb the equilibrium; thus, whilst supply and demand remained the same, the price would remain unchanged. There were also other assumptions built into equilibrium theory. For perfect market knowledge and rational economic behaviour, it was assumed that *firms* would always act to maximise profits. Such a mechanistic model denied choice, as there was only one obvious course of action to be taken. However, criticisms from Hayek (1949) and Mises (1949) emphasised mutual learning about the state of the particular market and the dynamic character of the market process. Firms may move towards equilibrium through learning more, but equilibrium as a theoretical construct should not be assumed to prevail in practice. This led to the resurgence of Austrian economics and the explicit characterisation of the market process as being entrepreneurially driven and speculative. It permitted the thought that judgement and decision-making in a state of less than complete knowledge were the operating conditions under which allocative decisions are made. Further, drawing on Knight (1921), entrepreneurial decisions are made in conditions of uncertainty about a future possibility or possibilities, amongst which the entrepreneur must choose (Shackle, 1979). The ability to be alert to such options is fundamental to informed choice and judgement.

Kirzner's work, building on Mises and the Austrian tradition, emphasises entrepreneurial discovery that takes place under *dis*equilibrium conditions and is 'a process of discovery driven by dynamic competition, made possible by an institutional framework which permits unimpeded entrepreneurial entry into both new and old markets' (Kirzner, 1997: 31). The theory propounds that old, less efficient and unimaginative courses of action are replaced by new superior ways in capitalist market economies. This theory of discovery juxtaposed entrepreneurship with equilibrium theory and highlighted the importance of entrepreneurial alertness in noticing hitherto unexploited opportunities. Hence the institutional framework and the competitive conditions under which entrepreneurial decisions are being taken are critical aspects of the context (Audretsch *et al.*, 2001).

Thus, the twentieth century revealed some interesting developments[15] that began to challenge neo-classical equilibrium thinking; Frank Knight focused specifically on the nature of risk and uncertainty, producing his seminal work in 1921; Joseph Schumpeter (1934) turned earlier theorising about the entrepreneur on its head by placing entrepreneurial activity at the heart of economic development; whilst von Hayek (1937) challenged the assumptions of equilibrium theory as being unrealistic. Other twentieth-century contributions that have had a lasting impact on current entrepreneurship theory include those of: T. W. Schultz (1975, 1980), who identified entrepreneurial behaviour as an ability and thus pioneered human capital theory; G. L. S. Shackle (1972, 1979), whose strong belief in free will underpinned his theory of choice and imagination; Israel Kirzner (1982a, 1982b, 1985), whose central concern in developing entrepreneurship theory is the importance of perception and alertness to profit opportunities within the market process; and Mark Casson (1982), who defines the entrepreneur as a judgemental decision-maker, operating within an equilibrium system.

Intellectual traditions

Over the course of the past three centuries different economists have defined the role of entrepreneur in different ways (see Table 2.2). Based on some work by Hébert and Link (1988, 2006), the roles can be separated as falling into either dynamic or static economic systems. Only within dynamic systems does the role of entrepreneur make sense, as the function of entrepreneur is that of an agent of change and development in a market economy.

Albeit simplified, Hébert and Link identify three major intellectual traditions with their roots in Cantillon. These they label as:

- *The Chicago Tradition*: Knight–Schultz;
- *The German Tradition*: Thunen–Schumpeter;
- *The Austrian Tradition*: Mises–Kirzner–(Shackle).

These traditions have various themes in common: perception, uncertainty

Table 2.2 Roles identified for the entrepreneur by economists

---

Dynamic theories
- The entrepreneur is the person who assumes the risk associated with uncertainty (e.g. Cantillon, Thunen, Mangoldt, Mill, Hawley, Knight, Mises, Cole and Shackle)
- The entrepreneur is an innovator (e.g. Baudeau, Bentham, Thunen and Schumpeter)
- The entrepreneur is a decision-maker (e.g. Cantillon, Menger, Marshall, Amasa Walker, Francis Walker, Keynes, Mises, Shackle, Cole, Schultz, Hayek and Casson)
- The entrepreneur is an industrial leader (Say, Saint-Simon, Amasa Walker, Francis Walker, Marshall and Schumpeter)
- The entrepreneur is an organiser and coordinator of economic resources (e.g. Say, Walras, Clark, Davenport, Schumpeter and Coase)
- The entrepreneur is a contractor (e.g. Bentham)
- The entrepreneur is an arbitrageur (Cantillon, Walras and Kirzner)
- The entrepreneur is an allocator of resources among alternative uses (e.g. Cantillon, Kirzner and Schultz)

Static theories
- The entrepreneur is the person who supplies financial capital (e.g. Smith, Turgot, Pigou and Mises)
- The entrepreneur is a manager or superintendent (e.g. Say, Mill, Marshall, and Menger)
- The entrepreneur is the owner of an enterprise (e.g. Quesnay, Pigou and Hawley)
- The entrepreneur is an employer of factors of production (e.g. Amasa Walker, Francis Walker and Keynes)

---

and innovation. They have all emphasised the *function* of the entrepreneur in an economy, as opposed to his or her *personality*, and the entrepreneur's role as a dynamic force or agent of change operating in a market economy. The entrepreneur bears uncertainty for the sake of profit and has the ability to perceive opportunities that others cannot see. He or she acts on his/her perception. It is this perception and judgement that distinguishes the entrepreneur from others.

On the issue of uncertainty they point out that 'uncertainty is a consequence of change, whereas innovation is a precept of change' (Hébert and Link, 1988: 156). The distinction between the roles of entrepreneur and capitalist is also now much clearer: for example, true entrepreneurial gains bear no relation to the size of capital employed in a business. They are a consequence of the entrepreneurs' ability to identify profitable opportunities and to back their judgement by acting on their perception. The capitalist or investor, in contrast, would expect his/her return to bear some relation to the amount of capital employed. However, one thing that the entrepreneur and capitalist have in common is that they both face an element of risk – and not only financial risk. This is because both must back their judgement whilst operating in conditions of uncertainty. Finally, it is worth reflecting on whether the entrepreneur is the person who instigates change or merely adjusts to it. Hébert and Link believe that it does not matter: either reaction requires perception, courage and action; failure in any of these departments will render the entrepreneur ineffective.

Concluding statement

This very brief survey of economic thought has demonstrated: a gradual and increasing awareness of the crucial role played by entrepreneurs in economic growth; a theoretical contradiction between equilibrium theory and the disruptive function of the entrepreneur (i.e. a person who deals in conditions of disequilibria); very different traditions in the ways that disruptions in supply and demand and market economics are dealt with; and very different traditions and treatments of the entrepreneur, with a strong British tradition that minimised his/her role and supplanted it with that of the capitalist.

There was an initial preoccupation with risk-taking in conditions of uncertainty as being fundamental to the behaviour of the entrepreneur. This, as a key characteristic of entrepreneurs, has since been questioned because entrepreneurs are seen to be adept managers of risk and to have special abilities that enable them to perceive market opportunities differently from other people. However, the jury is out as to whether entrepreneurs bear risk, uncertainty or both (Loasby, 2002). The entrepreneur has come to be viewed as a decision-taker who exercises choice amongst action alternatives. It is the entrepreneur's ability to make correct judgements that differentiates him/her from others.

There are various approaches to explain the entrepreneur's motivation, although they may be boiled down to the profit motive: to 'buy cheap and sell dear', to exploit a profit opportunity and to be aware of new developments in technology in order to reduce the costs of production and gain a competitive advantage.

Philosophically, the economists that have been reviewed view the entrepreneur to be someone who operates in a market economy, but they vary as to how they approach equilibrium theory and various methodological assumptions. Traditional economic theories are deterministic, emphasise rational objective behaviour and assume that outcomes are predictable. The economic theories outlined in this chapter have, to varying degrees, questioned the deterministic nature of economic behaviour: for example, Knight argued that some decisions are based on information that is known and probable outcomes that may be predicted, whereas Schumpeter's concept of creative destruction suggested a point in time where prediction was impossible (Casson, 1982). Kirzner suggests that entrepreneurs perceive and are alert to opportunities, and that their behaviour is logical and self-interested. To this extent behaviour is predictable, although the entrepreneur is still operating in conditions of uncertainty. Kirzner's entrepreneurs are operating in concrete reality – the opportunities exist and to that extent there is objectivity – whereas Shackle's entrepreneurs are operating entirely in their imaginations, which is where the opportunities are constructed. To this extent Shackle's philosophical position is subjective. Pittaway (2000: 50) suggests that Shackle puts forward an anti-equilibrium thesis where individual choice is central – choice that is concerned with imagined futures, all of which are deemed possible. Hence, the judgement of the chooser depends on their experience, their personality, ambitions, aspirations and knowledge. The choice of a particular sequence of future possibilities is an action that is required now to ensure that the most desired imagined future is realised. Shackle termed this 'enterprise'.

There is recognition and inference by different economists of various psychological and behavioural characteristics of entrepreneurs that distinguish them from other business owners. Such characteristics have included *foresight*, a *keen awareness* of possibilities, a *creative imagination, confidence* in their decision (i.e. a willingness to gamble on their imagination) and an *agent of change*. Entrepreneurs are not simply overseers, superintendents or 'caretakers'; they actively pursue and initiate change. This has been taken to mean, by some, that they are innovators insofar as the pursuit of change is not change for change's sake. In the Schumpeterian sense, they might develop new products, exploit new markets, introduce new technologies, capture a new source of supply, use imaginative ways of investing in the business, reorganise systems and structures to accomplish efficiencies in operations and/or bring about the reshaping of an industrial sector.

These economists have also indicated where the boundary lies between their own approach to understanding the function of the entrepreneur and that of other discipline bases. Of principal concern in this book is the ability to develop an understanding of the nature of entrepreneurs and entrepreneurship from a psychological perspective. This will be the task of ensuing chapters. In the next chapter, however, I shall consider the socio-economy, that is, the context in which entrepreneurs make decisions.

Notes

1 http://cepa.newschool.edu/het/profiles/cantillon.htm and http://en.wikipedia.org/wiki/Richard_Cantillon.
2 The Physiocrats dealt with knowable, material realities and were concerned to identify principles that would allow for perfect prediction. They identified three social classes: landowners, farmers and craftsmen. They believed that the farmers were the only ones who could produce a surplus. Prior to industrialisation, agriculture was absolutely central to the French economy and way of life (http://www.uta.fi/entrenet/english/internetix/fsioEN.htm).
3 Kregel (1990) makes the point that Smith's notion of self-interest is not of unbridled greed, but is modified by what he believes to be socially acceptable.
4 Hébert and Link (1988) argue that Schumpeter should be placed in the German school, following Thunen. This is certainly debatable; we have placed him in the American school for reasons that will become apparent.

 5 http://cepa.newschool.edu/~het/schools/austrian.htm. Carl Menger is often linked with Jevons and Walras, as founders of neo-classical economics.
 6 For an overview, see: http://cepa.newschool.edu/~het/profiles/menger.htm.
 7 Arguably, Schumpeter (1934) covered all aspects of innovation and not merely technological innovation (see below).
 8 Although Schumpeter was Austrian by birth, he was never a foot soldier of the Austrian school (hhtp://cepa.newschool.edu/het/profiles/schump.htm). He is said to be largely unclassifiable, except perhaps as a founder of 'evolutionary economics'. His status as president of the American Economic Association in 1948 enables us to place him somewhat ambivalently in the 'American school'.
 9 Source: Wikipedia.
10 The *Austrian Economics Newsletter* (Spring), 1983; http://www.mises.org/journals/aen/shackle.asp.
11 http://en.wikipedia.org/wiki/Israel_Kirzner and http://www.econ.nyu.edu/user/kirzner/.
12 'Derek Trotter', affectionately known as 'Del Boy', was a market trader in a television sit-com *Only Fools and Horses*, in which he invariably bought cheap goods that he stored in his council flat and was unable to sell on either through his market stall or dubious contacts.
13 'Entrepreneurship' by Mark Casson: *The Concise Encyclopedia of Economics*, Library of Economics and Liberty. (http://www.econlib.org/library/Enc/Entreprneurship.html).
14 It is worth considering the role of the 'right hand man' as discussed in Chell and Tracey (2005).
15 This chapter does not include work in industrial economics; however, an interesting article by Audretsch, Baumol and Burke (2001) makes links to Kirznerian economic theory, for example.

3 The socio-economic environment

Introduction

The previous chapter presented a historical approach to understanding significant aspects of economic thought in relation to entrepreneurship and the entrepreneur. Some of the outstanding criticisms and indeed insights that should be borne in mind are not independent of historical and contextual detail. The industrial revolution shifted swathes of people from the country to the towns in search of a living; factories sprang up and so did the concept of organised labour. This latter development brought with it a further entrepreneurial behaviour: the organisation of resources for the exploitation of an opportunity to produce goods and create wealth.

In this chapter, some of the building blocks of social constructionism will be laid down and explored through the explication of Giddens' structuration theory. This permits consideration of how individuals operate in society and how context (structure) may be conceived of in affecting individual behaviour. This adds a further dimension to the entrepreneur as agent in society, or more specifically within a socio-economy. If it is assumed that an entrepreneur's function is transformative, then there is a duality to be resolved – the freedom to act within social constraints and cultural rules and financial regulations. I shall explore this duality of free will and determinism as it pertains to entrepreneurial behaviour. Hence, I shall focus on the socio-economic framework in which entrepreneurs take business decisions. Layers of context from the macro- to the micro-environment will be assumed to form the structural background. The aim is to dig deeper into this complexity, assuming a theoretical frame of structure and agency. The treatment of the macro-environment will include understanding of the institutional framework that constrains or enables human action; at the meso-level I focus on the firm as an organising framework in which entrepreneurial decisions are taken, and at the micro-level I shall deduce the implications for entrepreneurs and entrepreneurial teams as dynamic economic decision-makers and agents of socio-economic change.

The macro socio-economic environment

Macro-environments as traditionally dealt with by economists have made deterministic assumptions about national and international contexts framing competitive behaviour. Trading conditions and the degree of environmental 'turbulence' have been pointed up as immutable contexts that shape and influence business and firm behaviour (Burns and Stalker, 1961; Miller, 1983; Casson, 2005). The environment is formed by a complex of socio-economic, political and legal sub-systems that are interwoven yet analytically distinct. Indeed, they are further complicated by the physical, the technological and the religious environments. There is a sense in which the environment is 'out there' (i.e. has a history and duration independent of the firm or entrepreneur), and another sense in which environments are internalised, produced and reproduced by actors and agents (Giddens, 1984; Craib, 1992). In grasping this complexity, we wish to consider how we might think of environments analytically: what the process is by which entrepreneurial behaviour is shaped and constrained or, indeed, enabled by the socio-economic environment. In pursuing this understanding, we should consider a number of theoretical issues. Crucial is the vexed question of 'structure and agency', in which functionalists overtheorise 'structure' and interpretative sociologists emphasise 'agency' (Gorton, 2000; Jack and Anderson, 2002). Giddens' solution is that of 'structuration theory' in which there is an intimate interplay between structure and agency, the agent producing and reproducing structure. Structure is constituted socially through signification (the generation of meaning), legitimation (the rules and norms that differentiate between appropriate and inappropriate, legal and illegal behaviour) and domination (the exercise of power and dominion over others). However, as will be argued below, it is important analytically to identify structure, agency and their interplay – structuration – as distinct and separable. Anticipating our conclusions, it is quite understandable at the macro-level of analysis to, as it were, overemphasise the dominance and power of socio-economic institutions in shaping behaviour and to underplay the role of individuals – agents – in recasting the rules and creating change and dynamism. Thus, there are questions of determinism and causation – the dominance of powerful situations – but also, following Giddens, questions of meaning and legitimation. Environments create situations, many of which will be recognisable and routine to the individual agent. They may manage these in a predictable and orderly manner, drawing on behavioural scripts and schema that they have learnt through previous encounters. The behaviour would be meaningful in the context of the known situation, approved and acknowledged by peers as being appropriate (in Giddens' terminology 'legitimate') and powerful to the extent to which the agent is managing the situation and influencing others. In such social contexts there are implicit rules, including social norms of what is considered appropriate, perhaps moral, and socially acceptable. In contrast, environments may also throw up new situations for which the individual has no prior experience and in which s/he must improvise. This freedom of action by which the agent may develop new ways of working and new procedures and rules also enables us to understand the character of the agent. However, structuration theory undertheorises the nature of agents, for example by omitting consideration of how things are done (Ryle, 1949; Weick and Roberts, 1993) and, indeed, how attributions are made in respect of that behavioural characteristic (Chell *et al.*, 1991; Chell and Pittaway, 1998).

The structures that comprise environments are institutions that make up the societies and nation states in which entrepreneurs and firms are located. Institutions vary from marriage, family, religion, banking and finance. Whilst knowledge of the workings of such institutions varies, such variation in knowledge is a factor that distinguishes amongst agents, more specifically business persons and entrepreneurs. The ontological status of such institutions and the systems they develop as a way of working is open to question. On the one hand, they have been reified as if they were 'concrete structures' making up a tangible reality, whereas, on the other hand, they have been given a phenomenological status (Giddens, 1984). The problem is that they are both: there is nothing more tangible than the 'red tape' of bureaucracy that ensnares small businesses, whereas the institutional practices, conveyed through different media of communication, through the exercise of power and the received normative aspects of what might be considered to be legitimate (or illegitimate) behaviour, are often intangible, implied (but not necessarily articulated) and tacit. The latter are all aspects of institutional behaviour that may be, and are, regularly contested. The institutional framework of government, politics, law, finance and banking, for example, has an external 'facticity' (Berger and Luckmann, 1967) that creates a sense of the tangible in the minds of business persons and other agents who are part of the assemblage of participants in a particular aspect of life. Indeed, institutions are not simply created through discourse; they have an existence, evidenced by publicly available information. Moreover, they have spatial and temporal existence that shapes the sense of presence in the world and is instantiated in physical, historical, geographical and social data. Place and time and concomitant associations that shape the nature of institutions, however much they may be contested through discourse, give an awareness of continuity that is the bedrock through which changes occur. Thus, there is a perception of the dominance of institutions in people's lives in developed capitalist societies, but this is not inevitable (Giddens, 1984; Craib, 1992). Moreover, they create an extensive network of decision premises and procedures that underpin the functional reality of various intensely interrelated social and, most particularly, professional groups (Simon, 1957; Choi, 1993).

Further, whilst institutions are rule-governed, and in one sense produced and reproduced through the actions of human agents (to follow Giddens), time, location, power and control separate the structure (comprised of institutions) and the agents. Whilst agents forge the rules of institutions, such rules become a part of the structure and separate from agency, not only because of the duration of the institutional structure/phenomenon but also because the agents' control over the structure is not absolute – it is always limited. Thus structures are independent of agency in the collective sense. Hence, structures as institutions shape the wider social, commercial and political environment of the agent and create situations and circumstances with which the person has to deal.

Institutional structures shape but do not determine the agents' behaviour. The operation of institutional rules constrains individual behaviour, but leaves freedom of action – choice – to the individual. Whilst people may need routine and order in their lives – provided by institutional structures – they also need flexibility and room to manoeuvre. Rules are not natural laws and may be broken for various reasons: cultural and circumstantial changes may render the rule defunct, that is, devoid of meaning; through changes in social movements the rule may be questioned and perceived to have little legitimacy; and weak rules cease to hold sway in many quarters of society – they cease to have general influence. Thus, institutions as phenomena are complex social structures that hold different meanings for different agents; they are often sites of contradiction – for more or less radical change and for the systematic questioning and transformation of routines (Craib, 1992: 159). Hence our understanding of modern societies is not based on order and rule-governed behaviour, but of much greater agentic power to contest the nature of social structures that affect everyday lives now and into the future. Further, this also underscores the 'messiness' of social existence, the disruptive nature of other people's actions, the unpredictable (good luck and misfortune), the unexpected and the unintended consequences of actions and behaviour on the fabric of people's lives. Agents – people – do not merely deal in the social world but also in the physical world, which impacts on people in its sheer physicality but also as a consequence of agents' actions and activities that cause devastation, depletion and denudation of natural resources.

Finally, the term 'agent' itself is so impersonal: it robs us of the sense of the personal and of individual differences. In Giddens' structuration theory there is presentiment of powerful social structures, even though that may not be what was intended. Agents act within the socially defined rules and therefore their behaviour is very constrained in Giddens' theory. Moreover, the domination of social structures suggests that people act in socially predictable ways much of the time. There is a conflation between determined action and socially responsible action (Archer, 1988: 93). There is, moreover, too great a focus on the social *roles* that agents assume, which leaves no space for a consideration of the agents' identity (sense of self or personhood). Giddens believes that people are motivated by what he terms 'ontological security', which arises from the routine nature of agents' lives, a routine that is preferred over disruption. Thus, 'routine' is a characteristic of

daily life. This in itself gives an impoverished sense of the person; it is as if they inevitably choose to have lives that run in predictable and familiar grooves, that they shy away from any form of change from the routine. This vision of human nature seems to hark back to an idyllic pastoral existence of, say, rural tranquillity or of the more recent past, the industrialised towns – the need to man factories and control people's behaviour, for example, through the instigation of time and motion routines. This would create the antithesis of conditions that would foster entrepreneurship and innovation. In the modern world life is not typified by routine but by change, which people deal with in their own ways. Hence, there is a need to develop the sense of the agent operating in different walks of life as a person with options, with a world view and with a more complex sense of the world in which s/he lives. This would necessitate a reinterpretation of the routine aspects of life to mean: leaving 'cognitive space' for deliberation over new situations, where the exercise of choice is pertinent and where further decisions may be made by taking into account other people's behaviour. It would enable an integration of interpretivism into macro-level social constructions of modernity, which is characterised by globalisation, rapid technological change, knowledge development, relativism, the abandonment of morality, a sense of impotence and danger, fragmentation through the juxtaposition of different social groupings, human rights to self-fulfilment, variability and breaks with the past and with tradition (cf. Craib, 1992). This would create the conditions in which the person has to make sense of his/her situation and the wider complex environment and a culture that lacks unity or integration. In this environment the behaviour of the entrepreneur should be considered.

Culture and agency

The conflation of structure and agency in Giddens' structuration theory is seen as problematic (Archer, 1988; Craib, 1992). Logically, it is important to be able to analyse structure separately from agency. This enables us to understand the nature of the engagement of the individual with the structure, whether that be industry, bank, marriage or whatever. Thus, logically, structures do not exist because of a person's awareness of them; they have separate temporal and spatial existence and it is that durability that adds to the sense of stability within society. As such, because an institution predates our experience of it, we can examine its nature (e.g. marriage) in a particular culture and we can consider what past, present and future actions may contribute to transformation of that particular institution.

Conventional approaches to culture suggest that a pattern of behaviour is evident: there is uniformity of action and shared meanings (Archer, 1988). For this to be true there should be logical consistency between the elements of culture – knowledge, beliefs, values, mores, norms, mythology, etc. However, this begs the question of cultural consensus: how is consensus arrived at? Further, it appears to deny pluralism, it undertheorises power relations within a given culture and also underplays the political context in which a particular version of culture is given expression. Such conventional approaches appear to be fixed to such an extent that the dynamics of culture (its ability to change and develop) are underplayed. In contrast, an example of the political system attempting to change the employment culture of white collar jobs in blue chip companies – 'enterprise culture' – was introduced as a cultural system and philosophy crafted by the Thatcher Government in the UK in the 1980s. The issue was how to introduce those ideas as a practical basis for action within society. No cultural system is passively received by the populace; it needs to be actively mediated and manipulated. Analysis of the speeches of the day (Fairclough, 1991; Selden, 1991) showed how this proposed change in the socio-culture was being carefully engineered. Moreover, there was not a harmonious acceptance of the 'enterprise culture' philosophy, as critical analysis has shown (Gray, 1998; Chell, 2007a). Rather, what was revealed was the interplay of political power in opening minds to new socio-economic practices such as 'going it alone', disengaging from 'safe and secure' employment to the acceptance of a challenging, potentially less secure future. Such measures were heavily overlain by the rhetoric of those holding political sway, which helped to generate legitimacy. This two-way interplay between ideas (the cultural system) and their expression (socio-cultural practice) facilitated change and social acceptance – in some quarters – and the integration of a cultural shift into the fabric of society as their underpinning innovative ideas were being sown.

Cultural shifts, however, are not simply carried through ideas embodied in language and linguistic codes, but also through power differences, social (strata) and class differences and symbolism. Dominance of the ruling class and the top-down imposition of culture are characterised and opposed by Marxism, where social transformation could only be achieved, it was argued, by undermining the dominant culture and its economic expression – capitalism – by members of the subordinate culture, the Proletariat. Whilst the idea of class and class structure as the basis of culture is too simplistic,[1] what such theories do introduce is the idea of 'counter-cultures' and the question of how opposing ideas may be selectively used to promote sectional interests.

Society is being increasingly characterised as dominated by science and technology, information and knowledge, especially in advanced industrial societies. These ideas are consistent with the economic view characterised as 'rational economic man'. Science and technology suggest purposive behaviour that is rational and objective. Moreover, we can see everywhere the transforming effects of science and technology. From the industrial revolution to the present day, societies have embraced technological developments that have produced cultural changes. At the socio-cultural level people[2] have acted out of self-interest, their desires for technological developments fuelling technological advancement. In advanced industrial and capitalist societies, people on the whole want the latest gadgets in their homes; the potential impact on the quality of their lives, as they see it, provides a sharp incentive. This mass desire at the socio-cultural level provides the socio-political legitimation, whilst mass production provides the socio-economic rationale. However, the apparent upward drive for the benefits of science and technology in industrialised societies is not the only source of interest and drive. At the political level (the institution of government) the national interest is vested in the competitive performance of industry, which is linked to innovation and foresight through leading-edge developments in science and technology. Hence, we see a complex interplay at various levels that is driving cultural changes at an unprecedented rate.

Archer (1988: 68ff) when discussing Habermas (1978) considers the issue of the emergence of an alternative (subordinate, as she terms it) culture to challenge this technocratic ideology. This could not be more relevant today post 9/11. Habermas proposed emancipation through cultural reflection (not terrorism). However, cultural constraints – those institutional structures that exist whether or not we are aware of them – that have found expression at the socio-cultural level in, for example, the arms race, colour and racism cannot easily be removed solely by thought and reflection. The desired (by the counter-culture) changed subjective state of emancipation could question the legitimacy of certain cultural constraints and if a legitimation crisis can be precipitated then structural transformation is likely to follow. However, the benefits of science and technology for societies (e.g. lasting improvements in health and welfare via medicine) are the kinds of developments that people embrace; they are facilitators of benefice and social change. But, contrary to Habermas' argument, such changes require not merely reflection on ideas, but practical expression in the socio-cultural system in order to gain general acceptance, integration and effect a cultural shift. This would be true also of any counter-cultural movement.

Structuration theory has been increasingly recognised as an approach that enables the theoretical development of entrepreneurship (Jack and Anderson, 2002; Chiasson and Saunders, 2005; Sarason *et al.*, 2006). Figure 3.1 provides an overall summary of a social constructionist view of the socio-economic and political regulatory environment in which entrepreneurs operate. It shows the 'signification-legitimation-domination' structuring concepts at the three levels (macro-, meso- and micro-) and the scope at each level for interpretation, synthesis of understandings and innovation. It would appear to show that demand for entrepreneurship and innovation is made manifest at the macro- and meso-levels of the socio-political economy, especially through government and industry, and is understood by firms and individuals who respond to that demand. However, this framework is constructed within current capitalist assumptions; historical analysis that precedes the Industrial Revolution and the Middle Ages suggests a significantly different cultural environment, which governs both the supply of and the role played by entrepreneurs within those societies (Baumol, 1990).

Structural level	Environment	Structural concepts			Agency	Structuration	Outcomes
		Signification	Legitimation	Domination			
Macro	Country, nation, region, scientific, artistic institution, etc.	Political and cultural meaning	Regulatory framework	Governmental power	Anonymous, e.g. the government, 'they'	Production and reproduction of structure, socio-political, socio-economic interpretation of structural framework	Laws, policies, governance, regulations, cultural norms
			National/dominant culture				
Meso	Firm, industry, organisation, institution, university, financial institution, etc.	Contested meanings	Formal and informal rules	Formal and informal control	Headship, e.g. CEO, vice chancellor, 'boss'	Production and reproduction of structure, enactment of rules, creation of local interpretative framework	Policies, norms, directed behaviour, structural enactment
		Ambiguity	Interstices Local culture	Loop holes			
Micro	Individual, team, intra-organisational behaviour, etc.	Contestation manoeuvring	Formality, informality	Control, power	Individual enactment, e.g. nascent entrepreneur	Production and reproduction of structure, social and personal exchange to create interpersonal interpretative formats	Understanding, shared meanings, contested areas, socio-cultural enactment
		Personal interpretation, interplay to direct and control meaning					

Figure 3.1 A social constructionist view of the socio-economic and political environment (based on Giddens' concept of 'structuration').

Using this framework in the next section I consider the socio-economic structure at industry and firm levels and, in the penultimate section, the micro-level of socio-economic behaviour of the entrepreneur.

The meso-level environment: the industry and the firm

The competitive environment within capitalism is the backdrop to behaviour of the industry and the firm at the 'meso-level'. It is a moot point as to whether any particular firm is aware of its competition, but theoretically the forces of competition, along with fiscal and other economic incentives, shape the environment in which strategic and tactical decisions are made at firm level. The point of this manoeuvring is to gain competitive advantage over rival enterprises. This, however, is a very simplistic overview of the industry and firm environment. From much of the strategic literature, theory considers primarily the strategic positioning of firms within its industry (Porter, 1980, 1990). However, the theory lacks a sense of the entrepreneur (Leibenstein, 1966), of business culture (Casson, 1995) and of the possibility of cooperative behaviour (Eisenhardt and Schoonhoven, 1996). Indeed, current criticisms also focus on the need for a well-developed theory of the firm that includes entrepreneurial behaviour as a key component (Witt, 1998; Casson, 2005).

At this juncture, we should take a step back to consider the assumptions of the economic theories to be discussed: on the one hand, neo-classical equilibrium theories, including transaction cost theory, and on the other hand, evolutionary- and resource-based theory. Neo-classical equilibrium theories take a realist view of the economic environment that comprises, for instance, 'objective' facts and opportunities that are purported to be external to, and there to be discovered by, the entrepreneur. Furthermore, equilibrium theories fail to take into account the impact of social relations on (socio-)economic decision-making (Granovetter, 1992). Where economists in this camp have developed a concept of social influences, it results in automatic behaviour – following customs, habits, and so forth. Rather, it is important, Granovetter argues, to understand how behaviour is embedded in 'concrete, on-going systems of social relations' (ibid.: 6). In contrast, evolutionary theory and, specifically, Penrose's Resource Based Theory (RBT) assume that the entrepreneur has a subjective view of the environment and that through his/her imagination envisages an opportunity. Hence, opportunities are not 'plucked' from the environment; they are formed through an interactive process in which the entrepreneur realises that an opportunity can be had through his/her interpretation of the socio-economic environment. In the ensuing pages these theories are outlined in some detail.

As argued above, institutional practices and prevailing (indeed, often conflicting) elements of culture constrain or facilitate particular behaviours. In entrepreneurship, these elements of the socio-economic and the socio-cultural environment would appear to be key forces that shape the context of entrepreneurial decision-making. The industrial economic environment, however, is characterised by uncertainty and risk. The familiar, the routine, are better understood, more certain and less risky and planning is possible, in contrast to innovative environments where there are potentially opportunities for growth, profit and capital accumulation. However, the nub of the issue is that decisions are made on the basis of incomplete information, in the context of particular business cultural conditions, in pursuit of imagined opportunities and business goals. Casson (1995: 83) summarises the next step in his argument, as follows:

> In an evolving economy, the division of labour will adapt as new problems arise and existing ones are solved. Environmental change is endemic because of population aging, resource depletion, wars and so on. But it is the *perception* . . . of problems that is important. Information lags mean that. . . . problems may not be immediately perceived, while cultural changes mean that new problems may be perceived . . . At the root of this is the subjectivity of problems.

People identify different problems due to their different perspectives, norms and tastes, sense of appropriateness and legitimacy, and goals. They also are likely to provide different solutions due to their different cognitive frames and differential knowledge and information at their disposal. However, overlaying this is identification with particular cultural sub-groups (ibid.: 92). Such factions may be influenced by, for example, religion, social class, family, local community (however composed) and trade union. This 'collective subjectivity' may be implicit, tacit and is likely to have developed over time. The values held by one culture (such as the collective benefits of scientific progress) may be challenged by another. But conflictual views and values within and between given cultures is part of the modern pluralistic view of society and social life. The values of one culture support and legitimise the beliefs and actions of members of that group, and lead them to pursue particular objectives and solve particular types of problem. This may reveal different comparative advantages between different sub-cultural and cultural groups. Such differences in beliefs and values are important to entrepreneurial decision-making, as they affect choices made at the personal, social and political levels. These in turn shape the context of what is possible: constrained as opposed to facilitated actions.

Cultural groups may be characterised by the relationships within the group: tight knit and cohesive, as opposed to loosely tied, even fragmented. Tight-knit social groups tend to reveal higher levels of trust (e.g. some religious groups – Quakers) and this has economic consequences insofar as there is the need for relatively low transaction costs (Casson, 1995). This set of socio-economic circumstances, however, tends to characterise the routine rather than the innovative and may reveal itself in greater efficiencies thus being competitive at that level (Leibenstein, 1966). Loosely tied networks of members of socio-economic or business culture lack cohesion, may negotiate economic relations opportunistically, experience broader and occasionally conflictual information flows and are better positioned to identify opportunities provided that they can manage the uncertainty and attendant risks. One entrepreneurial skill they require, however, is judgemental decision-making (Penrose, 1959; Casson, 1982).

The judgemental decision is defined by Casson (2005: 329) as non-routine and involves synthesising publicly available and private information, making assumptions about the environment in which the entrepreneur is operating and arriving at a subjective assessment of the risk and the decision to invest or not in a project/opportunity. However, for Casson the environment comprises a tangible and intangible structure that impinges on the entrepreneur/entrepreneurial firm and provides an external flow of information that informs his/her decision-making. From a socio-cultural view, however, the judgemental decision may be recast as a subjective judgement as to what is the right thing to do. From a socio-economic structuration perspective, it is a subjective judgement based on a synthesis of knowledge (perceived information in time and space) of what would be a meaningful, personally valuable and powerful solution to a perceived circumstance that results in decisive action. In other words, the judgemental decision from a structuration perspective is one that would 'make a difference' and have the dynamic of creating desired change (Giddens, 1984).

The competitive environment and theory of the firm

I have established that entrepreneurial behaviour is constrained (and at times facilitated) by institutional, market and socio-cultural structures. Industry is part of this environmental structure and, through industry associations, business clubs and other socio-economic facilities, provides a conduit and a network of agents through which knowledge and information flows. However, industry structure in itself has a spatial and temporal existence predating the birth of many small firms and, through structural features, such as industry concentration or fragmentation, it provides a potential constraint on firm behaviour. At the level of the firm, each strives differentially to gain a competitive advantage and deploy its resources efficiently and effectively. However, this begs the question of whether the firm as opposed to the market is the appropriate vehicle for the exploitation of an opportunity? The normal answer by economists is that it is only appropriate when there are information asymmetries or when transaction-specific assets invite opportunism. Coase, however, took a different view by identifying the role of entrepreneur as the authority that has the power to allocate resources within the firm and wider economic system (Coase, 1937: 389). The reason for establishing a firm, he argues, is that the costs are lower than they would be if one were to attempt to organise production through the pricing mechanism (e.g. there would be the costs of negotiating each contract separately, the problems associated with long-term contracts and the issue of control). Hence, there are costs of operating within the market but, by allowing the entrepreneur to form a firm through which s/he can direct resources, some costs are saved. Factors of production are lower than through the market mechanism. However, a critical problem arises when attempting to forecast consumer wants in conditions of Knightian uncertainty. The problem – 'what to do and how to do it' – rests with the entrepreneur; s/he is the 'deciding function' that within conditions of uncertainty is able to *forecast* consumer wants through good judgement and confidence in that judgemental capability. Management, in contrast, *reacts to* price changes. In attempting to deal with future contingencies that are not specifiable, the entrepreneur is able to coordinate the allocation of resources that are under his/her control and deploy them rapidly. This is far more efficient than a situation where resources are disparate and therefore more costly to deploy.

Theoretically, to introduce the entrepreneur into the theory of the firm the assumptions of equilibrium theory, that is, perfect competition and perfect distribution of knowledge, are relaxed (Mises, 1949; Penrose, 1959; Kirzner, 1973). A given firm is able to realise competitive advantage, because it comprises resources that are not possessed by its rivals. These resources are information (about the possible opportunity) and skills (the ability to marshal resources in order to exploit it). Penrose (1959) takes this argument a step further by suggesting that firms qua bundles of resources that compete in this way are not static entities, they aim to grow and evolve.[3] Hence, resource-based theory of the firm has two dimensions: *dis*equilibrium and evolutionary theory (Foss, 2000).

Penrose (1914–1996) assumes that 'history matters', that growth is evolutionary and based on cumulative collective knowledge and learning. She considers that a firm is a collection of productive resources, within an administrative (i.e. organising) framework. Her theory owes something to the classical management scholars of the 1930s (e.g. Mayo, 1933; Barnard, 1938; Follett, 1940), who identified the importance of internal coordination and cooperation as the basis for efficient and effective organisation.

Penrose (1959: 36) takes a subjectivist view of entrepreneurial qualities, noting in particular that *entrepreneurial versatility* comprises imagination and vision, both of which are logically prior to *entrepreneurial judgement* (ibid.: 41). An entrepreneur's *expectations* are not 'objective facts'; they have limited knowledge and experience, but they are supposed to be able to work out the consequences of their actions (ibid.: 55). The climate in which the firm operates is one of uncertainty and risk, and in this situation plans must be developed *for the future*. These plans are based on *subjective expectations of possible outcomes*. Uncertainty too is based on *subjective judgement* and refers to an entrepreneur's *level of confidence* in his estimates and expectations (ibid.: 56). The firm *as a pool of resources is organised in an administrative framework* (ibid.: 149–150). Such an administrative framework has been underscored by organisational theoreticians (e.g. Barnard, 1938; March and Simon, 1958). However, over the years products change; indeed, there needs to be continual change and adjustment in both the productive services and knowledge in line with *external* changes[4] and changes in opportunities. This adjustment is facilitated by the development of absorptive capacity helping to connect productive services with productive opportunities. Change also requires the firm to adapt its operations in order to *maintain a competitive position*, whilst acknowledging that competitors create restrictions on the firm's activities (ibid.: 151). Such changes in external circumstances prompt strategic changes, including the need to change managerial capacity to meet growth in demand and innovation, changing the techniques of distribution and the organisation of production management. Thus, there are critical points in the process of expansion (evolution), in particular the need for new administration and *leadership skills* to meet increasing *specialisation, transformation and transition* to a further stage in growth and development (ibid.: 161). Penrose, of course, did recognise external constraints, which she refers to as 'competitive handicaps' (such as finance), and the position of small firms relative to their larger counterparts – the latter enjoying more extensive market connections, better standing in the capital market, larger internal funds, a successful past record, greater accumulation of experience, ability to take advantage of technological developments and economies of scale (ibid.: 218). The small firm is up against financial and fiscal (structural) constraints of limited access to capital, high interest rates, credit limits and problems of raising capital. Furthermore, growth and evolution of particular firms is not an inevitability. Under conditions of high churn, low profitability and low technical progress (e.g. the UK clothing industry), one should not expect growth. However, even within such conditions, prospective entrepreneurs with unusual ability, original ideas and considerable versatility have a wider choice of economic opportunities than the average. In this regard, they are able to identify the 'interstices' where profitable opportunities have not been pursued (ibid.: 223).

Penrose's theoretical approach to the theory of the firm is consonant with Austrian economics and enables us to tie in entrepreneurship (Foss, 2000; Alvarez and Busenitz, 2001). The subjective nature of entrepreneurial capability – developing insights through trial and error, heuristic methods – is the cognitive capability that characterises the Austrian school's concept of 'alertness to opportunity'. Such insights enable the entrepreneur/ entrepreneurial firm to learn what resources are needed and how they might be configured to exploit an opportunity, that is, they develop a new 'means–end framework': knowledge that that moment of realisation is particular to the firm in the act of opportunity formation and therefore rare and difficult to imitate. It is this process that confers a competitive advantage on the firm. However, there are two key acts inherent in this process: the creation of the opportunity: and the organisation of resources – knowledge and capability – that enable exploitation. Arguably, this knowledge, which has been arrived at through a serendipitous, non-linear process, may include tacit elements and for that reason is difficult to imitate. This in itself provides an *ex post* barrier to competition by rival enterprises. The new combination of resources that the entrepreneurial firm is able to put together may not be well understood, particularly initially by rival firms; this 'causal ambiguity' also prevents rivals from imitating and thus limits competition (Alvarez and Busenitz, 2001: 766). Furthermore, the particular combination of human resources – personnel and their capabilities – makes up the tangible and intangible assets of the firm. This expanding knowledge and 'absorptive capacity' (i.e. the ability to soak up ideas within a specific domain and exploit them) are also part of the entrepreneurial firm's competitive advantage (ibid.). This process becomes cyclic and virtuous because the more the ability to recognise and exploit opportunities, the greater the absorptive capacity and the greater the ability of the firm to sustain continuous innovation.

Firms are heterogeneous and only a proportion develops an idiosyncratic, socially complex set of capabilities that enable them to exploit opportunities and gain a sustainable competitive edge. Socially complex resources are not only difficult to imitate, but are initially likely to be located outside the firm and as such must be recognised and garnered. This raises an interesting issue, the interaction between the entrepreneur and broader society creating a context in which learning occurs and generates a socially complex asset. The latter initially are the competencies required to facilitate opportunity exploitation that generates other intangible assets such as reputation and the development of an effective firm or corporate culture. Where the innovation is of a complex technology, the firm needs socially complex resources for its exploitation. As such, entrepreneurial firms comprise idiosyncratic knowledge bases and competencies; this fact accounts for the different visions that an entrepreneur has that will lead him/her to take a different decision and adopt a different plan from other non-entrepreneurial firms or firms that do not possess sufficient of the same capabilities. These choices, particularly in the early history of a small firm, give it its unique character, but also may have 'path-dependent' implications for the firm (Alvarez and Busenitz, 2001: 769). One possibility is that the novel may become routine and the competitive advantage that was once enjoyed may evaporate. Path dependency,[5] in particular path determination, implies an overtheorised concept of structure (and, in this case, causation) and an undertheorised role for the entrepreneur or agent. Within the limitations of this theory, it is important that the firm engages in continuous innovation practices if it is to maintain a competitive advantage.

The social context to the firm both internally and externally has been addressed by a number of scholars (e.g. Witt, 1998, 1999; Alvarez and Barney, 2004). Witt (1998) is concerned that both imagination and leadership are identified as crucial elements in the evolution of the firm. He argues that the transaction cost economics approach focuses on the internal organisation of resources through formal governance procedures, but fails to explain adequately the role that ideas play in the development of the firm over time. The evolutionary approach suggests firm-specific competencies that highlight the significance of the firm as an organisation for acquiring and using productive knowledge profitably. Hence, the evolutionary approach moves away from a focus on the procedural – the application of known 'routines' and processes – and by focusing on the substantive (concepts and ideas) it is able to explain how firms evolve and how knowledge, ideas and imagination are necessary to achieve technological change, continual reorganisation and the founding of a sustainable enterprise. Thus, there is both an entrepreneurial and a cognitive element in the theory of the evolution of the firm.

Witt asks two important questions: (a) whose imagined venture is to be followed?; and (b) how can firm members be induced to follow one particular imagined business conception and for how long? This, Witt argues, requires a reappraisal of the role of the entrepreneur as leader. The role of leader should be considered within the social-cognitive milieu of the firm, which includes intense communication of ideas within the group, social learning and the development of ideas held in common and the opportunity for the entrepreneur qua leader to shape those ideas. The success of this transmission process is crucial and the mode is through informal communication that facilitates the development of socially shared ideas, tacit understanding and knowledge and shared actions. This reduces the possibility of the emergence of rival concepts, which would signal a lack of effective leadership. There is no room in transaction cost economics and the associated formal governance approach to accommodate this style of leadership (ibid.: 173).

Witt (1998) also addresses why a multi-person firm (or nascent enterprise) may be necessary to realise an entrepreneurial vision and which business concept survives. Put simply, the number of transactions involved is too great for a single entrepreneur. Further, given the starting premise that the business concept is based on entrepreneurial imaginings (Shackle, 1972, 1979), a 'competitive sorting process' occurs. In the case of the nascent enterprise, this sorts out whether the business concept is strong enough to generate an appropriate level of income and results in a decision whether to become an entrepreneur or an employee. This is based on the logic of opportunity costs that each person, including personnel in extant firms, will consider for themselves. It does not preclude the possibility that some judgements may prove to be wrong. Further, this evolutionary approach to the firm also addresses certain issues of firm culture (ibid.: 174). Compliance with the entrepreneur's vision not only reduces opportunism from rival conceptions, but is managed through a combination of social skill (persuasive communication in particular), informality, asymmetric information and bounded rationality, social learning, initiative and creative situational problem-solving. This underscores the necessity of effective leadership in an entrepreneurial context. Essentially, there is in place a social cognitive process by which the entrepreneur achieves 'buy in' to her/his business conception. Where, in an aging firm, this control over the entrepreneurial business concept has slackened, and where routine administration overtakes entrepreneurial leadership, the interactions in the firm change their character and individual initiative and innovativeness are discouraged. This is likely to 'render the firm immobile' and reduce its effectiveness in a competitive and innovative environment. The works of Kanter, for example, have testified to this in her series of popular business books that address the decline in competitiveness of the US corporation in the 1980s (Kanter, 1983, 1989, 1995).

Alvarez and Barney (2004), in contrast to Witt (1998, 1999), take a transaction costs plus resource-based view to develop an alternative theoretical approach to the entrepreneurial firm. They place greater emphasis on formal governance mechanisms, the entrepreneur's behaviour and the existence and scope of the entrepreneurial firm. They do not acknowledge the above evolutionary theory nor do they appear to recognise the issue of the germ of an idea, the role of imagination and subjective judgement. Their starting point is the Kirznerian position that 'a small number of economic actors know about the rent-generating opportunities associated with a particular competitive imperfection' (ibid.: 623). However, such opportunities are recognised and part of the external structure, not, as in the case of evolutionary theory, substantive ideas forming in the entrepreneur's head. Thus, for Alvarez and Barney (2004) to pursue an opportunity the entrepreneur must assemble the necessary resources, be able to appropriate at least some of the surplus that should be generated and do this at the lowest possible cost.

There are two types of economic actor: the arbitrageur, who controls all the resources necessary to generate a surplus and whose organising tasks are trivial; and the entrepreneur, who does not control all the necessary resources and whose main task is to gain access to those resources in such a way that s/he can make a profit. The paper focuses on the latter economic actor and seeks to identify those 'governance structures' such as 'isolating mechanisms' and the type of knowledge that would best enable him or her to achieve these twin goals. Taking knowledge first, explicit knowledge is easier to imitate, whilst tacit knowledge is not and is unlikely to be diffused quickly amongst potential competitors. This 'diffusion of knowledge' issue is relevant to the decision that the entrepreneur makes. To manage explicit knowledge, the most likely governance structures are through the market, for example setting up strategic alliances, licensing agreements and contracts of various kinds. However, this approach is not without its dangers from competition; the first to spot the opportunity[6] (the prospector) needs to involve others in the act of prospecting – by giving away knowledge, s/he also gives away the negotiating power to extract all the value from this opportunity, and the question is to what extent. If s/he tells no one s/he does not have the resources to extract all the wealth from the opportunity acting alone. Hence, this is known as the 'prospector's paradox'. In such circumstances, the entrepreneur/innovator may use various forms of intellectual property protection to try and isolate the opportunity from the competition. If such mechanisms are successful and can be enforced at low costs then they are likely to be preferred over hierarchical governance (i.e. the creation of a firm) for organising resources needed to capitalise on the explicit knowledge underpinning the opportunity. Where intellectual property protection mechanisms are unlikely to be effective then the alternative – hierarchical governance – will be preferred.

Where tacit knowledge is involved, Alvarez and Barney argue that hierarchical governance (the creation of a firm) would be preferred because this enables greater control over that knowledge and reduces the risk of opportunism; the analogy is that of the craftsman–apprenticeship relationship. The craftsman knows more than he can tell; the apprentice is willing to subordinate himself whilst he learns and this enables the organisation to realise the economic value of the opportunity whilst managing associated costs. The sole criterion used to choose is the cost–benefit of the particular organisational form. In reality, however, knowledge associated with a particular opportunity is likely to have a mix of explicit and tacit knowledge associated with it; the choice then would depend on weighing up the balance and exercising judgement. Alvarez and Barney present these choices in the form of an algorithm (ibid.: 630). As such there are four routes:

1   The economic actor controls the required resources and the outcome is *arbitrage*.
2   The economic actor does not control the required resources and knowledge is *explicit*. This leads to the use of effective isolating mechanisms (intellectual property protection) and the outcome is a *non-hierarchical form of governance* through market mechanisms.
3   The economic actor does not control the required resources and knowledge is *explicit*. The judgement is that the use of isolating mechanisms is likely to be ineffective and *a hierarchical form of governance* is required through firm formation.
4   The economic actor does not control the required resources and knowledge is *tacit*. The judgement is that the use of *hierarchical organising mechanisms* in the form of a firm is appropriate.

Hence, this theory covers the economic conditions under which different kinds of entrepreneurial behaviour are most likely. The theory explains the existence of the firm and the conditions that affect its likely scope. It assumes that opportunities exist externally to the firm/entrepreneur and await discovery. Indeed, in that narrow sense they are open to all. However, this theory has limitations. Whilst the authors identify a possible entrepreneurial resource as tacit knowledge, only formal mechanisms of control are considered as being open to the entrepreneur. As argued by Witt (1998, 1999) in the case of option 4 above, transaction cost theory does not elucidate entrepreneurial behaviour at the individual and group level. To capture this, we should assume that tacit knowledge is linked to the envisioning process of the entrepreneur and that a skills set that includes leadership and social/interpersonal competencies is required to handle the embedding of ideas. Informal processes are the appropriate prerequisites. However, in options 3 and 4 above, Alvarez and Barney (ibid.: 633) argue that the reasons for and therefore the way that governance is played out will be different. In option 4, where knowledge is tacit, governance is concerned to control opportunism and to 'create the context within which subtle, tacit and difficult to understand knowledge can be communicated'.[7] This appears to assume that the firm already exists. In the case of option 3, where the relevant knowledge is explicit, Alvarez and Barney (ibid.: 633) argue that hierarchy is important because it slows down the diffusion process and the emergence of competition. Finally, this theory develops the transaction-cost-based approach by explaining why the firm comes into existence. However, we would argue that it is, in Granovetter's terms, an undersocialised account of firm development because those socio-economic linkages that enable firm development are missing (Granovetter, 1973, 1985, 1992). In the example below a socio-economic analysis is developed, and in the ensuing section we consider further such socio-economic constructions of the emergence of the entrepreneurial firm and entrepreneur at the micro-level.

Eisenhardt and Schoonhoven (1996) approach the exploitation of opportunities through the creation of strategic alliances. They are critical of the transaction cost approach, which they argue does not account for the strategic and social factors that are critical to alliance formation in a dynamic environment. They adopt resource-based theory and emphasise the firms' strategic needs for cooperation. Alliance formation occurs when firms are in a vulnerable strategic position and where the pay-off for cooperation is high. They argue that economic action is embedded in a social fabric of opportunities to interact and that these social relations include: personal relationships, status and reputation, strong social position and the lure of the provision of additional resources that would enable the firms to compete effectively. They demonstrate that: (a) firms with many competitors and more technically innovative strategies showed a greater tendency to engage in alliance formation; (b) firms in emergent-stage markets (as opposed to growth or mature) were more likely to engage in alliance formation; and (c) firms with large top management teams that were experienced and well-connected formed product development alliances at higher rates. These key findings were all statistically significant. In contrast, firms with low rates of alliance formation had few resources, mundane technologies and small, less well-connected, less-experienced top management teams. Such management teams, they argue, offer few attractions to potential partner firms. They conclude that in highly uncertain situations firms seek, not avoid, alliance formation. At industry level, they suggest that firm actions are shaped by market factors, competition, barriers to entry and market stage – in the language of structure, they include the systems and rules that shape institutional forces. At firm level, the study emphasises firm-level differences that create heterogeneity based on differential capabilities and characteristics that yield a different quality of action and performance outcomes. Thus, both industry- and firm-level influences are relevant to alliance formation. Within the firm, they point to a set of *internal* cognitive factors such as consensus-building, risk-taking, communication, social integration and willingness to change. Additionally, these firms showed a set of *external* social characteristics such as status, reputation and contacts. In essence they demonstrate that more resources beget more. For established firms in an industry there are thus additional ways to capitalise on opportunities.

Casson (2005) draws together a number of issues in respect of the need to integrate entrepreneurship into the theory of the firm. He takes an 'institutional' approach, combining 'managerial perspectives with economic insights' and defines an entrepreneur as someone who specialises in judgemental decision-making. He assumes that superior judgement on the part of the entrepreneur stems from access to privileged information and that perceptions of risk are subjective. 'A confident entrepreneur may perceive no risk where others perceive considerable risk' (ibid.: 331). The precipitating combination of personal characteristics is confidence and optimism relative to others. Whilst an entrepreneur's judgement may be wrong, if it is not, his or her decision to exploit an opportunity will be profitable, otherwise s/he will endure a loss. Successful entrepreneurship is sustainable because it generates profits.

Casson sets the firm in an environment that may be volatile and thus his firm may be subject to environmental 'shocks' from which he deduces probable managerial/entrepreneurial responses. The link between the entrepreneur and firm is, according to this theory, through the entrepreneur's information about the environment. Moreover, maintaining current information is costly and time consuming so the entrepreneur must devise cost-effective ways of acquiring information to enable him or her to make judgemental decisions about how to respond to different types of environment shock. For short-term contingencies, routines will have been devised, whereas for long-term volatility, decisions would need to be improvised. The individual who is most able to do this is the 'classic entrepreneur'; he 'synthesises information from diverse sources in order to take an important and risky decision' (ibid.: 333). The information generated as a consequence of volatility will enable the entrepreneur to identify new investment opportunities. However, 'the innovative entrepreneur and routine-driven manager perform complementary roles within a typical firm' (ibid.). Casson continues to discuss and classify environmental shocks into demand- and supply-related and tangible and intangible. He concludes that 'combining all these four dimensions together provides a reasonably comprehensive basis

for analysing how different patterns of volatility lead to different manifestations of entrepreneurship, which lead in turn to different sizes and
structures.' (ibid.: 334).

Competition is a further source of volatility that entrepreneurs should
monitor and keep a 'weather-eye' on. Competition in the product market
arises from market-making initiatives of rival firms and generates 'short-
term, tangible, specific and demand-related shocks'. However, this theory of
the firm concerns flows of information to the entrepreneur whose key job is
to monitor this in respect of the volatility of the environment. Hence, this
view of the business system focuses on the flow of information that affects
decision-making; the economic problem is identified as that of devising an
appropriate division of labour to process information and to invest in an
infrastructure that will support it.

Entrepreneurial activity concerns the identification of changes in patterns
of demand and to create new markets to meet these demands. These activities of 'the market-making entrepreneur' are attributed by Casson to the
Austrian school, although the latter he claims assert that:

> [M]arkets are always out of equilibrium and that entrepreneurial inter-
> ventions tend to move markets towards equilibrium ... This inter-
> pretation presumes that the markets already exist ... Radical forms of
> market-making entrepreneurship, however, involve designing products
> or specifying services that did not previously exist and for which there
> was, therefore, no market.
>
> (Casson, 2005: 336)

This suggests that there must be careful integration between production and
market-making; it is thus incumbent on the entrepreneur who has developed
a new product (or service) to invest in appropriate production facilities. This
would mean integrating backwards where irreversible investment in production is required. Under this view the producer and market-maker are one
and the same. Such a tactic takes care of potential competitive rivalry and
ensures quality control. Further, the market-making entrepreneur does not
necessarily have to invest in fixed capital assets (which may be leased or
rented) but s/he does have to invest in working capital, including stock and
work in progress. The extent of this investment is based on the entrepreneur's expectations and judgement of future demand. Hence, in contrast
to the assumptions of neo-classical economics, the theory of entrepreneurship emphasises the riskiness of investment in inventory. Small firms may
thus experience cash flow problems, which suggests that efficient inventory
control and cash flow management are vital for the stability of the firm.

A further refinement of Casson's theory of the entrepreneurial firm is that
the 'organiser-entrepreneur' and the 'ideas-based entrepreneur' should be
one and the same because, he argues, there is not a market for ideas except in
the sense of patentable ideas and, secondly, were one to separate out these

two then there would be divergent expectations. Hence, normally the entrepreneur must take responsibility for implementing his/her ideas, which suggests s/he requires financial resources and organising skills. This also implies that entry into entrepreneurship is not free; both financial endowments and organising skills are significant barriers to entry. However, what this part of Casson's theory appears to overlook is the role of partnerships and/or team entrepreneurship (Chell and Tracey, 2005).

A further element of the theory is that the entrepreneur[8] is more optimistic than other people. Optimism creates an opportunity, whilst pessimism creates a barrier to entry:

> If the entrepreneur's judgement is correct, then the greater this psychological barrier, the more profit is likely to be made for if other people share his optimistic estimates, they then will compete for the same resources, driving up their buying price, competing for the same customers, driving down the selling price, and eliminating the margin from which the entrepreneur derives his profit (Hayek, 1937). If on the other hand, other people are very pessimistic then there will be no competition so the entrepreneur will be able to exploit his market power to the full.
>
> (Casson, 2005: 340)

However, the entrepreneur also needs the cooperation and support of others (including employees and suppliers) if s/he is to be successful. This means influencing other peoples' opinions to align with his/her own. By getting these others to share in his/her optimism s/he can reduce her/his fixed costs. Hence, in these kinds of ways Casson has produced a theory of the entrepreneurial firm that predicts various kinds of managerial (institutional) behaviour. Furthermore, he claims that the role that he has cast the entrepreneur in as information-manager 'explains a great deal about the personality of the entrepreneur' (ibid.: 342): for example, *his/her optimism, self-confidence, effective social networking and low aversion to risk*. Entrepreneurs are thus considered to be highly *plausible* in enhancing their *personal image* and in *self-promotion*. Such plausibility has been captured in terms like 'charisma' and phrases such as 'larger than life'. As such they are well able to motivate their staff, set ambitious targets and build consensus. Such a view is consonant with Witt's argument (presented above) of 'leadership' as a crucial attribute of the successful entrepreneur. However, Casson's position is quite different from that of Witt as this view is based on transaction, or more specifically information costs; the entrepreneur assesses the cost of monitoring external volatility and builds that into his/her calculation. 'It is, therefore, quite unnecessary to depart from the paradigm of rationality in order to explain the administrative procedures adopted by entrepreneurs' (ibid.: 343). Furthermore, Casson's entrepreneurs operate by a system of rules: 'Indeed, it could be argued that the rules selected by an entrepreneur as a basis for his organisation are the nearest thing to a fixed factor within the theory of the firm because they are the single thing that is most costly to change' (ibid.). This is close to Giddens' view of institutional behaviour that such structures endure and are difficult to change. Rules can become so immured that they are indistinguishable from the institutional fabric. They are part of the culture – the modus operandi – shaping expectations of how things are done. Yet by the same token, such rigidities, such inflexibilities, do *not* sit well with our understanding of entrepreneurial behaviour. Rather, such behaviour (as Casson illustrates) was typical of large firms in the 1980s and 1990s – firms that Kanter (1989) argued needed to 'learn to dance'.

Casson's theory of the entrepreneurial firm clearly links the entrepreneur to the environment. Whilst his entrepreneurs specialise in judgemental decision-making, it is the volatility of the environment that throws up opportunities and creates a market for this skill. Thus, Casson adopts a realist position with respect to the discovery (rather than the formation) of opportunities by the entrepreneur. Further, Casson claims that his theory is more 'true to Schumpeter' as it is applicable to all markets and not simply the technological or the radically innovative. He also argues that, whilst the assumptions of his theory are consistent with transaction economics, he takes a broader view of information asymmetry (ibid.: 345). Finally, Casson argues that his theory of the firm has a longer intellectual tradition than the resource-based view attributed to Penrose (1959), because of its 'greater breadth' insofar as it relates the entrepreneur's capabilities to the nature of the business environment (arguably, Penrose does this too) and 'greater depth', because it generalises the rational decision-making model to multi-stage decision-making. Penrose, however, adopts the position of subjective decision-taking, where the entrepreneur responds to the perceived environment, whereas Casson is reluctant to move away from 'rational choice'. Subjective decision-making is consistent with the theory that entrepreneurial decision-making is idiosyncratic, and may even be counter-intuitive.

The micro-level environment: the entrepreneur and socio-economic context

In the above section, I have argued that economic approaches such as transaction cost economics undertheorise the socio-economic environment and therefore provide an incomplete account of entrepreneurial firm emergence. In this section, I consider current theoretical approaches that attempt to address the socio-economic conditions that affect firm emergence, acting either as constraints or enablers. To do so I draw once more on sociological theory, specifically Giddens and also the work of Granovetter.

Jack and Anderson (2002) combine Giddens' structuration theory with the concept of social embeddedness to develop an explanation of entrepreneurial firm formation and entrepreneurial effectiveness in a remote area in the Scottish Highlands. Embedding, they argue, is how an entrepreneur becomes part of the local structure and creates a contextual competitive advantage. Embeddedness is more than a network of socio-economic roles: being part of the social structure enables the entrepreneur to identify and realise opportunities. The concept of embedding links structure and agency in a dynamic relationship. It involves the entrepreneur (a) not only becoming part of the local structure, but understanding it; (b) enacting and re-enacting the structure and thereby forging new links into the local community; and (c) being enabled to maintain both the links and the structure. The researchers found that there is no one way in which embedding occurs, but that it does involve developing one's credibility and understanding of how business is done in the locality. This influenced how the entrepreneurs managed and developed their businesses. This paper emphasises the social aspect of entrepreneurship, the entrepreneurial process and, through entrepreneurial agency, the ability to recognise opportunities in the structure. There is a dynamic between structure and agency – the recognition of a local need (within the structure) – whilst the entrepreneurs also drew upon the locality to support their business. Knowledge was crucial in two respects: the entrepreneurs developing their knowledge of the local area; and the locals developing their knowledge of the entrepreneurs and their businesses. Thus, the relationship became a two-way exchange, with trust and understanding being a socially derived outcome.

Chiasson and Saunders (2005) adopt Giddens' structuration theory to critique a number of approaches to opportunity recognition and formation. They argue that structuration theory dissolves the recognition–formation dichotomy to suggest that opportunities are both formed and created through *scripts*. Structure is linked to action through scripts, which are 'recipes' that enable people to get things done. They are a form of 'behavioural grammar' that informs everyday action. However, they are not as regularised as linguistic rules; as socially constructed ways of dealing with the everyday, they are subject to modification. Scripts have a number of attributes based on Giddens' theorising: signification (meaningfulness), legitimisation (legitimacy) and domination (power). Thus, scripts are meaningful if an individual can act on them quickly within a business setting; they are not only understood, but they conform to a set of expectations that are valued and this gives them legitimacy; they are powerful if they enable the agent to 'get things done'. Modification and change in scripts can arise intentionally or unintentionally, through deliberate experimentation or by chance. Within structuration theory, entrepreneurs would not necessarily be aware of script use but they would act reflexively to monitor the outcomes of their use, thus eliciting knowledge about business and social structure. 'From this definition, entrepreneurial *experience*, could be defined as a person's previous exposure to successful and unsuccessful scripts in the production of meaningful, powerful, and legitimate business outcomes' (Chiasson and Saunders, 2005: 753).

In this paper, Chiasson and Saunders review critically six different approaches to opportunity research that span the recognition-formation spectrum. Opportunity recognition is identified with structure, where an agent identifies and reinforces (unintentionally) the extant structure through pre-existent scripts, whereas for opportunity formation the entrepreneur forms a new and unique script. '[Structuration theory] suggests that both are correct, implying that, while the general form of the scripts may be unaffected by entrepreneurial action, the selection, shaping, and use of many common and uncommon scripts within a setting are under their control' (ibid.: 754). Furthermore, there is always an initial stage in the process that concerns *recognition* and draws on the knowledge/awareness of rules and resources within the structure. This should not preclude idiosyncratic knowledge. The entrepreneur formulates this knowledge as a 'business script'. Departing from the paper, we suggest that the entrepreneur would then *intentionally* enact the script[9] (Bird, 1989). Alternatively, s/he may choose to ignore the script (i.e. opportunity). The extent to which s/he will ignore or enact the script is crucial to understanding the extent to which the structure is changed. By reinforcing and changing the script, structure is modified and the script is further developed accordingly. In this way, opportunity scripts are formulated over time.

For the purposes of this discussion we shall focus on two of the six approaches to entrepreneurship discussed by Chiasson and Saunders: neo-classical equilibrium theory (NCET) and embeddedness, which they bracket with effectuation and relationality theories (EER). With regard to NCET they make the following observations:

1   Opportunities are independent of the entrepreneur and available to all.
2   There is uneven exploitation depending upon *who* recognises them and this is a function of individual differences.
3   Recognition is more important than formation.
4   NCET is particularly relevant in industries with strong industrial norms.
5   The problems with NCET are:

   a   Studies of personality characteristics have been unable to predict consistently individuals who will identify opportunities. There is a need to consider the setting and industrial context.

   b   Structuration theory suggests that opportunities are re-enacted through scripts, thus the focus on psychometrics will at best only capture those individuals who can mimic that narrow set of scripts, which limits prediction.

   c   NCET ignores the legitimacy and power dimensions of script imitation, the social and political aspects that affect costs and the decision to become an entrepreneur.

For embeddedness, the following observations are made:

1 Embeddedness emphasises *forming* opportunities by pulling together resources close at hand and thus the entrepreneur draws on readily available scripts to exploit new product/service possibilities.
2 The entrepreneur develops social relations inside and outside the organisation to foster local and specific advantages.
3 Embeddedness is thus deemed to be important for social integration and entrepreneurial success.
4 All scripts unintentionally reinforce and only occasionally change broader business and social structures. Thus within (and they specifically refer to the Jack and Anderson version of embeddedness described above) embeddedness the script structure is limited by these broader structural constraints.
5 We might add that this version of embeddedness emphasises strong local ties *only*. It might be worth recalling Granovetter's (1973) argument in respect of the strength of weak ties. In this version of embeddedness the successful entrepreneur purposely develops relationships in remote and disconnected parts of an initially potential network. This suggests that the entrepreneur should prepare multiple scripts at different levels in the network and draw on widely different and remote sources of knowledge and resources that enable him/her to formulate and pursue an opportunity effectively (Chell and Baines, 2000).

Sarason *et al.* (2006) take further the idea that structuration theory can usefully shed light on the individual–opportunity nexus put forward by Shane and Venkataraman (2000). In focusing on the entrepreneurial process in this way, they avoid investigating the nature of the entrepreneur or the nature of the opportunity separately. Rather, they focus on the dynamic interaction between the two. The entrepreneur, they argue, is a reflexive agent who specifies, interprets and acts on sources of opportunity. The individual–opportunity nexus is viewed as a duality in which entrepreneur and opportunity come together and are intertwined such that neither is independent of the other. Hence, opportunities do not exist a priori. Further, because of this complex interdependency, the process is idiosyncratic and path-dependent. This enables a consideration of the idiosyncratic nature of the nexus rather than on the potential imitability of an opportunity. As such, entrepreneurship is concerned with interpreting extant relationships in a new way. In contrast to the traditional view, which holds that entrepreneurs identify and fill market gaps, structuration suggests that entrepreneurial ventures are recursive processes that evolve. Sources of opportunities are constructed and reconstructed over time.

Hence, taking structuration as the theoretical framework, entrepreneurs create and do not simply discover opportunities 'out there' and the new venture is not a deterministic reflection of a market gap. This presents a subjective ontology that constitutes an alternative to positivism and post-positivism. Moreover, taking the entrepreneurial process to be loosely defined as 'discovery, evaluation and exploitation', they suggest that, within structuration, the discovery process concerns the interpretation of a meaningful opportunity (structure); thus, signification structures are more important at this stage. Evaluation concerns the assessment of opportunities that emerge from discovery and, as such, legitimation structures are more salient. Finally, domination that in this instance would concern the power to control and transform resources is arguably more salient in the exploitation phase.

This paper attempts to recognise fully the subjective nature of the entrepreneurial process: that it represents a 'double hermeneutic', subjective and reflexive, where the entrepreneur has the ability not only to reflect on but also to change that which is being observed. Further, the theory recognises that the socio-economic system is dynamic and subject to change, dynamically creating opportunities based on subjective interpretations. In this way, we can say that it builds on earlier economic theorists such as Shackle (see Chapter 2), and is also evolutionary in its approach – again this could be seen to link to extant economic theory, some of which we have referred to in this chapter. Our criticisms are that, as presented, it may be oversocialised; moreover, it fails to recognise that institutional structures, for example, may temporally precede the individual–opportunity nexus whilst also forming a constraining or enabling structure. Finally, we note that that the individual–opportunity nexus is labelled 'idiosyncratic'. In this theory, we presume that another agent could not act as a substitute. We therefore need to consider further the extent to which the individual–opportunity nexus could be considered unique (i.e. not substitutable) in all cases of entrepreneurial venturing. This will be a subject that we shall come back to in our concluding chapter.

Conclusion

In this chapter I have outlined critically an interdisciplinary approach – the socio-economic theoretical frame that encompasses the socio-economic environment and the role of the entrepreneur in a social and economic setting. This broadens the economists' assumption of an entrepreneurial *function* to a consideration of socially derived rules and norms that affect the entrepreneurial role and behaviour at different societal levels. The three principal parts to this chapter, macro-, meso- and micro-, represent three different levels of analysis. At the macro-level, Giddens presents a grand theory of society in which he theorises about the impact of institutional structures on agentic behaviour. His particular contribution of structuration theory indicates that structure and agency are intimately interlinked and that institutional structures are produced and reproduced through agency. However, we also saw how important it is to consider structures as having temporal and spatial existence independently of agency, which gives those structures 'facticity' and an ontological reality that presents an ongoing presence of stability within society. The complexity of this social constructionist approach is more pronounced when we also consider Giddens' notion of 'rules and resources' that drive agency-structure engagement. Rules – socially derived – are unlike linguistic rules and vary in their strength and flexibility. Further, meaning is highly variable and presents the individual with the means to construe situations; status and social position give legitimacy and power to transform events. Hence, structure is not wholly deterministic; it is counterbalanced by agentic freedom to act. Thus an entrepreneur operating in this milieu performs a socio-economic role. However, that role is circumscribed by socio-economic and socio-political demands; this leaves open the nature of the supply of entrepreneurs to fulfil such demands.

At the meso-level there is an evident struggle between business economists who have adopted a more conventional route – say, transaction economics – and those who have developed a theoretical approach or approaches based on the subjective nature of entrepreneurial decision-making in their different attempts to answer the question: why are firms formed and how? Transaction economics assumes that firms exist to fill a gap in the market, that decision-making concerns issues of cost efficiency and that management of firms is through formal procedures of governance to reduce the possibility of malfeasance or opportunism. Several theorists have found this approach wanting. First, they argue that it does not explain how firms come into existence; to explain this we need to understand how resources in the environment are organised in order to exploit a perceived opportunity. Resource-based theory addresses this issue by assuming disequilibrium conditions and the evolution of the firm. This gives a clear role for the entrepreneur. Second, it is essential to understand the behavioural element in firm formation. Entrepreneurs work within the limits of their knowledge and experience in taking decisions; they are also working in conditions of uncertainty and need to make judgements based on their subjective assessments of the perceived market opportunity, and the capabilities and resources that can be garnered in order to create a strategic advantage over rivals. Firms are heterogeneous and only a proportion of them develop an idiosyncratic, socially complex set of capabilities that enable them to exploit opportunities and gain a sustainable competitive advantage. This suggests that the entrepreneur must interact within broader society, gleaning knowledge and information, and learning in order to construct a socially (and, occasionally, technically) complex set of resources that is difficult to imitate. Entrepreneurs are thus constrained, but are also free to make decisions that create their future and that of the enterprise. However, the theory fails to address the supply of entrepreneurs.

Entrepreneurs who develop an extensive network of weak ties within the socio-economy put themselves in a stronger position to identify and absorb the resources they need in order to realise an opportunity. The development of a personal network is part of the strategic armoury of the entrepreneur. Internally, when firms are forming, contrary to transaction economics, these nascent firms do not possess a formal internal structure (see Chell *et al.*, 1991). Rather, as Witt argues, the 'firm' is primarily a vision based on the imagination of the entrepreneur and the important questions are: (a) are the ideas of the entrepreneur convincing; and (b) is the entrepreneur sufficiently persuasive that others will join him/her to enable the firm to evolve? This emphasises the role of entrepreneur as leader, creating a social-cognitive milieu through intense informal communication of ideas within the group: social learning occurs – the ideas develop and are held in common. This promotes shared understanding and tacit knowledge and reduces the likelihood of rival conceptions. This underlines a further point that, to survive, the nascent enterprise must have a configuration of resources that at least initially is difficult to imitate. It also underscores the autonomous nature of entrepreneurs, as they take on the responsibility to assume a leading role in directing and shaping the future of the enterprise.

The firm and entrepreneur are linked to the socio-economic environment by several researchers. Eisenhardt and Schoonhoven approach the exploitation of opportunities through the creation of strategic alliances and emphasise the importance of cooperative tactics and social factors in alliance formation. Casson, on the other hand, views the economic environment as turbulent, throwing up unexpected occurrences that create opportunities but also affect entrepreneurial judgemental decision-taking. He also takes an 'institutional approach' and casts the entrepreneur in the role of 'information manager'. This, he argues, has implications for the personality of the entrepreneur. Casson's position, however, is quite different to that of Witt, in that his theory is based on transactions and information costs; a rational view of entrepreneurial behaviour is assumed in which entrepreneurs operate with a system of rules. However, the system of rules appears to be quite rigid and this does not sit well with our view of entrepreneurial behaviour as requiring considerable flexibility. But one assumes that the answer to the question of the supply of entrepreneurs would be met by the assumption of profitable opportunities; however, it does not explain whether such economic incentives would be sufficient to increase the supply of individuals with the requisite capabilities.

Further, at the micro-level several theoreticians introduce Giddens' theoretical framework in order to link the entrepreneur closely with the socio-economic environment. The development of a general theory of entrepreneurial behaviour is produced by Chiasson and Saunders (2005); it focuses on the recognition–formation spectrum of opportunity research. Initially the entrepreneur recognises a knowledge-information-resource configuration that s/he interprets as meaningful (i.e. has potential), valuable, will fit in with the expectations of significant others and is such that it empowers him/her to act. In interpreting this as a potential opportunity the entrepreneur draws on his/her experience and knowledge and forms a plan or business *script* of how to take the opportunity forward. This further stage is the formation of the opportunity: the creation of a new and unique *script* that is enacted. This develops over time as the entrepreneur reflects on how elements of the structure going forward constrain or enable it. However, by reinforcing and changing the script, the structure is changed and the two co-evolve over time. Thus the entrepreneur learns how to play the game, iteratively developing an opportunity and testing it against perceived and experienced structures creatively and deftly.

Sarason *et al.* (2006) add that by taking the entrepreneurial process to be loosely defined as 'discovery, evaluation and exploitation', they explain how, within structuration, the discovery process concerns the interpretation of a meaningful opportunity, evaluation concerns the assessment of opportunities that emerge from discovery and exploitation concerns the power to control and transform resources. This approach could be usefully explored through the use of case studies as the particularities of the socio-economic context will affect how structuration is played out. Furthermore, structure and, indeed, agentic elements should be developed further to achieve a more rounded view of the particular case. Structuration theory fails to theorise about the nature of the agent – at best, agency is a role – and this leaves a void in which we might be forgiven for believing that in the case of the entrepreneur anyone can fulfil this role. However, even if we take the concept of 'embedding', this presumes the ability of the entrepreneur to formulate social and economic bonds and relationships that are close and others that are more distant but nonetheless important, which suggests at the very least the importance of social and interpersonal capabilities. Such capabilities enable the entrepreneur to leverage and garner resources for the development of his/her vision or plan, thereby creating both social awareness and a market for the good (Jack and Anderson, 2002). This particular aspect of theory could be said to tie the entrepreneur into a specific socio-economy and arguably hints at either different types of entrepreneur or the flexibility of entrepreneurs that enables them to adapt to specific local socio-economic conditions.

Social constructionism is able to explain the importance of the socio-economic and political environment and its impact on entrepreneurial behaviour. However, that explanation is largely confined to the demand for entrepreneurship and innovation and the role that may be played out by entrepreneurs at different socio-economic levels. In the next two chapters, consideration is given to the supply side issue; can anyone be an entrepreneur or does an entrepreneur have particular characteristics that can be identified and measured? Thus, I next consider the trait approach to characterising the entrepreneur.

Notes

1 For an expansion of this thesis, see Archer (1988: 47–59).
2 Archer (1988) uses the term 'actors', which I eschew as society in my theory is not populated with actors, acting out roles, but with social beings, who are inter-

preting situations based on the information available to them, often from a wide variety of sources not confined to the institutional, as in the Giddens' rule-driven sense.

3 Some economists, who knew Edith Penrose, allege that she was not a 'resource-based theorist' (Mark Casson, Brian Loasby, private communications). This section suggests that she was primarily an 'evolutionary economist' whose ideas have since been taken to underpin current resource-based theory.

4 By external changes we presume that Penrose assumes an external structure that shapes the firm's environment.

5 Path dependency (which may vary and is common) appears to be being used by these authors in the sense of path determination (which is rare), but from a methodological perspective has a strong positivist overtone.

6 This example underlines the realist position they have adopted in respect of the discovery (as opposed to the creation) of opportunities. Shane (2003) adopts a similar position. The idea was explicitly rejected by Richardson (1960) and implicitly by Penrose (1959).

7 The issue of the internal management of tacit knowledge is dealt with extensively by Nonaka and Takeuchi (1995) and also by Witt (1998, 1999), albeit in rather different ways. Witt's approach as discussed in this chapter is readily applicable to the nascent enterprise, whereas Nonaka and Takeuchi assumed an extant firm.

8 It is a moot point as to whether what is meant is that entrepreneurs are generally more optimistic people, or that their optimism is project-specific.

9 Theoretically and in practice an entrepreneur could unintentionally enact a script. However, it is difficult to argue that this is consistent with, for example, entrepreneurial alertness.

4 The search for entrepreneurial traits: 'The Big Three'

Introduction

In the previous two chapters we have considered: (a) how economists over the past three centuries have viewed the entrepreneur essentially as a functional role in an economy, but also in some instances as an individual with some implied personal attributes; and (b) the socio-economic and socio-cultural contexts in which entrepreneurs do business. In this endeavour a theoretical foundation based on social constructionist premises has been laid to explain entrepreneurial behaviour. From the economics of the entrepreneurial process it was clear that: entrepreneurs use their imagination in the recognition, formation and exploitation of opportunities; garner resources; exercise judgement and leadership; and, usually but not exclusively, found firms in order to manage the process. Moreover, entrepreneurs enact this entrepreneurial process within a context, and to explain interaction within the context Giddens' structuration theory was assumed. However, structuration theory tends to undertheorise the agent. This leaves open the question of whether and, if so, how might the agent be best described.

Furthermore, as long as nations trade competitively and seek to increase the standard of living of the population generally, entrepreneurship and innovation will be part of the government's agenda. Thus there will be a demand for entrepreneurship, but what of the supply? There are two theoretical perspectives that attempt to answer this question: (a) supply may be manipulated through incentives – making the environment more conducive to entrepreneurship – and people with appropriate *human capital* will rise to the bait; and (b) the supply is limited to individuals who have the appropriate *personality* characteristics. In this chapter the aim is to concentrate primarily on the latter perspective. However, before doing so, I will briefly outline some of the human capital issues.

Human capital theory

Human capital, according to Schultz (see Chapter 2), concerns abilities that enable a person to exploit a profitable opportunity. This theory of human capital has since been extended to include, for example, parental occupation, gender, ethnicity/race, education, work experience and inherited wealth (Burke *et al.*, 2000; Delmar and Davidsson, 2000; Minniti *et al.*, 2005). One problem with such research is that it aids prediction of self-employment,[1] but not entrepreneurship per se. Human capital theory may, however, be linked to institutional theory (and the theoretical underpinnings discussed in Chapter 3), where culture in the form of patriarchal pressure, for example, hinders women from entering self-employment (Delmar and Davidsson, 2000), and the view that women find it more difficult to identify with small business men as a group (Aldrich and Zimmer, 1986). Other human capital factors, such as education, show mixed results and are related to the type of industry (e.g. knowledge intensive).

Thus, human capital theory identifies some of the personal factors that limit or, in some instances, enable self-employment. It goes some way towards enabling the prediction of self-employment, given large cohorts, and reveals overall differences between countries (e.g. Delmar and Davidsson, 2000; Minniti *et al.*, 2005), but it does not explain why or how some individuals who enter self-employment manifest superior entrepreneurial performance whilst others are unable to grow their business, drop out or just remain self-employed. To develop an explanation, it is necessary to ask whether there is something about the personality of entrepreneurs that enables them to exploit opportunities successfully, in a sustained way, resulting in socio-economic benefits.

I now turn to a general discussion of personality theory, before reviewing evidence for (or against) a select number of traits that have dominated entrepreneurial trait theory, namely achievement motivation, locus of control and risk propensity.

The relevance of personality theory

The fundamental problem is to arrive at an understanding of the nature of personality in general, given the considerable revisions in thinking that have taken place in recent years. These issues have been recounted in some detail in the first edition of this book and include a 'crisis of confidence' in personality theory (discussed in detail in Chapter 6 of this volume). The question of what is 'personality' and what is the basis of the trait construct are fundamental to such concerns. The lay person uses the term 'personality' in a very different way to that of the psychologist. The lay person uses it in the sense of 'distinctiveness of character', even 'celebrity', seeing the whole 'type' of person rather than a single dimension. The psychologist refers to personality structure and dynamic inner processes that are private. Hence, ' "personality" refers to stylistic consistencies in behaviour, which are a reflection of inner structure and process' (Furnham, 1992: 15). Thus, when the lay person uses the term 'entrepreneur' they are referring to a type; they can 'recognise one when they see one' because they believe that they have sufficient public information to label that individual as an entrepreneur. This is not the same, clearly, as the scientific process that a psychologist engages in – the ability to isolate traits that are predictive of specific behaviours; in this case it is the belief that there is a trait or set of traits that characterise an entrepreneur and are predictive of entrepreneurial behaviour.

A trait is a single dimension of personality, which is made up of a number of components. Take, for example, the trait of neuroticism. This is made up of a mix of behaviours and cognitions of guilt, depression, low self-esteem, anxiety, phobia and psychosomatic illness. However, neuroticism is identified as a key part of the structure of personality – a general trait – whereas entrepreneurialism would at best be considered to be a specific trait. The questions then for the psychologist and the psychometrician that still need to be addressed are: Is there a trait 'entrepreneurialism'? Or, if not a single trait, can the components of an entrepreneurial personality be identified, and should a measure of either the single trait or the constellation be developed? It is not that difficult (although it is time consuming and not inexpensive) to construct such a measure; the problem is constructing one that is conceptually and theoretically grounded, has the appropriate psychometric properties and is externally valid (i.e. has predictive utility). As indicated, a further question to consider is whether (if it exists) the entrepreneurial personality is uni-dimensional (comprising a single trait) or, indeed, whether it is multi-dimensional and can be described by a constellation or profile of traits.

During the 1980s, the counter-argument was expressed that entrepreneurialism is a 'contact sport', it is about 'doing' (i.e. behaviour) and not 'being' (trait characteristics); we should therefore focus on the 'dance' and not the 'dancer' (Gartner, 1989). Such a line of argument does not itself negate the possible influence of personality, as personality and behaviour are related. However, the theoretical position that behaviour is solely a function of personality may not hold up in the case of the expression of entrepreneurship. Rather, it could be argued that behaviour is a function of personality and situation, and their interaction (Chell, 1985a).

Hence, I suggest that it is necessary to start by examining personality structure. Throughout, one should bear in mind the following questions:

- What theory of personality is being espoused?
- What are the fundamental dimensions of personality structure?
- Do personality factors predict behaviour in the work context?
- Is personality stable or variable over time?
- Is personality inherited or learnt?
- Can personality change or be changed?
- How can personality be measured reliably?
- What other individual differences, apart from personality, predict behaviour?
- How are relevant traits related to one another?
- Are traits the same as types?

- How can our knowledge of personality be applied in the study of entrepreneurs in the identification of entrepreneurs and prediction of their behaviour?

The classic structure of personality and traditional trait theories

Traditional or classic trait theories assume that the trait (P) causes behaviour (B); personality (P) – the cause – is known as the independent variable, and behaviour (B) – the effect or overt expression of P – is known as the dependent variable. There are several different trait approaches:

- Single trait approach. A single trait is identified and measured, for example locus of control (Rotter, 1966).[2]
- Multiple trait approach, where a profile of traits is assumed to predict specified behaviour.
- Personality structure, where a trait system is identified and the trait profile is measured (e.g. Eysenck, 1967; Cattell, 1971).
- Cognitive traits. A trait dimension is identified in cognitive terms, for example belief systems such as conservatism (Wilson, 1973). Cognitive traits refer to the ways people perceive the world and make judgements and decisions (Baron, 2004) and/or to their cognitive style, that is, a person's preferred approach to information processing (Allinson *et al.*, 2000).
- Biologically based traits. Some traits such as neuroticism (Eysenck, 1967) are assumed to have a biological basis to them, hence a person's behaviour reflects biological differences.
- Normal/abnormal traits. Traits such as depression, psychopathy and hypochondria are measured as an aspect of abnormal behaviour.
- Psychodynamic theories. Freudian theory claims to measure deep-seated unconscious needs and fears, formed in childhood.

The measurement of single traits or trait profiles does not include all the approaches psychologists have taken to personality; other approaches include interactionism, social psychological and the cognitive approaches that have been developed over the past two decades and will be discussed in some detail in Chapter 6. Probably the most prominent approach has been that of research to determine the structure of personality. The history of trait psychology can be traced back to the nineteenth century and the work of Sir Francis Galton (1884), and in subsequent decades to the development of statistical techniques such as factor analysis. However, the father of trait psychology and personality theory is generally considered to be G. W. Allport (1937). Allport assumed a normal distribution of traits in a population and thereby opened the door to the exploration of the science of trait psychology, including the construction of psychometric measures to assess a

dimension or dimensions of personality. The procedure involves questionnaire construction for personality assessment. Each dimension is measured
by a single scale that must adhere to a number of psychometric properties –
reliability, stability and validity. A personality inventory may include scales
that measure more than one trait or dimension of personality. When applied
to a population, the data collected will be factor analysed and the norm for
that particular population established. Populations or statistical samples
may be gathered from known groups that are targeted for research purposes, such as occupational groups. In this way norms for the population in
general and for identified sub-groups may be compared.

Factor analysis enables the psychometrician to manage a vast amount of
data, in particular trait descriptive adjectives. The general idea is to explore
whether there might be an underlying structure to these traits. For example,
Matthews and Oddy (1993) identified three personality dimensions – conscientiousness, agreeableness and intellectance – from twelve trait descriptive adjectives by means of factor analysis and correlation techniques. This
gives a sense of hierarchy amongst personality traits, some traits being
broader and more encompassing than others. The attempt to identify primary trait dimensions that may be correlated to form secondary traits (such
as extraversion) is the basic concept of psychometric attempts to identify the
structure of personality.

The identification of primary traits began with the work of Raymond B.
Cattell (1946, 1971) and the Sixteen Personality Factor questionnaire
(16PF), which became a standard measure (Cattell *et al.*, 1970). Further
work has meant improvements to internal consistency, though there are
important differences between the 16PF5 (Conn and Rieke, 1994) and
earlier versions. Studies have been undertaken of various occupational
groups, with considerable face-validity (Cattell and Kline, 1977). However,
criticisms of the construct validity of the various scales remain (Matthews
et al., 2003: 19).

A highly influential personality theory that has enjoyed forty years
of pre-eminence is H. J. Eysenck's three-factor model (Eysenck, 1967,
1997). Eysenck identified three broad personality factors – neuroticism,
extraversion–introversion and psychoticism (see Box 4.1). The current
version of this self-completion questionnaire is the Eysenck Personality
Questionnaire Revised (EPQ-R: Eysenck and Eysenck, 1991).

The most recent major work on personality structure is that of 'The Big
Five' factor model (Costa and McCrae, 1992; De Raad, 2000). The Costa
and McCrae NEO-PI-R inventory comprises 240 questions, 48 that measure
each of the five dimensions. These dimensions are called neuroticism, extraversion, openness, agreeableness and conscientiousness (N, E, O, A and C).
Matthews *et al.* (2003) point out that the personality inventories of Eysenck,
Costa and McCrae, and others are not the same as personality theories;
they are current, 'best attempts' to measure personality structure but they
are always subject to revision. The current view of personality structure,

Box 4.1   Eysenck's three-dimensional structure of personality

The neurotic individual (high N – neuroticism) is anxious, worries, loses sleep, tends towards depression, may allow emotions to affect their judgement and is preoccupied with things that might go wrong. The low N scorer recovers quickly after an upsetting experience and is generally calm and unworried. *The extravert* is sociable, craves excitement, takes chances, likes laying practical jokes, may be unreliable and has a tendency to lose their temper. *The introvert* tends to be quiet and retiring, fond of books rather than people, is serious, keeps feelings under control, is reliable and has high ethical standards. *The psychotic* is solitary, troublesome and often cruel, lacks the ability to empathise with others, is aggressive and has unusual tastes. The traits of neuroticism and psychoticism were intended to describe normal personality dimensions even though when taken to extremes they are descriptive of abnormal behaviour or personality disorders. Eysenck also suggested that there is a biological basis to personality (Eysenck, 1967). Indeed physiological studies have suggested that, for example, the extravert is someone who requires stimulation, whereas the introvert does not and so tends to avoid situations that may be overstimulating.

however, is that 'The Big Five' explain much of personality, that is, five factor solutions have now been arrived at from a number of disparate sources (see Matthews *et al.*, 2003: 25–38 for an overview of this evidence). In a seminal paper, 'Personality Traits are Alive and Well', Deary and Matthews (1993) focus their attention in particular on the 'Big Five', as indeed does Hampson (1988) in her assessment of personality structure.

Personality theory continues to be controversial, with important issues being debated. McClelland (1996), for example, asked the question: 'Does the field of personality have a future?' This clearly is an issue that scholars of entrepreneurship have raised in respect of the so-called 'entrepreneurial personality' (Chell, 1985a; Gartner, 1989; Chell *et al.*, 1991). McClelland again raises problems associated with methodology, for instance he suggests that a considerable proportion of research uses self-report measures of conscious cognitive variables. Self-report data of this kind can be unreliable. He advocates greater use of implicit measures that can tap unconscious personality traits. Further, he suggests that personality psychology needs to place more emphasis on content, rather than on processes, and that there is too little use made of time sampling procedures and narrative life stories, as well as a lack of emphasis on validity.

A further area of debate is that of personality and culture studies, which since the 1960s have largely disappeared but now, with progress in trait psychology, their revival is feasible. A review of evidence on the consensual validity, longitudinal stability, heritability and structure of personality traits suggests new approaches to old issues. At the trans-cultural level, claims of universality are addressed. At the intercultural level, associations are sought between mean levels of personality traits and corresponding culture-level variables; cultural institutions may be either causes or effects of personality. At the intracultural level culture-specific manifestations of universal traits are documented. The new discipline of personality traits and culture draws on multiple methodologies to understand human nature in social context (McCrae, 2000).

Critique of the trait approach as applied to the entrepreneur

The application of classic approaches to measurement of the entrepreneurial personality would require careful design and appropriate 'populations' identified and systematically tested. Unlike most studies within occupational psychology where the target population is reasonably well defined (e.g. police officer, salesperson, classroom teacher, etc.), defining an entrepreneur is a significant question. Many studies, as will be discussed throughout this book, have foundered due to the difficulty of identifying target populations and being able to develop consistent (across projects and populations) sampling frames. Furthermore, it is difficult to conceive of such studies without an analysis of relevant contextual variables and their effects. Once such a measure is introduced the research becomes considerably more complicated, with questions about what might be considered 'relevant' contextual variables (see Chapter 6, section on Interactionism). However, many experts in entrepreneurship do consider business venturing to be a process and the part played by the individual entrepreneur to be considerably diminished. For example, Stevenson and Sahlman (1989) have taken a highly critical view of attempts to identify and measure the personality traits of the 'entrepreneur' using conventional psychological techniques:

> At the heart of the matter is whether the psychological and social traits are either necessary or sufficient for the development of entrepreneurship. Character traits are at best modalities and not universalities, since many successful and unsuccessful entrepreneurs do not share the characteristics identified. Further, historical studies do not show the same character traits in earlier entrepreneurs. Also, the studies of life paths of entrepreneurs often show decreasing 'entrepreneurship' following success. Such evidence at least raises a question whether the nature of entrepreneurship is immutably embedded in the personality from early stages of childhood development. Finally, while many authors have purported to find statistically significant common characteristics of entrepreneur, the ability to attribute causality to these factors is seriously in doubt.
>
> (Stevenson and Sahlman, 1989: 103–104)

This indictment gains further credence when one considers that research findings on entrepreneurial traits have yielded equivocal results. Different schools of thought have offered alternative explanations of entrepreneurial behaviour, but there seems to be little agreement regarding the profile of the entrepreneur. From the psychological literature, entrepreneurs were thought to be moderate risk-takers (as discussed in Meredith *et al.*, 1982), deviants (Kets de Vries, 1977), high in need for achievement (McClelland, 1961, 1965) and to have an internal locus of control (Brockhaus, 1982) and a tolerance of ambiguity (Schere, 1982). Further, the characteristic of a Type A behaviour pattern has been identified as a promising indicator for differentiating entrepreneurs from managers (Boyd, 1984; Begley and Boyd, 1985). The Type A construct is intended to measure the degree to which a respondent displays extremes of competitiveness, aggressiveness, impatience, striving for achievement and feelings of being under pressure. So, is there more recent evidence to corroborate such a view? In the ensuing section, we ask: 'who is an entrepreneur?'; is there evidence of an entrepreneurial trait or traits that differentiates entrepreneurs from other leaders or managers and, indeed, from the general population?; and were the above-named traits the most appropriate ones to use as a basis for judging the nature of a possible entrepreneurial personality?

Who is an entrepreneur?

The question of 'who is an entrepreneur' has proved to be highly controversial (Carland *et al.*, 1984; Chell, 1985a; Gartner, 1989; Shaver and Scott, 1991). Initially it was suggested that a single trait might be identified and from the early literature three possibilities were proposed: need for achievement, locus of control and risk-taking propensity. In the following section I review research that has focused on each of these contenders.

The 'Big Three': need for achievement, locus of control and risk-taking propensity

Need for achievement

The work of McClelland, in the 1960s, suggested that the key to entrepreneurial behaviour lies in achievement motivation. The need to achieve is a drive to excel, to achieve a goal in relation to a set of standards. A person endowed with such a need will spend time considering how to do a job better or how to accomplish something important to them. McClelland distinguished this type of person from the rest, suggesting that they were 'high achievers'. High achievers are said to like situations where they can take personal responsibility for finding solutions to problems. They like rapid feedback on their performance so that they can judge whether they are improving or not. They avoid what they perceive to be very easy or very difficult tasks and they dislike succeeding by chance. They prefer striving to achieve targets that present both a challenge and are not beyond their capabilities. This ensures worthwhile effort and results in feelings of accomplishment and satisfaction.

McClelland's theory, which was developed with greater mathematical precision by Atkinson (Atkinson and Birch, 1979), has been criticised on methodological grounds, for example in his extensive use of the Thematic Apperception Test (TAT: Sexton and Bowman, 1984). Furthermore, the predictive power of McClelland's theory has been questioned. Brockhaus (1982) has pointed out that McClelland's empirical research did not directly connect need for achievement (NAch) with the decision to own and manage a business. This problem is corroborated by the findings of Hull *et al.* (1980), who found NAch to be a weak predictor of an individual's tendency to start a business. A relationship so described may, in fact, only serve to obscure the operation of the achievement motive.

The reasons why people start their own business have been shown to be a mixture of 'push' and 'pull' factors, which may or may not be associated with the need to achieve. Given that there are a variety of reasons for setting up in business, it follows that business owners will vary in their motivational structure and may not be limited to those who enjoy a challenge. Other criticisms relate to McClelland's attempt to relate economic development to the prevalence of achievement imagery (Wilken, 1979). The cultural basis of the achievement motive may be relevant to Western capitalist countries, in particular the USA, and its effects are open to speculation. Further, historically the British culture was such that its 'high achievers' were 'creamed off' for top jobs in administration and government. Self-employment was not regarded as an attractive option until the popularisation of the 'enterprise culture' in the Thatcher era of the 1980s. This British attitude towards self-employment together with the stigma attached to business failure is not so evident in the USA, for instance, where it is suggested that failure is viewed as a positive learning experience.

McClelland's theory also includes the idea that the achievement motive can be inculcated through socialisation and training. Such work has been carried out in several Third World countries, including India, Malawi and Ecuador. In the UK, attitudes towards the training and development of entrepreneurial aspirations and behaviours may be shifting as the impact of various enterprise programmes introduced into the educational system begins to take effect. Despite these criticisms there is some empirical support for the idea that entrepreneurs have a higher motive to achieve than people in general: for example, neither Hornaday and Aboud (1971) nor Begley and Boyd (1986) used the TAT. Even if achievement motivation exists as a stable characteristic and is consistently found to be more prevalent amongst entrepreneurs (as opposed to business owners generally), there is still a question of its relation to business performance. McClelland has confirmed that training courses designed to develop achievement motivation have improved small business performance significantly in terms of increased sales, profits and numbers employed (McClelland and Winter, 1971; Miron and McClelland, 1979). More recently, he has addressed the question as to whether there are other key personal characteristics needed for entrepreneurial success (McClelland, 1987). A critical issue in research is whether such findings can be replicated. Begley and Boyd (1986) found very little relationship between various psychological characteristics of founders and non-founders and measures of business performance.

Fineman (1977) reviewed the development of the achievement motive construct, evaluated the psychometric soundness of various instruments and examined the convergent validity of numerous measures of the achievement motive. He found only 22 significant correlations among 78 measures calculated of the achievement motive, including the TAT used by McClelland. However, he did not specifically consider the research results of studies of the achievement motive and the entrepreneur. This was left to Johnson (1990), who built on Fineman's conclusions to evaluate research in entrepreneurship. To this end Johnson selected eight different measures of achievement motivation. Despite variability among the studies regarding samples, operationalisation of achievement motivation and its measurement, a positive relationship between achievement motivation and entrepreneurship was found in 20 of the 23 studies reviewed (Johnson, 1990: 47). However, Johnson qualifies his findings with a number of important caveats: (a) consideration should be given to the construct validity of different measures, that is, not only are they measuring what they purport to measure, but the measure is measuring the same construct; (b) the heterogeneity amongst small business owners and entrepreneur populations should be addressed and only where one can clearly define the two can one claim to differentiate between, say, entrepreneurs and non-entrepreneurs; and (c) the purpose of scientific measurement is to examine causal relationships and the notion of achievement motivation is such that it results in observable achievement-oriented behaviour, which suggests that such a psychological disposition will result in firm-level outcomes and the need for multi-dimensional models of entrepreneurship. Johnson considered the possibility of adopting an open-systems model to incorporate the multi-dimensionality of the business creation and growth process, the interrelation of various internal processes and the impact of key environmental variables in order to have a 'better understanding of the whole "entrepreneurial animal" ' (ibid.: 51).

Sagie and Elizur (1999) sought to understand what the 'achievement motive' purports to measure. Different studies have measured different attributes of the achievement motive (e.g. 'personal responsibility', 'readiness to face uncertainty', 'inventiveness' and 'inclinations to work hard'), suggesting that all such attributes differentiate between people with high entrepreneurial orientations and others. Sagie and Elizur point out that, whilst there has been support for the first two of this list of attributes, conflicting support has been found for the others. Crucially, they point out, 'these ambiguities may be the result of variations in the ways the two constructs have been defined and measured' (ibid.: 376).

Hence, notwithstanding such criticisms, is there any evidence to suggest that entrepreneurs have a stronger need to achieve than other members of the population? Langan-Fox and Roth (1995) developed a typology of the female entrepreneur on the basis of psychological characteristics of 60 Australian female business founders. In this study, a number of projective and self-report measures were used to assess multiple dimensions of personality within the theoretical framework of McClelland. Other variables influencing the motivations of entrepreneurs, for instance motives usually attributed to managers, were explored and included self-attributed need for power and influence, ability to influence/have power, resistance to subordination, internal locus of control, job satisfaction and achievement values. Analyses revealed three psychological types of female entrepreneurs: the need achiever, the pragmatic and the managerial entrepreneur. The need achievers had high need achievement scores, the managerial entrepreneurs had high self-attributed need for power and influence scores and the pragmatic entrepreneurs were moderate on both motivations of achievement and power.

Returning to the study of Sagie and Elizur (1999), consideration was given to how the achievement motive might be deconstructed and measured. The authors suggested that three facets could be identified: (a) *behaviour modality – instrumental, affective* and *cognitive*; (b) *type of confrontation – readiness of the individual to take on a challenge and cope with it* or *not*; and (c) *time perspective* – calculation of risk occurring *before* the task is performed, focusing one's efforts to cope with difficulties and solve problems *during* performance and facing personal responsibility and satisfying the need to succeed occurring *after* the task is done. They suggested that the achievement motive was primarily an instrumental behaviour that includes *feelings toward the behaviour*, whilst beliefs (i.e. the cognitive element) would be peripheral. The authors tested the hypothesis that readiness to face uncertainty, take personal responsibility, calculate risks, confront difficulties and solve problems characterise persons of high entrepreneurial orientation. The test was conducted on two classes of students – those studying small business with the intention of founding a business and those studying economics and business. Small business students were found to score higher than their business and economics colleagues on most of the achievement items. Statistically significant differences between the samples were found on four achievement components: the readiness to face uncertainty, calculating risk, undertaking personal responsibility and solving problems. The authors felt that the results would have been stronger had their sample been composed of experienced workers rather than students. Clearly, a repeat study with nascent entrepreneurs who were not students would be desirable.

But do psychological constructs, like the achievement motive, predict a proclivity for entrepreneurship? The following study includes three classic themes of entrepreneurship: achievement motivation, risk-taking propensity and preference for innovation (Stewart *et al.*, 1999). A survey of 767 small business owner-managers and corporate managers was assembled from a 20-state region, primarily in the south-eastern USA. The participants completed a questionnaire composed of the Achievement Scale, the Risk-Taking and Innovation Scales of the Jackson Personality Inventory and questions pertaining to individual and organisational variables. Respondents were divided into two groups: corporate managers and small business owner-managers. Subsequently, the owner-managers were further categorised as either an entrepreneur or small business owner, using the widely cited Carland *et al.* (1984) theoretical definitions (see Chapter 1). Entrepreneurs were defined by their goals of profit and growth for their ventures and by their use of strategic planning. Small business owners focus on providing family income and view the venture as an extension of their personalities. In this study, both groups – entrepreneurs and small business owner-managers – were simultaneously compared with employed managers. The results indicated that those owner-managers labelled as entrepreneurs were higher in achievement motivation, risk-taking propensity and preference for innovation than were both the corporate managers and the small business owners. This profile of the entrepreneur as a driven, creative risk-taker is consistent with much of the classic literature concerning the entrepreneur. However, there is a serious criticism of this research design: did the sampled individuals develop those characteristics identified *after* they became corporate managers, entrepreneurs or lifestyle small business owner-managers? This would suggest that the characteristics were acquired. As there are no 'before' data, this question cannot be answered.

Nonetheless, not all of the owner-managers fit this profile. When compared with corporate managers, the small business owners did not demonstrate higher need for achievement or preference for innovation; however, they did demonstrate a significantly higher risk-taking propensity. In terms of the constructs studied, the small business owners were more comparable to corporate managers than to entrepreneurs. Stewart *et al.* (1999) argue that a major issue is whether there is a connection between the owner's psychological profile and the characteristics of the venture, including performance. Some owners will be more growth-oriented than others, and performance should be assessed in the light of the owner's aspirations for the venture. Moreover, owners should be aware of their own personality, including risk preferences, which may be more or less suited to different venture circumstances, including those with relatively high levels of risk. Furthermore, planning in small businesses appears to enhance venture performance. Those labelled entrepreneurs in this study have goals of profit and growth and tend to engage in more planning The authors concluded that an awareness of these psychological preferences and concomitant attention to planning behaviours have the potential to improve the performance of the venture, irrespective of owner aspirations.

Other research on the achievement motive has addressed the issue of whether it travels across countries and cultures. For example, Utsch *et al.* (1999) investigated the differences between entrepreneurs and managers in East Germany. They argued that the situation was weak in respect of the decision to become an entrepreneur. Thus, they expected a stronger relationship between personality traits and behaviour. They measured the traits of autonomy, innovativeness, proactiveness, competitive aggressiveness and achievement orientation and were able to discriminate between entrepreneurs and managers on most of the variables, with the exception of proactiveness. They conclude that personality *is* important in founding a business.

Lee and Tsang (2001) focused their attention on demonstrating the extent to which NAch is associated with venture growth among Chinese entrepreneurs. The authors investigated the effects of certain personality traits, background and networking activities on venture growth among 168 Chinese entrepreneurs in small- and medium-sized businesses in Singapore: personality traits included the need for achievement, internal locus of control, self-reliance and extroversion; background factors were education and experience; and networking activities consisted of size and frequency of communication networks. A structural equation modelling technique was used to estimate the relationship between personality and background of the entrepreneur and venture growth. The results indicate that experience, networking activities and the number of partners, as well as internal locus of control and need for achievement, all have a positive impact on venture growth. Two other personality traits, self-reliance and extroversion, were found to have a negative impact on the number of partners and a positive impact on networking activities, respectively. The effect of education on growth, however, is moderated by firm size, being positive for larger firms and negative for smaller firms. The findings indicate that, among all the factors considered, an entrepreneur's industrial and managerial experience is a dominating factor affecting growth. The authors conclude that need for achievement is the personality factor that has the greatest impact on venture performance. However, they also state that personality traits in general are not important factors affecting growth. Furthermore, they suggest that, given the importance of experience, there is a need to shift attention from entrepreneurial traits to entrepreneurial skills (ibid.: 597).

These later studies suggest that it is not enough to focus solely on traits. Rather, researchers should design their studies to assess the impact of personality within a rather more complex model of the process of business venturing. An example of a study designed along these lines is that of Korunka *et al.* (2003). Their interdisciplinary study analysed configurations that comprised entrepreneurial personality, resources, environment and organising activities in the context of the start-up process. A configuration was defined as a multi-dimensional entity that emphasises patterns and interrelations. As such the development of an organisation can be 'reconstructed as a chain of configurations' (Korunka *et al.*, 2003: 25). The personality configuration consists of measures of need for achievement, internal locus of control and risk-taking propensity, personal initiative, security and self-realisation motive. Additional measures for the configuration areas of personal resources, environment and organising activities were constructed and compiled into a single questionnaire.

A representative sample of 941 useable questionnaires for nascent entrepreneurs and new business owner-managers was examined. The new business owner-managers data set ($n = 627$) was analysed and used as a bench mark. Of these, 153 fulfilled a set of success criteria. The configuration of this group was shown to be characterised by a strong need for achievement, a strong internal locus of control, strong personal initiative and a medium risk-taking propensity. The configurations for resources, environment and organising activities were moderate for this group. With a low standard deviation for the personality configuration, the authors suggested that this was a relatively homogeneous group. Of the nascent entrepreneurs, three start-up configurations were found that reveal different patterns of personality characteristics. The clusters were labelled 'C1: nascent entrepreneurs against their will', 'C2: would-be nascent entrepreneurs' and 'C3: networking nascent entrepreneurs with risk avoidance patterns'. These clusters were interpreted in the context of aspects of the environment, the resources and the start-up process. C1 had a low profile on personality characteristics and a 'fatal combination' of other factors (e.g. social support), with a strong push factor – the fact that they were unemployed. C2 (comprising a high proportion of women) had a strong locus of control, security and self-realisation motives. The single most important negative factor was their unfavourable financial situation. C3 indicated a favourable start-up position, strong risk avoidance tendency in relation to the other personality characteristics and a strong consideration of possible failure. C3 also indicated strong social support and networks, used information intensely and reported few organisational troubles. They had strong resources and little outside pressure. These findings suggest that at the nascent stage the patterns that emerge reflect different economic conditions, namely necessity versus self-realisation, that the start-up process is heterogeneous and that there are strong external influences. The researchers conclude that it is inappropriate to investigate the personality characteristics of nascent entrepreneurs and new business owner-managers in isolation from the wider contextual factors that affect patterns of activity.

Hansemark (2003) investigated the impact of NAch and Internal-External Locus of Control (I-ELOC) on entrepreneurial activity using a longitudinal design. She argued that previous studies that measured the personality characteristics of established business owners were of little value scientifically because they do not provide a basis for the prediction of future entrepreneurial activity. She pointed out that no previous studies had sought to identify whether gender might be a discriminating factor. In order to answer these questions she designed a longitudinal study. The subjects – males and females – were assessed using both objective and projective measures of NAch and Rotter's measure of I-ELOC 11 years prior to any entrepreneurial activity. The average age of the 'before' group was 22 years, and at the post-test stage the average age was 33 years. She used an experimental and a control group (group affiliation), from which she was able to extract data by sex of participant.

Hansemark found that after 11 years a higher proportion of the experimental group (48%) had started a business compared with 21% for the control group. This difference was statistically significant ($p > 0.05$). When gender was taken into account, although fewer women proportionately started a business than men, this result was not statistically significant. Further, there were no significant results for NAch, but those subjects that scored below the median on internal economic locus of control were shown to be more likely to found a business than subjects scoring above the median on that measure. This difference was statistically significant ($p > 0.038$). For all subjects, *none of the personality measures predicted start-up activity*. However, whether the subjects belonged to the control or experimental group did have a significant impact in predicting business founding ($p > 0.006$). When subjects were divided by sex, NAch failed to predict start-up for both men and women. Locus of control marginally predicted start-up for men ($p = 0.058$). Also for men, group affiliation showed a statistically significant difference in respect of the prediction of start-up ($p = 0.011$). None of the results for the women showed statistically significant differences.

Hansemark (2003) concluded that as regards NAch, most prior studies have been carried out on extant entrepreneurs. This suggests that personal characteristics may have been developed after or because of entrepreneurial activity, and thus NAch *was not an important prerequisite or predictor of entrepreneurship*. The study showed that group affiliation had a significant impact on predicting entrepreneurial activity. However, there was an over-representation of men in the experimental group. Fewer women in the experimental group started a business compared to the women in the control group. This suggested that there may have been a problem with the entrepreneurship programme that the women in the experimental group attended. Finally, the advantage of the longitudinal design is that it enables one to look at causation and separate out dependent (founding) and independent (personality) variables. The results suggest the importance of such a design and demonstrate that it may be premature to conclude that there is no relationship between personality and entrepreneurial activity.

Utsch and Rauch (2000) considered the effect of achievement orientation on venture performance. They designed a 'mediation model' that linked personality to behaviour and performance outcome. They demonstrated how their measure of achievement orientation was mediated by two factors: innovativeness and initiative. In other words, profit growth and employee growth of a venture were shown to be a consequence of the impact of achievement orientation on the mediating variables, with innovative behaviour being the stronger link to performance outcomes.

Subsequent work that has incorporated the achievement motive has tended to examine the role of achievement and other personality factors in the context of a more complex multi-dimensional model. For example, Baum *et al.* (2001) incorporated environmental variables, strategic management variables and ten personal characteristics to create a composite of trait, skill and motivation. They found that motivation and organisation factors had direct effects on organisation performance, whilst trait and skill affected performance indirectly through motivational and organisational factors. In a further study, Baum and Locke (2004), following Carsrud and Krueger (1995), suggested that need for achievement, risk-taking propensity and locus of control are the wrong traits for empirical study. They identified a set of traits and 'new resource skills' that they posited were closer to the situation of venture founding behaviour. This study will be discussed in further detail in Chapter 5.

Collins *et al.* (2004) realised that, whilst McClelland's achievement motivation construct has been widely employed, criticised and discussed, there remained outstanding questions that should be addressed. This paper usefully summarises and tests some of the key concerns that have bedevilled the need for achievement construct. It looks at: (a) the degree of support for the construct; (b) the evidence for a relationship between achievement motivation and entrepreneurial performance and entrepreneurship career choice; and (c) the validity of the various measuring instruments that have been used. The researchers raised a number of issues:

- Does it matter how we define entrepreneurs? Should they include small business owner-managers or should the definition be limited to business founders only?
- Over time people tend to self-select jobs, occupations, careers, etc. and those that remain in them become more homogenous in respect of personality, values and attitudes. It should therefore be possible to identify stronger associations between achievement motivation and entrepreneurial behaviour in occupational groups rather than at the individual level of analysis.
- People with a high need for achievement are more likely to choose occupational careers that meet this particular need.
- As some managerial jobs require NAch, some managers (argued McClelland) are likely to be entrepreneurs. If this supposition is correct, then measures of NAch should differentiate better between entrepreneurs and non-entrepreneurs (e.g. general population) than between entrepreneurs and managers.
- People with a high NAch should *perform better* in an entrepreneurial role as there will be a better fit between their personality and work environment.

- However, NAch should better predict *career choice* than entrepreneurial performance *if it is true* that people high in NAch are more likely to choose an entrepreneurial career.
- McClelland argued that need for achievement is developed in childhood and operates subconsciously. Thus, a projective measure (TAT) will be a better predictor of entrepreneurial behaviour than would questionnaire measures. The Miner Sentence Completion Scale (Miner and Raju, 2004) is also a projective technique and its predictive power should be explored.

In total, 41 studies were meta-analysed, including many of the studies discussed earlier in this section. They found:

1 There was no statistically significant evidence to suggest that how the entrepreneur was defined made any difference to the relationship between achievement motivation and entrepreneurial activity.
2 The group level of analysis showed stronger associations between NAch and entrepreneurial activity.
3 Achievement motivation was significantly related to choice of career, specifically entrepreneurial career.
4 Achievement motivation was shown to differentiate between entrepreneurs and non-managers in comparison to studies that sampled managers only.
5 Achievement motivation was significantly related to entrepreneurial performance.
6 Contrary to expectations, NAch was a better predictor of performance than of career choice. This difference was statistically significant.
7 There were no differences between the type of measure used and it was suggested that it would be better to use the questionnaire as it is easier to use and score accurately.

They concluded that these results *do* support McClelland's theory that achievement motivation is related to both occupational choice and performance in an entrepreneurial role. Specifically, they state that achievement motivation appears to be an important characteristic of entrepreneurs. They suggest that NAch is not a better predictor of career choice, because individuals with high NAch may be attracted to different types of careers. The finding that NAch is a better predictor of performance suggests that achievement motivation may be of practical use to differentiate between successful and unsuccessful entrepreneurs and to select entrepreneurs who may take advantage of entrepreneurial finance and other support. Collins *et al.* (2004) believe that we should not be surprised that achievement motivation distinguishes better between entrepreneurs and all other professions than it does with managers, 'as managers' jobs often have entrepreneurial elements, and entrepreneurial jobs typically entail management activities' (ibid.: 112). They also make a very interesting point about achievement motivation itself: that it is not a one-time influence on behaviour. Rather, there are repeat opportunities for the achievement motive to affect an individual's decisions and behaviour over the lifespan. Hence, even though the construct may account for very little of the variance, its cumulative effects over time may be substantial. They acknowledge that there are issues about the non-inclusion of studies of entrepreneurial 'failure' and that because the bulk of the studies are correlational there is a problem of direction of causality. Finally, given that there are many factors that affect venture growth, they raise the question as to whether achievement motivation would play a significant role in a multivariate study.

Locus of control

Rotter (1966) developed the notion of 'locus of control of reinforcement' (LOC) as part of a wider social learning theory of personality. People with an internal locus of control are those individuals who believe themselves to be in control of their destiny. In contrast, people with an external locus of control sense that fate, in the form of chance events outside their control or powerful people, has a dominating influence over their lives (Levenson, 1973). However, it is worth highlighting that Rotter's concept was a learnt behavioural response and not a trait (Chell, 1985a: 47). This suggests that it may be important to discover the conditions that may affect the development of this particular response in entrepreneurs. Given this generalised sense of a LOC, it might be expected that most business owners have a higher internal LOC than the population at large (Brockhaus, 1982). After all, it is the nature of the management process that control be exerted over those factors that they identify as having an influence on their business. Indeed, this reasoning may be applied to CEOs, senior management, and so on. It is perhaps not surprising, therefore, that one study reported that no evidence had been found to distinguish between business founders (entrepreneurs) and non-founders (business managers) (Begley and Boyd, 1986).

Another line of investigation is the relationship between NAch and LOC. It would seem logical to suppose, as did Rotter (1966), that these two characteristics should be positively related. That is, people who have high NAch believe in their own ability to control the outcome of their efforts. Borland (1974, cited in Brockhaus, 1982) suggested that a belief in internal LOC was a better predictor of entrepreneurial intentions than NAch. Hull *et al.* (1980) disagreed with Borland in that they failed to find a relationship between LOC and entrepreneurial activity, but agreed that NAch was not the most important variable. To complicate the issue further, Brockhaus and Nord (1979) found that internal LOC scores failed to distinguish between entrepreneurs and managers. On the other hand, a study by Brockhaus (1980a) showed some promise for distinguishing between successful and unsuccessful founders. The criterion of success was that the business remained in existence three years after the LOC scores were obtained. The founders of the 'successful' businesses had a higher internal LOC than the founders of those businesses that had subsequently ceased to exist.

What should one conclude from such conflicting evidence? There are two possible ways forward that we will consider: to examine critically the measure of a LOC; or to question fundamentally whether LOC is a key distinguishing characteristic of entrepreneurs and is not part of a wider, more generalisable orientation to the business. Furnham (1986) has indicated a fundamental weakness in the LOC scale as developed by Rotter (1966): its claim to uni-dimensionality. It would appear that people view the effects of chance and of powerful others differently. Further, different researchers have applied the LOC measure to a variety of settings: health, religious beliefs, education, political behaviour and behaviour in organisations. In the latter case, researchers have used or adapted generalised LOC scales rather than attempted to modify or adapt the concept to economic or organisational issues. For this reason, Furnham (1986) developed and tested his own economic LOC scale. He demonstrated that its multi-dimensionality – internality, chance, external-denial and powerful others – showed clear differences in response according to a number of demographic variables: sex, age, education, voting behaviour and income. Further, Bonnett and Furnham (1991) compared boys and girls aged 16–19 participating in a Young Enterprise Scheme to a control group using four measures: Protestant work ethic, internal economic LOC, achievement motivation and perceived parenting. They found that the entrepreneurial group scored higher on the measures of Protestant work ethic and economic LOC, but no differences were found for the other variables.

In the 1991 edition, we felt that there was a need to seriously question the adoption of the LOC measure as a core trait of entrepreneurs. Then we asked: how do business owners view factors associated with LOC? We suggested that some business environments are very turbulent, some industrial sectors are more competitive than others and business owners vary with respect to their preference for constant change or relative stability. Fluctuations in the performance of a firm give a temporal dimension that may, at any single point in time, influence the business owner's sense of control. Moreover, how does LOC relate to other business behaviours, such as confidence, decisiveness, judgement, business success, and so on? Further, this underscores the point that LOC is likely to be a learned behaviour. Thus, the research design should reflect this.

This analysis suggests that the link with the cognitive process of developing and implementing plans and strategies in an effort to steer the business along a successful course is a specific instance of an individual's attempt to control and manage the environment. The strategy is designed to create a situation where the odds of success outweigh possible failure. Cumulative experience is also indicative of experiential learning. In exercising judgement and attempting to be 'realistic', the business owner should be aware of the power of situations and of other people, whilst simultaneously trying to reduce their influence. This suggests that in a business context contextual factors and probable outcomes associated with the judgemental situation need to be carefully considered. Such factors should be viewed in relation to firm-specific performance outcomes. It is not unusual for business owners to suffer setbacks or occasionally experience business failure. This suggests that it is likely that the extent of their 'internality' would be tempered by experience. To date, research on the LOC of the entrepreneur has yielded conflicting results. If further work is to be carried out using the LOC concept, multiple measures need to be taken within a stratified sample of business owners and compared with a sample of nascent entrepreneurs and a control group of non-entrepreneurs. One way forward might be to: (a) collect sufficient background information to examine the possible mediating effects of other variables, including adverse experience; (b) use ratings of possible mediating factors expected to be associated with internality or externality and thus to relate such measures to the LOC scores; and (c) examine these measures in relation to a series of performance outcomes. Thus, in the light of further research, the continued adoption of LOC as a differentiator between entrepreneurs and other populations and its ability to predict entrepreneurial outcomes should be reviewed.

Much has been written regarding the organisational changes needed to achieve entrepreneurship in established companies (Engle *et al.*, 1997). Many corporate strategists conclude that, above all others, a firm's 'rank and file' have the intimate knowledge of business operations necessary to discover innovations within a corporation. However, little attention has been devoted to discovering a measure to identify the employees within a corporation who may be entrepreneurial and likely to produce innovations. This exploratory study used external entrepreneurs as proxies for corporate internal entrepreneurs. The purpose of this study was to examine the effectiveness of two measures – Kirton's Adaptation–Innovation Inventory (Kirton, 1976) and a version of Rotter's LOC Scale (Rotter, 1966) – in distinguishing entrepreneurs from a population of employees. Participants (54 entrepreneurs and 79 employees) completed the two measures. Entrepreneurs were found to be more innovative and less adaptive than employees. Also, they had less respect for rules and authority structures. There was no difference found between entrepreneurs and employees on the LOC measure, but an unusually large percentage (84.3%) had an internal LOC. The researchers concluded that there was support for Kirton's inventory as a differentiator between the two groups and they recommended that in a future study the unabridged version of the LOC be used.

Mueller and Thomas (2000) tested whether the LOC construct along with a measure of innovativeness was generalisable across cultures. They also used these measures to categorise respondents as being high or low on entrepreneurial orientation (ibid.: 64). The survey was administered to business, economics and engineering students across the USA, Canada, South America, and a number of Asian and European countries. National culture character-istics were scored using Hofstede's (1980) study. The analysis showed rela-tionships between national culture characteristics and the trait measures. They found stronger support for LOC in countries with individualistic cultures than for innovativeness, which produced non-significant results on both dimensions of culture – individualism–collectivism and low/high uncertainty avoidance cultures. The authors concluded that traits such as LOC and innovativeness are learned and not immutable. They suggested that the population in general has predispositions to behave entrepreneur-ially, although only a proportion actually found businesses. This, they argue, confounds studies that attempt to distinguish entrepreneurs from the general population. Thus, in their study, by concentrating on the potential entrepreneur but not practising entrepreneurs, they suggest that they have a basis on which to predict an increase in the likelihood of venture initiation (ibid.: 68). They would expect a range in the distribution of individuals with entrepreneurial potential across different cultures.

In a separate study, Lee and Tsang (2001) tested the hypothesis that internal LOC is related to venture growth among Chinese entrepreneurs. They interviewed 168 entrepreneurs over the telephone. They collected vari-ous demographic data, including firm size, which enabled them to analyse separately owner-managers of large and small firms. They demonstrated that entrepreneurs of large firms with higher growth rates exhibit more internal LOC. They concluded that there is overall weak support for entrepreneurial traits and that entrepreneurial skills are likely to be more important. Further, they suggest that firm size is an important moderating factor that previous studies have failed to take into account. Finally, they suggest, in line with Mueller and Thomas (2000), that entrepreneurship is a culturally embedded phenomenon and that the economic growth of the Asian Pacific region, with its 'underlying entrepreneurial spirit', requires greater attention.

Hansemark (2003), whose study is discussed in the above section, was only able to demonstrate that LOC has predictive validity (i.e. predicts 'Start a new Business') for men, not women.

Research on LOC as a characteristic of entrepreneurs and a predictor of entrepreneurial behaviour is by no means convincing. More recent studies have tended to combine the measure with that of other personality traits rather than consider LOC as a single measure of the entrepreneurial per-sona. However, doubts have been expressed. In response, researchers have developed more sophisticated models and measures and have continued to search for other characteristic traits that might be prototypical of the entrepreneur.

Risk-taking

Considerable research has been undertaken in pursuit of the notion that a fundamental characteristic of the entrepreneur is his/her propensity to take risks (McClelland, 1961; Kilby, 1971; Palmer, 1971; Brockhaus, 1982). The usual interpretation of a risk-taker is someone who, in the context of a business venture, pursues a business idea when the probability of succeeding is low. Lay or stereotypic notions of the entrepreneur assume that s/he is typically a risk-taker. However, one line of thinking does not entirely agree with this idea: Timmons *et al.* (1985), following McClelland (1961), advocate that entrepreneurs take calculated risks. Indeed, Carland *et al.* (1984), following Schumpeter (1934), suggest that risk-taking is a characteristic of business ownership or, more specifically, capital investment.[3] The empirical evidence was found to be equivocal when reviewed in the earlier volume of this book (Chell *et al.*, 1991). For example, Hull *et al.* (1980) found potential entrepreneurs to have a greater propensity to take risks. Their definition of 'entrepreneur' included anyone who owned a business, assumed risk for the sake of profit and had the explicit intention of expanding the business. However, Brockhaus (1980b) defined 'entrepreneur' as an owner-manager of a business venture who is not employed elsewhere, and he confined his sample to people who had very recently decided to become owner-managers. He could not distinguish the risk-taking propensity of new entrepreneurs from managers or from the general population. Brockhaus avoided the complication of whether the 'entrepreneurial' venture was a success. He speculated that established entrepreneurs might appear to be more moderate risk-takers, because those entrepreneurs with a propensity towards low or high levels of risk-taking might cease to be entrepreneurs at a greater rate than those with a propensity towards moderate risk-taking. Other researchers have taken this line of argument further and made a strong connection between success and the degree of risk-taking. It has been argued that, given that some risk of failure must be attached to any business undertaking, the successful entrepreneur is the one who takes calculated risks (Timmons *et al.*, 1985).

According to Meredith *et al.* (1982: 25):

> [Entrepreneurs] enjoy the excitement of a challenge, but they don't gamble. Entrepreneurs avoid low-risk situations because there is a lack of challenge and avoid high-risk situations because they want to succeed. They like achievable challenges.

This interpretation agrees fully with the McClelland and Atkinson research on achievement motivation, where the high achiever has been demonstrated to be someone who takes medium-level (calculated) risks (McClelland, 1961; Atkinson and Birch, 1979). It is consonant with a study conducted by Julian *et al.* (1968), who found that people with an internal LOC were less likely to engage in risky behaviour than were those with an external LOC. It would seem to follow from this research that owner-managers who have an internal LOC will be medium risk-takers, whereas those owner-managers who are 'externals' will tend to take low or high risks. Other evidence, for example a study by Miller and Friesen (1982), showed that CEOs with an external LOC were conservative in their decision-making, whereas CEOs with an internal LOC were more prepared to adopt 'bold and imaginative' strategies. It was concluded that 'internal' CEOs were more innovative and, consequently, more entrepreneurial.

The propensity to take calculated risks is indicative of judgemental decision-making and associated with the strategic behaviour of the entrepreneur. This assertion gains support from the work of Hoy and Carland (1983), who have suggested that strategic behaviour differentiates between entrepreneurs and small business owners, whereas 'selected personal traits [did not hold up] as distinguishing characteristics' (ibid.: 164). What is to be made of such evidence? One issue appears to be: from whose perspective is the decision or action considered to be risky? A multiple perspectives approach facilitates clearer thinking. Thus, from an observer's perspective the business person or entrepreneur may be viewed as a risk-taker. However, in the sense in which risk-taking has been defined, even a decision to do nothing may involve risk. From the business person's perspective, s/he may see themselves as 'hedging their bets' and attempting to minimise risk. The adoption of a risk minimisation strategy may be said to rest on: (a) information-seeking and awareness; (b) the ability to devise imaginative solutions to problems; and (c) supreme confidence in the solution and hence the decision. It is in these senses that the entrepreneur might be said to take calculated risks and why it is evident that some entrepreneurs express an aversion to risk-taking (Burns and Kippenberger, 1988). Subsequent research begins to address such different approaches to risk.

Palich and Bagby (1995), for example, suggest that entrepreneurs do not see themselves as more likely to take risks than managers in large corporations (but they may perceive less risk). They conclude that entrepreneurs may not think of themselves as being any more likely to take risks than non-entrepreneurs, but they are nonetheless predisposed to think of business situations more positively. Hence, entrepreneurs view some situations as 'opportunities', even though others perceive them to have little potential (i.e. the latter view these situations as risky ventures that offer disproportionately low returns relative to their associated risks). The researchers suggest that their findings offer the potential to develop a taxonomy that may help to identify entrepreneurs, a tool that would be useful to firms interested in assessing individuals' natural potential for entrepreneurial behaviour. At the same time, systematic differences in cognitive processes may permit the differentiation of entrepreneurs from small business owners, which would be useful since these groups often cannot be determined from the size of an enterprise (i.e. both tend to be associated with smaller ventures).

The concept of risk, risk-taking and risk management is seemingly so fundamental to business venturing that it is hardly surprising that this construct continues to be heavily researched. For example, Sarasvathy *et al.*

(1998) compared entrepreneurs with bankers in their perception and management of a variety of risks. The problems included financial risk, risk to human life and health and risk of a natural disaster. The analysis of think-aloud protocols revealed some very interesting and perhaps not altogether surprising differences. Entrepreneurs accept risk as given, express more perceived *control over returns* and focus on *controlling the outcomes* at any given level of risk; they pick some acceptable level of risk and then *push for larger profits*. They appeared to select the project with the best–worse case scenario and expressed *confidence* that they could make the reality better than the probable worst case (ibid.: 213). They also frame their problem spaces with *personal values* and assume greater *personal responsibility* for the outcomes.

Bankers appeared to believe that they could go *for the highest possible return* and *work on minimising the risks*. Thus, their strategy was one of *high risk/high return* followed by trying to *reduce the risk through various strategies*, such as insurance, damage control; and so forth. They focus on target outcomes – attempting to control risk within structured problem spaces and avoiding situations where they risk higher levels of personal responsibility. In such cases where human health and safety are involved, bankers did not appear to feel compelled to address these issues, whereas entrepreneurs assumed that such issues were part of their responsibility and thought of creative ways in which the full cost of totally solving the problem could be met. The authors suggest that it may be differences in work experience that cause entrepreneurs and bankers to construct and cognitively represent problems differently. However, they also toy with the idea that differences in cognitive representation might have led entrepreneurs and bankers to choose their widely different careers in the first place (ibid.: 217).

Stewart *et al.* (1999) compared entrepreneurs, small business owners and corporate managers on a number of measures, including risk-taking and need for achievement. They found that entrepreneurs had a 'proclivity for entrepreneurship'. This means that entrepreneurs are driven to succeed and have a higher propensity for risk-taking; put succinctly, an entrepreneur is 'an achieving, creative risk-taker' (ibid.: 204). Small business owners had a relatively higher propensity than corporate managers to take risks. Further, they found that small business owners are less risk-oriented and are not so highly motivated to achieve as entrepreneurs. This finding supports earlier studies.

Stewart and Roth (2001) tested the propositions that entrepreneurs are more inclined to take risks than managers because the 'entrepreneurial function entails coping with a less structured, more uncertain set of possibilities' (ibid.: 146); and that classic achievement motivation (NAch) is coupled with fear of failure. This theory suggests that those people high in NAch set moderately challenging goals and, as such, are moderate risk-takers. As both entrepreneurs and employed managers are high achievers, they should both be found to be moderate risk-takers and indistinguishable on this measure.

The authors defined entrepreneurs and small business owner-managers after Carland *et al.* (1984), positing that there would be marked risk propensity differences between growth entrepreneurs and income-oriented small business owners. Using a meta-analysis of the literature, they demonstrated: (a) income-oriented small business owners had a lower risk propensity than growth-oriented entrepreneurs; (b) income-oriented owner-managers had a higher risk propensity than (contractually employed) managers; and (c) growth-oriented entrepreneurs had a higher risk propensity than (contractually employed) managers. Their results tend to confirm that entrepreneurs are more likely to take risks than managers. Finally, they point to Brockhaus (1980b), which indicated no risk propensity differences between entrepreneurs and managers; they suggest that the results for the field as a whole 'differ greatly from those of Brockhaus'.

However, Miner and Raju (2004) take issue with Stewart and Roth's (2001) conclusion; they suggest that Stewart and Roth have based their conclusion on insufficient evidence (in fact, three studies only in respect of risk propensity and growth orientation). In an attempt to rectify this, Miner and Raju meta-analysed data from 14 additional studies that compare the risk propensity of entrepreneurs with that of managers. The studies had used the Miner Sentence Completion Scale (MSCS) to measure risk. They found that entrepreneurs were *less likely* to take risks than the control subjects. This result is the opposite of that of Stewart and Roth, suggesting that entrepreneurs are *risk avoidant*. They consider whether the use of different psychometric measures (self-report versus a projective measure) might account for the discrepancy. They combined the Stewart and Roth data with their own; the result suggested that entrepreneurs may not have a propensity for risk. In attempting to explain this additional discrepant result, they adduce evidence of managerial decision-making from a study by Shapira (1995). This study suggests that 'managerial decision-making is characterised by considerable risk-taking' (ibid.: 10). This is because processing of information by managers was found to be riddled with biases. Hence, the implicit decision-making model adopted by these managers was not a rational model. This notion of greater risk acceptance by managers again contradicts the findings of Stewart and Roth. Miner and Raju suggest that such an approach also typifies entrepreneurial decision-making. They claim that, in processing information, entrepreneurs may emerge as risk avoidant, although making certain start-up and investment decisions may give the appearance of high risk. In considering how entrepreneurs and managers might make decisions, they conclude that:

> It looks as if managers tend to believe in their ability to exercise post decisional control and thus avoid risk ... (Whereas) the research on entrepreneurs ... suggests a belief in pre-decisional control, which means that risk is removed in a completely different manner.
>
> (Miner and Raju, 2004: 10)

Finally, they speculate that the two different techniques – projective test and self-report measures – could yield different or indeed contradictory results because they are measuring different memories, drawing on unconscious or conscious experiences. This is not a particularly satisfactory conclusion, but they acknowledge that they do not know what the relationship is between implicit and self-attributed motives and risk propensity/avoidance behaviour. Hence, they conclude with a call for further research to investigate the causes and manifestations of risk on decision-making and associated actions of the entrepreneur and growth of the firm, and on possible entrepreneur–manager differences. Importantly, they believe that there is a need to consider other skills, abilities, motives, cognitions and cognitive styles, as well as biases and heuristics, if a well-founded view of what factors influence the risk behaviour and decision process of entrepreneurs is to be achieved. Indeed, it may be worth recalling the study reported above, which suggested that it may be that start-up conditions also affect attitude towards risk (Korunka *et al.*, 2003).

Summary and conclusions

Competition amongst capitalist nations and a desire to raise standards of living for all have meant that entrepreneurship is much in demand. This chapter therefore addresses the issue of the supply of entrepreneurs. Briefly I examined human capital theory and conclude that this approach has predictive value in respect of self-employment, but the problem is that the self-employed include sole owners, lifestyle 'entrepreneurs', trades people and small business owners and only a minority of people who will found high-growth, sustainable businesses. This approach leaves open the question of whether it is possible to identify traits that characterise entrepreneurs who will perform entrepreneurially and produce entrepreneurial outcomes (i.e. high-growth profitable businesses employing significant numbers of other people).

Trait theory suggests a personality structure and a dynamic inner process, which are reflected in stylistic consistencies in behaviour. There are different theories that attempt to account for personality structure, the latest suggesting five components – neuroticism, extraversion, openness, agreeableness and conscientiousness. Measures of structure may be applied to populations such as occupational groups, to assess any statistically significant differences between them. This would suggest a standard personality profile for a group, and raise the question whether particular individuals (e.g. potential recruits) fitted the profile. It is clear that one could construct populations of sales personnel, police officers, publicans, and so forth, and produce test results. This approach to the entrepreneurial personality has, on the whole, not been taken; rather, researchers have chosen to identify possible specific traits that they believe to be typical of entrepreneurs. Specific traits are said to be relevant to some populations and not others. Criticisms of the trait approach as applied to entrepreneurs have abounded (e.g. Chell, 1985a; Gartner, 1989; Stevenson and Sahlman, 1989). In this chapter I have chosen to focus primarily on just three highly researched traits and to review the evidence. Table 4.1 summarises this evidence.

Table 4.1 Trait theory of entrepreneurship: summary of findings

Study	Findings
Achievement motivation	
McClelland (1961)	Entrepreneurs are high in need for achievement (NAch)
Hornaday and Aboud (1971)	Empirical support for NAch in entrepreneurs
McClelland and Winter (1971)	NAch improved business performance
Fineman (1977)	Critiques the soundness of the NAch construct
Miron and McClelland (1979)	NAch improved business performance
Atkinson and Birch (1979)	Entrepreneurs are high in NAch
Hull *et al.* (1980)	NAch is a weak predictor of business founding
Begley and Boyd (1986)	Empirical support for NAch in founders; no relationship with business performance
Johnson (1990)	Reviewed 23 studies; 20 showed a positive relationship between NAch and entrepreneurship; important caveats
Langan-Fox and Roth (1995)	Three types of female entrepreneur: need achiever, pragmatist and managerial entrepreneur
Sagie and Elizur (1999)	Small business students more achievement-oriented than business and economics students
Stewart *et al.* (1999)	Entrepreneurs higher in NAch, risk-taking propensity and innovation than corporate managers and small business owners, and were growth-oriented
Utsch *et al.* (1999)	Discriminated between entrepreneurs and managers on autonomy, innovativeness, proactiveness, competitiveness and achievement orientation
Utsch and Rauch (2000)	Achievement mediated by innovativeness and initiative impacted venture performance
Lee and Tsang (2001)	NAch, internal LOC, experience, networking and number of partners had impact on venture growth; but experience more important than personality traits
Baum *et al.* (2001)	Traits and skills affected venture performance indirectly

(Continued overleaf)

Table 4.1 Continued

Study	Findings
Korunka *et al.* (2003)	New business owner-managers had high NAch, internal LOC, initiative and medium risk propensity; also three configurations of nascent entrepreneurs that reflected different economic conditions; personality factors should be viewed in wider context
Hansemark (2003)	No significant results for NAch; internal LOC showed men more likely to found; NAch not a prerequisite
Baum and Locke (2004)	NAch, risk-taking propensity and LOC are the wrong traits
Collins *et al.* (2004)	NAch predicts entrepreneurial performance but not career choice
Locus of control	
Julian *et al.* (1968)	Internal LOC associated with less risky behaviour
Borland (1974)	Internal LOC is a better predictor of entrepreneurial intentions than NAch
Brockhaus and Nord (1979)	Internal LOC did not distinguish between entrepreneurs and managers
Hull *et al.* (1980)	No relationship between LOC and entrepreneurial activity; NAch not the most important variable
Brockhaus (1982)	Business owners have higher internal LOC than the general population
Miller and Friesen (1982)	CEOs with external LOC took more conservative decisions, whereas those with an internal LOC adopted bold imaginative strategies – the latter were adjudged to be more entrepreneurial
Begley and Boyd (1986)	Internal LOC does not distinguish between founders and managers
Furnham (1986)	Developed economic LOC scale
Bonnett and Furnham (1991)	Students on Young Enterprise Scheme scored higher on Protestant work ethic and economic LOC
Engle *et al.* (1997)	No difference between entrepreneurs and employees on LOC, but on Kirton's Adaptation–Innovation Inventory entrepreneurs were more innovative and less adaptive
Mueller and Thomas (2000)	Stronger support for LOC and countries with individualistic cultures; LOC and innovativeness learned
Lee and Tsang (2001)	Entrepreneurs of large firms with higher growth rates exhibit higher LOC; overall weak support for traits; skills more important

Hansemark (2003)	LOC predictive validity for men, not women
Risk-taking propensity	
Schumpeter (1934)	Risk-taking is a characteristic of capital investment
McClelland (1961)	Entrepreneurs have a propensity to take calculated risks
Palmer (1971)	Entrepreneurs have a propensity to take risks
Kilby (1971)	Entrepreneurs have a propensity to take risks
Atkinson and Birch (1979)	High achievers take calculated (medium-level) risks
Brockhaus (1980b)	Risk-taking propensity did not distinguish new entrepreneurs and managers or general population
Brockhaus (1982)	Entrepreneurs have a propensity to take risks
Meredith *et al.* (1982)	Entrepreneurs take medium-level risks
Hoy and Carland (1983)	Strategic behaviour (that includes propensity to take calculated risks) differentiates between entrepreneurs and small business owners
Carland *et al.* (1984)	Risk-taking's a characteristic of business ownership
Timmons *et al.* (1985)	The successful entrepreneur takes calculated risks
Burns and Kippenberger (1988)	Entrepreneurs hedge their bets and attempt to minimise risk
Palich and Bagby (1995)	Entrepreneurs perceive less risk than managers in large firms; they view business opportunities more positively
Sarasvathy *et al.* (1998)	Entrepreneurs accept risk and attempt to control outcomes; bankers go for the highest possible return and work on minimising risks
Stewart *et al.* (1999)	Entrepreneurs are driven to succeed and have a higher propensity for risk-taking than small business owners or corporate managers
Stewart and Roth (2001)	Entrepreneurs are more likely to take risks than managers
Miner and Raju (2004)	Meta-analysed 14 studies; found entrepreneurs were *less likely* to take risks than managers and suggested that entrepreneurs are risk avoidant

Table 4.1 and the preceding discussion show mixed results. Whilst there is, for example, rather a lot of evidence in support of achievement motivation, a number of caveats have been raised by a range of researchers. For LOC there were mixed results, raising a number of similar methodological concerns and also possible gender effects. The findings from studies on risk-taking indicate a need to consider fundamentally how risk is constructed. The methodological issues of general concern are: (a) how the measure is constructed, using an inadequate measure; (b) the research design, e.g. use of control groups, composition of the sample (e.g. nascent entrepreneurs,

single-occasion measures, lack of before/after or longitudinal studies, absence of controls for other variables such as sex, prior founding experience, the effect of learning); (c) the relationship with performance issues. Some researchers have suggested that environmental variables should be part of the research design and that other attributes, such as skills and abilities, are likely to be more important than traits.

In conclusion, more sophisticated research designs are required to provide more convincing evidence that any of these three traits are prototypical of entrepreneurs and predictors of entrepreneurial behaviour and firm performance. Studies that include a multivariate design, focusing on variables that encapsulate person, environmental, resource and organising factors, would appear to have considerably more potential from an interdisciplinary perspective. This type of approach and a greater in-depth analysis of risk-taking are key areas warranting further research. In the next chapter, I consider research that has attempted to identify other traits of entrepreneurs, the measuring instruments used and the conclusions that have been drawn.

Notes

1 Self-employed refers to those individuals who work for themselves but do not employ other people; this is often characterised as a lifestyle choice as it does not constitute the entrepreneurial act of wealth creation or business founding.
2 Locus of control was originally conceived as a socially learnt behaviour. However, since Rotter's original work it has been treated as a trait construct.
3 See Chapter 2 of this volume.

5   New entrepreneurial traits

Introduction

The supply of entrepreneurs is an issue in any growing economy, so the question 'can anyone fulfil the role and function of an entrepreneur?' is fundamental. In the previous chapter, attention was focused primarily on trait theory, specifically whether solid, rigorous evidence could be found in support of three 'big' (in the sense of predominant) entrepreneurial traits – need for achievement, internal locus of control and risk-taking propensity. At best, research on the 'Big Three' exposed some crucial methodological problems, including the requirement that other factors, such as gender and specific environmental dimensions, should be considered, which would necessitate multivariate analyses. It was also evident that the conceptual basis to traits such as risk propensity should be explored further in order to understand how, for example, risk is constructed and enacted by nascent entrepreneurs, venture capitalists, bankers and other significant groups. This approach might be extended to the language associated with the achievement motive.

The apparent problems of inconsistent, equivocal findings in respect of the application of these three attributes to entrepreneurs encouraged researchers to identify other measures of different, but purportedly relevant, attributes. These I have termed 'new entrepreneurial traits'. However, some researchers have extended their thinking to include additional person attributes, such as skills, abilities, attitudes and strategic behaviour. Furthermore, attempts have been made to develop measures of a profile of attributes such as entrepreneurial orientation, using a mix of person descriptors, suggesting the possibility of inclusion of such a measure in a theoretical model within human capital theory. However, such a model should be very clear about the nature of the dependent variable – self-employment is not a sufficiently rigorous indicator of entrepreneurial performance – and should be tested with the same cohort over time (e.g. nascent entrepreneurs with the intention to enter into entrepreneurship) and after two further time periods to demonstrate sustainability of the entrepreneurial performance and association of the characteristics with that outcome.

The crucial questions that researchers continue to ask in order to identify entrepreneurial traits are: is there just one trait or a constellation of traits that can be singled out, and how might they be measured? Further, are there traits that are linked to successful or, indeed, superior entrepreneurial performances? Single traits (other than the 'Big Three') that have also been identified include tolerance of ambiguity (Schere, 1982), which acknowledges the uncertainty-bearing role of an entrepreneur. Schere demonstrated a statistically significant difference between entrepreneurs and managers on this measure. Sexton and Bowman (1984) demonstrated that entrepreneurs have a significantly greater tolerance for ambiguity than do managers. Gooding (1989) showed that entrepreneurs viewed equivocal data more positively than did managers. Sexton and Bowman (1985) identified a 'high need for autonomy' – a characteristic that has found some support in both the sociological and psychological literature; it has been variously described but more usually as a 'high need for independence' (Hornaday and Aboud, 1971; Fagenson, 1993; Brandstätter, 1997) or 'a propensity to act autonomously' (Lumpkin and Dess, 1996). Schrage (1965) found that 'veridical perception' was more important than achievement or power motivation in identifying the successful entrepreneur. Hornaday and Bunker (1970) attempted to discover whether 21 different characteristics applied to the *successful* entrepreneur and in the follow-up study referred to above; Hornaday and Aboud (1971) suggested that high need for achievement and independence, low need for support and the importance of leadership differentiated the *successful* entrepreneur from a control group. Timmons *et al.* (1977) suggested that there were more than 20 characteristics that discriminate between entrepreneurs and others.

The problems associated with the trait approach, or indeed the identification of any person attributes linked to the entrepreneur, have not necessarily gone away. The melange of possible traits, the lack of conclusive evidence, questions over sampling design, sampling on the dependent variable and the appropriateness of various measuring instruments have led to considerable disillusion with the traditional trait approach to understanding entrepreneurial behaviour and character (Low and MacMillan, 1988; Thornton, 1999). Nonetheless, as theory developed, some researchers felt that there are compelling aspects of an entrepreneur that surely make them stand apart. Thus, attention has swung back to take a further look at the possibility of identifying new trait differentiators (Collins *et al.*, 2004; Stewart and Roth, 2004). To do so researchers have adopted different approaches, for example: they have developed and designed new measuring instruments and identified new traits from economic theory (e.g. alertness to opportunity) and organisation theory (e.g. proactivity); and others have attempted to put together a profile of entrepreneurial characteristics. These I will review in the ensuing pages. First we will consider different measures of entrepreneurial traits, some of which were specifically designed for the task, and then examine any fresh evidence for new traits (other than the 'Big Three') that have been identified as candidates that purportedly characterise the entrepreneur.

Thus, in sum, the purpose of this chapter is: to examine this further evidence of alleged entrepreneurial attributes; to look critically at some of the measuring instruments that have been developed, used and evaluated; and to evaluate the state of knowledge of descriptors of the entrepreneurial persona.

Specific measures of entrepreneurial characteristics

To identify either a single trait or a constellation of traits, the measures must be reliable, valid, have predictive capability and provide incontrovertible evidence (Hornaday and Aboud, 1971; Hogan *et al.*, 1977; Nicholls *et al.*, 1982). Moreover, they should tie into theory (McClelland, 1961). A number of research studies have attempted this, as discussed above. The trait measures that are clearly designed for the purpose rather than using general personality inventories should be tested and developed using nascent entrepreneurs (i.e. individuals with the intention to become involved in entrepreneurship and who have taken some steps in that direction). Individuals with prior experience of entrepreneurship should act as a separate cohort from inexperienced nascent entrepreneurs so that social learning of entrepreneurial behaviours and skills can be identified. Carefully constructed control groups should also be included in the research design. In addition, demographic data, parents' employment details, sex of the respondent, ethnicity, education and work experience should be included (Delmar and Davidsson, 2000). However, these thoughts are not entirely new; there are some very early studies that also suggest that a basket of measures including motives, values, demographic characteristics and specific traits measures should be adopted (Hornaday and Aboud, 1971).

Entrepreneurial attitude orientation

Robinson *et al.* (1991) considered alternatives to the trait approach. They argued that personality measures often lose their efficacy when applied to specific situations, such as entrepreneurship, and that demographic characteristics are fatally flawed as predictors of future actions (ibid.: 16). They suggest that attitude holds greater promise as a predictor of behaviour. Based on a body of research on personality and entrepreneurship, they developed 'The Entrepreneurial Attitude Orientation (EAO) Scale'.

This scale has four sub-scales:

1   Achievement in business (ACH) – based on McClelland's concept of need for achievement and referring to concrete results associated with start-up and growth of the venture.
2   Innovation in business (INN) – based on Kirton's adaptors and innovators measure and relating to perceiving and acting upon business activities in new and unique ways.

3   Perceived personal control of business outcomes (PC) – informed by the construct of locus of control (Rotter, 1966; Levenson, 1973) and concerning the individual's perception of control and influence over his/business.

4   Perceived self-esteem in business (SE) – from Crandall (1973) and pertaining to the self-confidence and perceived competency in an individual in respect of his/her business affairs.

Each of these sub-scales consists of three components – affect (feeling/emotion), cognition (belief) and conation (desire or intention). The variable criterion to distinguish entrepreneurs from non-entrepreneurs was the act of business creation, specifically 'a start up entrepreneur, who had founded more than one business, the last one being within five years, using some type of innovation' (Robinson *et al.*, 1991: 20). Groups of entrepreneurs and non-entrepreneurs (primarily professionals, such as accountants and engineers) were put together and the EAO Scale administered. It was found that the scale could discriminate between entrepreneurs and non-entrepreneurs, especially the sub-scales of innovation and personal control, although as innovation was a defining characteristic this is perhaps unsurprising.

Further work carried out by Huefner *et al.* (1996) used the EAO and three additional scales – the Entrepreneurial Quotient (EQ), Myers-Briggs Type Indicator (MBTI) and Herrmann Brain Dominance Instrument (HBDI) – to seek sources of discriminating factors between entrepreneurs and non-entrepreneurs. These authors wished to know whether, by using several types of scales, they could enhance prediction and understanding of entrepreneurship. It should be noted that the authors did not select any standard 'trait' inventories, such as the Jackson Personality Inventory and Personality Research Form E (JPI/PRF-E) or the Edwards Personality Preference Schedule (EPPS). Rather, their choice was for two entrepreneurship-specific scales and two general scales:

The *Entrepreneurial Quotient* is entrepreneurship specific and was originally designed to enable a life insurance company to hire agents who were entrepreneurial (Northwestern Mutual Life Insurance Company, 1985). This scale does not appear to be readily available for general usage and so does not appear to have been widely used, tested or validated.

The *Myers-Briggs Type Indicator* is a general and widely used scale that enables people to gain self-insight and insight into other people. It comprises four bi-polar scales that are based on Jungian theory of individual differences in perception and judgement, encompassing the following scales:

• *Extraversion–Introversion* (E–I): a person's preferred way of interacting that reveals either a focus on people and objects or the inner world of concepts and ideas.
• *Sensing–Intuitive* (S–N): a person's preferred way of perceiving, either sensing the moment or focusing on insight, relationships and meanings.

- *Thinking–Feeling* (T–F): a person's preferred way of exercising judgement that is either logical and analytical or inferential based on values and feelings of others.
- *Judging–Perceiving* (J–P): a person's preferred way of dealing with the environment that is either based on a desire for planning, order and structure or an orientation that is flexible and sensitive to new information.

The classification for each dimension results in 16 possible types. From previous research it was expected that the sub-scales S–N and T–F would differentiate between entrepreneurs and non-entrepreneurs.

The *Herrmann Brain Dominance Instrument* aims to categorise people into left-brain right-brain categories based on their learning preference or style. There are four types:

- Quadrant A: typified by activities that are logical, analytical and mathematical.
- Quadrant B: typified by activities that are controlled, planned and sequential.
- Quadrant C: typified by activities that deal with emotion, are people oriented or spiritual.
- Quadrant D: typified by activities that are imaginative, holistic and require synthesis.

Herrmann (1988) predicted an entrepreneurial profile that has a high score on quadrant D and moderate to strong in the other three quadrants, but he does not appear to have tested the prediction.

Huefner *et al.* (1996) differentiated their sample into four groups: non-entrepreneurs who, according to self-report, were not entrepreneurs and had never owned and managed a business; owner-managers who, in accordance with self-report, were not entrepreneurs and had owned and managed one or more businesses; entrepreneurs who reported that they were entrepreneurs and had owned and managed one or more businesses; potential entrepreneurs who reported that they were entrepreneurs but had not owned and managed a business. The sample was drawn from students at Brigham Young University, their friends, family and acquaintances; it was thus a convenience, and not a random, sample. The results of this study revealed some interesting findings and a selection of the key, statistically significant results is presented here.

The EQ demonstrated two results: (a) an effect of sex, with male respondents showing a much higher mean for entrepreneurship than women (the authors, however, point out that the measure may be sex-biased, as it has not been normed, and recommend that it should be revised); and (b) a strong differentiation between entrepreneurs, owner-managers and non-entrepreneurs.

The EAO sub-scales revealed: (a) differentiation between males and females on self-esteem (SE) and innovation (INN); (b) SE, PC and INN differentiated between entrepreneurs and the other two groups, with entrepreneurs scoring much higher on INN (mean = 73.6) than owner-managers (mean = 63.1) or non-entrepreneurs (mean = 67.2) and INN being the strongest predictor; and (c) a slightly surprising result that ACH did not differentiate between the groups and the authors' suggested cultural bias – the American culture being strongly achievement oriented.

The MBTI showed no differentiation between men and women, but this scale is sex-normed. The Sensing–Intuitive sub-scale differentiated between groups, with entrepreneurs achieving a higher score on Intuitive and owner-managers and non-entrepreneurs achieving a higher score on Sensing. However, standard deviations were large, which suggested that the differences were perhaps not clearcut – this may also come down to the accuracy of classification initially into groups. There was a significant difference between groups on Judging–Perceiving: entrepreneurs were higher on Perceiving, whilst the rest scored higher on Judging. Again, there were large standard deviations and the authors strike a note of caution in drawing the conclusion that all entrepreneurs are 'Intuitive–Perceiving' types. The overall classification for entrepreneurs was ENTP, whereas for the owner-manager/non-entrepreneur group it was ISFJ. The authors feel that this suggests a possible norm for the entrepreneur using the MBTI.

The HBDI revealed some differences by sex, but the only significant group difference occurred with sub-scale D – the right-brain metaphor – with the highest score for entrepreneurs. It indicates a preference for activities that require imagination, are holistic and require synthesis.

Finally, this research investigated whether there was any particular combination of scales that was the best at correctly classifying entrepreneurs and minimising the number of owner-managers and non-entrepreneurs misclassified. They found that the EQ gave the best overall classification. The best combination was EQ/EAO/MBTI, with EAO/MBTI a near second. However, the proportion of misclassification for each of these combinations was relatively high (upwards of 30%) and the authors suggested that it would depend on what the research questions were as to which combination of measures should be used. It should be noted that there is also a problem of improving the ability to classify subjects correctly into the different groups. This research shows an attempt to thoroughly analysis the EAO instrument. Further work is needed to model the relationship between broad trait measures (such as those in the MBTI) and specific entrepreneurial trait measures and other person factors such as attitude that may mediate entrepreneurial performance. Any repeat survey should use random rather than convenience samples.

Entrepreneurial orientation

Lumpkin and Dess (1996), using a scale of Entrepreneurial Orientation (EO), include measures of a propensity to act autonomously, a willingness to innovate and take risks and a tendency to be aggressive towards competitors and proactive relative to marketplace opportunities. Furthermore, they suggest that the five dimensions of the EO scale may 'vary independently, depending on the environmental and organisational context' (ibid.: 137). We should also note that this approach – to develop a measure of Entrepreneurial Orientation – is moving away from the idea of a single uni-dimensional trait measure that differentiates the entrepreneur from others, to an explicit recognition of the multi-dimensionality of the entrepreneurial persona.

The unit of analysis in Lumpkin and Dess is primarily the firm, although the measures of EO are of entrepreneurial behaviour. This clearly raises issues of the unit as well as the level(s) of analysis. The authors seek to examine the relationship between EO and firm performance and to identify sets of contingency factors that mediate the relationship; these include environmental and organisational factors. They conceptualise four additional contingency models of the EO–performance relationship (Lumpkin and Dess, 1996: 156): (a) the 'moderating effects model' in which the strength of the EO–performance relationship is moderated by organisational structure, specifically mechanistic versus organic structure (Burns and Stalker, 1961); (b) the 'mediating effects model' in which EO is the antecedent variable, firm performance is the outcome variable and the integration of organisational activities is the mediating variable (Kanter, 1983); (c) the 'independent effects model' in which 'environmental munificence' and EO affect firm performance independently; and (d) the 'interaction effects model' in which the characteristics of the top management team, such as tolerance of ambiguity or need for achievement, are believed to interact with EO to influence firm performance. The researchers develop the conceptual framework and a set of propositions and pose a number of interesting questions to be addressed and tested through further research. These questions should also include; what are the most appropriate entrepreneurial characteristics that should be measured and are the measures validated?

Assessment/development centre approach

Moran (1998) reports on the development and testing of a method for profiling the small business owner-manager (which is equated with 'entrepreneur') against a range of personality dimensions utilising a form of Assessment/Development Centre (ADC). Moran argues for the utility of adopting a multi-dimensional approach using a wide range of instruments to tap different aspects of motivation, cognition and ability and relating these to the individual perceptions, plans and needs of nascent[1] owner-managers. A basket of measures, including a decision-making and prioritising exercise, a problem-solving exercise and a group exercise based on a crisis scenario, was used to assess individuals' enterprise. The personality measures included standard personality inventories: the Myers-Briggs Type Indicator (MBTI: Briggs and Myers, 1993); Learning Styles Questionnaire (Honey and Mumford, 1986); Leadership Opinion Questionnaire (Fleischman, 1957); Team Role (Belbin, 1981); Survey of Personal Values (SPV) and Survey of Interpersonal Values (SIV) (Gordon, 1984); measure of creativity, specifically 'Alternate Uses' (Guildford *et al.*, 1978); and ability measures and general enterprise tendency.

This method has the advantage of being able to profile the individual. However, Moran also wanted to relate these measures to the Growth Orientation (GO) of the individual. He distinguished between High, Medium and Low GO on a number of explicit criteria. Moran found no significant differences between High, Medium and Low GO owner-managers on the MBTI, although the ENTP profile was more pronounced with the High GO group. Dominant learning styles were 'activist' followed by 'pragmatist', and again they were more closely associated with High GO. The results of the Leadership Opinion Questionnaire suggested the need for a strong leadership orientation and that this tends to increase with increasing GO. The preferred team roles were: Shaper, Company Worker and Chairman. However, for the High GO group the preferences were Shaper, Chairman and Plant, suggesting an ' "entrepreneurial combination" of high drive, leadership and creativity' (ibid.: 27–28). On the SPV the results for the overall sample revealed high scores on Variety and Practical-mindedness, whereas on the SIV high scores were found on Independence and Leadership. The lowest ranked values were Achievement and Orderliness on the SPV and Benevolence and Conformity on the SIV. Separating out the results for the high GO group in respect of SPV, they scored significantly higher on Decisiveness and lower on Orderliness. These results suggest that nascent owner-managers with High GO value opportunities for rapid decision-making and being able to impose their own views but are less likely to value order or system. The measure of creativity did not differentiate between GO groups. This study raises questions about this particular mix of measures and whether such a study could be designed using larger samples and a control group.

Further work using the MBTI

Gardner and Martinko (1996), using the MBTI to study managers, outline the psychological types and the psychometric properties of MBTI and evaluate the scale on a number of criteria. On the whole, the authors excluded change agents, organisation development consultants and entrepreneurs from this study, and provide a critical review of some methodological issues associated with the studies they evaluated. This gives a useful and rigorously considered view of the utility of this psychometric instrument. They conclude that 'the low quality of much of this research has undoubtedly undermined the MBTI's reputation and created scepticism about its utility' (Gardner and Martinko, 1996: 58). Some of the interesting dimensions that they extract include decision style, risk perceptions, judgement, performance and intuitive type.

Further, these authors considered four 'decision styles': ST – a practical, realist approach; NT – a logical and impersonal approach; SF – an evaluative approach based on personal values; NF – a pro-social approach that attempts to serve the needs of people in general. They examined evidence for decision style under different levels of uncertainty. Research that examined the compatibility of the decision environment with the individual's decision style found that 'incompatible settings elicited more risk aversion' (Gardner and Martinko, 1996: 69). However, this was found to be true for STs only: 'the other styles saw less risk and were more prone to adapt' (ibid.). It was suggested further that SFs, NTs and NFs perceive more and are risk averse in compatible settings because they fear that like-minded persons will see through their arguments. Alternatively, they may know more about the dangers inherent in 'compatible settings'.

They also note, for example, that different psychological types have different preferences for the way information is displayed. There were clear differences between Sensing–Intuitive types in dealing with graphical raw, graphical summarised, tabular-raw and tabular-summarised formats. Specifically, Sensing types appear to favour concrete and factual data for decision-making purposes, whereas Intuitive types rely on hunches and heuristics. Sensing–Thinking types take longer over decision-making than Intuitive types. Also Intuitive types view graphs as more useful than tables, however, when operating under time pressure, they perform worse with them and are less confident (ibid.: 71). They adduced evidence to support the view that Thinking types are more assertive and less cooperative than Feeling types, which they suggest may have implications for managerial approaches to conflict resolution. Additional evidence was adduced to support the view that Intuitive types were more prominent in middle and top management positions, performed more novel and creative tasks and were more adept at strategic planning (ibid.: 76). Finally, these authors suggested further research using designs that separated out managers (at different organisation levels) and owner-managers and entrepreneurs. They suggested that there is considerable scope to examine various organisational and managerial behaviour dimensions of type-related behaviour, ranging from leadership style, communications, goal-setting, time management, reactions to job stress, impression management, strategic planning and other behaviours, including risk aversion. Importantly, they point out that there is also a need to consider possible moderating effects of situations between type preferences, behaviour and effectiveness. Critically, however, any repeat of this research should use a sample of nascent entrepreneurs, a control group and a matched sample of managers and/or owner-managers. The groups should be matched on (at least) age and gender, include other demographics such as education and work experience and also measures of other person characteristics as indicated above.

Reynierse (1997) took as his starting point the work of Carland *et al.* (1984), which distinguishes between entrepreneurs who are growth oriented and small business owners who pursue lifestyle goals, and applied the MBTI scales to test the proposition that one can distinguish entrepreneurs by both type and conduct. He also wanted to show the value of trait psychology for understanding entrepreneurship. Prior work of the Carlands (Carland *et al.*, 1988a, 1988b) using MBTI revealed entrepreneurs as Intuitive–Thinking types and small business owners as Sensing–Judging types. Also, an earlier study of Reynierse (1995) suggested that it would be useful to include a measure of bureaucracy, on the grounds that bureaucracy indicates stability and resistance to change, whereas entrepreneurialism is indicative of the opposite tendency. Reynierse argued that the JP (Judging–Perceiving) type represents a broad continuum from bureaucracy to entrepreneurialism in which the entrepreneurial preference P tends to initiate and promote change, whereas the bureaucratic preference J tends to encourage established order and resist change. It was found that relative to small business owner-managers, entrepreneurs were intuitive (N), thinking (T) and Perceiving (P) types. They are more likely to go with their hunches, but can also be impersonal and analytical; they are also open, flexible (P) and outgoing (EP). Compared with managers, entrepreneurs were also found to be more outgoing (E), intuitive (N) and open to change (P). When comparing small firm entrepreneurs with lower level managers, entrepreneurs were more likely to be E, N and P; paired temperaments for entrepreneurs included EP, NT, NP, EN and TJ; and for the complete type, 20 entrepreneurs were ENFP and 23 were ENTP – all these results were significantly different to those for lower level managers. Thus, the extravert (outgoing), intuitive (speculative, hunch-making) and perceiving (spontaneous and open to change) dimensions of personality were apparent for entrepreneurs. A further comparison was made between a sample of fast-growth entrepreneurs and executives. This showed a different profile in that I (Introversion) and P (Perceiving) were overrepresented for entrepreneurs. Both IP and EP paired temperaments were overrepresented for fast-growth entrepreneurs, as was SP, NP and TP, whereas EJ, NJ and FJ pairs were underrepresented for these entrepreneurs. This adds weight to the notion that entrepreneurs are more likely to be Perceiving (open to change) than Judging (organised, close-minded, controlling) types.

In summary, Reynierse found that higher levels of P relative to J were found for entrepreneurs compared with business managers; entrepreneurs showed relatively high frequencies of E, N, T and P and there was also found to be an overrepresentation of the ENTP type. He concluded that predictions of entrepreneurialism could be made on the basis of P plus E, N or T. Also, I-type entrepreneurs showed a tendency to be NTP and this was particularly so for fast-growth entrepreneurs; F-type entrepreneurs tended to be ENFP types, especially for small firm, but not fast growth, entrepreneurs. This contrast makes sense in that F types seek warmth, loyalty and commitment to values – closeness that might typify the more family-oriented or lifestyle business, whereas fast-growth entrepreneurs are more demanding, TJ (analytical, organised) types. The J type tended to be underrepresented for most types of entrepreneur. Reynierse also observes that whilst N and P typify the entrepreneur, N is also typical of business executives in American companies. This evidence supports the view that small business owners differ from entrepreneurs or managers. Further, it was suggested that the SP-type entrepreneur was possibly underrepresented in the samples studied. Finally Reynierse concluded that the mindset of the entrepreneur and the bureaucrat is fundamentally different: an entrepreneur's experience is a source of opportunity, discovery and new directions – the antithesis of the bureaucrat. Thus:

> [T]he entrepreneur has an external orientation that promotes opportunity recognition (E), tends to be innovative and can detect patterns and shifts (N), and is highly flexible, promoting an action orientation and responsiveness to change (P). By contrast, business managers in large bureaucratic organisations have an inward orientation toward their own practices (I), are particularly attentive to immediate events within their span of control and influence (S), and generally adhere to internal policies, structure, and plans, a commitment that is antagonistic to flexibility, action and change (J).
>
> (Reynierse, 1997: 17)

It is essential in studies such as this that they are applied to nascent entrepreneurs to ensure predictive validity. Sampling on the dependent variable, as in this study, invites the criticism that entrepreneurs learnt the behaviours that were being picked up in the MBTI data analysis. A cohort of nascent entrepreneurs might be matched with a cohort of MBA students or apprentice managers on various demographic dimensions and measures taken over a period of say ten years. This would facilitate measurement of performance outcomes and the possibility of the development of learnt behaviours and styles of operating.

Entrepreneurial Potential Questionnaire

Müller and Gappisch (2005) devised a pencil and paper test based on King's (1985) Entrepreneurial Potential Questionnaire, which measured six traits: Need for Achievement, Internal LOC, Problem-solving Orientation, Risk-taking Propensity and Manipulation/Assertiveness. Six new items were constructed to measure: Need for Autonomy, Level of Arousal, Stress Resistance, Emotional Stability, Intuitive Problem-solving and Tolerance of Ambiguity and Interpersonal Reactivity. Eighty-five entrepreneurs took part in the study. A principal components factor analysis was conducted to determine the typological structure of the 12 traits being measured. A five-factor solution was found that accounted for 70.5% of the variance. The authors suggested that the test showed similarities with the typologies of Miner (1997) and the MBTI (Reynierse, 1997). By factor analysis the authors identified five types of entrepreneur:

1   *Creative Acquisitor* – the idea generator or intuitive type and a sales-person type; could be described as an 'innovation-oriented salesperson' who has a risk-taking propensity.
2   *Controlled Perseverator* – emotionally stable and able to absorb stress; has an analytical problem-solving orientation. This type could be described as an entrepreneur who applies their affective potential in a well-directed manner.
3   *Distant Achiever* – has a high need for achievement and personal autonomy.
4   *Rational Manager* – is assertive and has an analytical problem-solving orientation and risk-taking propensity.
5   *Egocentric Agitator* – described as a maladapted type with low inter-personal reactivity (i.e. low ability to empathise with others, socially inflexible and low ability to enthuse others).

Müller and Gappisch (2005) also correlated the type scores with ratings of job and life satisfaction. Type 2 (Controlled Perseverator) correlated positively ($p = <0.05$) on both measures, and Type 5 (Egocentric Agitator) correlated positively on job satisfaction. There were no other significant correlations.

A critical appraisal of this study suggests that while reliability and validity tests were made of the measures, some (e.g. the alpha coefficients of internal consistency) were relatively low, ranging from 0.6 to 0.79. A further difficulty is that the study was of actual entrepreneurs with an average of 13 years of experience; there were no before or after measures of job or life satisfaction. There are no measures of business performance. The labelling of the factors to indicate entrepreneurial personality types is problematic and there is no attempt to relate the personality style to environmental issues. An earlier study by Miner (2000) dealt with some of these issues by assessing type-specific attitudes of graduates after they had left university and their prediction of entrepreneurial behaviours. The issue of job and life satisfaction could be used more generally in entrepreneurial research as one measure of outcomes.

The 'Big Five'

Thus far I have considered a number of new scales that have been designed to measure entrepreneurship as a multifaceted set of characteristics and also the application of the MBTI, which views subjects as exemplars of 16 possible ideal types. However, during the period of 'crisis' in trait psychology (see my discussion of this as it applies to the entrepreneurial personality: Chell, 1985a; Chell *et al.*, 1991), lexicographers and psychometricians were working on a new structure to personality in general. This would contrast with Eysenck's three-factor solution (extraversion, introversion and neuroticism) as outlined in Chapter 4 and Cattell's 16-factor structure of personality. This new structure – termed the Big Five – is described below, with some examples of its application to the entrepreneurial personality.

The 'Big Five' has been put forward as a five-factor solution to the structure of personality. The Big Five dimensions include Neuroticism (N), Extraversion (E), Openness (O), Agreeableness (A) and Conscientiousness (C) (Deary and Matthews, 1993). Each dimension comprises six facets or sub-scales. The claims are: there is a convergence between many researchers on the conceptual similarity of personality dimensions obtained from different structural models of personality; some researchers believe that the five-factor solution is a better psychometric account than previously proposed models; and research has been done to correlate factor scores found using different measuring instruments and the Big Five. These measuring instruments include the MBTI, the PPQ (Professional Personality Questionnaire), the Eysenck three-factor model and Cattell's 16PF. Deary and Matthews (1993) also point out that the arguments of critics of trait theory were fuelled by the fact that there were so many different personality measurement instruments that it was hardly surprising that it was so difficult to provide solid evidence of reliable and valid indicators of predispositions. Table 5.1 shows the facet scales of the Big Five. Claims are made that there is close agreement with Eysenck's three-factor solution (Deary and Matthews, 1993: 301) and, furthermore, Cattell's 16 factors have been analysed and reduced to five factors (Krug and Johns, 1986). McCrae (2000) has also explored the revival of personality and cultural studies and makes out a case

Table 5.1 The 'Big Five' based on Costa and McCrae's (1992) model of personality structure

Neuroticism	Anxiety, angry hostility, depression, self-consciousness, impulsiveness, vulnerability
Extraversion	Warmth, gregariousness, assertiveness, activity, excitement-seeking, positive emotions
Openness	Fantasy, aesthetics, feelings, actions, ideas, values
Agreeableness	Trust, straightforwardness, altruism, compliance, modesty, tender-mindedness
Conscientiousness	Competence, order, dutifulness, achievement-striving, self-discipline, deliberation

for the scientific assessment of the prevalence of the five-factor model across, between and within cultures. Our particular interest, however, is the work that has been undertaken to use this approach to personality in order to analyse the entrepreneurial persona.

Amit *et al.* (1993) examine the relationship of the entrepreneur's personality to long-term venture survival. They measure survival in two ways: (a) the likelihood that the venture will survive for at least 8 years; and (b) the overall lifespan of the venture. They used the 'Big Five' personality scales to assess entrepreneurs on extraversion, emotional stability, agreeableness, conscientiousness and openness to experience (see Table 5.1). As hypothesised, the entrepreneur's conscientiousness was positively related to long-term venture survival. Contrary to expectations, they found a negative relationship between the entrepreneur's openness and long-term venture survival. Extraversion, emotional stability and agreeableness were found to be unrelated to long-term venture survival. This study suggests that it may be important to also measure some specific entrepreneurial traits and not simply the very broad general traits of the 'Big Five'.

Envick and Langford (2000) also turn their attention to the application of the Five-Factor Model of personality and its application to the entrepreneur. They label the Five Factors:

1   *Adjustment* (stable/confident . . . nervous/self-doubting).
2   *Sociability* (warm/optimistic . . . independent/ reserved).
3   *Conscientiousness* (dependable/responsible   . . .   impulsive/careless/ disorganised).
4   *Agreeableness* (team-oriented/trusting . . . self-interested/sceptical).
5   *Intellectual Openness* (imaginative/curious to practical/unimaginative/ literal-minded).

They cite the work of Brandstätter (1997) – reported in detail below – who found that business founders were more stable, independent and open to new experiences than heirs or managers. They hypothesise that entrepreneurs would score higher on Adjustment and Openness than managers, whilst managers would score higher on Sociability, Conscientiousness and Agreeableness. A survey instrument developed by Howard *et al.* (1996) – referenced in Envick and Langford (2000: 12, 16) – was used. No significant difference between entrepreneurs and managers on Adjustment, Sociability and Intellectual Openness scales were found. However, they did find that managers scored significantly higher on Conscientiousness than entrepreneurs, thus suggesting that they are more organised, cautious and plan more than do entrepreneurs. Managers were also found to score higher on Agreeableness, suggesting that they are more team-oriented and considerate than are entrepreneurs. A major problem with this study is that both entrepreneurs and managers had been in situ for many years; their behaviour could have been learnt as a consequence of 'on-the-job' experience.

Founders of privately owned businesses – the definition of entrepreneur in this study – with an average of 14 years experience would be exposed to management tasks over a lengthy period. Likewise, managers would be exposed to decisions concerning innovation and change within the organisations that employed them. It is thus crucial that apprentice managers and nascent entrepreneurs are sampled prior to employment or self-employment and that follow-up measures are taken at a subsequent date or dates.

A further study conducted by Ciavarella *et al.* (2004) examined the possibility of a relationship between long-term survival of a venture and the entrepreneur's personality as measured by the 'Big Five'. They used the five-factor model as described by Barrick and Mount (1993) to include Extraversion, Emotional stability, Agreeableness, Conscientiousness and Openness to Experience. The authors suggest that 'entrepreneurs with personalities that enhance their ability to perform in various situations should have a greater probability of sustaining the operations of the venture for the long term when compared to entrepreneurs with personalities not suited to venture ownership' (ibid.: 469). These authors found that neither Extraversion, nor Emotional stability nor Agreeableness was predictive of the long-term operation of the venture. Conscientiousness was positively related to the venture's survival for at least 8 years and also the overall lifespan of the venture. Openness to experience and long-term survival of the venture was significant in the opposite direction to that predicted. The authors surmise that the findings appear to indicate that 'those who stick to the task at hand rather than being open to a variety of opportunities are more suitable to guide the venture into maturity' (ibid.: 475). After carrying out further analyses the authors concluded that only Conscientiousness emerged as a predictor of firm survival. The result on Openness suggests that this characteristic might have greater influence on firm closure as entrepreneurs are more open to try new ideas and take risks in an environment that has insufficient resource to fully exploit the opportunities. It is clear from what is known from other research that these results are counter-intuitive and should be treated with caution and tested rigorously through careful sampling. It is surprising that the research team did not use before and after measures in this study. The cohort was identified in 1968–1973 when they were students and surveyed for biographical (but not personality) data. In 1995 the cohort was screened to include 'only true entrepreneurs' and these 111 individuals were used in the study. No control group from the original cohort was identified. Further, despite the fact that the researchers noted that the Big Five factors show potential for entrepreneurial leadership, no comparison was attempted with a cohort that became senior managers in their field. It might also be helpful to use the Big Five Inventory alongside other measures of entrepreneurship behaviour and firm performance.

Proactive Personality Scale

The concept of proactivity has a distinguished pedigree. For example, Schumpeter (1934) suggests that the entrepreneur is a dynamic and proactive force; Smith (1967) described 'opportunistic entrepreneurs in similar terms; Miller and Toulouse (1986) suggested that growth-oriented chief executives adopted a proactive and analytical decision-making style; and Chell *et al.* (1991) found the proactive characteristic to be prototypical of an entrepreneur.

Bateman and Crant (1993: 104) define proactive behaviour in dispositional terms: '[it is] behaviour that directly alters environments'. The distinction is between those people who change the world and those who adapt *to* the world. The proactive individual is an active agent as opposed to someone who is passive (Harré, 1983). 'Proactive people scan for opportunities, show initiative, take action, and persevere until they reach closure by bringing about change. They are pathfinders (Leavitt, 1988) who change their organisation's mission or find and solve problems. . . . People who are not proactive exhibit the opposite pattern – they fail to identify, let alone seize, opportunities to change things' (ibid.: 105).

A measure of the proactive construct was developed and assessed in relation to the 'Big Five', three specific traits (LOC, NAch and Need for Dominance) and three criterion variables (civic activities, personal achievements and transformational leadership). Bateman and Crant (1993) hypothesised that the proactive scale would correlate positively with Extraversion and Conscientiousness, but not with Agreeableness, Neuroticism or Openness. This result was confirmed. It was assumed further that the proactive construct would overlap with the instrumental traits – need for achievement and need for dominance. This was confirmed at appropriate levels of significance. Further, it was assumed that proactive individuals would be more engaged in the world around them and thus would more likely engage in activities whose mission is to effect change. Furthermore, individual scores on the proactive scale would be related to individual personal achievements and to positive identification by peers as transformational leaders. These three measures of criterion validity also correlated significantly with the proactive scale. As the authors point out, the findings were significant without having to consider situational factors. They suggest, however, that using an interactive design might increase the construct's predictive power. The measure was tested on three different student cohorts, including an MBA class. It is clear that it should be tested on a more varied population and its predictive capability assessed.

Crant (1996) took the Bateman and Crant research further when he examined the extent to which having a proactive personality is associated with entrepreneurial intentions. Using the Proactive Personality Scale, he explored individual differences in intentions toward entrepreneurial careers, defined as owning one's own business. Using a sample of 181 undergraduate and MBA students, entrepreneurial intentions were found to be significantly associated with gender, education, having an entrepreneurial parent and possessing a proactive personality. He also found that students who reported higher entrepreneurial intentions tended to be: male rather than female; MBA students rather than undergraduates; and had at least one parent who owned a business. The research should be replicated on a sample of nascent entrepreneurs from the general population.

Using a sample of 215 small company presidents,[2] Becherer and Maurer (1999) examined the relationship of the president's proactivity disposition to his/her entrepreneurial behaviour. Proactivity was measured using the 17-item scale developed by Bateman and Crant (1993). Entrepreneurial behaviour was measured in terms of starting versus not starting a business, the number of start-ups and the types of ownership (start, purchase, inherit). The relationships of proactivity to the firm's entrepreneurial posture, its performance and the extent of the president's delegation of authority were also examined. Their findings were extremely interesting: the proactivity of the company executives was positively correlated with the entrepreneurial posture of the firm and increased sales – both results were statistically significant. The relationship between proactivity and profitability of the company was not significant. However, proactivity was related significantly to the number of businesses founded by the company executives. The authors were also able to show that the company executives with a higher proactive disposition were more likely to have founded their business and to have purchased it. There was no relationship found between decision style and proactivity. Becherer and Maurer conclude that proactive executives scan the environment for opportunities, take a bold and aggressive approach to the market (entrepreneurial posture of the firm) and, as such, actively shape their environment. Further, they suggest that these leaders are aggressively growing their firms strategically within the marketplace. Moreover, there are clear external indicators of entrepreneurial behaviour, such as founding more businesses that are also positively related to the executives' proactive personalities. Finally, the fact that proactivity was not found to be related to decision-making style, they suggest, shows that the proactive executive is more likely to be oriented toward the 'bigger picture' than phenomena related to organisation structure and processes.

Once again, later studies focus rather more on the entrepreneurial process; for example, a study by Kickul and Gundry (2002) tested an entrepreneurial process model that examined the interrelationships among a small firm owner's personality, strategic orientation and innovation. In the first part of the model, it was posited that a proactive personality would directly influence a prospector strategic orientation. This type of strategic orientation would then be a key factor in determining the type of innovations introduced and implemented within the business. Using a sample of 107 small business owners, results revealed that the prospector strategy orientation mediated the relationship between proactive personality and three types of innovations: innovative targeting processes, innovative organisational systems and innovative boundary supports. This and the Becherer and Maurer study should be replicated using nascent entrepreneurs and then followed up over a period of years to test for causation (i.e. is proactive personality predictive of entrepreneurial behaviours?). As yet the evidence is not conclusive.

Cattell's 16PF, the 16PA and situational characteristics

Brandstätter (1997: 160) appears to build on the prior work of Wärneryd (1988), who asked the question: who is an entrepreneur? First he tested the separate propositions that 'founding' and/or 'ownership' is a fundamental cause of entrepreneurial behaviour. For this purpose he used a shortened version of Cattell's 16PF, which he labelled the 16PA. He then identified a set of situational characteristics that are common to all entrepreneurs: an absence of other people giving orders; risk and insecurity inherent in entrepreneurial situations; the need for emotional stability; demand for social contact; and readiness to respond to change and to try out new ideas. All these characteristics were posited to be fundamental to entrepreneurial behaviour, and to Brandstätter they suggested the need to measure, for example, emotional stability, social extraversion and openness to new ideas. The resultant 16PA adjective rating scales employ self-descriptions of personality characteristics (Brandstätter, 1997: 166) that measure 'norm orientation, emotional stability, independence, rationality and extraversion' and are similar to the 'Big Five'. In addition, entrepreneurs were tested on a scale that measured their satisfaction as an independent entrepreneur. The samples studied were founders, heirs, would-be entrepreneurs and managers, and include both men and women of a range of ages, educational achievement and size and kind of business managed.

Brandstätter (1997) demonstrated that founders were more stable and more independent than heirs and that aspiring entrepreneurs were similar to founders. Looking at patterns of high–low (HH/LL) combinations of emotional stability with independence, 37% of founders exhibited an HH combination and 27% an LL combination, in contrast to heirs, who showed the reverse pattern, specifically 21% HH and 48% LL. Aspiring founders fell somewhat in between, but were closer to the founders' pattern. The result was statistically significant. Using multivariate analysis, Brandstätter found that founders were more stable, more independent and less rational (i.e. more imaginative and open to new experiences) than heirs. These differences held for men and women. Managers were found to be less stable and less independent than heirs or founders. Founders exhibit greater satisfaction with their role than do heirs. Attributions of success and failure are also worthy of note: in the case of success, attributing this internally (i.e. to oneself) correlated significantly with emotional stability, independence and expected future success. Failure, unsurprisingly, is less attributed to the self. Men show a greater preference for internal attributions for both success and failure than do women, and heirs attribute failure or success more to themselves than do founders. All these findings reached statistical significance.

From this study Brandstätter concludes that these personality differences influence both the decision to set up in business and entrepreneurial success. He also argues that both founders and heirs find themselves in similar business situations, therefore it is unlikely that personality differences are caused by differences in situations. It is more likely that people who are emotionally stable and independent 'develop the courage and initiative necessary for setting up a private business' (Brandstätter, 1997: 172). This is supported by the similarities between the personality profiles of would-be entrepreneurs and actual founders. Extraversion was not found to be a critical requirement of entrepreneurship; indeed, given the time that entrepreneurs need to put into their enterprise, this result is perhaps not surprising. Finally, Brandstätter suggests that '[e]motional stability and independence indeed seem to foster (a) the courage (self-confidence) to take reasonable risks in trying out new ways of providing goods and services, (b) the well coordinated, flexible and persistent actions in pursuing the goals successfully' (ibid.: 174). This study included a sample of would-be entrepreneurs and also looked at issues of success and failure. The key policy implication of this study is that in evaluating the effects of economic policies and training programmes aimed at entrepreneurs it is important to consider the personality structure of the entrepreneur: to consider the compatibility of the personalities wishing to be entrepreneurs and the demands that they will face. Misfit between personality structure and task structure may be a major cause of failure; clearly this is a hypothesis worthy of further research.

Job Stress Questionnaire

The idea that risks are associated with taking entrepreneurial decisions is not in doubt, but do entrepreneurs suffer stress-related behaviours (such as irritability) as a consequence? Begley and Boyd (1986) found no difference between founders and non-founders on a measure of Type A behaviour, where Type A characteristics are associated with stress behaviour. However, Buttner (1992) found entrepreneurs to experience higher levels of stress due to role ambiguity, to have more health problems, be less able to relieve work-related tensions and be less satisfied with their work than were managers. The measurement of stress, however, has been problematic. One approach has been to examine 'Person–Environment Fit', which examines the interplay between specified environmental/occupational variables and stress and strain. The resultant Job Stress Questionnaire (JSQ), developed by Caplan *et al.* (1975), was modified and used by Harris *et al.* (1999) to evaluate job stress in a sample of entrepreneurs. They administered the modified JSQ to 169 male and 56 female entrepreneurs.

The JSQ measures four sources of environmental stress: excessive work-load, role conflict, role ambiguity and underutilisation of skills. Caplan's JSQ was modified by deleting three items, which resulted in a 10-item scale with three sub-scales that measured Workload, Role Ambiguity and Skills Utilisation. The alpha coefficients of these sub-scales were 0.81 (Workload), 0.59 (Role Ambiguity) and 0.63 (Skills Utilisation). The alpha coefficients for the latter two sub-scales show low to moderate internal consistency.

Entrepreneurs were compared with three other occupational groups – white collar workers, blue collar workers and professionals. Entrepreneurs scored significantly higher than the other three groups on Workload but significantly lower on the other two scales. The results suggested that Workload is the greater source of stress for entrepreneurs, who spent on average 56 hours per week on work-related activities. The other occupational groups tended to work set hours per week. Entrepreneurs experienced less stress from 'underutilisation of skills' than the other occupational groups and likewise they suffered lower levels of stress from role ambiguity.

It was suggested that entrepreneurs might have less emotional investment in education and skills than other groups that are likely to have trained for particular trades or occupations. These results may be due to the nature of entrepreneurial activity, which is often characterised by heavy workloads, long hours and a self-established role in the organisation. Finally, entrepreneurs usually headed up their enterprise and were the primary decision-taker, suggesting that their role was self-established and unambiguous. This research appears to miss what some would consider to be pivotal in the role of entrepreneur compared to other occupational groups, that is, the management of risk inherent in the decisions taken, particularly at strategic and higher operational levels. The JSQ fails to take account of this potentially important source of stress.

Tolerance of ambiguity

It has been evident for the best part of the nineteenth century (e.g. Knight, 1921; see Chapter 2) that entrepreneurs, in particular, deal with situations and innovation opportunities that are less than clearcut. Whilst economists thought of this as a decision-making process in conditions of uncertainty from which risk could be assessed, psychologists framed the issue rather differently. It was, on the one hand, viewed as a problem of information processing (Schere, 1982), and on the other as a problem of stress management arising from ambiguous cues in the environment (Begley and Boyd, 1986). Thus, the work of Schere suggested that entrepreneurs have a high tolerance for ambiguity and a low aversion to uncertainty, and Begley and Boyd were able to show that entrepreneurs had a greater tolerance for ambiguity than did managers. Gooding (1989) demonstrated that when entrepreneurs and managers were presented with unequivocal (i.e. unambiguous) data they processed it in the same way, whereas entrepreneurs viewed equivocal data more positively than managers. As reported above, entrepreneurs experienced lower levels of stress from role ambiguity than did blue or white collar workers (Harris *et al.*, 1999). There is a need to take a sample of nascent entrepreneurs and assess whether this measure is predictive of entrepreneurship.

Fresh evidence of other traits that might characterise an entrepreneur

Opportunity recognition

The concept of opportunity recognition as a defining characteristic of an entrepreneur is by no means new. The work of Timmons *et al.* (1977, 1985) and McClelland (1987) discussed this construct. For example, Timmons *et al.* (1985: 153) claim that the key to entrepreneurial success is understanding opportunity:

> We do not believe that there is any single set of characteristics that every entrepreneur must have for every venture opportunity. The 'fit' concept argues the opportunity is quite situational and depends on the mix and match of key players and on how promising and forgiving the opportunity is, given the founder's strengths, advantages, and shortcomings. Significantly, among the hundreds of growth-minded entrepreneurs with whom we have worked, *not one* possessed *all* of the highly desirable characteristics . . . to a high degree. A team might show many of the desired strengths, but even then there is no such thing as a 'perfect entrepreneur', as yet.
>
> (Quoted from Chell *et al.*, 1991: 46)

Opportunity recognition is considered to be a cognitive construct that results in a behaviour pattern identified as 'opportunity recognition'; it may be a learnt behaviour or competence and not necessarily a trait. As such, it has been suggested that entrepreneurs are operating with a 'future time frame' (Bird, 1989) that appears to be about the alertness to domain-specific information that enables the entrepreneur to identify opportunities (Kaish and Gilad, 1991). More recently, researchers have identified and explored this characteristic of opportunity recognition further. Many of these developments have emerged from new theoretical perspectives on the entrepreneurial process. For example, Alvarez and Busenitz (2001) argue that entrepreneurs have the capability to recognise new opportunities and assemble the resources to exploit them. Indeed, one theoretical line of enquiry – the notion of alertness to opportunities – can be traced back to Kirzner (1973): that entrepreneurs possess or obtain specialised knowledge and use it to create or exploit opportunities (see Chapter 2 of this volume). Shane remarks, however, that within Austrian economics, the possession of information enables some individuals to recognise opportunities, whereas for the psychologist the ability is an individual-level attribute (Shane, 2000). Park (2005) provides a review of work focused on 'opportunity recognition'. He identifies 'entrepreneurial self-efficacy' and 'entrepreneurial intent' as the fundamental characteristics that are the best predictors of entrepreneurial behaviour, specifically opportunity recognition, thus treating opportunity recognition as a dependent variable. However, the opportunity recognition literature is still underdeveloped, with competing paradigms and models of the process. For example, Gaglio (1997) puts forward a four-stage model comprising prevision, vision, elaboration and launch that, Park argues, omits 'the extremely important refinement stage, a critical part of market entry' (Park, 2005: 746). Prior experience of technology and markets is also considered crucial if entrepreneurs are to have the tacit knowledge and insight required for opportunity recognition (Baker *et al.*, 2001, and Craig and Lindsey, 2001, quoted in Park 2004).

Gaglio and Katz (2001) argue that opportunity identification is the most distinctive and fundamental of entrepreneurial behaviours. If this is so, how it is defined and elaborated as a set of traits, practical skills and/or knowledge is also crucial to know. The authors adopt a Kirznerian approach, that is, they suggest that entrepreneurs who exploit opportunities are in a position where information is differentially distributed, such that they and they alone can recognise an opportunity; specifically, anyone in theory can notice an opportunity, but in practice it depends what they are interested in, their extant knowledge and absorptive capacity. This suggests that entrepreneurs, sensitised by their understanding of the particular industry, technology and/or market context, are able to identify the opportunity. Others without that prior knowledge/experience would not be in a position to recognise the opportunity (Shane, 2000).

Dutta and Crossan (2005) complicate this further by suggesting that there are two contrasting views: Schumpeterian and Kirznerian. Their discussion reflects different paradigmatic positions (explored in Chapter 7) that assume, on the one hand, positivism – opportunities exist *out there to be discovered* – and, on the other hand, the constructionist or interpretivist view that *opportunities are created* from the entrepreneur's actions within his/her environment or situation. Thus, they argue that Schumpeter's entrepreneur creates opportunities through a process of innovation of such enormity that it upsets the economic equilibria, and could even destroy an existing industry as the new industry is born; this process he terms 'creative destruction'. The process starts with an idea that is centred on the inventive mind of the individual – the entrepreneur. Moreover, Schumpeter's entrepreneur takes on the role of 'heroic initiator of change in the economy', thus attributing personal traits and motivation to the entrepreneur (Schumpeter, 1934). These traits include intuition, creativity and the power to overcome scepticism and hostility. Thus personal attributes rather than personal knowledge play a role. This led Lumpkin and Dess (1996) to identify those

attributes that comprised an 'Entrepreneurial Orientation': autonomy, innovativeness, risk-taking, proactiveness and competitive aggression (as discussed earlier in this chapter). This view contrasts with Kirzner's position,
which suggests that entrepreneurs have superior knowledge that is tacit and
therefore difficult to replicate; alertness to opportunities and implicit knowledge go hand in hand (Chell and Oakey, 2004). This alertness and idiosyncratic knowledge combines with imagination and interpretation and
leads to the creation of opportunities (Dutta and Crossan, 2005: 432). For
both Schumpeter and Kirzner, a person is an entrepreneur only when s/he
engages in what they each differently define as entrepreneurial acts.

Whichever economic position one takes, there is an explicit suggestion
that the character of the entrepreneur plays a crucial role in this process.
Being in possession of scarce knowledge appears to be a necessary, but not
sufficient, condition for the creation of opportunity, as both positions suggest that the entrepreneur has particular attributes that are either cognitive
(Kirzner's position) or personality (Schumpeter's position), but precisely
what these personal attributes are requires further in-depth research. However, there is a third position not brought out by Dutta and Crossan (2005):
that imagination is both a necessary and sufficient condition (Shackle, 1979)
for the creation of opportunity. Certainly the view that the prototypical
entrepreneur is 'opportunistic, innovative/imaginative, an agent of change/
restless, adventurous, and proactive' (Chell *et al.*, 1991: 154) gains some
support from this discussion. However, later chapters will pursue these
issues further as the need to build and test theory on opportunity identification and development is clearly apparent (Gaglio and Katz, 2001; Ardichvili
et al., 2003); this will be achieved by pursuing theories of entrepreneurial
cognition (Mitchell *et al.*, 2004). Further, there is the view that by taking a broader view of personal constructs rather than traditional traits,
'opportunity recognition' may be included as a personal construct within a
model of the nascent entrepreneurial process predictive of entrepreneurial
outcomes.

Independence/autonomy

There is both psychological and sociological evidence for the desire for
independence/autonomy. For example, Blackburn and Curran (1993: 190)
coined the phrase 'fortress enterprise' to typify the small business owner-
manager's stalwartly independent nature – a tendency to, as it were, batten
down the hatches against external interference, influence and intervention.
From the psychology literature, Brandstätter (1997) compared founders of
businesses with inheritors of businesses and demonstrated that founders and
aspiring founders are more independent than heirs to a business. Lumpkin
and Dess (1996), also discussed above, included in their scale of Entrepreneurial Orientation a propensity to act autonomously, and suggested
that the five dimensions of an EO may 'vary independently, depending on

the environmental and organisational context'. Sexton and Bowman (1985) showed that the entrepreneurs they sampled had a high need for autonomy. A much earlier study by Hornaday and Aboud (1971) examined potential differences between two racial groups of business men. Using the Kuder Occupational Interest Survey (OIS), Gordon's Survey of Interpersonal Values (SIV) and Edwards' Personal Preference Scale (EPPS), they measured need for achievement, need for autonomy and need for aggression using these objective scales. They showed that entrepreneurs scored higher on scales for achievement, independence and effectiveness of their leadership than men in general. However the EPPS for autonomy did not yield a significant result, even though the SIV for independence showed a significant difference between white entrepreneurs and the general population and all entrepreneurs and the general population on this measure. However, this dimension does raise a number of issues, such as what is meant by independence? Small business owners may treasure their independence, but they are not necessarily entrepreneurial – many own 'lifestyle' businesses and do not wish to grow. However, as part of a basket of traits (as in Entrepreneurial Orientation) it may have more credence. The measure should be tested on nascent entrepreneurs as a potential predictor of entrepreneurial outcomes.

Entrepreneurial self-efficacy (ESE)

Work that is associated with ESE has focused on entrepreneurial intentions (Bird, 1989). Bird explains 'entrepreneurial intention' as:

> . . . [a] conscious state of mind that directs attention (and therefore experience and action) toward a specific object (goal) or pathway to achieve it (means). Entrepreneurial intentions aim toward the creation of a new venture or new values in existing ventures.
>
> (ibid.: 8)

Boyd and Vozikis (1994) proposed that ESE is 'an important explanatory variable in determining both the strength of entrepreneurial intentions and the likelihood that those intentions will result in entrepreneurial actions'. They build on Bird's model of intentionality to integrate antecedent factors that explain the relationship between intentions and behaviour. To carry out one's intentions, there is a need for perceived behavioural control, which is very close to the construct of self-efficacy (Ajzen, 1987). Self-efficacy beliefs are strengthened in a number of ways: enactive mastery, observational learning, social persuasion and judgement of one's own physiological state (such as anxiety or emotionality) that may make one vulnerable to reduced performance. Attitudes and perceptions are prerequisites of social learning and self-knowledge that influence feelings of self-efficacy and strengthen a person's resolve, that is, the intention to pursue (or not) a particular course of action. Krueger and Brazeal (1994), moreover, anchor self-efficacy in their model of entrepreneurial potential and propose that ESE constitutes one of the key prerequisites of the potential entrepreneur.

Chen *et al.* (1998) suggest that ESE involves five key skill areas: marketing, innovation, management, risk-taking and financial control are key differentiators between people actively interested in setting up a business and those who have already started. They carried out two studies: one with students and one with entrepreneurs and non-entrepreneurs. They demonstrated that higher self-efficacy scores were predictive of the entrepreneurial decision to start a business. For the student group, having entrepreneurial friends and relatives increased the prediction, but gender was only marginally significant at $p = 0.10$. Founders had a higher ESE score than non-founders, and those individuals with high ESE scores were more likely to be entrepreneurs than those with low ESE scores. Within the specialist domains, it was ESE of risk-taking and innovation that differentiated between entrepreneurs and managers. The researchers suggest that ESE is a key component of entrepreneurial potential and, assuming this to be true, should be included in a model of nascent entrepreneurship. However, they also raise the issue of the stability of ESE as a construct and point out that there are complex issues to be addressed when modelling the relationship between ESE and enterprise performance. Hence, ESE may affect entry to entrepreneurship rather than entrepreneurial performance. Clearly there is a need for more sophisticated models to test such relationships. One practical implication identified is in training nascent entrepreneurs, and key points to look out for are the cognitive and belief system of potential entrepreneurs and the impact of the environment on the belief strength of ESE. In other words, where there is a support environment, nascent entrepreneurs are more likely to feel efficacious.

Studies continue to show, however, the strength of character and resolve that is needed to found a business. For example, Markman *et al.* (2002) investigated the link between general self-efficacy and regretful thinking amongst technological entrepreneurs and non-technological entrepreneurs. The entrepreneurs were found to have a significantly higher self-efficacy than non-entrepreneurs ($p = 0.5^*$), more intense regrets ($p = 0.5^*$) and different types of regret. They also found that inventors with high self-efficacy earned more. The implications of this study indicate the importance of self-efficacy for leveraging one's capabilities and that it is crucial in many entrepreneurial undertakings.

Markman *et al.* (2005) took their previous study further by investigating the co-occurrence of perseverance and self-efficacy with regretful thinking. They measured two types of perseverance: perceived control over adversity and perceived responsibility for the outcomes of adversity. It was suggested that entrepreneurs may exhibit some positive attributes – self-efficacy and perseverance – and some that are less desirable, such as regrets. Their study used the same random sample of 217 patent inventors in the medical industry (surgery devices) as in Markman *et al.* (2002). The results indicate that entrepreneurs score significantly higher than non-entrepreneurs on self-efficacy ($p < 0.02^*$) and on two distinct aspects of perseverance: perceived control over adversity ($p < 0.05^*$) and perceived responsibility regarding outcome of adversity ($p < 0.05^*$). Also, although entrepreneurs report the same number of regrets, their regrets are stronger and qualitatively different from those reported by non-entrepreneurs. These findings suggest that perseverance and self-efficacy are distinct attributes that do indeed co-occur with personal costs (we discuss the co-occurrence of traits in Chapter 6). Furthermore, post hoc analysis revealed that the higher the overall perseverance scores of patent inventors, the higher their annual earnings. Thus, income might be used as a proxy for personal success. Some implications of this study include the idea of training nascent entrepreneurs with respect to their perceptions of adversity; such training could transform a possible sense of helplessness into mastery. There are some problems associated with the categorical constructs 'entrepreneurs and non-entrepreneurs', especially when considering the life course. Furthermore, there is also a question of the direction of causality, although it would seem sensible to posit that self-efficacy and perseverance precede entry into entrepreneurship and that feelings of regret occur subsequently. Finally, the authors do not appear to distinguish between entrepreneurship and business management – the examples of regrets appear to reflect management decisions rather than entrepreneurial decisions.

Previous research on entrepreneurship has guided hypotheses regarding the relationship between entrepreneurial traits and skills (passion, tenacity and new resource skill) and situationally specific motivation (communicated vision, self-efficacy and goals) to subsequent venture growth (Baum *et al.*, 2001; Baum and Locke, 2004). Data from 229 entrepreneur CEOs and 106 associates in a single industry were obtained in a 6-year longitudinal study. Specific clusters of factors were measured: traits, competencies, motivation, strategies and environmental variables. All these factors were shown to affect venture growth, including the interrelations between the factors. In particular, at the individual level the traits and motivation affect the development of strategies, vision and high-growth goals. Skills and competencies are needed to develop an effective strategy. Hence traits affect (mediate) other more composite behaviours. Technical and industry-specific competencies had significant direct effects on venture growth and may form distinct competitive advantages. There were also issues about the measurement of strategy, as low cost and focus strategies *à la* Porter did not hold. Unfortunately the study used extant owner-managers of small businesses and there were no control groups or comparative groups of nascent entrepreneurs.

Forbes (2005) examined the way that strategic decisions made in new ventures exert a significant influence on the entrepreneurial self-efficacy of entrepreneurs who manage them. The findings showed that decentralisation of decision-making, decision comprehensiveness and the use of current or real-time information were all positively and significantly related to ESE.

Forbes argues that decentralisation affects the entrepreneurs' level of ESE by exposing them to persuasive argument. This is because sharing of decisions with employees increases positive feelings towards the entrepreneur; it results in positive feedback and a general sense of self-efficacy. Furthermore, decentralisation is likely to affect employees' feelings, including solidarity, sympathetic understanding and support. Decision comprehensiveness is important for two reasons: carrying out a comprehensive search for information in the course of making strategic decisions develops a sense of 'enactment mastery'; and comprehensiveness is related to the ability to articulate and explain one's reasons for adopting a particular strategic decision – this creates decision confidence, which in turn, affects feelings of self-efficacy. The use of real-time data enables an entrepreneur to develop a depth of understanding of internal operations as well as temporal context of the environment. Importantly this enables entrepreneurs to decide when to act; it enables them to avoid the potentially detrimental impact of surprise and unanticipated events.

Social competence

We learn again from sociological studies about the ability of the entrepreneur to network effectively (Aldrich and Whetton, 1981; Birley, 1986; Johannisson, 1995; Chell and Baines, 2000). So is there any evidence from psychology to suggest that entrepreneurs have greater social competence, a spirit of collaboration and networking capability? Envick and Langford (2000) found that managers are significantly more conscientious and agreeable than entrepreneurs. They are also more social, but not significantly so. Entrepreneurs were found to be more adjusted and open than managers, but this result did not reach significance levels. The study did not compare entrepreneurs with the general population.

Two studies in contrasting industries – cosmetics and high-tech – were mounted to investigate the social competence of entrepreneurs. The research was based on the idea that an entrepreneur's effectiveness in interacting with others (i.e. their social competence) may affect business success (Baron and Markman, 2003). These researchers tested the prediction that the higher an entrepreneur's social competence, the greater the success of the business. A survey was conducted with a questionnaire designed to measure four aspects of social competence: *social perception*, which measures accuracy in perceiving others; *impression management* – the ability to induce favourable reactions in others; *social adaptability* – the ability to adapt to a wide range of social situations; and *expressiveness*, which measures the ability to express emotions and feelings in an appropriate manner. Information on the financial success of the business was also collected.

These authors found that *social perception* was positively related to financial success for both groups of entrepreneurs. *Social adaptability* was found to be related to financial success in the cosmetics industry and *expressiveness* was related to financial success in the high-tech industry. These findings suggest that social competence may influence financial outcomes across a wide range of industries and settings. Entrepreneurs in the two industries work in sharply contrasting business environments and there was a gender difference in the composition of the two groups: the cosmetics industry entrepreneurs were entirely female and the vast majority of entrepreneurs in high-tech were male. This study, in fact, focuses on entrepreneurs' behaviour rather than their traits. However, as these authors suggest, there is a growing body of evidence to substantiate the view that social competence is a strong predictor of success in business (e.g. Wayne *et al.*, 1997). However, social competence is likely to be one of several factors that determine the success of individual entrepreneurs. The contrasting patterns of social competence might be explained by the fact that in the cosmetics industry there is a great deal of face-to-face interaction with complete strangers, and thus the ability to adapt to different social situations is highly desirable and enhances effectiveness. This behaviour is labelled as the characteristic of 'social boldness'. In contrast, the high-tech firms were small, with founders in close contact with employees. The ability of these founders to *express themselves* appropriately and generate enthusiasm would help to motivate and encourage employees, thus contributing to the success of the business. Entrepreneurs from both industries would need to read other people accurately and therefore *social perception* was crucial and found to be related to financial success. Emotional intelligence did not emerge as a factor that determined financial success. However, Baron and Markman are critical of this factor, pointing out that other research has shown that only social perception has emerged as a reliable dimension of emotional intelligence. Clearly a limitation of this research is the direction of causality: is social competence causing success, or vice versa?

These studies are a reminder of the need to consider the context of the behaviour and the complexity of opportunity realisation in practice. Social competence should be linked to other factors and indeed might also draw on the now extensive networking literature. In this regard, a study by Davidsson and Honig (2003) investigates the impact of social and human capital factors on the enterprise start-up process. These factors were significant predictors of venture start-up amongst nascent entrepreneurs but were less effective at later stages of the 'discovery–formation–exploitation' process. Researchers pursuing this kind of model should consider the inclusion of measures of personality variables discussed in this chapter.

Those researchers who wish to include entrepreneurial outcomes should also consider that successful entrepreneurs typically engage in a combination of activities to pursue and exploit opportunities, rather than just one (Kodithuwakku and Rosa, 2002). For example, one successful entrepreneur was involved in rice processing, buying and selling farmland, acting as a farmland broker and rice milling. Successful entrepreneurs were also able to manage their limited time and resources in more efficient ways than did the unsuccessful entrepreneurs. Success, therefore, was not only about the pursuit of opportunity (doing the right things); it also required that they do things right. In addition, successful entrepreneurs were more likely to have larger social networks that they used to pursue and exploit opportunities.

Intuition

The idea that entrepreneurs are able to envision future possibilities (Kirzner, 1973; Filion, 1991), where others see none (Timmons, 1989), is now viewed as an essential element of entrepreneurial behaviour. They are said to have a 'knack' for sensing these possibilities and use 'hunches' and 'gut-feeling' to aid decision-making (Bird, 1988). Bird (1988, 1989) argues that rational analytic and cause-and-effect-oriented processes underlie formal business plans, opportunity analysis, resource acquisition and goal-setting, whereas intuitive, holistic and contextual thinking inspire vision, hunch, an expanded view of untapped resources and a feeling for the potential of the enterprise. The argument is further bolstered by the view that entrepreneurs are able to exercise judgement where there may be insufficient information to conduct analysis (Busenitz and Lau, 1996). As reported above, Carland (1982), using the MBTI, found that entrepreneurs were ITP types, whereas owner-managers were more likely to be SFJ types. However, not all researchers were convinced of the importance of intuition: for example, Miner (1997) identified intuition as an important characteristic of 'expert ideas generators'; and Olson (1985) suggested that its use will vary over the different phases of the entrepreneurial process, in particular the invention/discovery process. Allinson *et al.* (2000: 36) summarised under what conditions intuitive thinking was more likely to predominate for entrepreneurs:

> It appears to involve operating in circumstances where there are high levels of uncertainty, few precedents, a lack of hard data and, often, a need to make decisions under time pressure.

These authors found that entrepreneurs were more intuitive than the general population and managers generally, but did not differ significantly from top managers and chief executives. This latter finding was consistent with the work of Mintzberg (1979), Isenberg (1984), Agor (1986) and Parikh *et al.* (1994).

Intuition has been measured using the MBTI (Gardner and Martinko, 1996; Reynierse, 1997) or more recently a measure of cognitive style (Allinson and Hayes, 1996). Whilst in general findings have led to the belief that entrepreneurs are more intuitive than lower or middle managers, research that takes the cognitive approach suggests the need for more detailed consideration. This will be discussed further in Chapter 6 where we examine entrepreneurs using the cognitive research approach.

Summary and concluding remarks

I commenced this chapter with a conundrum: the idea that there are trait descriptors that individuate an entrepreneur but a lack of any consistent evidence to substantiate such a view. In Chapter 4, the most researched traits – need for achievement, locus of control and risk-taking propensity – were found still to be problematic and so in this chapter I have sought to consider 'new traits'. Key problems include conceptualisation and measurement of particular traits, designing appropriate measuring instruments and creating samples for test purposes.

In this chapter I have done two things: (a) examined the measuring instruments that have been used and the evidence they have produced; and (b) brought to the fore new traits and characteristics that scholars believe show promise. The conclusions are these: there is still a need to do more work on the design of measurement instruments; more attention needs to be given to the creation of samples for survey work – I recommend that samples should be created of nascent entrepreneurs, that is, people with a serious intention of setting up a business, in order to increase the predictive validity of research findings; and more attention needs to be placed on research design, control of variables, reliability and validity of the measures, sample sizes and source of the population being sampled. It is clear from the way that many of the research studies are so designed that some researchers believe that entrepreneurial traits alone do not account for sufficient variance, and that other factors also should be measured – they include other person characteristics and also contextual factors. In the next chapter I will develop this theme further.

There is evidence of 'new traits' that show considerable promise. They include the proactive personality, entrepreneurial self-efficacy, perseverance and intuitive decision-making style. Other traits that require further work include social competence and the need for independence – for example, how consistent is the evidence for these two traits? I suggest that by carrying out more research on decision-making style, researchers will uncover more about how information is taken into account, how risks are tempered and how judgements made. This suggests the need for more qualitative design work before developing trait measures or person constructs.

What of the measures that have been used? It seems clear that there is further work that could usefully be done using the MBTI, Entrepreneurial Orientation, the Entrepreneurial Potential Questionnaire, the Big Five, the Proactive Personality Scale and the 16PF/16PA. Constructs such as 'Opportunity Recognition', 'Self-efficacy', 'Social Competence' and 'Cognitive Decision-making Style' should be developed and researched further.

In sum, the various studies are pointing to the need for investigators to design more complex models that may include demographic and other human capital variables, motivation and attitudinal variables and selected person constructs. Dependent on the aims of the particular study, such models should attempt to assess the impact on outcomes, such as venture growth, entrepreneurial performance, entrepreneurial well-being and feelings of success. The conceptualisation of trait or person constructs should have emerged from theory (e.g. Markman *et al.*, 2005) and should also consider the possibility of the indirect effects of trait/person constructs (Baum *et al.*, 2001; Baum and Locke, 2004). Models should also be sensitive to contextual issues such as the different stages in the opportunity development process and that opportunity recognition may also be conceived of as a person construct (Chell *et al.*, 1991).

In the next chapter I develop the theme of interaction between the person and their environment or situation further, and I also consider cognitive approaches to understanding entrepreneurial behaviour. In subsequent chapters, however, I will explore analyses of entrepreneurial behaviour through a different paradigmatic lens. For the moment let us turn to a development in psychology that became evident in the early 1970s, that of interactionism. This is the subject that opens the next chapter.

Notes

1 I use nascent in this context to suggest individuals who had serious intentions to found or purchase their own business.
2 The target population was 683 small business presidents and the response rate was 31%.

6 Interactionism and cognitive approaches to personality

Introduction

The idea that a trait or set of traits could be identified that described the entrepreneurial personality and distinguished the entrepreneur from non-entrepreneurs was the subject of the last two chapters. There, I examined what traits were being identified and measured and the nature and effectiveness of the measuring instruments. From this review, I was able to show that whilst there was some evidence of the importance of personality, it accounted for only a small amount of the variance. Furthermore, there continue to be problems of sample composition, sample size and design of the measures. However, there was additional work to investigate further possible traits, such as 'opportunity recognition', proactive personality, confidence/self-efficacy and decision-making style.

Trait psychology per se is believed by psychologists to be no longer the issue, however many psychologists believe in interactionism (Hampson, 1988; Pervin, 1990) and it is to this theoretical perspective that I first turn. One of the strongest critics of trait theory, Mischel (1968, 1973), advocated a reconceptualisation of traits. I consider this development and its latest formulations, which hypothesise a combination of cognitive and affective elements as integral parts of the system of personality expression (Mischel and Shoda, 1995, 1998). Further, I describe Mischel's concept of 'behavioural signature', which introduces both the contingency nature of behaviour and distinctive character (Mischel et al., 2002). This leads to a consideration of the cognitive-adaptive theory of person–situation interaction (Matthews, 1999), followed by a lengthy section on cognitive research applied to the entrepreneurial personality. I conclude by highlighting the importance of introducing both cognitive and affective dimensions into the theory of the entrepreneur in the process of business venturing and in particular noting the lack of integration of theories of creativity into current cognitive theories.

Interactionism

The precursors of interactionism can be traced back to the 1920s (Ekehammer, 1974). However, it was not so much the rediscovery of this early work, but criticism of existing schools of thought that led Argyle and Little (1972) to arrive at interactionism through a criticism of trait theory, whereas Bowers (1973) reached a similar position from his critique of situationism. There are three positions to be separated. The traditional view of traits as primary determinants of behaviour can be summed up in the formula $B = f(P)$, where B stands for behaviour and P for personality. Situationism, on the other hand, emphasises environmental or situational factors as the main determinants of behaviour and can be summarised as $B = f(E)$, where E indicates 'environment' or 'situation'. Interactionism implies that neither personality nor situation is emphasised, but the interaction of these two factors is regarded as the main source of variation – hence, $B = f PE(P \times E)$. One issue for the interactionist school is the interpretation that may be placed on 'interaction'. Is it *physical* and thereby mechanistic [personality and situation variables (the independent variables) *cause* the behavioural response (dependent variable)][1] or *psychological*, where perception of the situation is paramount? (Endler, 1983). Here the interpretation and the meaning of the situation to the individual 'cause' him or her to behave in a particular way[2] (see Chell, 1985a: 19–23). In other words, the assumption of traditional trait theory is that a person would exhibit a particular trait similarly across all situations, showing little or no variability; situationists, on the other hand, theorise the dominance of the situation, where there is no variability in behaviour shown by people finding themselves in like situations; and in the interactionist model people show variability in their behaviour across situations, that is, people behave in particular ways in some situations but not others. This means that the psychologist should consider both the aspects of person and situation in order to specify or predict behaviour (Argyle and Little, 1972).

Measuring both personality and psychological aspects of a situation is a tall order, particularly in field settings, and would require a very sophisticated research design in order to capture data from behaviour across a broad spectrum of situations and over a reasonable time period. Applications of interactionism in the field have been undertaken with some success (see, for example, Hacker, 1981; James and Sells, 1981; Ivancevich and Matteson, 1984; and, more recently, Brigham *et al.*, 2007). One situational characteristic that entrepreneurship scholars have singled out is that of founding versus non-founding. Begley and Boyd (1986), for example, compared a sample of owners ($n = 239$) who were either founders or non-founders. The founders scored higher than non-founders on risk-taking propensity, the need for achievement and tolerance of ambiguity. They found no differences on measures of locus of control or Type A stress behavioural tendencies. Sexton and Bowman-Upton (1986) measured conformity, energy level, interpersonal affect, risk-taking, social adroitness, autonomy, change, harm avoidance and succorance. They sampled females from the following groups: entrepreneurship majors ($n = 54$), non-entrepreneurship business majors ($n = 73$), managers ($n = 96$) and entrepreneurs ($n = 105$). Among their findings, they reported five of nine strong similarities between entrepreneurs and the entrepreneurship majors and four significant similarities between business students and business managers. Furthermore, practising entrepreneurs were found to be lower in conformity and higher in energy level, risk-taking and autonomy than business managers.

The influence of situations on behaviour and the inability of traits to predict behaviour accurately was the line of attack made by Mischel (1968). Situationism per se (i.e. the idea that behaviour can be explained wholly by the situation a person finds himself in) was found to be untenable (Bowers, 1973). Mischel (1973, 1981) therefore argued for a reconceptualisation of personality from the position of a cognitive social learning theorist, that is, he assumed that behaviour was a learned response and that past experience had a part to play in how people interpreted situations and reacted to them. Furthermore, what is learned depends on the person's construction system (Kelly, 1955). This view accepts that people form consistent conceptions or impressions of others but challenges the scientific status of traits and their applicability to real-life situations. However, the classic theories of traits do not predict behaviour in a single, specific situation; rather, they demonstrate stylistic consistencies in behaviour across a number of situations and over time (Kenrick and Funder, 1988). To demonstrate the predictive validity of the trait, the situation should be relevant to the trait and observations should be made over a number of occasions. For example, to demonstrate anxiety, one would measure the trait before an anxiety-creating situation, such as sitting an exam, and take the measure before several exam sittings to reduce error variance due to uncontrolled situational variables, such as the student being ill on a particular occasion or having a liking for a particular subject being assessed (Epstein, 1977). Kenrick and Funder (1988: 31) conclude that the best predictive coefficients can be obtained if: raters familiar with the persona being rated are used; multiple observations are made, by multiple observers, of dimensions that are publicly observable; and behaviours are used that are relevant to the dimension in question.

The person–situation debate was a wake-up call to psychologists that has resulted in new guidelines for improving predictive validity. However, Funder (2001) notes that there is a need to improve the measures of behaviours and situations. There is still, arguably, too much dominance of laboratories, use of questionnaires and of college students. Other criticisms suggest the atheoretical nature and lack of practical use of trait research (Endler and Parker, 1992), that it is trivial and non-cumulative (Carson, 1989), but that traits can predict behaviour *if* core aspects of relevant situations are taken into account (Matthews *et al.*, 2003: 52). Clearly, there is no room for complacency by trait psychologists. Moreover, there is scope for social psychological explanations of personality and behaviour. Mischel has identified the centrality of the situation as a factor that affects behaviour and demonstrates how this aspect improves the predictability of the trait (Wright and Mischel, 1987).

Mischel's cognitive social learning person-variables and the entrepreneurial personality

Concerns over measurement of traits and the equivocal findings from trait research of the entrepreneurial personality (Chell, 1985a; Chell and Haworth, 1987) led to an exploration of a social psychological approach. This initial reconceptualisation was based on Mischel's 'cognitive social learning person-variables', which are '. . . the products of each person's total history . . . that in turn regulate how new experiences affect him or her' (Mischel, 1981: 345). They are:

- *Competencies*, which are the skills or abilities of the person.
- *Encoding strategies and personal constructs*, which describe the different ways people represent and think about incoming information or particular aspects of the situation they are in.
- *Expectancies*, which suggest that how a person performs in a given situation depends in part on what he or she expects might happen. There may be different behavioural possibilities and the person will weigh up the alternative courses of action open to him or her.
- *Subjective values*, which indicate that people may choose different courses of action because the outcomes of that action are differently valued.
- *Self-regulatory systems and plans*, which indicate that people have different goals and standards that they try to achieve and/or maintain. They adopt contingency plans and rules in order to reach their goals; this activity specifies the sequencing and organisation of their behaviour. It also enables a person to overcome the 'power of situations'. 'We can actively *select* the situation to which we expose ourselves, in a sense creating our own environment, entering some settings but not others, making decisions about what to do and what not to do' (Mischel, 1981: 350; quoted in Chell, 1985a: 49).

In an early study of the entrepreneurial personality such person-variables were applied to entrepreneurial behaviour (Chell, 1985a). The entrepreneur has to deal with a multitude of different situations that are shaped by environmental conditions. Some will be novel and others familiar; some require radical responses and others routine. However, the entrepreneur will identify the situation, consider the course of action open to him or her, adopt a plan of action for dealing with it or avoiding it, do this more or less skilfully and observe and evaluate the outcome.

It was suggested that the interaction between person and situation would be 'organismic' and not mechanistic, as the meaning of the situation is the aspect of psychological significance. As such, the person learns how to handle situations by learning the rules that govern them. This model is shown in Figure 6.1, which shows the process of the entrepreneurs' interaction with their environment. Entrepreneurs have an economic function that they may express through a variety of roles, such as opportunist, pioneer, inventor, marketer, trader, innovator, and so forth. In acting out the appropriate role, the entrepreneur engages in various activities from a behavioural repertoire. Some roles within a single project are likely to include activities that are not specifically entrepreneurial, such as managerial roles and responsibilities. Two main purposes are associated with these activities: to be practical (to manage the situation) and to be expressive (to convey impressions to others). The latter is a key aspect of social behaviour in order to develop style and reputation. Furthermore, actions are often executed with particular judges and audiences in mind. For instance, in dealing with customers, the entrepreneur may attempt to please and convey an impression of reliability, friendliness, orderliness and general business capability in order to win orders and maintain the relationship. This provides a model of broad dimensions of what the entrepreneur brings to each situation and suggests how the meaning of each situation translates into practical activities of learning rules governing each situation, developing and exercising skills and building up a reputation.

The model assumes interpretation of situational contingencies, unlike the 'pure' interactionist account, which would emphasise a stimulus–response regime, where the response is moderated by a host of contextual variables due to the centrality of social learning: 'the observer's cognitive schemas filter and organise the environment in a fashion that makes it impossible ever to completely separate the environment from the person observing it' (Bowers, 1973: 328). This model enables us to see the importance of interpretation, social learning and adaptability to situational contingencies.

Shaver and Scott (1991), building on the interactionist approach, consider a psychological approach to new venture creation that involves cognitive processes. 'We need to know how the business world is represented in the cognitions of people who do, and people who do not, found new ventures' (ibid.: 26). They argue that central to human behaviour is free will and choice. Human action is determined by mental activities such as deliberation and decision-making – choices between options – for which there are observable regularities that can be understood and could form the basis of prediction. However, this predictive capability is not the same as hard determinism that is evident in the physical sciences. Furthermore, the focus should be the person not the personality; the person processes information from the environment, using their combined cognitive, affective, attitudinal and motivational faculties. Environment is critical, because the creation of a business is fundamentally a social activity. Factors like 'opportunity

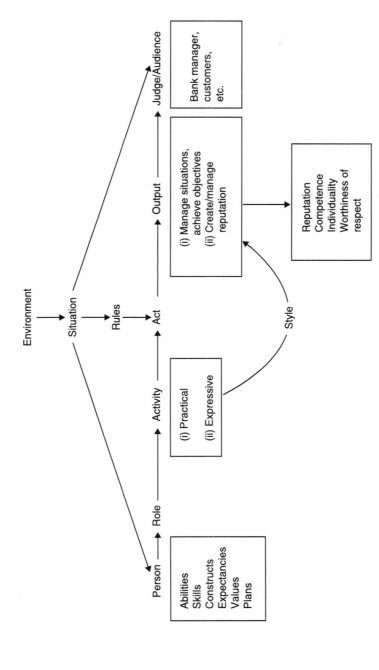

Figure 6.1 Person and situation influences that shape entrepreneurial behaviour (reprinted from Chell, 1986: 113).

recognition' raise a number of questions such as: how does the person process the incoming information and how do people make judgements under conditions of uncertainty? People use: *cognitive heuristics* (short cuts), such as being influenced by the information that is currently available; judgements that are conditioned by the assumption that a person or thing represents a relevant class of item; and judgements that are anchored according to proximity (e.g. local as opposed to national statistics). Further, the exercise of choice depends on two questions from the perspective of the potential founder: can I make a difference? (perceived control) and do I want to? (motivational processes). Perceived control is situation-specific, the key issue being freedom (or loss of freedom) to choose. Intrinsic motivation is high where a person feels that their behaviour is self-determining rather than being controlled. Being able to make a difference is not the same as wanting to. Reasons for business creation have been documented (Cromie, 1988); the psychological issue, however, is how the person evaluates their reason and turns it into a specific action.

Wright and Mischel (1987) have continued work that examines the expression of person-variables in context. According to Matthews *et al.* (2003: 43), Mischel sees a trait statement as a 'conditional probability of a category of behaviours in a category of contexts'. This model of interactionism has been further developed by Mischel and his co-workers and is labelled the 'cognitive-affective personality system' (CAPS).

Cognitive-affective personality system (CAPS)

Mischel (1981) and Wright and Mischel (1987) continue to criticise trait theory on a number of counts:

1   *The personality paradox*: personality is assumed to be stable and enduring and evident from situation to situation, however people's behaviour varies across situations. How, therefore, can psychology resolve this paradox of the intuitive assumption of stability and the evident variability of behaviour across situations?
2   *Assessment of cross-situational consistency*: the method used has been to *average* people's psychometric scores across situations in order to estimate a person's dispositional tendency on a trait, and the variability around the average has been discarded as 'error'. But, is that variance really error or were psychologists discarding valuable information?
3   *Classification of situations*: such classifications have been nominal – they have been adjudged in terms of their location characteristics, such as at the cinema, in a classroom, on a bus, etc. The problem is that this does not reveal the psychological aspect of the location, with which the person engages and which affects their behaviour.

Mischel and Shoda (1995) and Shoda and Mischel (1996, 2000) show that cross-situational variability could be explained by taking a process perspective; personality should be conceptualised as a stable cognitive-affective system that mediates how people select, construe and process social information and generate social behaviours. Such a knowledge structure thus comprises the processing of personal feelings towards a situation and also includes social learning elements. They suggest that behavioural variation across situations is a meaningful expression of personality, and not simply error; as such, it is important to understand profiles of person–situation relations and the underlying dynamics that have caused them.

In contrast to the trait approach, Mischel and Shoda (1995) suggest that emotions influence behaviour and should be incorporated into a social psychological model of behavioural expression. People interpret and label situations, but they also have feelings (positive or negative) about them and, arguably, such thoughts and feelings are inseparable. Furthermore, some such reactions may be automatic or 'pre-conscious'. Hence, emotion is a key aspect of individual differences in social information processing and should be included as an element of any personality system (see Table 6.1):

> Such cognitive-affective representations are not discrete and unconnected, rather 'cognitive representations and affective states' interact dynamically and influence each other reciprocally, and it is the organisation of the relationships among them that forms the core of personality structure and guides and constrains their impact.
>
> (ibid.: 253)

Table 6.1 Cognitive-affective units (based on Mischel, 1981; Chell, 1986; Mischel and Shoda, 1995)

---

1   *Encoding strategies and personal constructs:* categories that encapsulate the different ways people represent, symbolise and think about environmental stimuli, incoming information, particular aspects of the situation they are in, including other people, and the self.

2   *Expectancies and beliefs:* arise from experience of the social world and suggest that how a person behaves will depend on what s/he believes might happen in particular situations; they include expectations and beliefs about other people and self, and reflexively develop beliefs about the situation and possible outcomes.

3   *Affects:* feelings and emotions about a situation and the affective response.

4   *Goals and subjective values:* people choose desirable courses of action whose outcomes hold particular values for them; they avoid the undesirable and thus aversive outcomes and affective states are also evident.

5   *Competencies:* the development of skills and abilities and ways of doing (style and the adoption of scripts).

6   *Self-regulatory plans:* plans and strategies for organising actions in respect of goals and standards that regulate reflexively what outcomes are being sought; affective states in respect of outcomes, one's own behaviour and internal states.

The CAPS model goes beyond 'cool cognitions' to recognise that thoughts are 'affect laden' (Shoda and Mischel, 1996). When certain psychological aspects of a situation are experienced, a characteristic subset of thoughts and feelings is activated through a distinctive network of connections in the encoding process. Only certain units are activated in response to a particular situation and they activate other units along the path of the network until, ultimately, they generate a behavioural response. This model is based on the Hebb (1949) model of neural assemblies, that is, understanding the connections in a network enables one to understand how a complex and coherent pattern of behaviour is produced. Hence, it is this organisation that is the key to understanding human information processing. Information processing differences are manifested in social learning capability, which helps to explain differences in responses to experienced situations: how these are perceived and felt. Ultimately, this organisation reflects the person's cognitive social learning history in interaction with their biological history (temperament and genetic-chemical determinants).

Shoda and Mischel illustrate the CAPS model with an example of a person who learns that s/he has contracted a serious, life-threatening illness. Rather than present their example, consider the application to a situation that may arise in business venturing. An entrepreneur discovers that a major contract for their product has been cancelled; this results in a degree of anxiety (affective state).[3] As the entrepreneur considers the situation further (attempting to glean more information), he is able to develop the options he believes to be open to him (exercise of perceived control). The new state of affairs, as he sees it, affects his expectations of the business going forward (future plans and strategies). He starts to conceptualise the likely scenarios: the worst situation would be to call in the receiver and liquidate the company; another is to downsize and make a proportion of the workforce redundant; and a third option is the possibility, even at this late stage, of securing a new customer. Each thought generates its own affective state and a behavioural response characteristic of that individual. Mischel terms this characteristic response the individual's behavioural signature.

This personality system will generate distinctive *if . . . then* situation–behaviour profiles of characteristic elevation and shape. The distinctive response pattern for an individual reflects the particular acquired meanings of situations – both the cognitions and emotions associated with them.[4] The variation that is generated across situations for any particular individual is not random; it reflects, at least in part, the individual's activated thoughts and feelings and the distinctive neurological organisation through which they are reciprocally interrelated. The organisation and strength of relations among thoughts, feelings and behaviours is such that they will remain essentially the same across similar situations. This suggests both stability and predictability in an individual's behaviour. It assumes that people are able to generate a range of potential behaviours that are fine-tuned to the particular circumstance. Furthermore, an individual's behaviour generates consequences that, in turn, affect the psychological features of events encountered.

Mischel and Shoda (1998) also attempt a reconciliation of the 'Big Five' and the CAPS. They point to the shortcoming of the Big Five – its ability to locate someone in 'the factor space' – but this does not necessarily explain or predict why and when someone behaves in characteristic ways. This cannot be achieved, they argue, without greater contextualisation. They point to research where a 'triple typology model' has been adopted, that is, typologies of person, situation and behaviour. 'This method makes it possible . . . to differentiate subtypes of hostile people in terms of hostile behaviour they are likely to manifest in different types of frustrating situations' (ibid.: 251). Table 6.2 provides a summary of some of the essential differences between the CAPS and trait approaches.

According to Shoda and Mischel (2000: 421–422):

> We adapt to situations while internally coherent; we are goal directed, planful, and future oriented while reactive, impulsive, automatic, and reflexive; we are influenced profoundly both by the social environment and by messages of our genes and biological pre-dispositions. We are the architects of our lives and their victims.

Indeed, they assert that novelists and others have long known that behavioural expression is nuanced; people 'read' other people's behaviour, which is likely to be adapted to the exigencies of different situations. What novelists, and people generally, call 'character', Mischel terms a person's 'behavioural signature'. This appears to go to the core of the 'entrepreneurial

Table 6.2 A summary comparison between the CAPS and trait approaches

CAPS	Trait
• Nomothetic plus ideographic methods	• Nomothetic methods only
• Intra-individual dynamics of single case; generalisation from identifying common types of dynamic	• Samples randomly selected from population
• Can explain cross-situational inconsistency	• Cannot adequately explain cross-situational inconsistency
• Can explain 'why'	• Can only explain 'that'
• Emphasises the meaning of situations	• Meaning for individuals not known
• Both power of the agent and person are identified	• Trait attribution does not extend to social situations
• The analysis of dyadic interaction is part of the social situation	• It is not possible to analyse the impact of a trait on another using psychometric data
• Incorporates six dimensions of personality and as such is more holistic	• May focus on the underlying structure of personality or specific traits

personality': that the lay person or observer assesses the character holistic-ally before drawing a conclusion. A crucial issue, however, is how many situations would suffice to be able to reliably identify someone's character-istic way of behaving? A problem of wrongful attribution of trait terms to a person may occur when too few occasions are sampled across too few situations (Kenrick and Funder, 1988; Johnson, 1999).

Cognitive-adaptive theory

An alternative model assumes that traits are concerned with information processing and represent individual differences in design or adaptation (Matthews and Dorn, 1995). In this respect traits indicate how well an individual is equipped to deal with challenges that they may face during the course of their life. This gives a deeper sense to the meaning of 'traits' (Matthews *et al.*, 2003: 401). The model assumes that traits comprise causal factors (the genetic make-up), basic components (neural processes) and information processing, which are responsible for individual differences in personality development, such as aptitude for acquiring skills and trait adap-tation. At the level of person–situation interaction, skills operate through self-regulation mechanisms, as the person attempts to achieve their goals in a particular situation. Self-regulation is governed by motivation, self-efficacy beliefs and emotions. Hence, personality is distributed across acquired com-petencies and self-regulative dispositions that modulate person–situation interaction. Moreover, social-cognitive learning builds consistent styles of self-regulation, for example extraverts develop high levels of self-esteem, self-efficacy and perceived control with respect to socially and cognitively challenging situations. Self-knowledge feeds back into skill acquisition and real-world adaptation (ibid.: 404). One can see how such a model could be applied to the entrepreneurial situation.

Cognition research in business and entrepreneurship

Cognitive heuristics

The role of free will and choice is assumed in the analysis of social psycho-logical approaches to personality. Behaviour may be predicted and in some instances predictable, but it is not wholly determined; people choose situ-ations in which they engage and they can influence and shape them through the process of interaction. Cognitive research has gone beyond the percep-tion of situations and other people to identifying the concepts and thoughts that are used to frame situations, the rules of thumb and short cuts that people learn in order to speed up decision-making. They include cognitive heuristics, cognitive schemata and biases that affect judgement and decision-making, and the use of metaphor and analogy to help conceive the essence of situations. Such cognitive constructs arise out of focusing attention on particular aspects of situations, problems, and so forth. Cognitive foci are a necessary result of division of labour, which facilitates knowledge and skills development. Choice of where to focus one's attention may result in opportunity costs.

Schwenk (1988) highlighted the importance of cognitive heuristics and biases in strategic decision-making. Personal cognitive maps consist of concepts about aspects of the decision environment and beliefs about cause-and-effect relationships between them. Such maps serve to enable the person to interpret a situation and select certain aspects to facilitate diagnosis, classification and decision-making. This approach may be used to represent an individual's world view, the shared assumptions with others (say, in a group or team) and to shed light on causal assertions made in respect of a particular problem domain. The approach also raises questions about how the set of beliefs arose, how differences in belief sets are resolved by a team and how, in the business context, entrepreneurs and managers conceive of their industry and environment. The added notion of multiple goals and causal chains to a particular outcome also underscores the potentially con-tested nature of cognitive space and the ability to influence and shape the understanding of situations. Hence, it has also been suggested that, beyond cognitions, people develop schemata, which have been defined as 'cognitive representations of attributes and the relationships between them which constitute common sense social theories' (ibid.: 46). Schemata again are short-hand ways of categorising and understanding particular situations or problems; applying the schema helps to frame the situation or problem. Analogies are part of a shared vocabulary that enables people to discuss situations and utilise shared images. Once again, they help to define and shape the environment. Reasoning by analogy has been shown to help with creative thinking, although adopting simple analogies may underrepresent the complexities in a situation and result in poor analysis and understanding.

Shaver and Scott (1991) apply the concept of cognitive heuristics to the entrepreneur by considering how cognitive heuristics might guide judgement under conditions of uncertainty. In setting up in business, there are many prior events that have to be managed and that suggest multiple situations and outcomes. When acting intentionally and tackling relevant various tasks, the successful accomplishment of any one task depends on the per-son's ability and effort and task difficulty, tempered by an element of luck. Of these factors, the greatest variability occurs in effort expended and luck experienced. The potential causes of failure could be lack of ability, insufficient effort, insurmountable difficulty of the task and sheer bad luck. However, a person forms a view as to what might have gone wrong and then makes causal attributions. For example, to attribute the cause of failure to bad luck suggests an external cause and that the problem was not of one's making, whereas to suggest low motivation and lack of effort suggests an 'internal cause' and thus one has only oneself to blame. New ventures are founded because of the deliberate choices made by individuals; hence it is important to understand two further cognitions: perceived control and expectancy. Perceived control is situation-specific (unlike locus of control, which is a generalised expectancy). This concerns how the entrepreneur *thinks about* their reality. Thus, an entrepreneur believes that they can 'make a difference' and that they are largely in control. Hence, for 'perceived control' to work, the entrepreneur must believe that he/she has a choice to make, has achieved some initial success that can be attributed to his/her own efforts and that this permits intrinsic interest in the project to be maintained. Being able to make a difference is not the same as wanting to do so. To switch from employment to self-employment, for example, a person must believe that they can carry out the various tasks successfully. Furthermore, in evaluating the options available to them, they must be confident that they would secure more attractive personal rewards from selecting the self-employment option compared to employment. Making choices assumes preferences that have associated with them a subjective probability, that is, an estimate that a particular (desired) outcome will ensue. This will depend on the individual's preference for security versus potential and also their aspiration, which is defined by the situation; their final choice will depend on an interaction between the two.

Intentionality and the realisation of entrepreneurial potential

Krueger and Brazeal (1994) attempt to identify entrepreneurial potential by arguing that, to be able to exploit an opportunity there needs to be pre-existing preparedness. They build on the theory of planned behaviour Ajzen (1991), the theory of displacement and the entrepreneurial event (Shapero, 1975) and the construct of self-efficacy (Bandura, 1986). The nub of the argument is that there is a gap between entrepreneurial potential and the intention to act entrepreneurially (see Figure 6.2). Thus, in the process of nascent entrepreneurship, there are two drivers of entrepreneurial behaviour: *perceived desirability* of setting up a particular business based on the entrepreneur's perceptions of what important people in their lives, the industry and the community want or would think about the proposed launch; *perceived feasibility*, that is, perceived *self-efficacy* or personal capability to found a venture. Self-efficacy is closely linked to one's personal assessment of one's competences and capability to carry through the tasks necessary to achieve the goal: venture launch. The combination of perceived desirability (social norms and support) and perceived self-efficacy (perceived personal capability), where the perceptions are veridical, give a sense of mastery and credibility. *Credibility* is necessary for the next step in the model – *propensity to act*. Propensity to act carries with it a sense of personal control and autonomy closely allied to initiative-taking. This produces the springboard of *entrepreneurial potential* – the self-awareness that they could take the plunge. However, what is then required is the trigger that displaces what would otherwise be inertia – the drag anchor of indecision where conditions

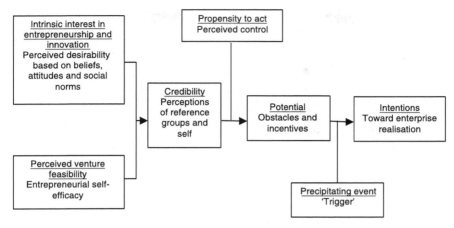

Figure 6.2 Factors triggering entrepreneurial potential (based on Krueger and Brazeal, 1994).

do not feel quite right. This displacement event could be positive or negative and is known as the *precipitating event*. This is often a sudden change in personal circumstances that produces the change in behaviour and influences the *intention* towards entrepreneurship. Krueger and Brazeal claim that their model fits both external entrepreneurial situations and also internal corporate venturing contexts. They point to the importance of understanding personal perceptions of context, the importance of volition and the processes underlying entrepreneurial activity. This model gives an opportunity for assessing entrepreneurial potential in two contexts: organisational and the general population. However, what appears to be the critical factor that can be developed or strengthened is *perceived feasibility*. Training, education and experiential learning can all help to strengthen a potential entrepreneur's self-belief in their ability to create and found a new business.

Intentionality and perceived entrepreneurial self-efficacy

Boyd and Vozikis (1994) also build on Bird's work on intentionality, by suggesting that self-efficacy influences an individual's entrepreneurial intentions. The model includes personal (personal history, personality and abilities) and contextual factors (socio-political and economic) that form the belief system. Such beliefs shape an individual's attitude towards a particular behaviour (such as whether it is feasible to pursue a business-founding opportunity). There are also two cognitive dimensions that comprise rational analytic thinking (leading to goal-directed behaviour) and intuitive holistic thinking (leading to the envisioning of possible future scenarios). Moreover, from this cognitive apparatus arise attitudes, perceptions and self-efficacy – whether the individual believes that they have mastered what is necessary to pursue a particular goal (in this case business founding). If all these elements are positive, then they will influence the intention toward business venturing and the likelihood of it occurring in practice, whereas any negative thoughts are likely to have the opposite effect. Bird suggests that it is possible to use her model to distinguish between entrepreneurs and potential entrepreneurs (those people with an intention that is not realised). Clearly beliefs shaped on career, work, risk, rewards and family matters would influence attitudes and also feelings of self-efficacy (e.g. lack of family support, conflicted goals and uncertainty around issues of risk and reward). Thus, Boyd and Vozikis conclude that a sense of self-efficacy is fundamentally important if an individual is to move from a position of entrepreneurial intention to action.

Chen *et al.* (1998) build on the work of Boyd and Vozikis (1994) by testing the model in the field. Entrepreneurial self-efficacy (ESE) has to be assessed at the specific task domain level to maintain its predictive power. They chose to measure ESE by referring to specific tasks involved in running one's own business. They developed a set of task requirements to derive a measure of the broader domain – business start-up. They retain intention and argue that ESE is a prerequisite of the potential entrepreneur. The kernel of their argument is that high-ESE people associate engagement in business venturing with rewarding experiences, whereas low-ESE people are likely to relate it to negative images such as failure, bankruptcy, stress, etc. Hence it is the former who are more likely to become entrepreneurs (Chen *et al.*, 1998: 301).

They measured three aspects of the entrepreneurial task-role domain: (a) *entrepreneurial capabilities*: uncertainty and risk, complementary managerial competence and creative opportunism; (b) *entrepreneurial roles*: self-achievement, avoiding risks, feedback of results, personal innovation and planning for the future; and (c) *tasks associated with stages of growth*: organisational systems, sales and marketing, people, production, strategic positioning and external relations. From this framework, they designed an assessment instrument comprising 26 items. They used it in assessment of two groups: 140 students from entrepreneurship, organisation behaviour and psychology classes and 175 small business owners and executives.

The results revealed that amongst the student group, those studying entrepreneurship scored significantly higher in ESE than both organisation behaviour and psychology students. This was attributed to their perceived self-efficacy in marketing, management and financial control (as they had not studied innovation of risk management). The entrepreneurs showed a significant difference between founders and non-founders, with innovation and risk-taking contributing to differences in self-efficacy. Founders had stronger ESE on innovation and risk-taking. The relationship between ESE and locus of control (LOC) showed that ESE scores were generally positively related to internal control but negatively to chance control. Further, they found that ESE distinguished better between entrepreneurs and managers than did LOC. In sum: (a) both students and executives indicated a significant and positive effect of ESE on the likelihood of being an entrepreneur; (b) ESE was found to be related positively to internal LOC and negatively to chance LOC; (c) the relative potency of specific task domains was demonstrated insofar as ESE of innovation and risk-taking differentiated entrepreneurs from managers; and (d) what differentiated entrepreneurship students from their management and psychology peers was not self-efficacy of innovation and risk-taking, but self-efficacy of various managerial functions. It was felt that this reflected course content and also the fact that the measurement occurred before students had an opportunity to develop competences in innovation and risk-taking, which they believed are more likely to be developed through real-world experience.

Entrepreneurial self-efficacy and regretful thinking

Markman *et al.* (2002) tested whether general self-efficacy and regretful thinking distinguish entrepreneurs from non-entrepreneurs. This study challenges the earlier work of Baron (2000) – that entrepreneurs have very few regrets – and pursues further the idea that self-efficacy is crucially important to those individuals pursuing entrepreneurial decisions and activities. Markman *et al.* (2002) identified a population of patent inventors (of surgical devices and related instruments). Within this category of inventors were people who used the patent to set up or continue to build their own business (*technological entrepreneurs*) and those who did not (*technological non-entrepreneurs*). A self-efficacy scale and a measure of regretful thinking were used to survey the sample of inventors. Regretful thinking measured the number of regrets, types of regrets and depth of feeling. They found that *technological entrepreneurs* tended to have higher self-efficacy, more intense regrets and different types of regrets (e.g. they experienced regrets over business opportunities that did not work out as expected, whereas *non-entrepreneurs* experienced regrets over career and education decisions). They found no difference between entrepreneurs and non-entrepreneurs in respect of the number of regretful decisions experienced. They also found that inventors with high self-efficacy earned significantly higher income. Unlike the Baron (2000) study, the sample was carefully and randomly drawn and of actual practitioners/inventors, whereas Baron's study was of student participants and included additional measures of types of regretful decision.

Markman *et al.* (2005) also consider the role of perseverance, self-efficacy and regretful thinking. Technological entrepreneurs demonstrate higher endurance and tenacity than non-entrepreneurs, because of the challenges they might be expected to deal with when setting up a new venture. This increased effort, if unrewarded, results in increased regrets and disappointments. Furthermore, technological entrepreneurs are likely to perceive a stronger sense of responsibility over outcomes, because of ownership of both the business and the invention, and a sense of responsibility for failure. As such, if things go wrong they are likely to experience high levels of regret. This is because of the high emotional energy required to persevere in the face of adversity, and also due to higher levels of commitment and personal costs. Furthermore, due to the need for considerable self-belief, if the venture did not thrive there is potentially both loss of face and disappointment.

Decision-making and the use of heuristics

The cognitive approach to studying entrepreneurial behaviour focuses on decision-making. Entrepreneurs often have little time to make decisions and must use heuristics (rules of thumb) to help them in their decision-making; this can lead to bias, overconfidence and errors of judgement (Busenitz and Barney, 1997; Baron, 1998, 2000). In contrast to executives, entrepreneurs often have to make decisions in situations where there is a paucity of information, such as the lack of historical trends, no previous performance data and little market information. Entrepreneurs are often opportunists: they are likely to act on an idea supported by limited information. Busenitz and Barney argue that such entrepreneurs tend to display overconfidence, that is, they proceed with an idea before all the steps and requisite information are known. Such overconfidence may help to convince other stakeholders of the value of the opportunity. Furthermore, they tend to generalise from small non-random samples of information (in contrast to executive decision-making, where access to large systematically collected data sets is more likely). The non-random sample of information often comes down to personal experience. Busenitz and Barney measured 'overconfidence' and 'representativeness' of a sample of managers and of entrepreneurs and demonstrated a significant difference between the two in the predicted direction. This not only suggests that entrepreneurs and managers think differently, but that entrepreneurs are prepared to *accept* higher levels of risk. It also suggests that entrepreneurs may not have a greater risk propensity than managers but, as risk acceptors, they try to understand how risk inherent in entrepreneurial opportunity might be managed.

Baron (1998, 2000) takes this line of argument further when he suggests that entrepreneurs are more likely to be exposed to situations that create conditions of cognitive bias and error (e.g. conditions of information overload, experiencing new situations and situations where emotions are running high). Under these circumstances, entrepreneurs are more susceptible to: cognitive errors, such as *counterfactual thinking* (imagining what might have been) and regret over missed opportunities; *affect diffusion*, where mood affects how a situation is perceived and judged; and *self-serving bias*, where they attribute success to personal capability and failure to external factors or persons. Whilst this bolstering of self-esteem can have some benefits, generally self-serving bias can lead to interpersonal friction and may be one factor that distinguishes between successful and unsuccessful entrepreneurs. Entrepreneurs also have *'cognitive blind spots'*, that is, their forecasts for the future are not anchored in the past, but on plans and glowing images of the future. This can result in overly bold forecasts that may cause serious trouble for the entrepreneur. Moreover, they are susceptible to the so-called *'planning fallacy'*, which is the belief that they can accomplish a project more quickly than is feasible. Where projects have staged investment, decision-makers (and entrepreneurs) may believe that they have put so much into the project they cannot quit now. This phenomenon of escalation in decision-making[5] (Staw and Ross, 1987; Drummond, 1996) results in increased commitment to a project when rational judgement would suggest pulling out. This phenomenon occurs because of: (a) feelings of responsibility for the decision and the difficulty of reversing it or backing away from it; (b) effort and intensity of initial commitment to the idea; (c) loss of face; (d) strong desire to justify one's initial decision; (e) the notion of sunk costs; and (f) group-think and group or stakeholder pressure. Baron concentrates on some of the practical implications of this work, whereby training and development of the entrepreneurs' awareness of such cognitive biases could aid them in decision-making and increase their chances of success. Table 6.3 summarises some of the potential biases of entrepreneurs.

Table 6.3 Potential heuristics and biases of entrepreneurs

Bias		Cognitive outcome
1	Information recall	Judgement based on ease of recall
2	Selective perception	Expectations become a source of bias
3	Illusory association	Belief that an association exists between unrelated factors
4	Conservatism	Failure to revise forecasts based on new information
5	Generalisability	Overestimate the extent to which small samples are representative
6	Wishful thinking	The likelihood of desired outcomes judged too high
7	Illusion of control	Overestimation of personal control over outcomes
8	Hindsight	Overestimation of likelihood of past events
9	Causal attributions	Misattribution of causes of failure/success
10	Overconfidence	Misplaced confidence in an outcome and/or one's ability to effect it
11	Information underload	Decision-making in the context of too little information
12	Information overload	May create conditions of stress resulting in errors and emotional decision-making
13	Regret	Imagining what might have been
14	Planning fallacy	The belief that a plan can be executed more quickly than is feasible
15	Escalation of commitment	Inability to pull out of a project

Simon and Houghton (2002) suggest that business decision-making contexts are sufficiently heterogeneous to influence how information is processed. They contrast two such contexts: entrepreneurs in younger companies versus entrepreneurs considering introducing new products. This analysis reveals that there are different pathways to the decision to pioneer that reflect different cognitive biases associated with the decision context. Entrepreneurs in these different contexts are both subject to different cognitive biases; such contexts suggest that in pre-established versus established firms there is a need to develop appropriate strategies, drawing on technical knowledge and market awareness, in order to take the decision to pioneer.

Opportunity emergence and evaluation

Keh *et al.* (2002) identified cognitive factors that influence opportunity evaluation. Opportunity evaluation is influenced by perception of risk; perceiving a lower level of risk is associated with more positive opportunity evaluation. The factors that cause entrepreneurs to perceive reduced risk are: (a) *overconfidence* (e.g. treating their assumptions as facts); (b) *belief in the law of small numbers* (e.g. by relying on small non-random samples of information); (c) *the planning fallacy* (i.e. where the current decision is treated as unique and divorced from past experience); and (d) *illusion of control*, where entrepreneurs have a strong preference for exerting control and consequently perceive less risk. In evaluating opportunities it would appear that entrepreneurs believe that they are able to control or hedge risks and thus influence future outcomes. Further, belief in the law of small numbers may not affect risk perception, because when opportunistic entrepreneurs evaluate business opportunities, potential benefits of the venture may be more salient than risks, since they are looking for reasons to accept ventures that help grow their companies. The results regarding overconfidence were not clearcut and require further investigation. Also, they found no evidence to suggest that the 'planning fallacy' affects opportunity evaluation. Further research should include an analysis of the 'benefits of the venture' and not only risk perception. Clearly, even though a formal cost–benefit analysis is not being suggested, people tend to weigh up the costs (i.e. risks) against the benefits and see them as being inversely related to each other. Modelling these processes can become quite complicated; Keh *et al.* also suggest that a future model might include some contextual factors and non-cognitive variables. However, this study was conducted on a relatively small sample – it is thus worth bearing in mind that the more complex the model, the larger the sample required.

Krueger (2000) and Shepherd and Krueger (2002) have pursued the idea of intentions-based cognitive models of opportunity emergence and the entrepreneurial process within organisations. They build on the work discussed above (Krueger and Brazeal, 1994): the need for potential entrepreneurs if entrepreneurial potential (i.e. opportunities) is to be realised.

Situations are categorised as opportunities or threats and as being controllable or not; the perception of these situations depends on people's mental models to interpret environmental cues, as signifying a threat or an opportunity. Furthermore, opportunity perceptions reflect an intentional process, self-belief (self-efficacy), a pre-existing belief that an activity is desirable and feasible and that there is a precipitating factor that overcomes situational inertia. To translate this into an organisational context (Krueger, 2000), the concept of collective efficacy is also required. Further, tangible and also subtle cognitive barriers should be considered. Shepherd and Krueger build on this work by focusing on the social cognition of entrepreneurial teams within organisational settings. They posit that the stronger the team's self-belief and perceived abilities, the greater will be its intention to engage in entrepreneurship. Also, this collective efficacy would influence the perceived feasibility of the entrepreneurial activity. In turn, collective efficacy is influenced by prior entrepreneurial experience. Lastly, the greater the perceived desirability of entrepreneurial intentions, the stronger the reinforcement of the team's entrepreneurial intention.

Cognitive scripts and cultural factors

Mitchell *et al.* (2000) approach the cognitive view of the venture creation decision somewhat differently. Their work attempts to develop a cross-cultural approach to venture creation and suggests that cultural factors affect three key aspects of social cognitions: knowledge or expert scripts associated with *arrangements* (i.e. the feasibility of a venture), *willingness* cognitions (i.e. the propensity to act) and *ability* cognitions, associated with venture desirability:

- *Arrangement scripts* include having the contacts, relationships, resources and assets necessary to start a venture and are the knowledge structures that individuals draw on concerning specific arrangements that support their own capability in a given domain. In the case of venture creation, four discrete areas of knowledge were identified: idea protection, having a venture network, having access to business resources and having venture-specific skills.
- *Willingness scripts* comprise commitment and receptivity to the idea of starting a venture and actionable thoughts regarding opportunity-seeking, commitment tolerance ('putting your money where your mouth is') and venture opportunity pursuit (i.e. getting on with the task).
- *Ability scripts* include knowledge, skills, attitudes, norms and capabilities needed to start a venture.

The authors hypothesised that all three of these knowledge scripts would be required in order to take a venture creation decision. They also consider interaction effects between combinations of pairs of knowledge scripts in order to understand the nature of the thought processes that shape this kind of decision-making.

Cultural values that influence the venture decision were posited to be individualism and power distance (Hofstede, 1980). A survey was carried out in seven countries (USA, Canada, Australia, Mexico, Chile, Japan and China) and 753 completed questionnaires were received. The results show two main effects: both venture arrangements and ability scripts were significantly related to the venture creation decision, and a significant interaction effect was found between arrangements and willingness scripts (i.e. arrangements are necessary, but are not sufficient without willingness). The analysis of cultural values on cognitive scripts showed surprising results: arrangement scripts did not differ significantly among the individualist or power distance countries. Willingness and ability showed significant differences among the country groupings. Individualism was found to moderate significantly the relationship between arrangement scripts and the venture creation decision. These results demonstrate both the importance of cognitive scripts and the fact that cultural differences explain some of the variance in venture creation decisions. As an exploratory study this showed promise in that it suggests ways of explaining differences between entrepreneurs and non-entrepreneurs and it explains (potentially) similarities and differences in venture decision-making among entrepreneurs across cultures. This, the authors suggest, offers the potential for a cross-cultural cognitive theory of entrepreneurship.

Why do some people recognise opportunities while others do not?

A further line of enquiry has been to pursue the questions: 'why do some people but not others recognise opportunities?' and 'how might our understanding of this process be increased by examining it from a cognitive perspective?' If it is true that entrepreneurs recognise opportunities without search, then is opportunity recognition a type of pattern recognition and, if so, what might be the features that the entrepreneur attends to? Baron (2004) suggests that people construct prototypes; the 'lay' prototype of 'opportunity' might have the features of newness, novelty and practicality for attraction of financial resources or for marketing purposes. Furthermore, in what sense does the opportunity exist? Baron suggests four possibilities: (a) it exists and the entrepreneur has picked up the signal – a 'hit'; (b) it exists, but the perceiver has failed to pick up the signal – a 'miss'; (c) it does not exist, but the perceiver wrongly believes that it does – a 'false alarm'; and (d) it does not exist and the entrepreneur correctly concludes that it does not – another kind of 'hit'. When combined with promotion, where accomplishment is emphasised, the person concentrates on hits, whereas when concentrating on prevention, the person concentrates on avoiding negative outcomes so that they make correct rejections and avoid false alarms.

Related to this issue, Gaglio and Katz (2001; see also Chapter 5) argue that entrepreneurs, especially successful entrepreneurs, possess a mental framework termed '*entrepreneurial alertness*' and, as such, should be able to notice change and market disequilibria. Gaglio (2004: 534) asserts that entrepreneurs do indeed think differently with regard to opportunities. They are more alert to changing circumstances, which prompt them to question the existing way of doing things ('means–end framework'). This begs two questions: how does the entrepreneur glean such insight that the extant means–end framework is no longer appropriate and how does s/he develop a new way of doing things? The answers, according to Kirzner (1979), are by veridical perception and veridical interpretation. In other words, the entre-preneur must perceive the changing situation accurately and also interpret it correctly. This means that the entrepreneur's judgement should be correct (Baron, 2004; cf. Casson, 1982). This may differentiate between the success-ful and the unsuccessful entrepreneur, or indeed growth-oriented entre-preneur and lifestyle business owner-manager (Chell and Baines, 2000). But, returning to Gaglio (2004), how do entrepreneurs do this, what are the steps in the process and what are the necessary and sufficient skills set?

Gaglio and Katz (2001) argue that working out how to achieve particular ends by entrepreneurs is heuristically driven (i.e. through experience and trial and error). However, being first to sense change requires perception and interpretation of an event as unexpected, followed quickly by the need to make sense of it and provide a solution to it. Further, entrepreneurs engage in mental simulations of the event – constructing and reconstructing it in their minds in order to work out what may or may not happen (Gaglio, 2004). This constitutes both mental rehearsal and imagined scenarios; it may include changing causal sequences, as a way of considering the more effective way that things could be. This latter process is called *counter-factual thinking*; it is, of course, not particular to entrepreneurs. Counter-factual thinking serves two specific functions: it allows a consideration of emotions – affective function – and also, through anticipation, a preparative function. What is required is that the entrepreneur can identify correctly the prior causal sequence, and the appropriate causal sequence that will produce the new, desired outcome. The supposition is that alert entre-preneurs will identify different signals earlier and respond quickly through the process of counter-factual thinking, whilst other business people would eventually pick up the signals and respond, but not until a pattern had already emerged.

More speculatively, do entrepreneurs engage in counter-factual thinking automatically – a spontaneous reaction – or elaborately (i.e. intentionally, deliberately and consciously)? The supposition is that counter-factual think-ing is intentional and, as such, more likely to lead to effective opportunity recognition. But, how is the thinking process structured? Do entrepreneurs, in constructing the mental simulations, work backwards or forwards? To work backwards is to presume a desired outcome and then imagine the sequence of events required to lead to it. On the other hand, by working forwards one assumes a particular start point and then constructs the causal sequence and its outcome. Given that the entrepreneur is presumed to have spotted the changed event, it makes sense to presume that the change is the start point and they work forwards to a particular outcome. However, existing knowledge of counter-factual thinking suggests that to be effective one must construct numerous counter-factuals and test them (Gaglio, 2004). Hence, it is proposed that alert entrepreneurs, in the process of opportunity-seeking, will test out various linkages in the casual sequence leading to the unexpected event and also generate many counter-factual possibilities and their consequences. Entrepreneurs who develop innovative ideas are more likely to show a preference for counter-factuals, using mental addition: this is more likely to produce a creative or novel response, because it goes beyond the facts of the original scenario. Further, whilst most people would go for 'downhill scenarios', 'opportunity finders' construct 'uphill' counter-factuals (i.e. introduce unlikely or surprising events); they imagine scenarios that challenge existing assumptions. A revolution at the time and an excellent example of counter-factual thinking is the automatic bank teller – the 'hole in the wall'.

A further step in the counter-factual thinking chain is that of evaluation of likelihood and plausibility. This involves the ease or difficulty of imagining and the depth to which one is willing to go in terms of identifying intermediate steps. This leads to the possibility of low likelihood alternatives, which the opportunity finders are less likely to reject. In other words, non-finders quickly reject counter-factuals as implausible, infeasible or difficult, whilst opportunity finders retain their counter-factuals and use additional counter-factual thinking to undo or redo the problematic parts. Evaluation and feasibility also depend on what the counter-factual is being compared to – the standard or anchor being used. When thinking about the future, the past and present are usually powerful anchors. Anchors can bias our assessments about the impact or timing of change – either underestimate or overestimate. Although, as Gaglio (2004) points out, Kirzner argues that these are precisely the kinds of mistakes that alert entrepreneurs do not make, due to their veridical interpretation capability.

Clearly Gaglio's focus is to attempt to unpack the 'black box' of cognitive thinking. Carolis and Saparito (2006) take this thinking a stage further, by developing a model that posits social capital as the contextual underpinning for cognitive biases in risk perception and the exploitation of opportunities. Social capital comprises four elements:

1   'Bonding' and 'bridging'. Bonding is where social capital is concentrated within the group, allowing the development of trust and agreed norms of behaviour that enable the group to more easily attain its goals. Bridging focuses on the individual's external social ties; social capital is used as a resource to explain how the entrepreneur uses his/her contacts to bring about personal gain.

2 Social capital benefits the entrepreneur through access to information and sources of influence. Entrepreneurs may, where they are on the edges of several networks, have the power to exploit different sources of information, by being able to put together apparently disconnected information in a way that an individual within his/her 'silo' cannot do (cf. Granovetter, 1973).

3 A further dimension of social capital is relational and concerns the development of trust. Trust facilitates the network connections because it suggests beneficial relations and continual reciprocity of arrangements. This suggests that the network ties and relations are strong.

4 There is a cognitive dimension to social capital, which concerns the shared understandings that develop between the different parties. This, ironically, limits the range of possibilities whilst providing a stronger basis for the preferred, probable way forward.

Human capital and opportunity recognition

Arenius and Minniti (2005) offer some empirical results from their survey of nascent entrepreneurs in which they measure economic, demographic and perceptual variables. These include human capital factors such as age, gender (technically sex), education, work status and financial resources (household income and/or family wealth). The perceptual variables included are opportunity perception, confidence in one's skills and ability, fear of failure and knowing other entrepreneurs. Further, due to the known effect of economic conditions, culture and institutional factors, they also posit a country effect. The sample size for this study was 51,721 individuals. Their analysis suggests that the make-up of nascent entrepreneurs comprises:

- Being a nascent entrepreneur decreases with age.
- Males are more likely than females to be nascent entrepreneurs.
- The employed are more likely than the unemployed, student or retiree to qualify as a nascent entrepreneur.
- Opportunity perception, confidence in one's skills and knowing other entrepreneurs are positively related to being a nascent entrepreneur.
- Fear of failure is negatively correlated with being a nascent entrepreneur.

A further analysis tested the probability of being a nascent entrepreneur. Five different models were analysed, with at best 25% of the variance being explained. *Model 1* included the human capital and economic factors only, and shows that 'entrepreneurship is a young man's game', that education is positively related to the likelihood of starting a new business, as is household income. *Model 2* included, additionally, the four perceptual variables. It was found to be better than Model 1 at explaining the probability of an individual being a nascent entrepreneur (explaining 21% compared to 4% of the variance). Age, gender and work status continue to be important and

education and household income less important, but the perceptual variables are all shown to be highly significant. Indeed, they go further and
state that the perceptual variables overall are powerful predictors of the
likelihood of being an entrepreneur. In *Model 3*, only the perceptual variables are included; all four are highly significant and explain almost 20% of
the variance. *Model 4* includes all the factors and tests the assumption that
gender changes the relationship between the dependent and independent
variables. It shows that the likelihood of being an entrepreneur and age,
household income and all the perceptual variables *do not depend on gender*.
In other words, both men and women who 'know other entrepreneurs,
who perceive the existence of good opportunities, and who feel that they
have the ability, skills and knowledge required for starting a new business,
are more likely to do so than their counterparts with different perceptions'
(ibid.: 242). Finally, *Model 5* tests for the possibility of country effects.
They found that the effects of age and gender were significant and negative.
Working and non-working respondents were just as likely to engage in
nascent entrepreneurship. All perceptual variables remain highly significant.
The effect for 21 out of the 28 countries was significant. Despite the significance of country effects, this does not reduce the cross-country importance of the perceptual variables. However, it does suggest that in the
21 countries identified there are strong local effects at work, reflecting the
theory that the macro-economic environments in some countries are more
conducive to entrepreneurship than in others. Finally, the authors acknowledge one shortcoming in the study, which is that the measure of perceptual
variables is subjective and may contain a biased response. Clearly, there is
scope for refining the measuring instruments and carrying out further empirical work to test our theories of nascent entrepreneurship processes and
practice.

Social and cognitive aspects of creativity

Creativity, as a process, comprises a complex set of skills, person and
environmental factors. It is an area of research that has suffered due to the
proclivity of academics to work within single disciplinary domains. Thus, in
business and economics, researchers have identified creativity to be innovation at firm level. This is somewhat ironic as the very acts of creative people require them to integrate knowledge and ideas from diverse sources
(Sternberg, 2003). Whilst there are a number of approaches that have been
taken, the social psychological/social personality and the psycho-economic
appear to have been the more fruitful and certainly the more relevant for
understanding the creativity of entrepreneurs.

Amabile (1983, 1990) has revealed a number of insights into the creative
process: socio-environmental influences, importance of personality, ability
and experience and the role of intrinsic motivation. When a person engages
in the process of creativity they draw on domain-relevant, creativity-relevant

skills and task motivation. Each of these is moderated by contextual factors. Table 6.4 shows these factors.

Domain-relevant skills include knowledge, technical proficiency and special talents. This cognitive component thus comprises scripts, algorithms or rules that the person may draw on as they set about the problem or task. It is not possible to have too much relevant knowledge, but it is possible to have algorithms that are applied inflexibly. Creative-relevant skills include a cognitive style that favours taking a new perspective on the problem, the application of heuristics in order to explore new cognitive pathways and a working style characterised as energetic and persistent (Amabile, 1990: 78). Associated personality characteristics are said to include independence, self-discipline, risk-taking, tolerance for ambiguity, perseverance and lack of concern for social approval. Intrinsic motivation is viewed as fundamental; indeed, Amabile goes so far as to suggest that this can make up for a deficiency in some of the domain-relevant skills. People who are intrinsically motivated are motivated by personal curiosity and inherent interest rather than by extrinsic factors such as pay, instructions, and so forth. The effects of this are that they are more likely to consider a wider range of ideas, make more unusual association of ideas, experience more positive emotions, depart more frequently from the more familiar algorithms and produce more creative solutions.

Sternberg (2003) points to a link between creativity and intelligence: creative people tend to show an above average IQ of about 120; in general, creative people tend to have high IQs, whereas people with high IQs are not necessarily highly creative. Cognitive approaches attempt to identify the cognitive processes that are applied to relevant knowledge domains. They suggest that, for example, skills other than the specific insight from divergent

Table 6.4 Components of creative performance (based on Amabile, 1983)

Cognitive: domain-relevant knowledge and skills	Ability: creativity-relevant skills	Motivation: task motiviation
• Domain-relevant knowledge • Technical knowledge and skills • Special domain relevant to 'talent'	• Appropriate cognitive style • Implicit and explicit knowledge of heuristics for generating ideas • Conducive work style	• Attitude towards the task • Perceptions of own motivation and understanding of the task
Depends on[a] • Formal and informal education • Experience	Depends on • Training • Experience in idea generation • Personality	Depends on • Initial levels of intrinsic motivation • Presence/absence of constraints • Ability to cognitively minimise constraints

[a] Assumes cognitive, perceptual and motor apparatus; and memory.

thought processes are often required. For example, to solve the nine-dot problem (Figure 6.3) requires that people think 'outside the box', but this insight alone is not sufficient; spatial thinking skill also appears to be necessary. (For the solution to this problem, see Figure 6.4 in the Appendix at the end of this chapter.)

Personality researchers have identified some key factors that include independence of judgement, self-confidence, attraction to complexity, aesthetic orientation and risk-taking. Such factors resonate with certain aspects of entrepreneurial behaviour. Further, boldness, courage, freedom, spontaneity and self-acceptance are some of the traits identified by Maslow (1968) that enable a person to realise their full potential. Work, however, that combines the cognitive-social personality and context are few; the work of Amabile is a prominent example. Csikszentmihalyi (1996), on the other hand, takes a systems approach to creativity, pointing out that the creative process comprises a domain, a person and a field. Within the field, judges apply rules that inform their judgement of what constitutes creativity within the particular domain. Finally, Sternberg and Lubart (1991) put forward a psycho-economic model of creativity. This theory they term 'investment theory', and it concerns the decision(s) to be creative.

Investment theory comprises six interrelated resources: intellect, knowledge, thinking style, personality, motivation and environment. These resources are summarised in Table 6.5. The deployment of each resource involves a decision, for example to use one's skills to generate ideas, evaluate and sell them. Whilst one's knowledge base is important, because without it one cannot think beyond it and add something novel, one needs to decide not to let it become a hindrance. The novel is by definition something that one would not commonly expect. Even where personality attributes are concerned, one must decide whether one is willing to take a risk, overcome obstacles and tolerate uncertainty. Some people do not take the necessary step because they allow others to block their creative output. Thus, to overcome such opposition, the idea is presented knowing that it is not valued and

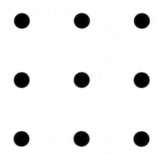

Figure 6.3 Thinking outside the box.

Instruction: connect the nine dots by drawing just four straight lines, and without lifting pen from the paper.

Table 6.5 Components of investment theory (based on Sternberg and Lubart, 1991, 1995)

Component	Manifestation
Intellectual skills	• Creative skill to see problems in new and unconventional ways • Analytical skill to recognise which ideas are worth pursuing • Practical (contextual) skill to be able to persuade others of the value of one's ideas
Knowledge	• Need to know enough to be able to move the field forward • Need to decide to use one's past knowledge, but not let it become a hindrance
Thinking style	• A 'legislative style' involves both a preference for thinking in new ways but also to think well • Thinking well involves being able to see the bigger picture as well as the fine details, to recognise which are the important questions and to think 'globally' as well as 'locally'
Personality	• Willingness to overcome obstacles • Willingness to take sensible risks • Willingness to tolerate ambiguity • Self-efficacy
Motivation	• Intrinsic motivation is crucial; creative work is driven by enjoyment and the love of doing what one is doing
Environment	• Should be supportive and rewarding of creative ideas; need to decide how to respond to environmental changes

then the creative individual must convince others of its value. Creativity is thus a confluence of several person-elements: the cognitive (decision and knowledge), the affective (attitudes, values and motivation) and behavioural (expression of skills and ability). Importantly, however, creativity can be nurtured and taught (Sternberg, 2003).

Summary and conclusion

This chapter does not attempt a comprehensive overview of studies of inter-actionism and cognition in respect of models of the process of nascent entre-preneurship and innovation. However, it does identify some of the key developments and issues. First, let me attempt to summarise the state of the art in respect of interactionism and cognitive approaches to personality, the entrepreneurial personality in particular.

I commenced this chapter by revisiting personality theory from the per-spective of 'interactionism', that is, the view that behaviour cannot be explained by recourse to an examination of personality traits alone, but the situation and the interaction between personality and context should also be taken into account. An alternative to traits was that of 'cognitive social learning person-variables' (Mischel, 1973). This was applied in the entrepreneurial context and a model of the process of entrepreneurship was developed (Chell, 1985a). Apart from the reconceptualisation of the person-variables, this model identified the importance of learning and cognition. It elaborated on a typical socio-economic context for the nascent or growth-oriented entrepreneur in which the entrepreneur enacts a role that is both practical and expressive; the aim is to manage the entrepreneurial situation competently and create good impressions. It underscores the importance of social competence and is consistent with later studies (e.g. Baron, 2000); it envisions possible future steps (Shackle, 1979; Chell *et al.*, 1991; Filion, 1991) and entrepreneurial alertness, where the entrepreneur starts with the changed event and envisions the future steps toward opportunity realisation (Kirzner, 1973; Gaglio, 2004). The model also highlights those skills that are relevant to successful entrepreneurial performance.

The theory has been developed further to include the combined cognitive and affective (thinking and feeling) aspects of behaviour; the CAPS process yields characteristic patterns of response to the *psychological* aspects of particular types of situation – a person's characteristic way of behaving, their *behavioural signature* (Mischel and Shoda, 1995). CAPS explains cross-situational variability in behaviour; the dynamic *cognitive-affective system* that is particular to a person is stable, but the way that this system works is on a contingency basis – the reading of situational cues suggests a particular behavioural response typical of that individual. Further, not only do people have thoughts about situations but also about feelings; hence, to every situational cue is a cognitive-affective response. People respond to categories of situation, drawing on their past experience to interpret the situational cues, but also being affected by mood and biological disposition. This theory is consistent with developments in the cognitive theory of the entrepreneurial personality.

Some of the initial cognitive theorising was largely divorced from feelings. The focus was on judgement, intentions and causal attributions when something goes wrong or is a success. Also introduced is the notion of choice and free will: a person's behaviour is not wholly determined; and s/he could not know all the factors affecting their judgement (Shaver and Scott, 1991). However, entrepreneurs are likely to want to 'make a difference'; hence they perceive themselves to be in control of situations, efficacious and self-confident.

Nascent entrepreneurs should have the potential and the intention to act entrepreneurially but those factors, whilst necessary, are not sufficient (Krueger and Brazeal, 1994). Acting entrepreneurially must be perceived to be a desirable thing to do, not simply to oneself but to significant others; it must be thought to be feasible and that one has the personal capability to carry out the requisite tasks. Hence, these conditions provide the springboard for 'taking the plunge'; such entrepreneurial potential, however, is latent and requires a trigger or precipitating event in order to overcome inertia. This trigger is usually a change in personal circumstances (redundancy, an inheritance) that fires the motivation necessary to realise intention. Later work (Krueger, 2000; Shepherd and Krueger, 2002) suggests that situations could be perceived as opportunities or threats and that this depends on people's mental models to interpret cues as signifying a threat or an opportunity. The model of self-belief – the idea that pursuit of an opportunity should be desirable and feasible – and that there is a need to overcome the inertia in a situation remain key parts of the theory; however, in addition to personal efficacy, social efficacy may also be assumed where entrepreneurship takes place within an organisation.

Several papers allude to the importance of an entrepreneur's self-efficacy beliefs (Boyd and Vozikis, 1994; Chen *et al.*, 1998). The latter study provides some empirical support for the theory that entrepreneurs tend to be self-efficacious and rely on a sense of personal control. Moreover, their self-efficacy is not a generalised tendency like locus of control, but is task- and situation-specific to risk-taking and innovation.

A further line of cognitive research focused on heuristics or short cuts, biases, overconfidence and errors in decision-making (Schwenk, 1988; Busenitz and Barney, 1997; Baron, 1998, 2000). Such biases include the tendency for practitioners to generalise from their own limited experience, making errors due to pressure and stress and having negative thoughts and feelings of regret. Errors in judgement arise from self-serving bias, over-optimistic forecasting, belief in the ability to accomplish a project more quickly than is realistic and escalation in decision-making, resulting in throwing good money after bad rather than cutting one's losses. Further work on information processing (Simon and Houghton, 2002) and the effect of risk perception on opportunity evaluation (Keh *et al.*, 2002) identified various cognitive bias effects, in particular, illusion of control. Markman *et al.* (2002) found that technological entrepreneurs had higher self-efficacy, more intense regrets and experienced regrets over opportunities that did not work out compared to non-entrepreneurs. Entrepreneurs persevere more than non-entrepreneurs and this increased effort, when unfulfilled, results in increased regrets and feelings of disappointment.

Mitchell *et al.* (2000) carried out a cross-cultural study of cognitive entrepreneurship that suggested that entrepreneurs should have the know-how and know-who that constitutes an *arrangement* script – who, what and where do I turn to start a venture? Secondly, entrepreneurs should have the commitment and the receptivity to the idea of founding (i.e. a *willingness script*). Thirdly, they should have the necessary competences and skills to get on with the task (*ability scripts*). They were able to show the importance of these scripts and that cultural factors explained some differences in venture creation decisions.

The greater part of the research, however, has been to show differences between entrepreneurs and non-entrepreneurs. Gaglio and Katz (2001) and Gaglio (2004) theorise that entrepreneurs use mental simulations in the envisioning process in opportunity development. Due to their heightened and veridical perceptual alertness to opportunities, entrepreneurs would be ahead in their thinking compared to non-entrepreneurs and they use counter-factual thinking to consider the various steps in the logic from the start point to a possible innovative solution. Moreover, entrepreneurs are more likely to pursue counter-factuals (imagined scenarios) that appear to have a low probability of success than non-entrepreneurs, who it is believed would abandon such ideas at an early stage. Clearly, entrepreneurs, when thinking through the steps of the desired scenario, are also considering how it might be made to work. One possible consideration is the marshalling of social capital resources (Carolis and Saparito, 2006) and the requirement of, at the very least, a partner, trusted subordinate or 'right-hand man/woman' to whom one can turn to effect successful implementation (Chell and Tracey, 2005).

Social psychological and psycho-economic theories of creativity enable this understanding to be taken a step further. New ideas are, on the whole, not liked and are undervalued. Entrepreneurs must manage this fact. Their socio-economic role therefore is to synthesise their knowledge and creative thoughts within the context of the business situation, but while such capabilities are crucial they are not sufficient. Intrinsic motivation helps to foster the conditions for them to produce novel ideas, and various personality skills and competences ensure that they persist and are able to manage obstacles and challenges that will inevitably arise.

The work summarised above comprises both theory building and empirical studies that help to edge our knowledge of nascent entrepreneurial and business creation processes forward. Both in social psychology and entrepreneurship, the idea of focusing on cognitions divorced from feelings and mood diminishes the theory and the likelihood of explaining variance and predicting outcomes. People, and entrepreneurs specifically, when dealing with problem situations go through a number of thought processes that include sense-making, imagining possibilities and harbouring thoughts and feelings about what various results might yield: opportunity of a lifetime? A successful product might be launched or a new factory could be opened? Better lifestyle? Such thoughts not only engage a person's imagination, but raise the question: what does that feel like? Indeed, what might the converse feel like – the missed opportunity? In these cases, regret, sadness and wondering what might have been are the types of feelings that most likely ensue (Markman *et al.*, 2002). This area continues to be a fruitful field for further research.

These studies help to identify additional gaps in knowledge, as well as the need to improve the methodologies employed. Shook *et al.* (2003) discuss various ways forward in these areas, whilst Baron and Ward (2004) add a set of issues that they believe have not been researched. However, the need to integrate creativity into any theory of entrepreneurial behaviour and process is, I would suggest, paramount. Whilst there is a general belief that both the pursuit of interactionism and cognitive research are steps in the right direction, there is considerably more work to be done to develop our knowledge of entrepreneurial behaviour and character.

Notes

1 This may be otherwise termed 'hard determinism'.
2 This may be referred to as 'soft determinism'.
3 See the case of Crowther's trouser factory in Chapter 8.
4 Consider, for example, the case of Anita Roddick (detailed in Chapter 8), when her husband was travelling in South America and she decided to set up a shop in order to have sufficient income for her and her children to live on.
5 The work on escalation was focused primarily on any person placed in a position of authority and/or control over a project where decisions to progress the project were to be taken in a staged way, for example the Taurus project in the City of London. As such, escalation of decision-making does not apply only to entrepreneurs.

Appendix

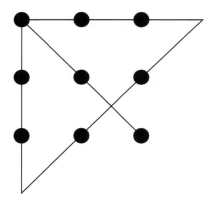

Figure 6.4 Solution to the problem in Figure 6.3.

7 Paradigms, methodology and the construction of the entrepreneurial personality

Introduction

It is clear from the preceding chapters that research in entrepreneurship and the entrepreneurial personality has been fraught with methodological difficulties, which should be addressed. Furthermore, it is requisite to an interdisciplinary approach that the depth of understanding of each discipline and its assumptions is made explicit and well understood. Hence, for purposes of integration and choice, the aim of this chapter is to expose various methodological issues and enable the construction of the entrepreneurial personality to be approached more clearly.

I commence by discussing epistemological assumptions, that is, the problem of knowledge and the issue of truth. In this section, ideographic (concerned with gaining insights into the workings of phenomena in a holistic way and theory building) and the nomothetic methods (concerning rigorous measurement of phenomena, objective causal analysis and theory testing) are compared and contrasted. These two approaches and their methodological assumptions have tended to be 'reified' in the form of paradigmatic approaches, which have been both helpful in highlighting certain contrasts and a hindrance in creating the issue of 'incommensurability' between the paradigms. Beyond this, the Burrell and Morgan (1979) paradigmatic approach is critiqued and an alternative, discourse analysis presented (Deetz, 1996).

In the third section, an exposition of social constructionism is developed in order to position the construction of personality. I build the argument by grappling with those aspects of sociology and psychology that have given rise to a public social constructionism and a private cognitive constructivism (Martin and Sugarman, 1996). I problematise the issues of maintaining a duality between the public and private and the mind and body (Ryle, 1949) and consider the specific problem for psychology of sensory perception. The ensuing section outlines the social construction of reality, based on the work of Berger and Luckmann (1967), showing how people develop 'typificatory schema' to account for the routine nature of behaviour and institutions, roles and social rules to give a sense of 'facticity'. I then consider the role that language plays in social interaction, its 'performative' nature and the socio-relational role of language as a prerequisite to thought and meaning (Derrida, 1978; Foucault, 1979; Wittgenstein, 1978). In this discussion the person is not apparent; this is addressed by reflecting on, and positioning, Hampson's approach to the construction of personality (Hampson, 1988). In the next section, Matthews *et al.* (2003) attempt to reconcile social psychology and trait theory. At the heart of their argument is the positioning of social constructivism and the social cognitive approach to understanding the link between personality, mind, the self and behaviour. Finally I summarise the implications for the 'Entrepreneurial Personality'.

The problem of knowledge

Homo sapiens is distinguished from other creatures due to the human capacity for conscious thought and the existence of mind. These characteristics have given the species the ability to learn, to know and become knowledgeable. They have led philosophers through the centuries to enquire into the nature of knowledge and mind: How do we come to *know* things about the so-called *external world*? How do we know that what we perceive is *true* and, indeed, how might we distinguish our beliefs and opinions from the 'truth'? Such philosophical problems pervade the whole of science and social science, have prompted a search for Truth,[1] have distinguished between knowledge and belief, refutation and denial, and the grounds of logical argument, amongst many other issues.[2] Believing that something is the case is not the same as knowing it to be the case; refuting an argument is not the same as denying its truth on, for example, the grounds of personal conviction. Conviction and strength of belief do not guarantee truth. Indeed, how do we move our claims beyond our perceptions that are partial and ephemeral, to knowledge of phenomena? Moreover, how do we know that what we claim to perceive is in some sense *real* and how do we know or claim to know other persons, our self and other minds? Such questions as these are fundamental to psychology and knowledge of personality.

Social scientists have adopted two distinctly different approaches to answering such questions: (a) how can something *be* – what is the nature of its existence, that is, its ontological status; and (b) how do we know the nature of that thing, that phenomenon, in other words, what epistemological assumptions are we making? These two approaches are the nomothetic and the ideographic. The psychometric study of traits is an example of the nomothetic approach; it typically adopts the scientific method, and uses quantitative methods for purposes of data analysis. Usually there is a theoretical or conceptual basis of the enquiry, from which a set of hypotheses are constructed and tested rigorously, through the collection of data about the phenomenon under investigation. The data are processed, analysed, interpreted and the results extracted, considered and formally reported. The process of statistical analysis of the data usually results in data reduction in order to achieve the best theoretical fit. This process of analysis *is considered to be* objective and rigorous, and enables the psychometrician to draw general conclusions – a process known as induction.

The ideographic method, in contrast, views investigation as that of getting close to the subject, exploring in detail their background, the context of their lives and the situations that they may be immersed in. This approach necessitates the analysis of subjective accounts and involves the inquirer in developing insights into behaviour, the nature of everyday events and how they are construed by particular 'actors' intimately involved in them. From a social scientific perspective, this approach commences from the observation of a particular case or cases, results in careful analysis of the case and the presentation of insights that have been revealed.

The nomothetic approach answers the question of knowledge by laying claim to the credentials of adopting a rigorous scientific methodology: variables are identified that are likely to be causal; conclusions are based on theory from which the independent variables are adduced, are tested rigorously and generalisations inducted from the *objectively* analysed empirical data. Even so, the conclusions and the knowledge[3] upon which those conclusions are based is only probabilistically the case; it is always possible that further experimentation could challenge, if not overturn, a prior set of conclusions.

The ideographic method may lay claim to have uncovered insights that are a truth about particular situations in everyday life in a similar way to that of a good novel, which may also lay bare truth. But the case may be seen as particular and subjective; it would not be seen as being replicable in the scientific sense, and would not lay claim to having discovered a 'universal truth'. So, technically, the social scientist adopting this method may not generalise from the findings of their particular case to 'other individuals who may find themselves in like circumstances'. This is clearly a problem for some social scientists who wish to adopt qualitative methods but also derive insights that may be generalisable beyond the particular case. Table 7.1 summarises some of the key differences discussed above.

It is clear that this difficulty may have arisen from the association of particular methods and approaches with the strict definitions of nomothetic and ideographic approaches. For example, 'objectivity' and 'subjectivity' in social science investigation is a matter of degree: it is not an absolute, but relative. In the scientific construction of psychometric tests, for example, the psychologist makes assumptions – explicit or otherwise – about the category of subjects under study and these assumptions may influence his/her choice of questions or statements that form the basis of the measure (Hampson, 1988). At all stages expert judgement must be made in interpreting data, drawing conclusions, and so forth. What may be *measured* is also an issue. Social phenomena are complex, multi-dimensional and comprising intangible elements that may defy measurement in the strict scientific sense. Measures must, if they are to meet scientific criteria, demonstrate validity

Table 7.1 Summary of key differences between nomothetic and ideographic assumptions of social science paradigms

	Ontology	Epistemology	Methodology
Nomothetic	'Real' tangible objects, things that enjoy an external reality out there in the external world	Knowledge and truth can be revealed through a systematic approach; the use of data and experimental manipulation to provide demonstration of what *is* the case. Truth is probable, not absolute. Knowledge is external, public and checkable	The scientific method assumes the objective existence of a datum that reflects or mirrors an external reality. Theory generates hypotheses that are tested through experimental and primarily quantitative methods (survey techniques). Inferences are made from analyses and conclusions drawn to establish knowledge and truth
Ideographic	Ephemeral, intangible phenomena, perception, mental states; existence within and between other minds	Knowledge and truth are always relative, formulated from the integration of various perspectives and a consequence of interpretation. Knowledge is a mental (private) phenomenon; truth is fleeting, interpersonal and relational	Mental phenomena (including interpretation) are unique to the individual. Phenomena are based on subjective experience. It is important to trace similarities and differences between subjective interpretations in order to generate insights. Detailed analyses of individual cases are required

and reliability and these criteria can, ironically, restrict severely what can be measured and thus what can be known. The alternative – a non-positivist theoretical approach – highlights and values the potential importance of the intangible in affecting social processes and phenomena. Capturing such phenomena for empirical and theoretical purposes in the pursuit of knowledge and understanding requires an alternative method of assessment. The problem of knowledge then becomes that of being able to demonstrate the phenomenon in a particular case, but the impossibility, argued by those who take a solipsist, indeed extreme, view of epistemological issues, of arriving at generalisations.

Solipsism is a conundrum, but it is not a tenable position, ultimately, for the social scientist to assume. It would be impossible for us to reflect on solipsism – the totally unique and solitary – if it were true. The nature of mind, the self and social intercourse is dependent on the ability to share perceptions, understanding and a language concerning the world and other people. Those shared thoughts, feelings, perceptions, and so forth enable us to develop our understanding of phenomena and move around in the world. Whilst we may ultimately be alone – the 'I' has only one referent – knowledge of ourselves depends on perceptions shared and communicated to others through the use of a common language. It depends on relations to the context and relationships to, and with, other people. However, whilst the language may be shared, this does not imply identical perception or interpretation; people may develop different perspectives and this in itself is a source of innovation.

Social science knowledge, arrived at through non-positivist means, requires special attention. It is not that something cannot be known to be true, but that the knowledge is multifaceted: built up from the perspectives of multiple observers. The issue is not that 'truth' is relative, but that what 'rings true' emerges from the whole context, including the language, the setting and the implicit 'rules of the game'. In contrast, knowledge (and truth) derived by positivist/empirical methods is based on probability, and the scientist, adopting this methodology, attempts thereby to establish physical (natural) laws. Social scientists, adopting positivist methodology, attempt to establish 'rules', but they are not immutable. Further, knowledge and 'truth', arrived at using non-positive methods, are based on evident shared meanings and shared understanding of a phenomenon, but they also encompass multiplicity and multiple layering of meanings and understanding, as the investigator gleans information from 'actors' perceiving a situation from their own point of view. Reliability may be achieved by 'playing back' the perspective to the subject, and checking understanding by seeking clarification and reflecting on that which is being done and said. This is essentially the reflexive process of 'getting closer to the subject' and thus empathetically understanding their perspective.

Knowledge and method of acquiring knowledge have been linked. However, it is apparent from this discussion that social scientists themselves have preferred methods of approaching their work (Reason, 1981). Drawing on Reason's classification, five dimensions are indicated (Figure 7.1). This set of

Figure 7.1 Dimensions of contrasting social science approaches to investigation.

dimensions creates a multi-dimensional space in which social scientists may be positioned. However, whilst analytical scientists tend towards the left-hand space of all five of the dimensions, some would argue that *imagination* is a crucial component of the development of scientific theories. Conceptual theorists are arguably strong detached thinkers who use their imagination to construct theories in the broadest possible way, exploring possibilities and thereby speculating with a view to being as general as possible. Humanists approach subjects through empathetic understanding, based on the personal, the interpersonal and the consideration of feelings. Conceptual humanists use imagination to explore subjects as subjects and in relation to themselves – the inquirer. Their theories are speculative and general, though they see multiple causes of behaviour and from their perspective knowledge and truth are problematic. Further, the 'particular humanist' tends to be the antithesis of the analytical scientist; they emphasise intense, personal sources of knowledge, use in-depth individual case studies, are interested in their subjects in a way that contrasts strongly with the 'detached observer' and, in exploring the particular, they see any attempts to generalise as being fundamentally counter to the ethos of their approach. This discussion serves to highlight some of the difficulties encountered in attempting to apply rigid categorisation systems applied to paradigms, discourses or systems of thought: (a) the categories are not clearcut; and (b) there is a false binary opposition. Moreover, what also emerges is the extent to which any scientist or social scientist can lay claim to 'objective truth' – a matter that we shall return to later in this chapter.

Paradigms

The objective of understanding theoretical positions was formalised in a hugely influential book called *Sociological Paradigms and Organizational Analysis* by Burrell and Morgan, first published in 1979. This work elevated the Kuhnian term 'paradigm' and contrasted four paradigmatic positions, giving pre-eminence to so-called Functionalism as the 'dominant discourse of the social sciences'. Furthermore, it established these four paradigms by dint of contrast between two spectra – 'social regulation versus conflict' and 'subjective versus objective'. Figure 7.2 shows the four resultant paradigms.

Social scientists approach their work by assuming a particular theory of knowledge and adhering to implicit views about the fundamental nature of society. Burrell and Morgan (1979) term this framework, and the set of meta-theoretical assumptions associated with it, a paradigm. Paradigms in social science are based on four sets of assumptions in respect of ontology, epistemology, methodology (as discussed above) and human nature. Further, the positivist quasi-scientific approach that assumes a tangible reality is distinguished from the anti-positivist approach that views reality as ephemeral and intangible. Human nature concerns the assumptions of free will or determinism; a deterministic view where everything is assumed to have

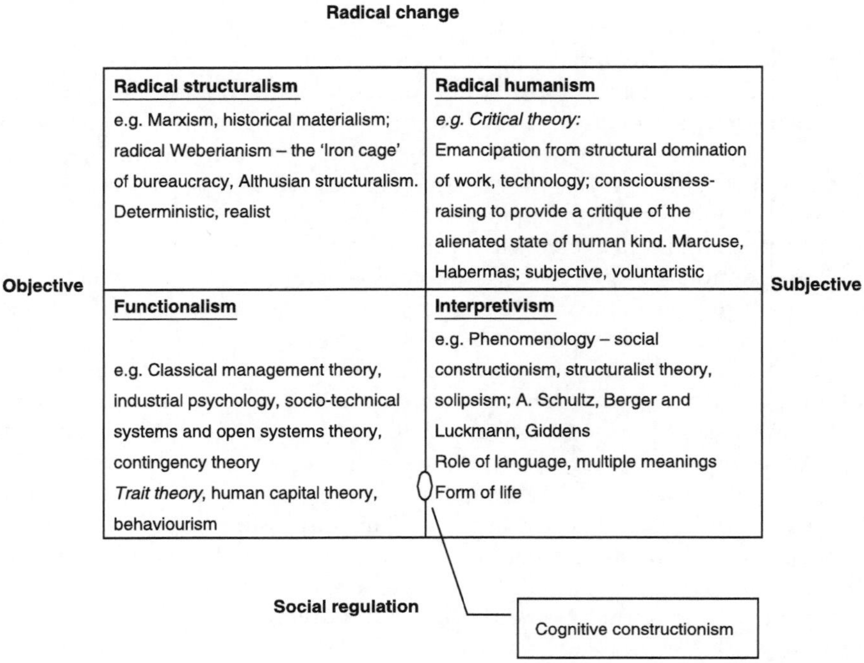

Radical change

Radical structuralism	Radical humanism
e.g. Marxism, historical materialism; radical Weberianism – the 'Iron cage' of bureaucracy, Althusian structuralism. Deterministic, realist	*e.g. Critical theory:* Emancipation from structural domination of work, technology; consciousness-raising to provide a critique of the alienated state of human kind. Marcuse, Habermas; subjective, voluntaristic
Functionalism	**Interpretivism**
e.g. Classical management theory, industrial psychology, socio-technical systems and open systems theory, contingency theory *Trait theory*, human capital theory, behaviourism	e.g. Phenomenology – social constructionism, structuralist theory, solipsism; A. Schultz, Berger and Luckmann, Giddens Role of language, multiple meanings Form of life

Objective ———————————————————————————— Subjective

Social regulation

Cognitive constructionism

Figure 7.2 The four paradigms (based on Burrell and Morgan, 1979).

Key: Cognitive constructionism on the boundary between paradigms (see also Chapter 3).

a cause (within positivism) is contrasted with that of the autonomous individual who has free will and choice (assumed by the non-positivist). Epistemologically, knowledge to the positivist may be viewed as either true or false. The anti-positivist, however, views knowledge in a relativistic way; it can only be understood from the point of view of individual subjects. Figure 7.3 provides a summary of these dimensions.

Where an investigator stands on ontology, epistemology and issues concerning free will will ultimately influence the method they choose to test knowledge and, in this way, influence the results and conclusions they make. If a researcher views the social world as an external 'concrete' or tangible reality then the method they employ would concentrate on the analysis of variables and empirical testing. They may seek to identify general 'laws' and concepts that describe that reality. If the researcher takes the opposite view of the social world, that it is the subjective experience of individuals who create, mould and interpret reality, the emphasis will be on explaining what is particular to individuals rather than what is general and universal. The debate in methodology, as discussed above, is between ideographic and nomothetic theories of method.

Several criticisms have been levelled at the Burrell and Morgan paradigms,

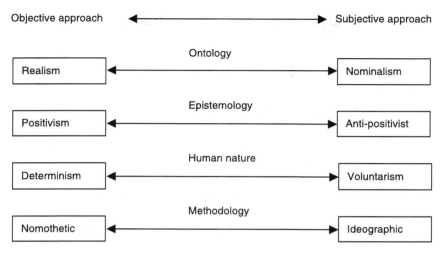

Figure 7.3 Assumptions made in social science inquiry.

including that of their incommensurability (Hassard, 1988; Gioia and Pitre, 1990; Holland, 1990; Jackson and Carter, 1991, 1993; Parker and McHugh, 1991). Even if one were to accept the utility of this four-paradigm approach, there is arguably a need for greater elasticity between paradigm boundaries to accommodate what, in actuality, is a multi-dimensional space. Rather, the two-dimensional space may be considered to be too simplistic (Davies, 1998; Chell and Allman, 2003). Further, the whole notion of the concept of 'paradigm' has been considered by many to be problematic. The meaning of 'paradigm' is unclear, especially in this sociological context, as it lacks rigour in the scientific sense in which it was originally construed[4] (Kuhn, 1962). Whilst some researchers take a more constructive view of the paradigmatic approach (Pittaway, 2000, 2005), Deetz (1996) has argued that Burrell and Morgan 'reify research approaches' by adopting this straight-jacket of the four paradigms; researchers' positions have to be fitted in, whereas the paradigms obscure important differences and contrasts in research orientation. 'Paradigms are incommensurable as they strive to maintain coherence but commensurable to the extent that they encounter the ultimately indeterminate outside world' (Deetz, 1996: 193).

Deetz (1996) questions the selection of dimensions that Burrell and Morgan have made, as he argues these are not the dimensions that reveal the differences and similarities among research approaches, which the researcher may then evaluate. In society, discourses are politicised by, for example, making contrasts between in- and out-groups, dominant and marginalised groups – the latter forming the status of 'the other' and being valued in different and often negative, sometimes derisory, terms. Deetz points out that Burrell and Morgan's articulation of functionalism as the dominant authority and source of mainstream discourse implicitly positioned the other three paradigms as 'the other', creating difficulties for researchers working in those other paradigms to express and position themselves. Furthermore, the 'regulation and change/conflict' dimension very quickly collapses into the subjective–objective dimension and, as such, any social research with a political agenda was assumed to be 'appropriately placed' in the subjective category.

Further, the debate concerning the subjective–objective distinction is misconceived (Deetz, 1996). Reasoning from a priori principles is to argue from a set of assumptions; however, if any of the assumptions are wrong, biased or incorrect, then the ensuing conclusions will also be misguided and incorrect. Hence, all scientific theory-building implicitly contains subjective elements; the assumptions made, the choice of what problems to research and the domination of a particular research community's work over that of another constitute value-laden issues.[5] Arguably, critical reflection is required to rid oneself of the *implicit assumption* of 'objectivity'. Positivism and its claim to 'objective knowledge' are associated with the development of powerful groups that are protected and privileged in both the academy and in society at large. However, much research now disputes the dualism between the subjective–objective and the internal–external split. Moreover, this spectrum between subjective and objective has also been aligned in some researchers' minds to a split between research methods: that qualitative methods should be associated with the subjective, and quantitative data collection and analysis with objective research. This implies that only rigorous and robust research can be carried out by adopting the latter methodology. On the contrary, in the sphere of social science all 'objects' are constituted in the sense that they are 'socially shared, historically produced and general to a group' (ibid.: 195). Hence, if both functionalists and interpretivists recognise this, it is possible for the latter to count things and for the former to recognise the relevance of those influences that constitute objects, determine problems and influence communities.

Deetz (1996) puts forward an alternative way of conceptualising research orientations: firstly, he makes the contrast between 'local/emergent' and 'elite/a priori' conceptions. The elite/a priori school operates with a 'consensus discourse' that works towards building a dominant structured knowledge base, whereas the local/emergent could be said to disrupt this structure through a discourse of dissension or, to use Deetz' term, 'dissensus' (see Table 7.2).

There are many points of contrast that can be made between these two positions: the elite/a priori group holds with the notion of expertise of a particular research community, research is heavily theory-driven and a particular technical language develops that provides consistency and assurance of the reliability of the research outcomes; whereas the local/emergent approach is open to new meanings that arise from the research enterprise and interactions within the research process – insights rather than truth, particular in time and place, are what emerge and aid understanding. In the latter

Table 7.2 Local/emergent versus elite/a priori approaches

Elite/a priori	Local/emergent
Privilege to technical/expert language	Knowledge has less lofty claims
Theory driven	Open to new meanings
Experience of the researched encapsulated in social science language	Problems and statements a consequence of interplay
Conceptual system viewed as a superior representation of reality	Concepts relative
Seeks the Truth	Seeks insights
Seeks generality of meaning	Insights are particularistic, but cumulatively may provide insight into other cases
Makes essentialist assumptions	
Findings freed from local/temporal conditions of production	Feelings, intuitions, multiple reasons assumed in generating insights
Production of rational knowledge	Self-reflexivity; recognition of subjectivity
Proclaims objectivity and value neutrality	Avoids the logic of objectivity and rationality
Expert observer	Skilled collaborator

case, insights result in concept formation and emergent theory rather than concept application from extant theory. Further, by making this differentiation between research orientations there are three advantages:

1 It acknowledges the social construction of both research positions and research objects that should be problematised.
2 It distinguishes between the production of different kinds of knowledge – the elite approach producing 'book knowledge' (i.e. knowing about) and the local/emergent producing practical knowledge ('knowing how' or 'knowing for').
3 It exposes the political alliances that may be associated explicitly, or implicitly, with particular concepts, such as managerial bias or reproducing a particular world view.

The 'consensus–dissensus' dimension is unlike that of Burrell and Morgan's 'regulation–change' dimension, as it is not primarily about class conflict. Rather, it concerns the idea of different discourses, and the ability to challenge critically 'dominant discourses' that can be limiting or suppressing of alternative perspectives: the points of view of the less privileged or marginalised groups. Deetz prefers to use the term 'discourse' rather than 'paradigm' to encapsulate different sociological approaches to talking about, and researching, social and organisational behaviour. He then goes on to describe the 'prototypical features' of each approach:

- The 'normative approach' pursues the basic goal of uncovering 'law-like relations among objects' and is reported in a 'scientific narrative style', for example classical management theories, leadership theories, contingency theories and the management of culture. I might add that the bulk of entrepreneurship theory has adopted the nomothetic scientific method and has assumed economic theory and the market mechanism as the context of entrepreneurial activity, and thus falls into the normative science category (e.g. McClelland, 1961; Storey, 1994).
- Interpretive discourse attempts to 'display a unified culture', assumes that people are active 'sense-makers' and that the researcher attempts, through ethnographic, hermeneutic or phenomenology, to arrive at a consensual culture of the subject of analysis (e.g. Weick and Roberts, 1993; Steyaert *et al.*, 1996). The goal is to show how particular realities are socially produced and maintained through rites, rituals, norms and other daily activities. Examples comprise the use of metaphor, for example organisations as 'well oiled machines' (Morgan, 1996), whereas metaphors used to give meaning to the entrepreneurial process have included 'journey', 'a race', 'parenting', 'building', 'war', 'lunacy' and 'passion' (Dodd, 2002).
- The 'critical' approach attempts to 'unmask domination' and adopts a directive, therapeutic style. The aim is to critique forms of domination, produce dissensus and open forums for building consensus, for example structurationists (Giddens, 1984, 1991), some feminist theory (Harding, 1991) and labour process theory (Knights and Wilmott, 1990). In entrepreneurship theory I cite a particularly enlightening discussion of Schumpeter's work by Ogbor (2000).
- The 'dialogic', deconstructionist approach attempts to 'reclaim conflict and is presented in an 'ironic, ambivalent style' (Deetz, 1996: 199). Deetz prefers 'dialogic' to 'postmodern' for a number of reasons, including the need to separate out this discourse from, for example, post-Fordist discourses that make realist assumptions. The dialogic focuses on: fragmentation and potential disunity in any discourse; domination, but not by any one group; the need to identify conflicts in everyday life; and the partiality and one-sidedness of reality (e.g. some gender studies) (Smircich and Calas, 1987). In entrepreneurship one problem has been to see males as the archetype of entrepreneurs, to use the male entrepreneur as the standard and to relegate and marginalise female entrepreneurs (Bowen and Hisrich, 1986). The dialogist questions 'taken-for-granted' assumptions about the nature of reality, and of social categories that are constructed but remain unquestioned.

Positioning the social construction of personality

The above section enables us to start to position personality theory. To move towards achieving this, there is a need to bring together several strands of thought that have been developed over the past twenty years. In this section I commence with setting out the problem for psychology in addressing the internal (mental) and external (physical) worlds and I consider some of the philosophical issues concerning the nature of the mind. This leads to an explication of the bridging paradigm of Martin and Sugarman (1996) and what it is to behave mindfully. However, before proceeding to a consideration of personality, it is also necessary to reflect on how reality is constructed. This sets the stage to visit Hampson's (1988) theory of the 'construction of personality'. Finally, I consider how this might be reconciled with trait theory and cognitive and social psychology.

The duality of internal and external worlds

There is a sense in which the disciplinary roots of social scientists shape their approach to their subject of investigation. Psychologists, broadly speaking, are engaged in understanding the psyche – the mind and mental processes, deep feelings and attitudes that account for someone's opinions and behaviour. However, psychology has a particular problem to explain in that there are events that occur in the physical world for which there is no corresponding event in the mental world, and vice versa. For example, electrical currents are part of the physical world but they are not an inherent part of the mind, whereas illusions and images may occur in the mind but have no place in the physical world. Sensations are subjective (phenomenal), belonging to the perceiver, as distinct from objective – belonging to the object and part of the physical order. Yet sensory qualities are also interpersonal and not entirely peculiar to an individual, otherwise they could not be understood. Nor are sensations confined to conscious experience; arguably the greater part of the mind is constituted of unconscious processes, ideas, and so forth that are not perceived and cannot be known through introspection (Hayek, 1952: 25). The problem for psychology is to explain the existence and nature of the mind in relation to behaviour and the physical world.

In approaching personality – a phenomenon that, arguably, is the external manifestation of mental processes – psychologists identify the latter manifestations (attitudes, behaviour, values, etc.) as objective phenomena from which may be inferred an *internal* sub-system, not only the mind but also personality. They do so by attempting to collect data about '*individual* differences' in these manifestations from which they derive general statements about human behaviour. However, such dispositional tendencies are indicative of *similarities*, not differences. In contrast, sociologists focus on the study of society and social institutions that affect human behaviour (see Chapter 3 of this volume). For psychologists the proper subject of study is the private 'internal world' of the individual, whereas for sociologists it is the external, public world of social groups and institutions. This fundamental divide raises a number of problems that I shall attempt to tease out.

Bouchikhi (1993) distinguished between cognitive constructivism[6] and social constructionism; the disciplinary roots of these approaches differ – constructivism has its roots in the psychology of the individual, and social constructionism in the sociology of the public and social world. This dichotomy has resulted in a *dualism* between the internal private world of individual mental processes and an external public world of social phenomena. Understanding how the public and private worlds interrelate is impossible to explain within either of these paradigms. Martin and Sugarman (1996) set out to develop a 'bridging paradigm' that, by placing the individual as agent in a socio-cultural frame, accounts for these interrelations.

The Martin–Sugarman paradigm rests on a number of premises: individual experience is shaped by the socio-cultural but is not reduced to it; psychological phenomena, such as thoughts, are expressed relationally through conversation – this implies a sharing of ideas, influencing processes and interrelating; and it is through language and reflexive processes that individual psychology is organised. However, individual understanding can transcend the immediate, because of the human capacity to remember and imagine. This means that past experience can be recollected and future possibilities imagined. This process is indeterminate in that the past events that may be retrieved by memory and considered cannot be predicted. Hence, human agency is not determined by the socio-cultural; it is constrained by it, but nonetheless actions occur within it. At the point of decision, people are free to choose. Thus, they apply their understanding of social events, conversation and behaviour; they actively interpret them in the light of their own lives and experience. As such, *cognitive constructivism* is thus limited but not determined: there is scope for the freedom of human agency. This means that human beings genuinely reflect on their experiences and, whilst much of that experience may be routine and understood, some experience is novel and is construed. People may use the familiar to construct an explanation of the unfamiliar, but new experience triggers the need to develop new ideas and new theory to explain one's reality. Hence, people develop personal theories to organise, anticipate, understand and manipulate their reality. This theory is consistent with views of entrepreneurial behaviour, where that behaviour is novel and innovative.

It is thus critical to this theory to realise that mind manifests itself through behaviour (human agency); it is able to construct reality through interpretation, presentation, manipulation, etc. of events, whether past or current. This dissolves the internal–external distinction; there is no duality, but a singularity of expression manifested in a split second. In this sense personality and its behavioural expression emerges from the situation (Bouchikhi, 1993; Chell, 2000). Ryle (1949: 13–24) presents further cogent arguments against the assumption of a dual reality; it creates a further problem of how one kind of thing – the mind – might affect, relate to or cause another kind of thing – the physical? Ryle refers to this as a 'category mistake'; the difference between the physical and the mental world is not only that the physical can be explained by mechanical causation whereas the mental does not adhere to the laws of mechanics, but also that the physical world is explained by laws that are deterministic whereas associated with minds are choice, responsibility and will.

The fact that a person can do mental arithmetic, read silently and 'hum' a tune *in their head* (sic) is not evidence of a receptacle in which mental processes supposedly take place. Rather, these mental processes are learnt behaviours that presume social interaction as a necessary feature of them being learnt at all. This also scotches the presumption that mental states can be reduced to the material, or vice versa. For example, we might jot a note on a piece of paper, but the *meaning* of that message cannot be found in the ink or the paper. Meaning is socially derived and developed. Accordingly, mind and matter are not 'logical oppositions', they exist in different senses. Mind, Ryle argues, is not a receptacle containing rules, propositions or prescriptions that a person must consider before they act; a person executes an act skilfully or not, intelligently or not, and in doing so they enact one behaviour, not two[7] (ibid.: 30). In preparing a cordon bleu dish a chef may need to refer to a recipe, but the creation of the dish cannot be reduced to knowledge of the recipe; expertise in the kitchen is mindful behaviour of a different kind.

Furthermore, the mind is not a mirror that reflects 'reality': or what is 'out there in the external world' (Gergen, 1999: 74). This issue is associated with 'realism' and, in paradigmatic terms, functionalism and positivism. The scientist lays claim to truth and the ability to present the facts 'as they really are' through the assumption of mind that is stripped of subjective influences; it thus operates in an objective way, without prejudice or bias. This alleged ability to accurately reflect reality is privileged and gains a sense of authority, as it is claimed that there is nothing there to distort the image of the world. But, argues Gergen (1999: 74–76), 'objectivity' cannot refer to a relationship between the mind and the world; rather, he suggests, objectivity is achieved by speaking and writing in particular ways: the scientist (a) distances the object in a depersonalised manner; (b) establishes his/her position and credentials; (c) 'purifies the lens' by ensuring the absence of any reference to his/her internal states (such as motives, desires, etc.); and (d) uses the rhetoric, standards and language of the scientific community. Such practices are part of the game; however, as Deetz (1996) and others have pointed out, scientists make a priori judgements, decisions and choices before embarking on a particular piece of research. The fact that such matters and any attendant feelings are not reported underscores the social and subjective elements of scientific behaviour. This does not make the judgements wrong, but it does serve to demonstrate the absence of publicly acknowledged reflection, possibly self-interested judgements, and the use of rhetoric to bolster the generation of scientific 'facts' (ibid.).

The social construction of reality

The social construction of reality is based on the phenomenological principles of Husserl and Schutz, and developed by Berger and Luckmann (1967). All perceptions and interpretations of behaviour, situations and events are the stuff from which reality is constructed. Further, the individual produces his or her own reality, character or nature and view of self. Berger and Luckmann suggest the term 'typificatory schema' to account for typical patterns of behaviour that people adopt in order to deal with routine and well-understood situations. Conceptualising how people behave, whether in familiar or unfamiliar situations, is both to attribute meaning to their actions and to label it by the use of appropriate adjectives. This comprises the external observation of behaviour: it is social and public.

The social construction of reality has also been construed as a process of sense-making (Weick, 1995). As such, it is about the ways in which people interpret what they perceive. To engage in sense-making is to construct, filter, frame and create 'facticity' and to render the subjective into something more tangible. However, these perceptions and understandings are also influenced by conversation, talk, discourses, texts, stories and media (Derrida, 1978; Foucault, 1984; Nicholson and Anderson, 2005). Furthermore, social constructionism highlights the role of public knowledge, of observable behaviours and the possibility of multiple perspectives on behaviour. Thus, lives are regulated by the external specification of roles and their associated activity, and rules of behaviour. Such institutionalisation of the ways things are done gives a further sense of objectivity (see Chapter 3 of this volume). Shared actions rather than shared meanings give a sense of social purpose. People develop routines for dealing with events and expectations that are situation-specific. Behaviour tends to take on patterns – ways of doing, ways of thinking about reality (framing events) and ways of being (the style and way of approaching events). We come to understand situations, problem-solving and handling issues through such processes of shared construction.

This construction is 'holistic' in the sense that it assumes that agents are viewed in context. Hence, the presumption is that understanding is not gained by abstracting the individual from the context; rather, knowledge and understanding can only be gleaned by seeing what the individual *becomes* while dealing with particular situations (Weick, 1995: 24). Such behaviour is labelled by others using a common language; as such 'evidence' may be used to support particular interpretations where reality is contested, it is this process that leads to dominant interpretations gaining acceptance. People thus construct an external factual order (Ring and Van de Ven, 1989).

It has been argued that *pure* social constructionism denies the reality of a mental life, as mental and cognitive processes are inaccessible (Martin and Sugarman, 1996). Behaviour, according to this school of thought, is driven solely by structuring events. Such a theoretical position, however, is ultimately untenable, because social intercourse can only take place through verbal and non-verbal communication. Such communications are shared and their meanings understood by other parties. Reflexivity allows for a consideration of one's self as well as the nature of other selves. Moreover, the ability to recall events from the past and, through the cognitive processes of imagination and projection, share these visions with others is *prima facie* evidence for the existence of mental processes. People reflect on situations and their choice of actions is influenced by imagined future possibilities and alternative scenarios. Our consciousness gives us the ability to think of possible actions, strategies or ways of dealing with a situation, to commit thoughts to memory and to imagine alternative scenarios, all of which presume the existence of social processes, including language. Primitively, we might have scratched signs on cave walls to indicate what animals we have captured, how many hides we have prepared and what our dream for the future is. As a child we read aloud and as we grow older we read silently. Images, drawings and language all become part of our public world, which we can learn to use more or less intelligently. Due to consciousness and the development of language we can consider all the possibilities before enacting one of them. Language precedes thought; it is a necessary condition for any thought to occur. But there is no receptacle in which that language resides; there is no dictionary in our head! Further, without social interaction, there would be no language. Intelligence is, in this sense, the extent of our ability to comprehend social interaction and to execute social behaviours adeptly or otherwise.

Thus, how things might be executed and strategies formulated indicates that human behaviour is *minded* (Ryle, 1949; Weick and Roberts, 1993). Crucially, what this means is that there is no separate duality between mind and body/behaviour; mind and body are intimately connected; thoughts are enacted and executed in particular ways. We might smile weakly, we might produce a robust argument or we might bat out an innings of cricket intelligently. Each of these actions is one action; there is not something going on in the mind that is private and another that is public – in other words the mind does not cause a particular public performance.[8]

The social construction of reality is *both* subjective and objective.[9] It is subjective insofar as the individual deals with a situation according to his/her perception and interpretation of it. It is objective – there is a sense of 'facticity' – insofar as people share knowledge and interpretations of situations and events, fixed in time and place and labelled as being events of particular type, note or consequence. Further, the existence of institutions that structure society also creates a further sense of the objective, because of the rules associated with institutional behaviour that shape people's lives: the bank closing at 3.30 p.m. is not a matter of perception! The assumption of general patterns and routines is presumptive of the social; the alternative is chaos and anarchy, that is, confusion and disorder at individual, social and governmental/political levels.

Individuals construct knowledge about themselves and other people by labelling and categorising their thoughts, feelings and experience. The act of naming is the mechanism by which people externalise their thoughts and articulate ideas, beliefs and views. Through experience and accumulated knowledge each person develops a personal set of labels to give meaning to present and future social situations. Further, they not only use this personal label set as a way of framing situations and enabling them to choose how they will act, but they also use it to understand and categorise the behaviour of other people. Behavioural acts, when repeated, form patterns that are used to label behaviour and recognise the characteristic way a person deals with a particular situation. This use of labels to explain other people's behaviour enables a person to attribute descriptors ('traits') and to develop concepts of 'types' of people and situations that they use to *guide* their behaviour. The subjective world is also labelled reflexively by the individual, thus externalising conscious thought. Furthermore, through the use of language people are able to store, exchange and describe experience and, as such, transcend the temporal and spatial aspects of their environment (Chell, 2000).

The performative role of language

In explaining the nature of mind and social processes, it has become clear just how important language is in enabling each person to gain an understanding of what is happening around them, the behaviour patterns and routines and, reflexively, their own behaviour. This analysis, however, is not complete without dealing with some key issues such as the 'performative' role of language, cultural relativism, truth and meaning that have been raised by various proponents of social constructionism, taking either a postmodern or dialogic approach.

A fundamental issue is how people are able to communicate meaning. Language (and the grammar of language) is not innate; words are not pictures – the relationship between word (the signifier) and object (the signified) is arbitrary. So how is meaning realised? One way is through social convention, but this begs the question of whose convention. Derrida (1978), using his method of deconstruction, suggests that language is a system of binaries: if something is black, then it is also not white. Hence, meaning depends on both presence and absence. Further, Derrida argues that we privilege one side of the equation: material versus spiritual, rational versus emotional. However, if language does not 'picture reality' what does it do?

Wittgenstein (1978) replaces the picture metaphor with that of the game.[10] In order to engage in the game one needs to know the rules, just as in the game of chess. We learn the rules governing the movement of each chess piece, but we also learn the objective of the game. We can learn to play the game of chess at various levels of sophistication, but the meaning of the pieces, the various moves (to 'castle', for example), the chequered board and the 32 different chess pieces are meaningless without the rules that govern playing the game. One cannot play this game – this 'form of life' as Wittgenstein terms it – without an understanding of the rules, the pattern of play, of actions and strategies, as well as the physical pieces that make up the whole game. This analogy can be applied to any 'form of life', such as marriage, the family or any institutional behaviour that has culturally evolved into ways of being. Meaning and understanding are embedded in the particular form of life. In this way behaviour is socially embedded.

Language is not simply a matter of labelling and categorising, but we do things with words. According to Gergen (1999: 35), in using language we enter into a performance – e.g. persuasion, explanation, rhetoric – and telling the truth is playing a specific form of game. Within the game of chess, it is either true or not that I have exercised a manoeuvre that has resulted in 'check mate'. Hence, 'truth' assumes the implicit rules of what counts as a proper description in the context of a game or 'form of life'. Telling the truth is like performing a specific game; we describe, explain and theorise about what may have happened, usually in narrative form. But our descriptions are circumscribed within the context, the form of life. We are not depicting the world when we tell the truth, but we are telling the truth within the conventions of particular groups; in a geography lesson we might declare that the world is round, whereas when we are describing the relative difficulty of a particular country walk the terminology of 'roundness' is irrelevant; 'flatness' or 'hilliness' would be more appropriate terminology in this context. If we look for truth in a local form of life, this avoids looking for truth *behind* the words. This does not preclude the fact that a further performative use of language may be ideological; it may be biased by personal or political motives. To engage in such an ideological critique is one political form of life and the attempt to criticise or supplant it may also be ideologically motivated.

A further concern is with the ordering effects of language (Foucault, 1979). Technical or specialist languages (such as medicine, psychiatry, sociology) create *disciplinary regimes*, the aim of which is to classify, describe and explain. Hence, a person may be described as healthy or unhealthy, normal or abnormal, upper or lower class. By offering ourselves up for classification in these ways, we give power to the specialist and subjugate ourselves to their scrutiny. What counts as mental illness is subject to the language of such specialists. Foucault's point is that such ordering effects not only give power but also *cultural discipline* insofar as we subjugate ourselves to scrutiny and possible invasion of privacy. On the other hand, social ordering is important, as it creates cultural traditions, ways of being, institutions and professional practices (Gergen, 1999: 41). These 'forms of life' give meaning to institutions such as the family, society, and so forth. Rather than wholesale rejection of these institutional practices, they should be regularly critically appraised to inquire into their negative and positive consequences. With such an appraisal, adjustments can be made, retaining the beneficial and discarding the harmful.

Thinking further about the social generation of meaning, words are not simply defined by other words, but are defined in relation to other people. Thus, meaning is gained from how words are used in relationship. Meaning is not logically prior to the social; it is not the product of an individual mind. Social settings, social groups and situations enable meaning to be gleaned from the language and words that are being used. Such relationships are logically prior to what is intelligible. They enable us to describe, explain and contest the 'here and now', as well as the future; as such, we are able to reflect on and consider competing constructions. In this sense, language as discourse creates structure, rhetoric and process. We use metaphors to suggest kinds of structure that represent our reality and we use rhetoric to persuade and conscript support. Discourse may take the form of narrative; we use the narrative form to tell a story. The narrative has a structure (a beginning, middle and an end), a point and a sense of explanation and insight. Narrative analysis examines how discourse can generate misunderstandings and conflict amongst people: how the way we define others and their behaviour has moral overtones of propriety/impropriety, good/evil, acceptable/ unacceptable. In such ways discourse about others creates the nature of the relationship and its consequences.

Thus, the ideas in this section have taken us beyond methodological individualism to theorise about the social aspects of context that shape behaviour and enable us to derive meaning from social situations and actions. This now facilitates a consideration of the construction of personality.

The construction of personality

Social constructionism, coupled with the severe criticisms of the 'traditional' trait approach to understanding personality, enables us to put into perspective the search for alternative methodologies. One such attempt to develop a fundamental shift in personality theory and to redirect attention to a novel methodology is that of Hampson's theory of the construction of personality (Hampson, 1982, 1988). The constructivist approach, as she terms it, is an attempt to take into consideration three perspectives on personality – the perspectives of the personality theorist, the lay person and the self. The personality theorist's perspective assumes an *explicit theory* of personality, that is, an attempt is made to describe what personality *is* by inferring the structure of personality from observations of behaviour. In contrast, the lay perspective assumes an *implicit theory* of personality, which comprises descriptive and intuitive beliefs. Furthermore, people have theories about their own personalities, which act as a guide and enable them to manipulate and control other people through impression management. Thus the self-perspective assumes the existence of *self*-constructs. Moreover, there are reciprocal influences of other people's perception of one's self. Awareness of these perceptions in turn affects one's own perception of one's self and this, consequently, affects how one projects one's self to others.

Hampson argues that the personality theorist has shown no interest in either lay views about personality or in the subjects' self-beliefs. Moreover, there is an assumption of objectivity about the way personality theorists conduct their investigations:

> The investigation of explicit personality is intended to be the objective measurement of inferred, underlying psychological properties of individuals. However, the claimed independence of the study of explicit personality from the lay and self perspectives does not stand up to close examination. Lay beliefs influence the choice of constructs to be studied and the way they are measured.
>
> (Hampson, 1988: 192–193)

A key issue is how the personality theorist decides which personality constructs to study. Hampson argues that these constructs have their origins in lay beliefs. The preparation of the psychological inventory, which has been assumed to be an objective, systematic exercise, is also criticised. It is suggested that the test designer relies upon his or her knowledge and beliefs about behaviour–trait relations in composing many questionnaire items. Hampson gives her own examples of where assumptions about the behaviour, purported to be indicative of the construct, have subsequently been shown to be erroneous.

Hampson concludes that:

> [T]he assessment of psychological equivalence of behaviours should be conducted prior to the empirical investigation of behavioural consistency and should take account of the lay and self perspectives.
>
> (ibid.: 194)

Research has shown that people share a common understanding of the behaviours they believe to be associated with traits and also the co-occurrence relations between traits. For example, it might be expected that people who are sociable are more likely to be helpful. The traits 'sociable' and 'helpful' are believed to co-occur. Hampson demonstrates that the psychologists' explicit theories and the implicit theories of the lay person have much in common. She then argues controversially (see, for example, Kenrick and Funder, 1988) that 'personality does not have an *objective* existence independent of the human observer' (Hampson, 1988: 195). Behaviour is only understood as being socially meaningful once it has been categorised and interpreted.

In sum, the personality theorist is concerned with the structure of personality that may be applied across a population and the ability, using a psychometrically constructed tool, to measure 'individual differences' in relation to particular trait terms. The observer's contribution, that is, how the person's behaviour is perceived and construed by others, is ignored, and so too is the person's own perceptions or awareness of him/herself.

Hampson (1984) addresses the issue of what she regards as a false dichotomy between the 'real' and the 'perceived' personality. Personality theorists regard personality as 'a set of characteristics which may be said to be within the individual causing her or him to behave in certain ways' (ibid.: 29). They are attempting to come to grips with the 'real' personality, whereas person perception is only concerned with people's beliefs about real personality.

Evidence has been adduced to suggest that both ratings of 'real' personality and of 'perceived' personality may be dismissed as figments of the imagination (Mischel, 1968; D'Andrade, 1974; Shweder, 1975, 1977; Shweder and D'Andrade, 1979). The problem is that personality may only be inferred; there is no true objective measure of personality:

> All rating scales vary with respect to the degree to which they refer to specific behavioural acts or require inference from a general impression . . . [Therefore] personality ratings even when taken under optimum on-the-spot conditions involving specific concrete behaviours, are inevitably a representation of reality that has been filtered through the human information processing system . . . There can never be truly objective ratings because ratings are more than just frequency counts of actual behaviours . . . A personality rating . . . involves the rater distinguishing certain events in the behaviour stream and drawing inferences from these events to a more abstract concept.
>
> (Hampson, 1984: 33–34)

This does not mean that perceived personality is merely a reflection of the similarity in meanings between personality terms used as labels on the rating scales. If it were, raters would be insensitive to the inconsistencies between the characteristics of the ratees and the semantic similarity between the rating scales. Immediate ratings have been shown not to accord with semantic similarity beliefs. Hampson concludes that the distinction between actual and perceived personality is in effect meaningless: 'A personality rating is the product of a constructive filter which imposes structure on what is seen' (ibid.: 35). Rather than personality being thought to reside within individuals, she suggests it may be located metaphorically between them.

What then do 'traits' refer to?:

> Traits are categories for social behaviour, and these categories only have meaning in so far as they have generally recognised social significance. We . . . share a common set of understandings about the meaning of social behaviour; personality traits are used as a way of summarising and communicating this meaning.
>
> (ibid.: 38)

Just as the manifestations of objects such as 'birds' are clusters of co-occurring attributes such as feathers, beak and wings, traits may be regarded as semantic categories 'referring to clusters of co-occurring behavioural and situational attributes' (ibid.). Hampson's constructivist theory thus assumes that traits are based on behaviour, which is perceived by observers and categorised in trait terms. The distinction between actual and perceived personality collapses as the trait categorisation of socially constructed personality replaces the idea of perceived real-world behaviour. This means that a different approach is needed to investigate personality traits:

> Socially-constructed personality traits ... are used as categories to apply to perceived behaviour. Observations of behaviour are never truly objective, but are *perceptions* and therefore open to the influence of the perceiver's information processing system ... For the constructivist ... evidence is required that observers are capable of perceiving patterns of behaviour on which to base the personality construction process. These patterns must 'exist' in so far as the trait labels applied to them are useful for communicative and predictive purposes. Thus the constructivist view is supported by evidence of behavioural consistency derived from observations of behaviour.
>
> (ibid.: 38–39)

As individuals, people share 'common understandings' to some degree. But there are multiple perspectives and interpretations of social behaviours and, as such, different perceivers might adopt different interpretations. Through discussion a social consensus may be arrived at. In order to do this the self-perspective may be crucial insofar as consideration is given to the individual's account of his/her own behaviour. Social interaction is a process of negotiation of situations and social encounters. The categorisation of behaviour and conclusions about the nature of an individual's personality is a consequence of this process.

A practical problem in terms of lay perceptions of personality is that people may make trait attributions on the basis of scant evidence and therefore may arrive at biased judgements as to the nature of the personality in question. On the other hand, psychologists using a single measure of a personality dimension may also be overconfident about the conclusions they draw with respect to the nature of personality. Ideally, multiple observations across a variety of situations conducted by more than one person are required to begin to assess the consistent nature of any one individual's personality (Kenrick and Funder, 1988).

A key implication of this theory is the criticism of the methodology of psychometric measurement using personality inventories. In essence, by making the lay theory explicit it is possible to devise new methods of assessing personality traits. The idea that traits operate like categorising concepts (personality-descriptive nouns or adjectives) may be taken as the key to this new methodology.

The basis of Hampson's methodology is the work of Rosch *et al.* (1976)

who have put forward a model of semantic categories for objects. The appeal of this work is that it assumes that criteria for category inclusion are imprecise and as such it incorporates Wittgenstein's notion of 'family resemblance' (Rosch, 1978). In other words, most categories do not have clearcut boundaries and so the idea that it is possible to devise a set of necessary and sufficient criteria for category membership is problematic. Categories may be conceived of in terms of clear cases that typify them rather than in terms of their boundaries. Essentially this is to seek 'prototypical cases' of a category. The prototype is the best exemplar of a particular category. For example, a mahogany dining table is more prototypical of the category 'table' than is a desk. However, as Hampson points out:

> Variations in prototypicality come about because membership of object categories is not an all-or-none affair; instead it depends on an object possessing a greater number of the distinguishing features of one category than those of another.
>
> (Hampson, 1982: 165)

For example, a patio window (or a patio door!) has many of the attributes of both the 'window' category and the 'door' category and is therefore difficult to categorise because it is not prototypical of either category. Such physical objects are categorised according to the function they serve, which is largely dependent on context. Whilst cakes and biscuits are examples of confectionary (being items that have been baked in an oven for human consumption), ice cream is not; this was rather important for Walls for marketing and other business purposes. A plastic bottle is an example of a container, but when empty (the salient context) it is reclassified as waste material. However, contextual modifiers, in this case the recycling process, may produce an entirely novel entity, in this specific case the 'fleece' jacket; as such, the bottle has now become an item of clothing! The ability to reclassify is in some cases fundamental to innovation. For example, Sir Clive Sinclair was considered to be an entrepreneur until he produced the C5.[11]

Cantor and Mischel (1979) have applied Rosch's framework to the categorisation of people. A primary concern was to develop an understanding of the function that categories serve in the perceptual process. These researchers drew a very strong analogy between object categorisation *à la* Rosch and person categorisation. Person-categories may also be described as 'fuzzy sets' (i.e. have ill-defined boundaries), which are best exemplified by the use of prototypical cases. Specific person-categories used by these researchers to illustrate their point are the extroverted person, the cultured person, the person committed to a belief or cause and the emotionally unstable person. These are noun phrases and some of the concepts adopted were not in everyday use. This also highlights the importance of contemporary or indeed historical usage, for example Amasa Walker's fourfold typology of entrepreneurs (see Chapter 2). Cantor and Mischel's work highlighted the distinction between personality nouns (from which one might arrive at a typology of people) and traits. Whilst nouns categorise people, adjectives categorise behaviours (Hampson, 1988). Such examples lend substance to the interpretivist approach. They also underscore the view of economists such as Schumpeter and Kirzner (see Chapter 2): that entrepreneurs are only entrepreneurs when carrying out such entrepreneurial functions as those that they each (differentially) attributed to that economic role: for Schumpeter the function was 'creative destruction' and for Kirzner it was 'alertness to opportunities'.

The main conclusions that may be drawn from Hampson's work are that personality can no longer be viewed as residing *within* the individual, and that it is a product of social processes resulting from observer and self-observer perspectives. The construction of personality has eight key features (Chell *et al.*, 1991; Chell, 2000):

1   Traits are categorising concepts that are inferred from behaviour.
2   Personality exists metaphorically between individuals (i.e. it is social and relational).
3   There are three types of perspective on behaviour (those of the personality theorist, the lay person and the self) and as such they should be reconciled and integrated into a composite theory of personality.
4   Traits are 'woolly' categories (i.e. they have 'fuzzy' boundaries).
5   Some behaviour has features that are typical of particular traits.
6   Other behaviour has features that are typical of more than one trait.
7   Traits are descriptive categories and are dependent on the interpretation of individuals.
8   Knowledge of personality becomes established through accumulation of data/evidence over time and situations and by the articulation and sharing of knowledge.

However, it could be argued that there is a sense in which Hampson is trying to have the argument both ways: that is, she espouses the view that 'personality resides between people', which suggests that it is constructed through social interaction and in relationships, but also she appears to acknowledge that a person *inherently* has a personality that may be discovered, measured and exhibits characteristics of stability over time. The latter may be adduced from her usage of the term 'constructivism', whose root derives from the work of Piaget and the view of inherent cognitive developmental structures in the individual.

The term 'personality' is rather like the term gravity; both are theoretical constructs that enable us to explain a phenomenon. Gravity cannot be found within the molecular structure of an object, so personality too cannot be found in the neural assemblage of a brain or the genetic material of the cells that make up our bodies. The purported existence of 'personality' within an individual is another variant of the 'Ghost in the machine' argument exposed by Ryle and discussed earlier in the chapter: it is a category error. In adopting the term 'personality' an abstract concept is being used to describe a pattern of behaviour that is publicly accessible. In describing a person's behaviour as, for instance, kind, we do not have to assume the existence of an internal measurable structure that is the trait 'kindness'. Indeed, the reasoning is circular: you behave kindly therefore you have a kind personality; or, because I have measured your personality and shown that you have the trait 'kindness', then I predict that you are likely to behave in a kindly fashion towards others.

If a conservative, unchanging and stable society is assumed in which people develop regular and routine patterns of behaviour at work, in their leisure and in the situations that are familiar to them, then it may not be surprising to see consistencies in behaviour. But, in this single sentence, there are assumptions about the nature of society, of individuals and of social and individualistic behaviour that are taken for granted. Further, if we say we are a product of the society from which we emanate, we surely should put a time and spatial frame on this. We also make implicit assumptions about the socio-cultural and historical influences on institutions that form the structure of our society and concomitant behaviour. Further, both language and meanings change over time and so, in reducing our descriptors of personality to single trait terms, can we claim to know what we (and others) meant in socio-cultural and historical context?

Hampson, however, recognised that 'personality' exists between people, that is, in relationships. It makes no sense to say that a person is shy and retiring, aggressive or kind, except in relation to other people; you can be none of these things in isolation. Your actions and behaviour are exhibited conjointly (Shotter, 1993). Hampson also suggested that there is no difference between personality perception and personality per se. This appears to be a rejection of an implicit internal structure termed 'personality'. In other words, the perception is the *reality*. Table 7.3 summarises and positions personality theories in relation to the assumptions of the social sciences.

Implications for the entrepreneurial personality

The 'entrepreneurial personality' is a noun descriptor and as such is descriptive of a type, not a specific agent or an individual; a person may be typical (or not) of that type (i.e. 'prototypical') (Chell *et al.*, 1991). Moreover, the concept of personality is an abstract concept that is used to explain and describe an intangible phenomenon. The entrepreneurial personality is a social construction; it is a description primarily of a function – social category – within the socio-economy. As such, behaviour is observed and attributions applied to particular individuals whom it is inferred fit the criteria: they operate within the 'form of life' known as entrepreneurship. In these terms, sense is made of their behaviour. These attributions may be in the language of 'traits', but from a lay perspective they are adjectival

Table 7.3 The positioning of personality theories in respect of assumptions of social science

Paradigmatic assumptions	Theoretical assumptions to personality		
	Trait	Social constructionism	Cognitive constructivist
Ontology	Realist – personality has a tangible objective reality; imposes totally on individual consciousness	Phenomenological – the product of conscious minds in relationship, interpreting and contesting subjective realities	Phenomenological – the product of cognitive structures that enable individuals to interpret reality subjectively and relationally
Epistemology	Positivist – knowledge of personality can be established as being true or false, knowledge established objectively	Anti-positivist – knowledge is experienced and interpreted in the 'form of life'	Anti-positivist – personality is primarily subjective experience, but knowledge of it may be established from observed experience
Human nature	Determinism – the expression of personality is determined by individual trait structure	Non-deterministic – the expression of personality is influenced in relationships, therein freedom to choose and construct reality	Non-deterministic – the expression of personality is limited by social circumstances, but not determined by them
Methodology	Nomothetic – adopts the scientific approach; assumes data are hard, tangible facts to be established. Seeks to measure and produce generalisations, especially about the underlying personality structure	Ideographic – attempts to understand the ways in which individuals create their world	Combined nomothetic and ideographic – attempts to combine methods to establish consistencies in behavioural expression of personality with the collection of data on subjective and relational experience. Potential for generalisation about personality in specified contexts

descriptions of behaviour that has been perceived. The entrepreneurial personality is also a cognitive construction; it is possible to infer that entrepreneurs have minds, make judgements and enact behaviour (that we term entrepreneurial) mindfully.

The entrepreneurial personality is a social phenomenon and as such there are social rules that 'govern' what constitutes entrepreneurial behaviour. Entrepreneurship is a form of life; there are implicit rules of the game that are embedded in the culture and socio-economy. To enact entrepreneurship is to understand those rules in a practical-expressive way. What entrepreneurship means in a particular context is socially derived from the situation, comprised of particular relationships and socio-psychological nexus that shape meaning and interpretation. Hence, it is analytically sound in a socio-economy to create a social category labelled the 'entrepreneurial personality' that has 'fuzzy boundaries' into which can be placed individuals who more or less fit the type. Indeed, further analysis might reveal subtle differences between types. However, one does not do this by measuring traditionally conceived traits, but rather socially meaningful person-attributes that it is agreed constitute entrepreneurial behaviour.

Current theory assumes that the essence of the entrepreneurial personality may be best described in cognitive terms: the ability to make judgemental decisions, be alert to opportunities and envision possible futures through creativity and imagination. Indeed, there is an intimate connection between mind and behaviour that reinforces the need to analyse the entrepreneurial persona in these terms. Hence, the theory enables the theoretical development of the entrepreneur as having some important attributes without recourse to *conventional* trait psychology.

Entrepreneurs may well be born with the psychological apparatus to behave entrepreneurially in later life, but the strong social component suggests that there is a role for social learning and personal development.

Social constructionism, social cognition and trait theory

There are clear differences between the three main approaches to understanding personality that have been highlighted in this volume. Table 7.4 summarises what I consider to be some of the key differences. The comparison between the social cognitive and trait theory is based primarily on a reading of Matthews *et al.* (2003: 204–237), whose principle aim is to find a rapprochement between trait theoreticians and social psychologists. For clarity, I have compared these two approaches with the social constructionist approach. Although Matthews *et al.* make a clear distinction between social constructionists such as Harré (Harré and Gillett, 1994) and social constructivists such as Hampson (Hampson, 1988), they argue that Hampson (as discussed in the preceding section) allows for three components of personality: 'the expert', the observer ('the lay perspective') and the 'self-observer'. Accordingly, 'these three aim to arrive at a mutually satisfactory construction of reality' (Matthews *et al.*, 2003: 206). This is problematic as it is unclear from a research perspective how these different perspectives are to be investigated and reconciled in order to construct personality.

Table 7.4 A comparison between social constructionist, social cognitive and trait approaches to understanding personality

Theoretical feature	Social constructionist	Social cognitive	Trait
1 Locus of personality	External social encounters/ interaction	Internal knowledge structures/schema in long-term memory	Internal/biological
2 Research method	Idiographic	Idiographic	Nomothetic
3 Observed behaviour/model	Variable, dynamic and emergent as person negotiates situations	Programmed by experience; processing routines result in revealed consistencies	Causally determined interactionism: P, S (P × S) = B
4 Stability	Individually construed in a range of discourses	Stability of action and behaviour	Stable behaviour patterns present an individual's characteristic style of interacting
5 Predictability	Not applicable	Idiographic methods predict a larger proportion of the variance	Predicts some of the variance
6 Mediating factors	Social context may be infinitely variable	Temperament affects social learning, which affects the development of knowledge structures	Nature of situational factors insufficiently researched
7 Sources of inconsistency	Negotiated relations	Level of activation of internal schema/ knowledge structures	Social feedback and social cues
8 Relationships (R)	Fundamental to the development of meaning and meaningful encounters; language plays a performative role in shaping R	Schema based on: (a) beliefs about R (b) motivation towards R (c) style of action within R	Traits, e.g. agreeableness: where high, expect low conflict/ competition; where low, expect aggression/hostility towards others
9 Psychological basis of personality (perceived or otherwise)	Historical and socio-cultural influences; form of life	Social learning and social influences, e.g. skills, self-efficacy	Socio-cultural beliefs and social influence by significant others,

(*Continued overleaf*)

Table 7.4 Continued

Theoretical feature	Social constructionist	Social cognitive	Trait
			e.g. authoritarianism, individualism/ collectivism
10 Critical issues	Lacks predictive power; language is a precondition of thought and social behaviour; focus is on performative role of language and social practice	Assumes inner theoretical constructs governed by person's genes; social knowledge understood idiographically	Trait explanation is circular; trait measures lack sufficient predictive power; determinants of behaviour should include context – how to measure the psychological dimension

The social cognitive approach theorises that individuals have developed a repertoire of 'processing routines', which enable them to handle social encounters. Individual differences in personality are a consequence of differences in particular social cognitions and associated processing routines. This view of personality assumes that there is an inner locus of personality, that there is some stability in expressed behaviour, that social cognitive dispositions are stored in long-term memory and that there is coherence to personality (i.e. beliefs, emotions, motivations and behaviours are interrelated). This social cognitive approach is consistent with the notion of an active mental life – mind – comprising mental structures, stored memories and constructs that are drawn on and used to construct possibilities in the here and now and also in the future and that may be communicated interpersonally to produce social knowledge and understandings.

However, Matthews *et al.* (2003) go further in an attempt to reconcile the social cognitive approach with trait psychology. 'Traits', they argue, also deal with social behaviour. Traits that deal with a person's characteristic style of interacting are a part of conventional trait theory. Traits predict social behaviour, although it is acknowledged that measures of social cognitions predict a greater amount of the variance in personality. Further, social cognitive processes *may* influence the development of personality traits; as social and self-knowledge builds up a stable cognitive core, personality is formed. Furthermore, if personality resides in social knowledge structures then social cognitive models should show how traits influence social behaviours in specific contexts. It is then incumbent on the psychologist to show how individual differences in social knowledge could be conceptualised and assessed nomothetically. For example the trait 'emotional temperament' is developed initially through interaction with role models and significant others; emotional responses are influenced through feedback, reinforcement and social learning, and people become aware of their emotional responses through discourse with significant others. Another example is the development of self-efficacy (Bandura, 1997, 1999) – a characteristic that is believed to be a crucial dimension of the entrepreneurial personality. Hence, it would appear that developmental psychology is the link between the compilation of a store of social knowledge, socially derived patterns of learnt behaviours and the understanding and application of a set of constructs that describe behaviour (technically traits, but in lay terms 'character').

The basis of social cognitive knowledge is the 'schema', which is a structured set of items of abstract or generic information that are stored in long-term memory.[12] In social psychology, there are self-schema and schema about other people and social roles. Knowledge of one's self is believed to arise through social interaction in which people feed back and reflect their perceptions of one. This process is never complete in that there may be aspects of the self that go unrecognised (for instance the unconscious aspects of the self, i.e. those aspects of which we are unaware) and those dimensions that are not necessarily reflected by others. A person will tend to identify with the social and cultural values of people around them and will make comparisons with others. Such processes help to shape one's notion of one's self. Different self-regulatory mechanisms are used to help ensure the integrity of the self. People feel uncomfortable holding in mind conflicting and inconsistent thoughts – a process known as cognitive dissonance. Hence, people tend to 'resolve' those inconsistencies by manipulation of information, denial and/or choosing what to believe. People also have imagined future selves, such as entrepreneurs enacting a role that involves imagined futures. This indicates the importance of temporal awareness and suggests a link with cognitive development and motivation.

However, these theories do not detract from (rather they tend to reinforce) the idea that personality is context dependent and may vary over short time periods and across situations. Personality may be 'negotiated' in interaction, whilst attempting to achieve their social aims, being accepted by others and conforming to social and cultural norms (Schlenker and Weigold, 1989). This line of thought suggests that personality is at best provisional and dependent on the sanction of others, lending support to the social constructionist view.

Self-knowledge may be potentially available, but not always accessible (Higgins, 1996). Some situations may serve to block some kinds of self-knowledge and its expression, for example, in pressured or stressful situations where a person might temporarily lose confidence. The interaction occurs where certain situations activate particular sorts of self-knowledge and beliefs, thus enabling a person to deal with the situation in a particular way. These self-beliefs might be negative, leading to dysfunctional behaviour or depression (Matthews *et al.*, 2003). This resonates with the work of Markman *et al.* (2005), which indicates that entrepreneurs who fail to realise an opportunity may engage in feelings of intense regret.

Matthews *et al.* (2003: 234) suggest that there are a number of issues to resolve, including the greater ability of ideographic methods to explain behaviour. To achieve this, an initial step should be to assess situations, as traits are more context dependent than has been recognised. The key issues, they suggest, are whether we believe that (a) social knowledge can be measured nomothetically and (b) that social knowledge is supported by cognitive structures in the individual. This brings to the fore the stark contrast between trait psychologists who pursue nomothetic methods and social psychologists who pursue humanistic or phenomenological approaches to personality. However, some social psychologists do accept (b) insofar as they believe that the self comprises a cognitive self-belief structure that organises behavioural expression and provides for a degree of consistency. Applied to the social construction of the entrepreneurial personality, this is consistent with the notion that entrepreneurs (like other people) develop their own 'label set' that they use to describe their own and other people's behaviour, although it leans towards cognitive constructivism insofar as there is an assumed stable structure. Kelly's personal construct theory (Kelly, 1955), moreover, sees the person as someone engaged in interpreting their experience using their own personal construct set. This is a radical interpretation of (b) in that it sees the cognitive structure as unique to the individual and thus at variance with the idea of scientific (in the nomothetic sense) measurement.

In sum, trait theorists assume that behaviours show some cross-situational consistency that relates to broad and narrow traits. However, social constructionists assume that personality is continuously created and recreated through discourse with people: personality resides between and not within persons. Social cognitive theorists assume that cognitive structures in long-term memory represent the person's social beliefs and motivations, giving consistency to behaviour. Such structures or schema are assumed to comprise relatively stable social knowledge that is generally context specific, is best captured through idiographic methods and is dependent on social learning. Social psychological approaches focus on the role of the environment in self-development (e.g. the development of self-efficacy beliefs) whilst social cognitive theories attempt to account for stable structures (the encoding of beliefs and procedural skills). This resonates with the idea of a broader set of person-constructs (see the work of Mischel described in Chapter 5, and Chell, 1985a). The presumption is that social knowledge controls behaviour (to some extent) in specific situations. On the other hand, psychometricians might counter that broad traits (e.g. agreeableness within the Big Five) may relate to social knowledge and social behaviour. This would be combined with narrow traits that may describe self-knowledge, attitudes and cultural values. Also, self-knowledge through the development of a cognitive core may control behaviour over multiple situations, whereas other elements may be linked to specific contexts such as those that cause anxiety (e.g. examinations) and are open to measurement nomothetically. Thus Matthews *et al.* (2003) conclude that there is room for both trait and social psychological approaches to personality!

This further analysis suggests that there is scope to readdress a number of issues in respect of the 'entrepreneurial personality'. Social (and economic) knowledge is context specific and learnt. Social cognitions process information that forms beliefs, skills and self-knowledge, which give consistency to behaviour. As such, they may be related to trait development, for example self-efficacy and opportunity recognition. Here, social knowledge may enable the entrepreneur to recognise a social need; the entrepreneur may be typical of a particular class and as such be 'in tune' with the social group. This social knowledge would then enable the entrepreneur to identify an opportunity that s/he believes is marketable. Hence, the link with trait development is that broad traits give the link to social knowledge and that narrow traits identify co-occurring attributes that are situation specific, for example knowledge, attitudes, skills and values in respect of risk-related behaviour. Clearly, this as yet speculative analysis belies the need for a considerable amount of further research.

Summary and conclusions

This chapter has adopted a meta-analysis of theoretical approaches to the problem of knowledge: how do we know what we know? If we cannot answer this question satisfactorily, how can we claim to inform debate and discussion about the entrepreneurial personality? In tackling this difficult subject head on, distinctions were drawn initially between the various paradigmatic approaches taken to epistemological questions. It was argued that it is crucial to understand the assumptions underlying a theoretical perspective in respect of ontology, epistemology and human nature as they influence fundamentally the choice of methodology. Paradigms are thus meta-theoretical approaches, which may also be thought of as organising discourses that focus attention on the adoption of appropriate tools for either building or testing theory. Social paradigms include a political dimension that tends to value one kind of discourse – the dominant theories that hold sway and are protected by gatekeepers – over the more fragmented, often dissenting voices that pursue novel, often challenging, lines of inquiry. This problem is evident in the pursuit of alternatives to the trait approach, which in psychology/psychometrics represents the dominant paradigm. It is also evident in what is broadly termed 'methodological individualism', where the view of the entrepreneur, for example as a heroic individual, holds sway over the idea that his/her behaviour has been shaped by social influences. This problem is quite stark when approaching the entrepreneur from an economic perspective (see Chapter 2).

This backdrop is important to understand the problem facing psychology:

understanding the nature of mind and its relation to behaviour and the physical world. This reflects an age-old problem, that of dualism: the presumed existence of two worlds – the public and the private. The work of Martin and Sugarman (1996) argues that these two spaces are linked. Human agency is relational: values, beliefs, attitudes and knowledge are developed through social intercourse. A person's reality is shaped by such thoughts – perceptions of their present situation – and an interpretation placed on them that draws on recollections of past events and shapes suggestions of possible futures. Hence, all human behaviour is minded in this way. Moreover, it bridges the notion that there is a dual reality; rather, what occurs is an emergence of actions and behaviour from the interpreted situation. This process is indeterminate in that what at any moment is framing the individual's understanding of future possibilities cannot be predicted.

Mind is not a receptacle for ideas that mechanically affect physical movements (Ryle, 1949), nor is it a mirror that enables some, particularly the scientist, to accurately reflect the external world (Gergen, 1999). Mind is consciousness. Thus, behaviour is 'minded', that is, people behave in particular ways such as intelligently, ineptly, cooperatively, stubbornly, and so forth. From experience and social learning, a person builds up a repertoire of action possibilities – some more familiar than others. They can thus choose how to behave on a given occasion, enabling them to shape further the situation they are managing. According to this analysis, the development of such a label set enables people to understand and categorise the behaviour of other people and, reflexively, themselves, whilst also drawing conclusions about the type of person with whom they are dealing.

Hampson's constructivist approach to personality and her critique of psychometrics was thus positioned. Knowledge of other people comes about through social interaction and, as such, personality resides in the interpersonal space between two interlocutors. Her theoretical position is not entirely phenomenological; she argues, for example, that trait terms tend to co-occur, that there are patterns to the expression of personality and that it is not simply down to the perceiver. Furthermore, she suggests that in order to really understand personality one should take a combination of expert, lay and self-perspectives. How these perspectives are to be combined is not elucidated. However, the development of 'label sets' of descriptors and terms to describe semantic categories is built up by the person recognising 'prototypical cases'. This label set is achieved by processes of recognition and resemblance, acknowledging the existence of ambiguous cases. In this way knowledge and understanding of phenomena, objects, events and other people is in a sense negotiated and may be contested. Thus, cognitive constructivist theory has enabled us to draw eight firm conclusions about Hampson's position (Chell *et al.*, 1991; Chell, 2000):

1   Traits are categorising concepts that are inferred from behaviour.
2   Personality is social and relational.

3   There are three types of perspective on behaviour: the expert, the lay and the self-perspectives.
4   Traits are 'woolly' categories, that is, they have 'fuzzy' boundaries.
5   Some behaviour has features that are typical of particular traits.
6   Other behaviour has features that are typical of more than one trait.
7   Traits are descriptive categories that are dependent on the interpretation of individuals.
8   Knowledge of personality becomes established through accumulation of data/evidence over time and situations and by the articulation and sharing of knowledge.

Some of the implications for the theory of the entrepreneurial personality are that the entrepreneurial personality is a noun descriptor and descriptive of a type, and as such a person may be typical or not of that type (Chell *et al.*, 1991). The entrepreneurial personality is a social construction of a social category within an economy. Individuals that are deemed to fit this social construction, operate within the 'form of life' known as entrepreneurship. However, the entrepreneurial personality is also a cognitive construction, as it is inferred that entrepreneurs make judgements and enact behaviours mindfully. The rules that govern the 'form of life' are embedded in society; thus, what entrepreneurship means in a particular context is socially derived. Adjectival attributions associated with classes of entrepreneurial behaviour suggest that natural categories of behaviour (skills, attitudes, etc.) are made on the basis that they are consistent with social (including business) criteria of what constitutes that class of behaviour; these attributions are inferred from observations and the association of co-occurrence of terms. This suggests that the entrepreneurial persona is primarily socially constructed.

However, given subsequent developments in theory, especially the restoration of trait theory from the challenges of the 1980s, there appeared a need to revisit current thinking in respect of the social cognitive, social constructionist and trait approaches. To this end, Matthews *et al.* (2003) attempt a 'reconciliation'. They highlight the importance of social cognition, memory and 'processing routines', which would suggest that the locus of personality resides in internal knowledge structures and cognitive schema. This is consistent with current entrepreneurship theory that focuses on cognitive as exemplified in the characteristic of 'alertness' (see Chapter 6). Moreover, the cognitive develops with experience and social learning. Hence, it is suggested that the social cognitive may influence the development of traits. For example, interpersonal interaction with significant others (family, friends, authority figures, etc.) affects the development of temperament, which is related to broad traits such as agreeableness. Significant others may also be considered to be role models, from which social attitudes and social mores are learnt. As such, interactions are based on relationships, are socially construed and so there is also the link with social constructionism.

These processes also build up self-knowledge, which shapes consequent social interactions.

This more speculative attempt to reconcile these different approaches suggests that there may be scope to address a number of issues concerning the entrepreneurial personality. Knowledge is context specific and learnt. Social cognitions process information that forms beliefs, skills and self-knowledge, which give consistency to behaviour. However, new situations may require the individual to improvise and learn new ways of handling social situations. Consistent behaviour is perceived by an observer in (trait) descriptive terms. Positive experiences may also be related to the development of traits, such as greater confidence and self-efficacy in handling situations, and opportunity recognition, where social beliefs and knowledge may belie the individual's ability to construct a situation as having economic potential. In sum, this analysis suggests that there is scope for developing further the theory of the entrepreneurial personality as a complex social construction.

Notes

1 We shall distinguish between Truth – the assumption that there is only one and only one absolute, certain and unconditional truth – and truth that is bounded, conditional and accurate within the parameters and circumstances pertaining at the time.
2 It is beyond the scope of this chapter to discuss in detail the various philosophical positions taken historically, but see, for example, Gergen (1999), *An Invitation to Social Constructionism*, for an introductory account.
3 Technically, general statements or propositions.
4 For clarity it is assumed that 'paradigm' in social analysis is being used as a meta-theoretical tool for positioning theoretical approaches at sub-disciplinary level.
5 Deetz also reminds us of the issue of ideology – belief systems that are adhered to by different social groups. Investigations may be carried out in a disinterested way (i.e. have no overt allegiance to a particular ideological position from research that has an evaluative component from the outset). Being 'disinterested' is not the same as being objective; there are still assumptions that may be being made that should be made explicit and recognised.
6 Cognitive constructivism is assumed to have its roots in the work of Piaget, whose concern was to explain child development through empirical means. The problem for many social constructionists is that this and later cognitive theory assumes the mind as an internal receptacle in which concepts and ideas somehow reside. This perpetuates the old dualism of mind and body, theorised by Descartes in *Discourse on Method* (1637), although arguably emanating from Greek philosophers such as Plato in his theory of the forms (ideas) and Aristotle's realist view.
7 The brain, with its neural networks and pathways that become activated through usage, is the source through which the individual is enabled to carry out an action more or less skilfully.
8 The performance of, say, Mozart's piano concerto no. 5 in D major is *not in the mind*, rather the pianist is consciously enacting the piece through coordination of fingers and keyboard. Another example is a diplomat handling a tricky situation:

his or her capability is *not in the mind*, rather it is in the adeptness by which a set of relationships is handled.

9 This ontological oscillation between subjective and objective accounts of reality is how things are. It poses a problem only for those who wish to argue for the reification and incommensurability between positivist and phenomenological paradigms. See the earlier discussion of Burrell and Morgan's paradigms.

10 Wittgenstein was not alluding to Game Theory, which concerns decision analysis in economics.

11 The C5 was a three-wheeled single-occupant vehicle so small that it immediately raised road safety issues. The question that started to tip the balance was this: could someone who was evidently unaware of likely social concerns over a product's on-the-road safety really be classed as an entrepreneur?

12 It is worth noting in relation to a social constructionism the computer metaphor, and the tendency to regard the brain as a receptacle.

8 The heterogeneity of entrepreneurs: cases and colour

Introduction

In the book so far I have reviewed many theories from many perspectives and disciplinary stands. As such, in the previous chapter the necessity for exposing underlying assumptions to position the theory was established; thus, it was possible to position both social constructionism and cognitive constructivism in relation to the trait approach to personality. Social constructionism elevates the voice of the subject, emphasising the socially construed world of the individual through language and discourse and postulating how individuals develop their own set of concepts by which to understand social events, behaviour, themselves and other people. Constructivism assumes an internal cognitive structure that enables the individual to remember past events and consider future possibilities, thereby theorising about how individuals have the freedom to create their own reality. These approaches stand in stark contrast to the methodological individualism of economics, which assumes that: (a) one can derive essential attributes of entrepreneurs by drawing inferences about *what they must be like* to fit the theory; (b) the social aspects of entrepreneurship are not relevant; and (c) behaviour operates mechanistically – it is assumed to be determined by environmental 'shocks' rather than through subtle interpretation and reflection, which rather removes the novelty of entrepreneurial behaviour and the ability of entrepreneurs to do the unexpected.

The aim of this chapter is to present some case studies of entrepreneurial personality, which will be analysed in respect of the tenets of social constructionism and cognitive constructivism. These analyses will attempt to demonstrate in some sense(s) that the entrepreneur attempts in subtle ways to shape and direct their reality and thereby to create a future that they desire. From a cognitive constructivist standpoint, it should be shown that the subject draws on accumulated experience (knowledge) that shapes future decisions. However, with Hampson's cognitive constructivism, I must cast myself in the role of expert observer and as such I am interpreting and judging the actions of the entrepreneurs in the cases. To do this I should reflect on whether there are socio-economically accepted ways of behaving that are indicative of entrepreneurship ('form of life') that I am implicitly drawing upon. Indeed I should attempt to make such criteria explicit. Thus Table 8.1 presents a summary of practical criteria for judging the existence of entrepreneurial potential and the associated expert personality construct.

Additionally, it is worth noting for completeness that practitioners and business economists would look for 'hard evidence' of entrepreneurial performance. For example, at the nascent level, such criteria might include the potential of the business proposition to employ others, for the business to be sustainable for three years or longer and that the business idea has the potential to generate growth and a profitable return on investment. Beyond the nascent level, serial or portfolio entrepreneurs found multiple businesses, employ large numbers, are able to establish their business globally and engage in continuous innovation practices throughout their business career. Furthermore, there should be evidence of the cogency of the idea that is supported by a team of expertise and not solely the entrepreneur/innovator.

In this chapter I will examine the above criteria against actual case

Table 8.1 Summary of practical criteria for judging the existence of entrepreneurial behaviour

Behaviours/skills	Expert term
1 Innovative/creative ability to generate novel ideas	Creativity/imagination
2 Recognition of opportunity	Alertness
3 Awareness of factors conducive to opportunity exploitation	Veridical perception and interpretation, discernment
4 Ability to develop an idea as commercial opportunity	Business acumen
5 Recognition of social need/gap in the market	Social/market awareness
6 Ability to garner necessary material resources	Resourceful
7 Ability to convince others of value of opportunity	Persuasiveness
8 Self-belief, self-awareness and able to make changes	Self-efficacy
9 Trust in own judgement	Self-confidence
10 Ability to manage other people	Leadership
11 Ability to differentiate amongst opportunities	Judgement
12 Ability to manage risk and shoulder responsibilities	Risk propensity, responsible
13 Networking and social embedding	Social competence
14 Ability to overcome institutional and other constraints	Political astuteness
15 Ability to learn the 'rules' and make the right move at the right time	Social learning, adeptness
16 Ability to endure and cope with difficulties	Resilience
17 Skills associated with different stages of business	Multi-skilled, flexible
18 Able to leverage opportunities	Manipulative, innovative
19 Able to go the distance	Commitment, stamina
20 Able to grow and sustain the enterprise	Strategic competence

evidence. The criteria, and in particular the expert constructs that denote them, are complex and multifaceted. For example, research has indicated that creativity requires a degree of playfulness and positive emotional energy (see Chapter 6). On the other hand, evidence of a 'sense of humour' could be interpreted as a means by which someone 'gets by'. Clearly not only should care be taken in applying the criteria, but also evidence of other attributes should be adduced. In the next section I outline the method I adopted.

Case study method

The case study is intended as an analytical tool, not simpliciter as a descriptive account of what is deemed an exemplar of a phenomenon, in this instance the entrepreneurial persona. However, the case is rarely chosen at random; it is selected for analytical purposes to produce insight into the phenomenon in question. The cases were selected primarily for their clarity (i.e. being 'prototypical') despite the 'fuzzy boundaries' of each construct (see discussion in Chapter 7). Case study analysis may be carried out on the assumption that each case is unique – this is consistent with one interpretation of social constructionism – or with the view that case analysis can be used to test theoretical propositions (Yin, 1994) – cognitive constructivism would lend itself rather more to this supposition. Of course, in the strict sense, it is indisputable that every case is unique in time, place and context. But, the tool of analysis is language; therefore the question is whether the entrepreneurial behaviours exhibited have sufficient commonality to be encapsulated in the same terms that would produce a meaningful and veridical account. Phenomenological accounts of behaviour are made explicable in relation to a 'form of life' (Wittgenstein, 1953). Hence Table 8.1 comprises phrases and summary descriptive terms that have emerged in the preceding chapters as redolent of a form of life known as entrepreneurship.

The cases drawn on, in the ensuing pages, are derived from two main sources: (a) face-to-face interview material of small business owners/managers/entrepreneurs and access to their enterprises; and (b) analysis of secondary sources of data of high-profile entrepreneurs/innovators. In drawing down the material from source (a) they cover a time frame that spans 25 years, though for the majority of cases it is less than 20 years. That fact enables me to say in many cases whether the firm still exists. The majority of these firms were developing or nascent enterprises yet to become fully established in their field. I also had data on the socio-economic contexts of many of these enterprises that were not reported at the time,[1] because each case was part of a larger sample. Thus, the results of the sample were reported rather than the individual case. I have also used secondary sources of data as in (b); these are arguably more valuable where they are comprised of biographical accounts. Casson (2005) has suggested a 'self publicist' tendency of entrepreneurs, whilst Ogbor (2000) has argued against the tendency to present entrepreneurs as 'heroes'. This raises the question of whether one can 'trust' auto- or biographical accounts of entrepreneurial behaviour. From a social constructionist perspective, claims to speak the truth are problematic (Gergen, 1999). Scientific knowledge has been privileged; its claims to objective knowledge assume accurate observation and reporting of a phenomenon and the ability of the mind to mirror nature. As minds perceive, interpret and select what shall be the focus of interest, the difficulty of maintaining the assumption of objectivity, where social issues are concerned, is deeply problematic. 'Truth' is dependent on applying social rules, which enable us to extract meaning that is conjointly understood. Thus, in addition, the relationship with the other is a prerequisite of that which is intelligible. Further, to understand whether a new piece of information 'rings true' is to ask whether it makes coherent sense relative to all other facts that we understand and believe to be true. In this sense we can both doubt everything and we can choose to believe (or not) the new information. Thus, as we critically contest the 'facts', we have choices as to what we believe or reject: it must be true because it fits our understanding of other 'facts'; it should be rejected because it does not fit our current understanding; it raises doubts about our current understanding and brings all our beliefs about that particular phenomenon into question. Hence, I shall approach the secondary sources of data with profound curiosity and criticality. I should also confirm that in none of the projects that I was engaged in over the past 25 years were any psychometric data collected. Observations of behaviour were primarily derived from textual analysis of transcribed interview data and reflections of visits to see the entrepreneur. Thus, to a degree, I have drawn on my own impressions and reflections when I (with my co-researcher) met many of these subjects.

I shall analyse each case using the 20 behavioural descriptors of skills and abilities and summary descriptive labels that are derived from the preceding chapters. It might yet be argued that this represents a selected list of attributes as there were surely other phrases and descriptive terms used, for example being 'proactive and taking initiative', 'being restless and adventurous' and as such a 'pioneering spirit'. Undoubtedly this is so, but the expert terms identified in Table 8.1 represent, on the whole, higher order constructs that are indicative of these terms: for example, term 19 encompasses energy (which may exhibit itself in restless behaviour) and terms 1, 2, 3 and 5 are indicative of 'being first in the field' (i.e. 'proactive' and 'pioneering'). In applying this profile of behavioural descriptors to the diverse selection of cases, I have adopted a five-point scale in an attempt to encapsulate 'shades of grey': 1 – not at all X; 2 – not very X; 3 – somewhat X; 4 – very X; 5 – highly X (where X signifies an expert term that summarises the behaviour or skill under consideration). As there are 20 terms, the lowest 'score' is 20 and the highest 100. This enables a more fine-grained analysis of entrepreneurial types based on their adjudged business performance. For example, scores above 80 would suggest superior entrepreneurial performance – indeed world class; a score of 60–79 would indicate a sound performance, whereas a score of 50–59 might be considered average, mediocre or even pedestrian. Scores of 49 or less might be considered to be uninspired or poor – possibly non-entrepreneurial. Whilst the cut-off points are necessarily arbitrary, they do resonate with earlier work that attempted to classify types of *enterprise* performance: e.g. Storey's 'failures', 'trundlers' and 'flyers' (Storey, 1993; Storey, 1994: 117).

It is worth considering the game or 'form of life' such as playing chess, in which both winning and losing are part and parcel of the game. To some extent it is the same in entrepreneurship: for example, an individual may pursue an innovation that fails to take off but on this occasion it is highly likely that the individual would not have met all 20 criteria; for instance, s/he is unlikely to have scored on criteria 5 (social and market awareness), 11 (judgement) and 15 (adeptness). (Here I would remind the reader of the case of Sir Clive Sinclair alluded to briefly in Chapter 7.) Thus, an individual's score may not reach the threshold that would be sufficient to influence observers to adjudge their performance to be entrepreneurial;[2] in lay parlance there would be sufficient evidence to raise doubts. In adopting a social constructionist analysis, it is clear that interpretation is involved at all stages. For research purposes some may be concerned that the approach is too subjective, but it can be made more rigorous by the use of additional judges. Indeed, this is an accepted method in psychology, where 'blind' judges are used to apply a set of criteria independently. The judgements are then compared and an assessment made of interrater reliability. Thus, the cases presented below are illustrative of the social constructionist method outlined above and the expert terms are being used as tools to indicate the form of life rather than an inherent trait within the individual.

The case studies

Table 8.2 comprises the results of analysis of each of the following cases by applying the 20 criteria listed in Table 8.1. These criteria are summarised in the left-hand column of Table 8.2 by adopting the 'expert terms' from the earlier table. In the ensuing pages each case is outlined to give a flavour of the person and his or her enterprise. Then some comments are made on the profile of the subject. Clearly space prevents a more detailed analysis being presented.

'Marilyn'

Marilyn's initial work experience comprised shop work as a teenager on a part-time basis and then on leaving school aged 16.[3] She also worked for a large insurance company as cashier and then telephonist. At 20 she was married and at 37 she was divorced. The latter was a crystallising life experience from which she formulated the desire to do something for herself. Initially, however, this was not running her own business, although the

Table 8.2 Analysis of case study material using 'expert terms' derived from interdisciplinary review

Criterion	'Marilyn'	Jacqueline Gold	Percy Shaw	Simon Woodroffe	Henri Strzelecki	Anita Roddick	Roger McKechnie	'George' of SRB	'Crowther'	Brin and Page
1 Creativity	2	4	5	4	4	5	5	2	2	5
2 Alertness	2	5	5	5	5	5	5	3	3	5
3 Veridical perception and interpretation	2	5	5	5	5	5	5	1	2	5
4 Business acumen	2	5	5	5	5	4	5	1	2	4
5 Social/market awareness	3	5	5	5	5	5	5	1	2	5
6 Resourceful	3	4	5	5	4	5	5	3	2	5
7 Persuasiveness	3	5	4	5	5	5	5	3	2	5
8 Self-efficacy	1	5	5	5	5	5	5	2	2	5
9 Self-confidence	1	5	5	5	5	5	5	2	2	5
10 Leadership	3	5	5	5	5	5	5	4	3	4
11 Judgement	2	5	5	5	5	4	5	1	1	5
12 Risk propensity	3	4	5	5	5	5	5	3	3	5
13 Social competence	3	5	4	4	5	5	5	3	2	4
14 Political astuteness	1	5	5	4	4	5	4	2	2	4
15 Adeptness	1	5	5	5	5	5	5	1	1	5
16 Resilience	3	5	5	4	5	5	5	3	3	5
17 Flexible	2	5	5	4	4	5	5	3	3	4
18 Manipulative	1	5	5	5	5	5	5	3	3	5
19 Stamina	3	5	5	5	5	5	4	3	3	5
20 Strategic competence	1	5	5	5	5	4	4	2	2	5
Score	42	97	98	95	96	97	97	46	45	95

thought had occurred to her. She started to work for a businessman who had just opened a new store. There were no systems in place and a lot of stock disappeared; Marilyn worried about the problem, until her new partner (also a small businessman) encouraged her to walk away from it. She started 'doing the markets' with her new partner (Tom) and then suggested that he 'put her in business'. They leased a shop on the edge of one of the markets and she started to sell women's lingerie and night attire. At first her weekly take was good and she employed part-timers on busy days such as Saturdays. Since that time she has seen a decline in takings.

I asked Marilyn about risks and opportunities. She now stocks the shop with more risqué items and she has some niche customers, in particular she mentioned transvestites. Marilyn claimed to be shrewd with money, but she clearly has a cash flow problem generated by the lack of cash coming in. Standing back from her personal situation, we considered some socio-economic changes that were taking place, specifically in respect of the activity of the traditional indoor market and the surrounding shopping area. Its general decline and the pervasive rumours that the market was to be closed down by the city council suggested an important aspect of the socio-economic context. What could Marilyn do? Why did she not get out? Had Marilyn identified any opportunities and acted on them?

Jacqueline Gold

By way of contrast, I now introduce a further case that I have derived from secondary sources of data – the case of Jacqueline Gold and the company known as 'Ann Summers'. Ann Summers had a male founder, who named the company after his secretary. In 1972 two brothers – David and Ralph Gold – bought the four stores in the Ann Summers chain. In 1979, David's daughter Jacqueline took work experience in the company (earning just £40 a week). She did not like the atmosphere; it was all men and it was perceived to be the sex industry. Jacqueline was to change all that. Two years later, she got the idea of launching Ann Summers' Parties from Tupperware. The parties were to be an all-women affair and were organised around a person's home. Jacqueline worked her way up to Director level in 1987 and in 1993 was made Managing Director and Chief Executive Officer. During that period and beyond she launched different ranges of swimwear, lingerie and sex toys. Ann Summers now boasts over 120 highstreet stores, mainly in the UK, and a turnover of over £140 million. Jacqueline Gold has won several awards for her business performance and she and Ann Summers have been the subject matter of several television programmes; indeed, as a businesswoman she has a high profile.

The social climate and cultural attitudes towards sex began to relax in the 1960s, which facilitated the establishment of the 'Ann Summers' concept in the early 1970s. This liberalisation and emancipation of women was, one suggests, a significant structural aspect of the opportunity that enabled Ann

Summers to take off. It is difficult to cast this concept in terms of a 'market opportunity', because it was so dependent on changes in social attitudes. Even so the company was to face some controversy; in 2000 she fought and won a Dublin court case to continue trading in the O'Connell Street store, Dublin; and in 2002/3 Jacqueline won the case against the government to allow advertising of Ann Summers in Job Centres.

So why, given such changes in attitudes, did Marilyn not succeed whereas Jacqueline's business was turned into a roaring, multi-million-pound success? Jacqueline, I suggest, was able to recognise opportunities, develop them and exploit them. Marilyn unfortunately did not demonstrate this capability. Marilyn was entrapped in a situation that was deteriorating and she had no practical ideas as to how to turn things around; nor did she appear able to cut her losses. For example, Marilyn might have tried the Ann Summers' Party Plan; it would have brought a source of income, some ideas and widened her network of personal contacts and potential customers. She might even have moved the existing business into a different location. All these possibilities were open to her. In this one case, I therefore take issue with the idea that 'anyone can be an entrepreneur'. In applying the criteria, Marilyn scores 42, whereas Jacqueline Gold scores 97. In this analysis Marilyn is someone who scores well below the threshold of what would count as embodying the form of life: 'entrepreneurship'. She is not totally devoid of some of the skills, but the analysis suggests that they should be developed much further. Jacqueline Gold in comparison learnt these skills initially in her twenties and honed them through experience. Jacqueline moved on from success to success whereas Marilyn stood still.

The inventor–entrepreneur: Percy Shaw

Percy Shaw (1890–1976) was born into a large (14 children) and very poor family in Halifax, West Yorkshire, UK. He left school at 13 to earn a living, however he took a commercial course at night school and he also became apprenticed as an engineer. Due to the very low wages he received, he abandoned the apprenticeship; however, he took on a variety of jobs in welding, boiler making and machine tool construction that were to add usefully to his experience. In 1912 he went into partnership with his father; initially they took on odd jobs, repairing household implements and the like. During the First World War several opportunities came the way of the Shaws', including the manufacture of cartridge cases and shell noses. After the war they went into road and path surfacing. By 1930 both parents had died and Percy continued in the same line of business. He made a narrow-type roller, which gave him an edge over his competitors, and he enjoyed 'tinkering' with motorcycles and cars. During this first 40 years there were numerous examples of learning, both through the formal education that Percy chose to do and through social learning (i.e. heuristically through doing, his father acting to some degree as a first role model).

After work Percy would drive over to the Old Dolphin public house in Queensbury. Halifax itself is surrounded by hills, moorland and the millstone grit of the Pennines. In the 1930s, Halifax and the neighbouring town of Bradford boasted many mill chimneys from the local woollen industry. The smoke from the chimneys combined with the mists and fogs that developed on the hillsides, particularly at night and in wintry conditions, made driving conditions particularly hazardous. The country roads between Boothtown and Queensbury are narrow and the land falls away steeply. Drivers would ordinarily have relied on the reflection of the car's headlights on the tram-lines in the road, but along Percy Shaw's route home there were no tramlines and indeed, with the demise of the tram in the towns, tramlines were fast disappearing. This presented a social problem and the realisation that some-thing needed to be done. The story is that Percy Shaw caught sight of a cat in his car's headlights as he was driving home through particularly dense smog. He stopped the car, alighted and realised that he was close to the edge of the road and a steep drop down the hillside. At that moment he had a flash of insight as to the solution to marking the road at night. The cat's eyes were his source of inspiration and in his spare time he set about producing his invention of Catseyes®, which was patented in 1935. Also that year his company, Reflecting Roadstuds, was incorporated, with Percy as Managing Director. Initially there was a problem of getting the company established, but socio-political issues, such as the blackout in the Second World War, helped put pressure on the authorities to get his invention adopted. Percy developed the plant to include a foundry to produce the cast iron base of the road stud, a rubber processing plant to produce the rubber insert and a glass manipulation plant for the production of the glass reflectors. By the 1950s he had achieved manufacturing independence. His next move was to expand into overseas markets, for which he was awarded an OBE in 1965. Although his invention made him financially secure, his lifestyle barely changed and he continued to live in the same house that he was brought up in at Boothtown.

Percy Shaw came up with an ingenious idea, through his problem-solving technical capability and determination at a time of considerable uncertainty. There was no extant market for his invention, but there was a social need that he clearly recognised. He therefore persisted, until others recognised both the need and the solution that he proposed. Percy Shaw was, in the old fashioned sense, a 'self-made man'; he was born with no social advantages and was self-educated. When the time was right he drew on his experience and the knowledge he had gleaned. These were his personal resources, from thence he harnessed the necessary external support and organised the other resources needed to go into production. My analysis gives Percy Shaw a score of 98; he is, in my judgement (and that of others, it might be added), a clear example of an inventor–innovator–entrepreneur. I gave scores of 4 on 'persuasiveness' and 'social competence' for the following reasons: (a) it was an external event (the onset of the Second World War) that precipitated the institutional decision to support Shaw's innovation, therefore it was not entirely down to his persuasiveness even though he was very persistent; and (b) his social competence was relatively high, however he lived in a very narrow world and chose not to break out of that even when he had the wealth to do so; in this respect his sphere of social competence was limited.

Simon Woodroffe

The extent to which prior experience is important is an issue that has been the subject of debate in the literature (Shane, 2000). We have already seen in the case of Percy Shaw that his accumulated experience facilitated his inventive genius, but can experience be transferred from one field to another? In the following case such transference of capability apparently took place. We[4] interviewed Simon Woodroffe in August 1997 only months after he founded 'Yo! Sushi'. Simon Woodroffe's background is in design; he owned a company that designed sets for big rock shows around the world. He knew the creative side of business from the music industry and the business side from 10 years running his own company. However, although he had been successful by the age of 45, he had never made a fortune. He insisted that he was highly motivated to be successful and he felt he could achieve this by moving into retail. Prior to getting the idea for a sushi bar from a Japanese businessman over lunch, he considered a wide range of options. But the idea of a conveyor-belt-style sushi with a brand called Yo! grew on him. He told us then that he had a hotel concept called 'Yo!tel', which he is now bringing into existence. His aspiration then was that 'Yo!' would grow into a worldwide brand; an aspiration that he has now realised.

There were two types of transference of knowledge that took place in the creation of Yo! First, as explained above, knowledge was transferred from running small businesses in the music industry, with particular emphasis on creativity and management experience. Second is the transference of the sushi and conveyor-belt-service concept from Japan to the UK. Woodroffe had conscious intent to establish a worldwide business in the hospitality industry and in this nothing was a matter of luck. The judgement and timing were crucial on a number of issues. Woodroffe researched his ideas and was driven, he told us, by a fear of failure, which he believed to be the most powerful motivating force. The cost of his research could almost be calculated, as he gave up his job and lived off his personal capital. He talked to a lot of people, using an extensive network of contacts, and got enthusiastic about the idea until he felt that he was 'acting as if' and believed he was going to do it: 'after a while you get to believe your own story'.

Critical judgemental decisions concerned marshalling the right resources, in particular the right property and the right financial deals. The process of opportunity recognition, development and exploitation was iterative over a period of 33 months. The milestones included: March 1994 when he got the idea; 1995 when he first met the chef; and 1996 when he had serious discussions with his bank, produced a business plan, convinced a top accountancy firm of the quality of the project, obtained a government loan[5] of £100,000, was turned down by a 'beer company', negotiated property deals on available sites (some of which fell through) and obtained a £30,000 sponsorship deal on audio and television equipment. All these moves depended on carrying out research and finding out information and developing relationships. The development of the opportunity was through the construction of information to produce meaningful ideas and relationships with key individuals. According to the latest website information:[6]

> Woodroffe sold his controlling interest in Yo! Sushi in a £10m deal, backed by private equity firm Primary Capital, which has since invested £3.5m to fund the group's expansion. Woodroffe retains a 22% stake and is now a world renowned business entrepreneur, presenting TV programmes and seminars as well as developing new brand adventures such as Yo!tel!

Using the analytical tool, Woodroffe scored 95: he was judged to score '4' on creativity because his idea was not original; he scored '4' on 'social competence' because, arguably, embedding the sushi bar in a cosmopolitan city like London did not demand the same degree of social competences as might have been the case, say, in the Highlands of Scotland; he scored '4' on political astuteness, primarily because it was not a major constraint; he scored '4' on resilience because, whilst resilience was necessary, the difficulties were relatively lower than those experienced by Gold and Shaw; and although he was flexible (scoring '4'), the different stages and skills required of him were arguably less than those demanded of, for example, Shaw, who had to painstakingly develop his invention before acquiring complex plant and equipment to produce it. Note: this is not to say that Woodroffe could not, if required, manifest greater levels of flexibility but the judgement and therefore the score are based on the extant evidence.

Henri Strzelecki of Henri-Lloyd

Henri Strzelecki[7] was brought up in Poland. His mother's family were in the road haulage business and his father was a civil servant. In 1946 Henri arrived in England as a soldier and remained in England after the Second World War. In those early years, he gathered a great deal of experience and motivation to set up a business of his own. He encountered post-war prejudice against employing non-British men by the trades union and discrimination (as he saw it) by employers towards him. He overcame all of these problems, but first he started at the bottom rung of the ladder. After several nondescript positions, including one in the Double Two shirt factory at Wakefield, he decided that it was time to consider his education and he applied to the Free Polish Government in London for financial assistance. He won a scholarship to Leeds College of Technology and took courses at the College of Art, the College of Commerce and Leeds University. However, his previous employer would only take him back as an order chaser and it appeared that the senior staff of the firm did not like Henri returning with new qualifications, so he looked elsewhere.

Henri's next move was to a clothing manufacturer, Berketex, located in Devon, as a trainee manager. Henri's job was to improve output and quality by achieving increases in efficiency and, if necessary, by replanning the whole department. After three weeks the boss came to see him. Henri told him he knew what should be done, but he could not get people to operate his ideas. He wanted to reorganise the factory floor, but people would not be moved. He realised that he lacked management skills. After six months he left; he and his now pregnant wife moved north so that she could be near her family and Henri took a job as Floor Manager with Alligator Rainwear Manufacturers; this job, he felt, would give him the experience he knew he needed in handling people. Whilst there, he was promoted to Production Manager. The company was experiencing financial difficulties and Henri was given the job of turning it round. He succeeded, but the promised bonus did not materialise; he had been let down again. Shortly after this incident, Henri left. He took a position as a Factory Manager/Designer in a company that produced workwear and protective clothing. Although this was useful experience, a disagreement arose over an under-costed order, which Henri believed would bankrupt the firm. However, he was unable to convince his co-directors and he resigned.

At the age of 38, Henri felt he had something to prove – perhaps only to himself. He knew that at times he was becoming critical and cantankerous. He felt he could do the job better himself and this was, in part, the cause of the disputes. There was only one way to resolve the matter and that was to set up on his own. He came close to purchasing a factory in South Manchester, which produced overalls, but the deal fell through.

Undeterred Henri tested out the sales potential of some outdoor leisure garments that he had designed and found that he could secure orders for this newly created yachting clothing. Now that he knew he had a saleable product, he joined forces with an associate Angus Lloyd and in 1963 Henri-Lloyd Ltd was founded on an initial capital sum of £3,000. The aim was to produce 100% waterproof, foul-weather protective clothing for yachtsmen and industrial uses – a specialised piece of clothing based on high technical standards. It took the company about 10 years to achieve a worldwide reputation. In doing so, Henri became well connected in the industry, attending exhibitions and shows and giving talks. By 1990 he was Director of the London International Boat Show and three other exhibitions over the previous three years and was voted on to the Board of Directors of National Boat Shows Ltd for another three-year term. Henri had also clearly learnt how to manage staff and knew everyone in his factories by name. He developed his own philosophy of management and business ethics. He also set high standards both for his product and the company image.

The decisions that Henri took once trading commenced in 1964 signalled the intention to grow the company rapidly. The key resource issues were: staff – but that was not too much of a problem in a location that boasted a clothing industry; premises – again, in an industrial area like Manchester, factories were available and a second factory was acquired in 1967; and specialist facilities for proofing the garments. The latter proved to be a problem, when the shock of imminent closure of the proofing plant Henri-Lloyd used was announced. Henri made an offer for it and succeeded in buying the necessary machinery and equipment and retaining the experienced workforce. He invited Harold Lindley, one of the top proofing specialists in the UK, to run the company. This proved to be a shrewd move; not only did the company lose only two days of production time, but Henri now had control over the processing and quality of the company's basic raw material.

Further crucial decisions were taken, as Henri consolidated operations in a purpose-built factory opened in May 1976. It was extended and doubled in size in 1978. In mid-1980, influenced by his links with Italian clothing designers, Henri and his co-directors made a strategic move into fashion clothing. After some deliberation, the company decided to produce the clothing themselves rather than sub-contract the operation. This was facilitated by the closure of a local clothing factory in nearby Wigan. Henri was able to absorb the experienced workforce of 35 and commence operations in 1985.

In 1987 a London-based public limited company wanted to buy out Henri-Lloyd. This was perceived to be a threat to the workforce; had he agreed to the sale, he felt that the factory could have been closed down within 12 months and production transferred to some other part of the world. Henri refused to accept the offer and it would appear that his fears were well founded, as the London firm was liquidated in 1989. Angus Lloyd, however, wished to sell his entire shareholding. To allow him to do this and to stave off the predatory London Plc, the Strzelecki family bought out Angus' shares with the financial backing of County NatWest, which became a new minority shareholder of Henri-Lloyd.

In 1983 turnover was £1.6 million with a workforce of 114, but by 1986 turnover had increased to almost £7 million with a workforce of 239. This rapid growth continued with the number of employees increasing to 300, aided by exchanging the Swinton premises for a new modern and larger factory in 1987, and opening an additional 30,000 square feet of factory space at Worsley later in 1988.

Administratively, the company is well organised. The company changed rapidly in its structure over the 1980s decade to allow continued growth in its core business of yachting clothing and its ever-expanding fashion market. A key factor in these changes was the formal appointment of Henri's two sons as Joint Managing Directors in July 1988, allowing Henri to step into the Chairman's role. Today all functional responsibilities are well taken care of, although in the very early days Henri did most jobs himself, including, if necessary, the general cleaning of the factory!

Henri owned few assets and lacked experience and an education when he first arrived in the UK as a young soldier. After demobilisation, he stayed in the UK and began to absorb useful experience, gain an education and take decisions that were to mould his future. Whilst the clothing manufacturing industry was (and still is) in decline in the UK, Henri identified a niche market area that he made his own. The design for his first foul-weather clothing was not taken up by his then employer and so he tested the market, found potential sales and backed himself to found his own company. This was not the only crucial entrepreneurial judgement that he was to make, however. There were several additional decisions that he made to establish the company with a worldwide reputation. Like Percy Shaw before him, he was to be honoured for his achievement, receiving an MBE for the company's export performance. The product may not have required the same imaginative vision as Shaw's invention, but what Henri insisted on was good design, technical excellence and quality in the product. In this sense Henri had a vision of what he wished to achieve and he made the decisions necessary over a period of time to ensure that his goals were met.

Henri's overall score is 96, which is indubitably adjudged to be entrepreneurial. The product was not an innovation in the sense that no one had produced foul-weather gear for yachtsmen before, although in quality and design it showed some innovative elements; he therefore scored '4' on this item. He was undoubtedly resourceful, but in the initial stages of the business his partner Lloyd provided one of the vital resources – finance; he therefore scored '4' on this item. Political astuteness was not demanded of him on a grand scale, but he did show his ability to overcome what he perceived to be institutional constraints; he was awarded a '4' on this item. Finally, it is arguable whether he should have scored '4' or '5' on 'flexibility'. He certainly showed himself capable of carrying out most of the jobs in his line of business; arguably his business partner reduced the necessity for Henri to engage in financial management at the early stages, though this could be contested. Overall, therefore, whether Henri is adjudged to have scored 96 or 97 does not matter, because he falls well within the bounds of the criteria for a successful entrepreneur.

'A vision is something that you see and others don't': the case of Anita Roddick

The above quotation is from Anita Roddick's book *Body and Soul*, published in 1992. Many people know the story of Anita Roddick[8] and the founding of The Body Shop, and, like Henri Strzelecki, one aspect of her business philosophy was ethical decision-making: making decisions not solely or even primarily on rational economic grounds, but rather with social and people's welfare considerations to the fore. The extent to which social considerations are taken into account varies between businesses from the social enterprise, where it is paramount, to the economic enterprise, where it takes second place. However, even in economic enterprises there are often social implications (Chell, 2007a) and The Body Shop is a prime example of this interplay.

Anita Roddick describes herself as a trader first; the model that she embodies is almost arbitrage but for the support of her partner, Gordon Roddick, who has provided many of the complementary resources that she acknowledges she lacks. In setting up The Body Shop, Roddick's motivation was simply to earn a living for herself and her family. As the daughter of an Italian immigrant, Roddick's background in the Italian community of Littlehampton, Sussex and her extended family relations in that small seaside town, she grew up in a small business atmosphere where most of the local cafés were owned by the Perellas. Although Roddick helped out in the Clifton Café, her education was sufficient to propel her to college and into the teaching profession.

She describes herself as a restless spirit. Indeed, rather than take up her first post as a teacher, she went to Paris; she hitched a ride to Greece, and then returned via Geneva, where she talked herself into a job with the ILO at the UN. She comments that she had self-confidence in her ability to sell herself. She then travelled further afield to Tahiti, where she noticed the silkiness of the women's skin, Australia and via several other places; she finished up in South Africa, where she was eventually thrown out for 'breaking the rules'[9]. On return home, she met her husband to be – Gordon Roddick – and they travelled to the USA with the idea of looking for a business opportunity but none was forthcoming. Back home, and now with two young children, the couple tried several small business ventures: a picture framing business, a B&B hotel and an American-style hamburger restaurant. Running the hotel and restaurant proved to be too exhausting. They packed in the restaurant and Gordon – 'an adventurer and dreamer' – took off to 'ride a horse from Buenos Aires to New York' – a mere 5,300 miles on his own for two years.

Anita wanted a small business to occupy her from 9 to 5 that would provide sufficient funds to keep her and two young children. She believed that she had identified a simple need: to sell cosmetics made from natural ingredients and bottled in cheap containers. Her motivation for this particular business opportunity (as she saw it) was her 'irritation with the cosmetics industry'. From her travels she already knew of 12 natural ingredients when she started to look for products for her shop; further, she states that she 'makes no claim for prescience of the rise of the green movement' (Roddick, 1992: 71). Her visit to the bank manager for a loan of £4,000 was turned down initially, until her husband took charge. Having now secured the loan against the collateral of the hotel, she attempted to garner other needed resources, including the premises for the first shop, acquired in 1976, located in Brighton. She required the assistance of a small manufacturing chemist to draw up a list of 25 possible products that the chemist was to produce. These products Roddick poured into containers of five different sizes. She started a recycling scheme with customers to refill the empty containers – a ploy, she states, that was done out of economic necessity rather than care for the environment!

There were several problems to overcome, but Roddick found that the shop appealed to a wide variety of customers; for herself she was 'passionate' about the business concept, and researched and experimented with ingredients and products. In the summer of 1976 – the hottest on record – Roddick decided to open another shop: this decision, by her own admission, was 'neither sensible nor pragmatic' (Roddick, 1992: 84). Roddick appeared always to think intuitively and trust her gut instincts (Allinson *et al.*, 2000; Sadler-Smith and Shefy, 2004). In a sense she could be said to 'specialise in judgemental decision-making' (Casson, 1982), but not in the 'rational-economic man' interpretation of that concept.

With her husband now abroad, Roddick visited the bank again and was turned down on the grounds that it was 'too soon'. Undaunted, Roddick procured the much needed finance – £4,000 – from a friend and associate's boyfriend in exchange for 50% of the business. The second shop was opened in Chichester in September with her associate, Airdre, running it. From an economic perspective this could be construed as a poor decision; on the other hand, it got the business up and running more quickly. Roddick took a further risk the following year, sourcing supplies of her products from a young herbalist. However, the risk paid off. On Gordon Roddick's return, he took over the bottling and they decided to sell the hotel. Gordon had further ideas for expanding the business. They opened two further shops and the idea of franchising was the way they moved the operation forward. In the next few years they opened shops in Brussels, Stockholm and Athens. The bottling operation was moved from the garage to an 'old furniture depository' and the young herbalist was invited to give courses to staff about the products. Anita attended seminars given by the big names in the cosmetics industry – Revlon, Estée Lauder, etc. – but she felt uncomfortable in this environment. The idea of 'connecting' socially, and not solely in a business sense, was fundamentally important to Anita. She even describes this need as a woman's way of doing business – an idea that resonates with a gender perspective of women's approaches to situations (Gilligan, 1982) and to ways of doing business[10] (Brush, 1992). There is a sense of the 'extended family' in the organisational model that she adopted to grow the business. Furthermore, she demonstrated considerable leadership (Witt, 1998), using informal methods and strongly communicated messages to persuade, cajole and muster the human and social capital required.

Arguably, Anita Roddick is a Schumpeterian-style entrepreneur: she disliked the cosmetics industry at that time; according to her, it had no creativity, it was dishonest and it spent an obscene amount on packaging and advertising, thus rendering the products exclusive and over-priced for the average woman. So, she innovated and created a novel product concept that was affordable to the average housewife and mother. She believed that she 'broke all the rules', even down to selling perfume as a simple raw ingredient (Roddick, 1992: 95). 'Everything in those days was a learning process . . . and we just loved change' (ibid.: 96). It is hard to argue that Roddick pursued her idea because she 'saw a market need', although 'alert to an opportunity' would be a reasonable description of both her and her husband's behaviour. But lighting on the cosmetics industry as she did was a gamble that she (and Gordon) made work through a combination of 'inspiration and perspiration', though in what proportions is impossible to calculate! It was a gamble because culturally there was not much interest in natural products in the 1970s; environmental concerns and the green movement did not take off until the mid-1980s. In that sense, Roddick was ahead of her time.

She claims, however, that she was primarily a trader and that the social issues were of secondary importance. What is interesting is how she balanced the issues of conscience (social) with the economic. Roddick revived what many businessmen had done before her: combining altruism and philanthropy to help support the poor and needy.[11] Roddick extended her net beyond the shores of her own country: for example, to create employment in Easterhouse in Scotland, to set up a Health Care Foundation (with Richard Branson), to support Amnesty International in Brazil, to open The Body Shop Day Care Centre in Romania[12] and to develop the 'Trade not Aid' campaign. Once again, Roddick declares that she felt that they were breaking the rules, but what they were now intentionally doing was raising the public consciousness of various social and environmental issues (Roddick, 1992: 129). Certainly in the 1980s, there was the development of an 'enterprise culture' where individuals were encouraged to 'go it alone' and wealth creation divorced from social issues was prevalent in the UK. Indeed, Thatcher famously was quoted saying 'there is no such thing as society' (see Chell, 2007a). By 2004 The Body Shop had swelled its number of stores to almost 2,000, serving over 77 million customers worldwide.[13] According to this source, The Body Shop was voted the second most trusted brand in the UK. From 1984 when she received the Veuve Cliquot Business Woman of the Year award, Roddick had received numerous awards from the OBE in 1988 to the Dame Commander of the British Empire in 2003. She continues to court controversy,[14] having in March 2006 sold The Body Shop to L'Oréal for a reported sum of £652.3 million.

In sum, Roddick is an instinctive entrepreneur who produced a sustainable and highly successful business concept, in conditions of considerable risk and uncertainty, primarily due to the fact that, at the time of founding, there was no discernable market. She was, however, sensitive to women's needs and reasoned that if she experienced a need for cosmetics that were sold in small quantities at affordable prices then that must be true of the vast majority of women and mothers. In this her judgement was right. However, she could not have known that; nonetheless she was confident in her judgement and backed it. Connectedness and a sense of real social issues were not far from her mind and balancing these was important to her, but trading and producing an income to support herself and her family was the primary motivation. She used her many talents to identify and capture essential resources and sources of supply and she was most certainly an innovator in her field. Since then, The Body Shop product concept has been copied by retailers worldwide – a testament to its perceived worth. She came up against powerful institutional structures, in particular the banks, but she was able to work around such obstacles with guile and ingenuity. She never suggested that the phenomenal growth of The Body Shop was solely down to her. She had a partner in her husband who complemented her in the skills and abilities he brought to the 'backroom' organisation of the business. Like many entrepreneurs, having someone at one's right hand is not unusual (Chell and Baines, 1998; Chell and Tracey, 2005).

Anita Roddick's overall score is 97; her business acumen fell down when she sold a 50% share in the business and on several other occasions she relied on her partner, Gordon, to supplement her business sense. Likewise her judgement (i.e. ability to differentiate between opportunities) only occasionally let her down. Her strategic competence was instinctive, and her desire to source products from around the world had a touch of brilliance about it, but the strategy of franchising the business was largely down to Gordon's influence. Thus on these three skills she is judged to score '4'.

Team entrepreneurship: Roger McKechnie

Towards the end of the 1990s decade there was a reaction to the idea of entrepreneurs as 'heroes' (Ogbor, 2000) and the notion that entrepreneurs created their businesses single-handedly (Birley and Stockley, 2000). This particular case was founded by a team, although there was a clear leader. We interviewed Roger McKechnie of Derwent Valley Foods in March and April 1993.[15] McKechnie, born in 1941, was educated at Newcastle University in Economics and took a job in Marketing with Proctor and Gamble. The training he received he viewed as 'absolutely invaluable'; he spent some time in London with the company before returning to the North East, where he married a doctor still completing her training. Roger left Proctor and Gamble and found a job in Peterlee at Tudor Crisps, where he was appointed head of marketing. The company was American owned, but because the company was doubling its turnover every 2–3 years they were left alone until around 1980, when they sold the company to Smiths Crisps. There was pressure on McKechnie to move to the London HQ, but he refused.

In 1979–1980, the UK was in the depths of recession and there were few Marketing Director jobs around, especially in the North East. McKechnie now started to consider what he could do for himself. He rejected the idea of marketing consultancy and considered his other option:

> [We] could get into snack foods; crisps or something that I knew. After it became clear that it ought to be snack foods because we saw a huge

number of opportunities that we were actually turning down in this big company [Tudor/Smiths] because they were too small. Whereas they [Tudor/Smiths] had a criterion of £5m turnover in the first year or it wasn't worth launching; we did an exercise, which said that, if you got £1m turnover on 4–5 products in the first year . . . we could pay ourselves the same money as we were getting at Tudor, earn £100,000 profit on £1m and start to build up the capital base. . . . . The only problem was a bit of cash . . .

McKechnie and a 'couple of mates' wanted to do their own thing; raising the money proved to be 'very easy' and as McKechnie had no job or alternative in view he believed that fate was pushing him in that direction. The company started in 1982 with four people working in a shed. They had raised half a million pounds with no product, no brand and nothing but an idea. The four took on different functional roles: two of them covered marketing, advertising and selling, one was experienced in production and the fourth assumed the accounting role. McKechnie describe the team as a 'team of oddballs' – different backgrounds, experiences, ages, attitudes and personalities. Roger was 'the dreamer', Keith had a terrific brain for figures, Ray was the 'finisher/polisher' and John was pragmatic. They discussed ideas critically and then Keith would 'do the numbers'; John could work out what was required to produce the goods and it would appear that there was sufficient know-how in the team to make rapid informed decisions.

The idea for the brand 'Phileas Fogg'[16] was McKechnie's. They believed that they had to do something different if they were to break into the snack food industry:

We actually had in our shed 2000 packets of snack foods from all over the world stuck on the wall. From that 2000, we selected six and did some very detailed research on that six. [We] identified the six, which we were absolutely certain would sell to adults in the UK at a crazy high price . . . Out of the six, we got down to the four that we could physically make . . . they were from California (corn chips), Mexico (tortilla chips), the Far East (Shanghai nuts) and France (croutons).

'Phileas Fogg' was the 'umbrella' – a product strategy that enabled them to tie together the four mini-brands. Developing the concept, they wanted the thing to be 'wholesome, natural, no "E" numbers, beautiful packaging . . .'. They recognised that this projected the product to the top of the range and so the packaging had to be perfect. The 'umbrella' also allowed them flexibility: if one of the products were to fail, they could remove and replace it without upsetting the overall concept. The concept also had to convey 'cosmopolitan', 'old-fashioned', 'interesting', 'up market', 'snooty' . . . not easy, but 'Phileas Fogg' captured it perfectly. After a full day's meeting, and not until they had consumed quite a few pints of beer, Roger came up with the idea, which they all laughed at and dismissed! The next day, undeterred, Roger brought up the idea again. Now they took it more seriously; they researched it and discovered that it was not a registered trade mark. Moreover, McKechnie had the idea that they should put a letter on the back of the packet from Phileas to his aunt Agatha: 'It actually enabled you to describe the product in the sort of words that you would never be allowed to use in advertising. . . . Also because they were funny products and we did not have a hole in the packet so people could see them . . . you had to do something to get people interested.'

The market response from the multiples was 'terrific': 'suddenly from doing one million in 3 years, in the second year we did £1.8m and in the third, we did £4.8m'. The strategy was simple: Phileas Fogg had to be the best in the business and 'we wanted the best customers in the business'. They targeted the best delicatessens, the top off-licences,[17] the premier pubs and the highstreet names in food retailing. Once established, working with these companies was demanding; they had to deliver to their quality standards and occasionally they had to conduct some 'quite tricky negotiations', but they always looked for a 'win–win' deal for both sides. McKechnie was emphatic that the marketing aspect of the business was crucial. The imaginative concept enabled them to make a decent margin; this compared favourably with other snack foods on the market – ordinary bags of crisps at 5p that were being undercut but could only compete on price or go under. Consequently, some of the big names in the industry were in financial straits at this time.

The team worked closely together and McKechnie felt that none of them could have achieved the establishment of Phileas Fogg and Derwent Valley Foods on his own. They shared problems, took each other's advice and respected each other's different contributions to decision-making. They were each educated to degree level and covered biochemistry, chemical engineering, classics and economics. This was coupled with experience in three blue chip companies in fields such as marketing and accounting. Ray initially trained with Unilever in marketing and subsequently worked abroad in several European countries. John (the chemical engineer) had worked for Chemical Pesta Foods, a subsidiary of Hovis-MacDougall, before joining Tudor Crisps. He then moved to Hinton's supermarkets where he was responsible for repackaging bulk items under their own label. Keith with a biochemistry degree initially worked at Torry Fish Research Station in Aberdeen. He did not like being a research chemist and became a bookie;[18] having decided that was not for him either, he took a degree in Personnel Management and a job as personnel manager at Tudor. He then side-stepped into marketing at Tudor and his career progressed from there. When they came together, as a founding team, their individual roles emerged naturally and informally. Indeed, the culture of the company is relaxed and informal, with a casual dress code. McKechnie explained that they 'thrived on change'; otherwise, without new challenges they would get bored.

We asked McKechnie whether he actively sought out opportunities. He initially replied 'yes', but qualified this by saying: 'you do not actively seek them out. Opportunities just tend to go past you and you grab them – a lot of people do not. A lot of people see them going past and say "Oh, we should have done that", but they did have the chance at one point'. This statement is open to some interpretation. On the one hand, it suggests that McKechnie recognised opportunities 'without search' (Shane, 2000). Also he believes that the opportunities were there in some (probably intangible) sense for others to recognise, but whilst he believed that they have perceived an opportunity, these 'others' did not enact it. It is only when they have seen it developed and enacted that they believe that they should have pursued it – that is, retrospectively. McKechnie elaborated on the process further. Initially 'opportunities' are merely ideas, which the team sift and test to see if they would work in practice – a sort of 'reality test'. If an idea does not pass that test it is simply discarded. Rather like Anita Roddick, they sourced ideas during their travels abroad. It is the team, however, that developed the idea: Roger and Keith tended to be the originators, whilst John works out how they can be developed as products and Ray 'turns good ideas into brilliant ones!'

This case is important because it highlights a number of crucial aspects of entrepreneurship. First, the case (like The Body Shop) raises the question of the motivation of entrepreneurs. McKechnie pursued the notion of working for himself out of economic necessity; he needed to earn a living, but had he chosen to relocate to London or abroad his career would no doubt have been assured. Personal and social reasons were a strong element in his decision. Second, a potential business starts with an idea, but this is not necessarily an opportunity. The idea must be tested against what is known (structural constraints) before it can be considered to be an opportunity. There is then the process of unknown and uncertain duration as the germinal opportunity is developed. Here, moving from 'snack food' to the Phileas Fogg brand constituted a huge leap in opportunity development. The next step was how to exploit the opportunity and how to make it work: did the sums work out? Could they make sufficient, pay themselves a living wage and make a profit? Did they have the know-how to produce the goods? This leads to the third crucial aspect of the process: the human and social capital that ensured sound judgement on key decisions. As a team, they had collectively considerable knowledge, know-how and experience. They had a wide range of contacts that enabled them to deal effectively with business, highstreet retailers, industrialists, district council, governmental agents and financiers. They had a mix of know-how that included product and industry knowledge: for example, they could work out likely sales in the pub chains; they were able to deftly negotiate with highstreet retailers; and they could estimate the likely size of the market, the margin and profitability. Their estimates proved to be conservative and, in fact, the business grew more rapidly than anticipated. However, at the time of the decision, facing an unknown future yet with a plan that was sensible, they were able to secure the initial loan capital they needed.

Ten years on, having made a success of Phileas Fogg, McKechnie and the team sold the business to KP – the reason? The business was becoming very big and required a further injection of capital. A company like KP, with the infrastructure of sales and marketing, was better equipped to take it to the next stage. McKechnie stayed on in a non-executive capacity to ensure that the product concept was protected as originally conceived. Later, he used some of his wealth to create a venture capital fund to support nascent entrepreneurs in the region. Where is he now? According to our sources he has recently set up another company based in Consett and to do so he has teamed up with one of his previous partners, Keith Gill. The social connections, relationships and sense of place are quite marked in this case.

I adjudged Roger McKechnie to score 97; his idea was brilliantly innovative and worthy of the '5', as evident in the instant success of the product. Whilst he showed 'political astuteness' it was probably most evident in the necessity to overcome some of the cultural constraints that is antipathy to entrepreneurial behaviour embedded in the North East. Fortunately for him, the regional authorities wanted to change this culture and needed exemplars such as Roger to 'fit the bill'. In that sense he was arguably pushing against an open door and for that reason he has scored a '4'. Likewise, on 'stamina' and 'strategic competence' he has scored straight 4s. He and his team did not 'go the distance' with Phileas Fogg and instead they sold out; this is not being judged to be the wrong thing to have done, rather it is the manifest behaviour that is being scored. Finally, it appears to be the case that, strategically, other members of the team should also be given credit and, perhaps, whilst the team might have scored a '5' each member's strategic competence would be adjudged on its merits.

When things don't quite work out: 'George' of 'SRB'

There are few reports of business failure and yet the vast majority of business start-ups fail within the first three years. In 1998 I reported on the critical details of a nascent business that failed due to malfeasance by a family member (brother), landlord and solicitor (Chell, 1998). Hopefully, only a minority of companies have such bad luck, but things can go wrong; in our experience it may only be one decision that can turn the fortunes of a nascent business attempting to establish itself into a failing business, losing turnover and profitability. Despite the fact that traditional industries may be in decline, many of our cases show that it is possible to swim against the tide if one has a resoundingly good idea and can develop a niche market around it. Our next case is in the Ship Repair Business and to protect the personnel concerned we will label the company SRB.[19] George was the MD and made the strategic decisions, looked after sales and the order book, while his business partner of longstanding, Bill, supplied the technical ingenuity. Also part of the team was Mary, who managed the office and was a first line manager on the administration side of the business, whilst Jack managed the workforce, which fluctuated, but in 2000 it was eight strong.

Between 1995 and 1999, SRB employed about 24 people and they were based on a much larger site, with good facilities for ship repair work. The aim was to become more involved in ship repair of medium-sized vessels; however, George had not considered the fact that there were too few medium-sized vessels in the area requiring repair to make a profit. This constraining situation necessitated taking on other kinds of work, which was less profitable. The rent and rates on the larger site proved to be too high, bumping up SRB's overheads. To make matters worse, shortly after moving to the larger site, a rival engineering company set up in direct competition with them further along the river (until that time they had no local competitors).

Despite these difficulties, George believed that SRB would have survived had it not been for another incident in 1998 that plunged them further into financial crisis. They tendered for a contract in partnership with a large civil engineering company that was to sub-contract the work to them. This contract was badly drawn up, with costs that were not made explicit and too much, apparently, was taken on trust. SRB lost £80,000 on that job. Most of the losses stemmed from the transportation and under-loading of underwater piles. SRB paid for the hire of barges to transport them, expecting to be reimbursed, but because there was no documentation to that effect they were left to foot the bill. The civil engineering company accepted the responsibility for what had happened, but they were not in a position to fund the losses incurred by SRB. However, they subsequently sub-contracted work to the smaller company – some of which was quite lucrative.

The 'bad debt' that SRB had incurred, combined with a downturn in the industry and the very high fixed costs of the company's premises, meant that SRB had to do something drastic in order to survive. This meant reducing the company's overhead costs – staff and property rental. They reduced the staffing complement from 24 to 12 and moved to much less salubrious premises nearby. They also shifted focus from ship repair to fabrication work that made lower margins. The company had survived and was now becoming profitable again. However, George admitted that the future of the company was still uncertain and, according to Mary, it was impossible to look more than one month ahead.

George had had an idea for growing and developing the business, but his judgement had, on this occasion, let him down. Both he and his co-owner had been in related businesses prior to moving into ship repair; they were both from the area and they had relevant and complementary skills. What perhaps was lacking in their judgement on this occasion was an economic purview of the industry and the direction in which it was heading. Despite the setback, however, they soldiered on; they could only have modest ambitions for the company, but they were determined not to let the rest of the workforce down. George's vision was to build new office space and a covered work area for the workforce. But he did not envisage making much money from the current business and he was developing a side line in e-commerce. The latter he believed could be run alongside the present business. He had clearly been stung by the flawed contract and he acknowledged that:

> In my heart and soul I know that's (the internet company) where my future is. Because if you look at this business, you could sell everything off, put the money in the bank, and make money in another business. . . . Why struggle just to pay wages? But at least we're keeping people employed. It's a hard world out there, it's a hard world.

George scored 46 and as such is adjudged not to have an entrepreneurial profile. In particular, his perception of factors conducive to opportunity exploitation (item 3), business acumen (item 4), market awareness (item 5), judgement (item 11) and adeptness (item 15) let him down badly. Only on leadership (item 10) did he reveal some of the ability required to be enterprising; on all other criteria he was manifestly below par.

'Frank Crowther'

There are several companies that I have visited over the years where there was a fine line between success and failure, and where the judgemental decision was crucial to get right. Take a modest sized company in West Yorkshire that produced men's trousers. At the time when we[20] first visited this company in 1987 it had doubled in numbers employed to 80, and in the previous year acquired a second factory about 10 miles away. The company produced to order to up to 600 independent retailers, many of which were household names. They were constantly looking for further orders and would add up to 100 new accounts per year. The owner and MD, Frank Crowther,[21] and his wife had bought the business 10 years ago and they were taking it upmarket in terms of quality of the product. Crowther appeared to be aware of the competitive climate in the industry generally. He could point to expansion of the business over the past 10 years, establishing a market and a brand name. Of course, they were operating within constraints; cash flow was an ever-present problem and typical for a small business, whereas other constraints were related to the nature of the industry and production process. A critical problem was the sourcing of supplies by the highstreet multiples from abroad in low-cost countries. However, they also had a problem of space and productivity that was a consequence not of technology, but of variation in orders.

Despite working in such a constrained environment, Crowther had steered the company well and the growth trajectory looked set to continue. In December 1987, they had a full order book and they were looking at the possibility of taking on more staff and expanding further. The company took on further workers to the point where it had expanded to a staff of 100. However, by May 1989 the company had gone into receivership. What had gone wrong? The turning point appeared to be reliance on repeat orders from the large highstreet retailers. One such large order had underpinned Crowther's decision to purchase and refurbish the second factory. Publicly[22] the company blamed high interest rates and the influx of foreign imports. In a sense this was probably true, because once their major customer[23] had defaulted on them, they were faced with what proved to be an impossibly difficult competitive situation. However, the company was sold as a going concern and 35 jobs were saved.

Crowther scored 45 and was manifestly not an entrepreneur. His profile is similar to that of George and was shown to be poor on judgement and adeptness. To a degree he was not culpable in that he was badly let down by a company that he had begun to supply; on the other hand, he misinterpreted the signals (item 3), demonstrated low levels of business acumen (item 4), was insufficiently aware of the market (item 5) and lacked strategic competence (item 20). On all the other dimensions his profile was below par to go as far as to consider him to be an entrepreneur.

When things work out: the World Wide Web and new ways of doing business – the case of Brin and Page and Google

The final decade of the twentieth century saw the development of an IT revolution that has created the potential for new arrangements and ways of doing business through information networks of global proportions (Castells, 1996). The creation of the infrastructure that enabled this phenomenon – the World Wide Web[24] and the internet – resulted in the emergence of the 'dot com' enterprise. The creation of websites made the internet accessible; nascent dot com businesses could produce their catalogue of products or services on line, enabling customers to browse 24/7 and place an order. This became known as the 'get rich quick' dream that youthful nascent entrepreneurs in the mid-1990s were to pursue. An inordinate amount of investment capital was thrown at such businesses on the assumption that they would become profitable. In 1998, for example, Lastminute.com was launched by Martha Lane Fox and her business partner Brent Hoberman; it was to be floated on the Stock Exchange at a paper value of £316 million. However, the dot com bubble was soon to burst. The valuation of e-commerce stock peaked at around March 2000 and by January 2001 values had dropped 25-fold or more and hi-tech companies listed on NASDAQ stock market index fell by 54%. Three hundred and ninety billion dollars had been wiped off the value of Microsoft; 210 dot com companies were shut down in the USA in 2000. This suggested the fragility of the 'new economy', but the greed that appeared to drive this phenomenon was by no means the whole story; socio-cultural and a range of structuring elements in the environment were also salient (Castells, 1996; Chell, 2004). This makes it particularly interesting to examine cases that actually came through and developed a sustainable business. One such case was Google.

Google was developed by Sergey Brin and Larry Page, whilst they were doctoral students reading computer science at Stanford. It took them just five years to turn this idea into a multi-billion dollar enterprise with global reach. How did they do that? The socio-economy and culture of Silicon Valley, the notion of technopoles and new industrial spaces are well documented (Saxenian, 1993; Castells and Hall, 1994). Further, the history of Stanford University as *the* west coast institution of higher education with a successful record of spinning out science and technology-based enterprises was robust and supported by a network of knowledgeable venture capitalists who had helped launch and develop such enterprises to become household names.[25] This cultural milieu structured situations and shaped attitudes, and it seemed that doctoral students like Brin and Page were actively encouraged to consider enterprise development and acquaint themselves with venture capitalists who visited Stanford (Vise, 2004).

Brin and Page were not typical entrepreneurs – or so it seems. Their parents were highly educated. Brin's parents were Russian Jewish immigrants who had fled their country due to anti-Semitism when Sergey was six years old. His father taught mathematics at the University of Maryland; Sergey was advanced for his age at Maths and took an undergraduate degree in Maths and Computer Science at 19 years of age. He received a National Science Foundation Fellowship after graduation that enabled him to study computer science at Stanford. Larry Page's father was an authority on Computer Science and artificial intelligence, based at the University of Michigan. His mother was a consultant in computer science with a Master's in that subject. He followed his father and brother by attending Michigan and taking an undergraduate degree there in computer engineering with various business courses. A few months into his doctoral studies at Stanford Larry's father died, aged 58.

Larry Page and Sergey Brin became good friends at Stanford, though their personalities and skills are said to be complementary. Brin is practical, a problem-solver and an engineer, with a lightening fast mathematical brain; he is also outgoing and enjoys sports. Page is more reserved, a deep thinker and curious, wanting to know why things worked (Vise, 2004: 35). Both were researching issues to do with searching the internet for information – a task that was not easy in the mid-1990s. Page started to use the search engine AltaVista and discovered that, unlike other available search engines, it threw up 'links'. He focused on what might be gleaned from such links. To do this he said that he would download the whole of the web on to his desktop!

The general idea was to be able to abstract relevant information from what were essentially huge amounts of random data. Page's theory was that the number of links indicated a website's popularity. Using this concept he developed a link rating system that he called PageRank. As with most technological innovations, the next stage was to develop a prototype, which was used internally at Stanford. PageRank went beyond matching search words with words on web pages; it put the search results in logical order. The next key step was to brainstorm the name and in 1997 they came up with the name Google. Brin kept the home page simple, in contrast to the busy web pages with flashy ads and dynamic computer graphics. To develop the concept further required considerable computer power and, whilst they received some support from Stanford, they needed considerably more cash. Their initial attempt to license the technology to AltaVista fell flat, but just as things were looking bleak they were introduced to the business angel Bechtolsheim who, reportedly, wrote them a cheque for $100,000. They left the PhD programme in a bid to look for ways to commercialise Google.

In 1998, they moved their nascent business into a garage and took on their first employee. After five months they were able to move to offices in Palo Alto, where they developed the business in an informal and relaxed way. The aim of the business venture was to enable people to find information on the internet faster; to produce a quality product fit for purpose. There were a couple of developments that facilitated their endeavour: the competition declined and they got some free publicity in PC magazine. The resources that they had invested in were just three: hardware, software and talented people to work for them. However, by Spring 1999 they were running out of funds; licensing did not seem to be an option, the finance they needed was larger than would be available from a business angel and so they looked towards the venture capital market. The key issue for them was how to get the backing *without* losing control of their business. The upshot was that in June 1999 they got two high-profile venture capital firms to support them and invest in Google Inc. to the tune of $25 million. There was still the problem, however, of how Google was going to make any money.

They were perhaps surprisingly economical with their purchases of hardware and other resource acquisitions. Their eighteenth employee, Reese, helped them devise software to ensure the reliability of Google. Within a month they had increased the number of computers to 2,000; they built redundancy into the system so that if one cluster of computers went down, another would be available with back-up copy. Brin and Page had an issue with flashy irrelevant advertising; pragmatically, they decided that focused relevant adverts were the answer if they were to create a sustainable business.

A number of things happened that helped Google Inc. to grow: the dot com bubble burst, releasing a pool of talent; Google Inc. moved to larger premises to house its by now 85 employees, where it developed a family atmosphere and culture that looked after its employees well. Microsoft lost a major legal battle and started to back off from entering certain new markets. From a survey at about this time, Google emerged as the leading search engine, thus giving it further impetus to look worldwide and develop the Google site into other languages. Now, with growing recognition, Google did a deal with Yahoo to provide Yahoo with its search engine capability. This now meant that by June 2000 Google Inc. was the world's largest and most comprehensive search engine – quite a feat in its very short history.

The Google story raises a number of issues. Search engines (albeit not very good ones) already existed, so does Google represent an incremental or a radical innovation? There were a number of institutional, structural and socio-economic factors that, arguably, shaped the environment in which Brin and Page were operating. Institutional factors include the history of technological innovation that had been emerging from Stanford since the success of Hewlett-Packard. Consequently, the Venture Capital industry directed at technological spin-offs from the university was well developed institutionally and well embedded in Silicon Valley. Socio-economic issues were also a feature; Brin and Page did not appear to be motivated primarily or initially by wealth creation, rather they recognised a problem that they were exercised to solve. This represented a challenge by anyone's standards and not only to attempt but to succeed to pull it off was quite extraordinary. Moreover, the concern for the quality of the product and the aim to enable people to find information more quickly was also of considerable social benefit. Arguably, there was a 'gap in the market', because the search engines that existed were of relatively poor quality, but that is perhaps a facile construction made by others with hindsight. It would appear that, in economic terms, there was a state of disequilibrium, especially as major players like Microsoft were temporarily disempowered and were backing off from the development of new products. This, in a sense, was a highly potent structuring factor that left an opportunity to be grasped. Furthermore, the association with Yahoo helped Google make a step change in size and speed at which the enterprise could be moved forward. Whilst they lacked control over resources, especially finance, Brin and Page showed considerable adeptness in leveraging more from less, thus demonstrating business sense. As 'agents', aspects of their personalities showed through: they were confident in their judgement and backed themselves to succeed; they had considerable technical and problem-solving capability; they had integrity; and they had an informal leadership style. Finally, we observe that there was also a strong sense of place, as is evident in several of the other cases we have highlighted.

I have given Brin and Page jointly a score of 95 on the grounds that it is very difficult from secondary sources of data to accurately delineate a profile for each of them. One could argue that there was so much support around that, in terms of business acumen, investors and others helped them to make the right decisions, though in some instances they held out and took the decisions they thought were right. They showed ability to manage other people, building up this competence slowly; they were aided by the fact that Stanford was socially embedded in innovation and spin-off business philosophy, and this meant that the institutional constraints (as I have termed them) were in their case facilitators. Being two, the multi-skills required to make a success of the enterprise were shared. Hence, in these particular skills (items 4, 10, 13, 14 and 17) I have adjudged them to score a 4; nonetheless they have indisputably demonstrated considerable entrepreneurial flair.

Discussion and conclusions

In the introduction to this chapter I have made explicit the criteria that have emerged from the socio-economic and entrepreneurship literature and then used the case study method to examine how a selection of enterprises emerged, were developed and were sustained (or not). There are many other cases that I could have discussed and in not doing so I may have left myself open to criticism. I have selected cases that span the twentieth century. The cases presented are highly heterogeneous, deliberately chosen from a range of industrial sectors, social backgrounds and time periods.

The cases were analysed by adopting a social constructionist perspective, drawing on face-to-face interview material and/or secondary sources that present the subject's story. Methodologically I assume that entrepreneurship is a 'form of life' and as such there are behaviours that, from social and economic perspectives, are recognised implicitly (or explicitly) as being indicative of the form-of-life entrepreneurship. In designing this chapter, I had a choice of whether to present one case, analysed in considerable detail that would be typical of the social constructionist approach, or a variety of cases; I chose to do the latter. This is because I have previously held the view that entrepreneurs are heterogeneous and that it is possible to differentiate them from non-entrepreneurs (Chell, 1985a; Chell *et al.*, 1991; Chell and Baines, 1998, 2000). To demonstrate this, it is necessary to compare and contrast. Further, in selecting a variety of cases I would hope to add to the robustness of the theoretical framework I have developed.

The 20 capabilities and expert terms shown in Table 8.1 above emerged from the analyses of preceding chapters. The method of analysis has given pre-eminence to the subject's voice, allowing him or her to describe how their reality as an entrepreneur (or not) was for them. Such details of their lives were then judged against the 20 criteria of the form-of-life entrepreneurship. The selection of cases was not random, but constituted clear cases that enabled the method to be demonstrated and both exemplars of entrepreneurs and non-entrepreneurs to be revealed by analytical means. Despite the many differences in circumstance, birth, upbringing, lifestyle, sex, place, time, industry, formal education and experience, the entrepreneurs – Jacqueline Gold, Percy Shaw, Simon Woodroffe, Henri Strzelecki, Anita Roddick, Roger McKechnie, Sergey Brin and Larry Page – were shown to have much in common in respect of those key criteria that denote the form-of-life entrepreneurship.

In sum, these entrepreneurs were all very or highly creative; of the criteria around opportunity recognition (2, 3, 4 and 5), scores showed high capability; they are all very or highly resourceful people, able to exert influence;

they showed high self-belief in what they were attempting to achieve and demonstrated, on the whole, sound judgement. They showed themselves able to manage risks, overcome difficulties – institutional or otherwise – and they were particularly adept at making the right moves at the right time. This did not simply happen, they each made it happen; and by exercising choice and making decisions they exerted control over their own futures. However, their achievements and successes did not happen 'overnight'; commitment, hard work and application were required over sustained periods, usually measured in years rather than months. This expenditure of energy required considerable amounts of stamina and self-belief. These entrepreneurs reached the top of their game; applying economic criteria of successful performance, they created wealth and employed people regionally, nationally and in some instances internationally; and from a social perspective through their products/services they also contributed to well-being. These cases were thus exemplars of superior entrepreneurial performance.

Three of the cases were selected because they represent clear cases of non-entrepreneurs in action. From economic theory, they each founded a business, but this has been shown not to be a necessary condition of entrepreneurship (see Chapter 6). These three business owner-managers differ in the following respects: industry background, sex, location and experience. Set against the 20 criteria, none demonstrated entrepreneurial capability beyond low to minimal levels and certainly below the threshold level. Critically important, they each lacked imagination and demonstrated difficulty in discerning opportunities. Moreover in all three cases their judgement let them down. They struggled within the institutional and industrial parameters of their situation, being unable to adeptly outmanoeuvre their circumstances. Despite some limited early success, and a degree of resourcefulness, they were unable to make the right moves at the right time. Unfortunately, in all three cases, each enterprise began to wither and showed tangible signs of demise. The cases demonstrated uninspired entrepreneurial performances that demonstrated implications for enterprise performance.

The issue of education and social learning is fundamental to social constructionism. All eight entrepreneurs received a formal education, though this varied considerably amongst them. It comprised post-experience education (Shaw and Strzelecki), 'O' levels (Gold – 8; Woodroffe – 4), Further Education (Roddick), degree (McKechnie) and doctoral (Brin and Page) level, but did not necessarily include any courses in business or management (Gold, Roddick, Woodroffe, Brin). What appeared to be more significant was the experiential and social learning that was absorbed and drawn upon when developing their business ideas. For example, prior experience of self-employment was apparent in the cases of Shaw, Roddick, Woodroffe and McKechnie, although not necessarily in the same industry (Woodroffe and Roddick both being able to transfer their generic skills and knowledge to another industry). Gold, Strzelecki, Brin and Page had, what might be termed, vicarious experience and role models from which they learnt about and absorbed the skills for business development. Gold came from a family of entrepreneurs, Strzelecki was employed in the clothing business for sufficient years to learn the trade and Brin and Page found themselves in a culture where developing and spinning off a business from the university was normal, supported and encouraged. Additionally, both Shaw and Roddick came from families that might be characterised as the petite bourgeoisie; Shaw and his father set up in business together, whilst Roddick's Italian family ran cafés in the vicinity of Littlehampton where she grew up. Only Page had no management or business background, but, arguably, this was made up for by having a more practically oriented business partner and a supportive environment where business angels and investors came looking for talent and business ideas worth backing. However, one should not overplay the role of experience because when a comparison is made with the business owner-managers both Marilyn and George had practical business and self-employment experience. Thus, prior experience in business and self-employment may be helpful in that it allows time for skills development, but it is clearly not sufficient to generate entrepreneurship capability.

Amabile (1983) has suggested that domain-relevant skills or technical knowledge are fundamental to creativity. Industry, business/market and technical skills and knowledge are the three main areas that should be considered in respect of their pertinence to entrepreneurship. Applying these criteria to the eight entrepreneurs, there is considerable variability in knowledge base: only Shaw and Strzelecki know the industry, have business and some knowledge of the likely market and also technical expertise. Gold rapidly put herself in a position to absorb knowledge of the industry and potential market, given that she was intent on creating change; McKechnie had worked in a marketing capacity for Tudor Crisps and so understood the snack foods industry and the market for such a commodity, whilst Brin and Page scored primarily on technical knowledge and also had a depth of understanding of the computer industry (arguably they picked up some knowledge of the markets as they developed the prototypes that preceded Google). Both Roddick and Woodroffe entered industries of which they had no prior knowledge or technical expertise – Roddick did not have the chemistry to be able to produce the products and Woodroffe was not a chef and had no experience of managing a kitchen or a restaurant. However, in both cases their resourcefulness ensured that they were able to garner the necessary expertise. Thus there was no one knowledge domain that all the entrepreneurs had in common; however, arguably, knowledge of the market was the most prevalent. That knowledge was variously gained and arguably based on surmise: Woodroffe transferred his knowledge of the success of sushi bars in Japan to their probably success in London and the UK; Strzelecki tested the market for his product to a degree; Roddick started sufficiently small and then built on what must have been unexpectedly rapid success; McKechnie and his team tested their business proposition in the marketplace and found that it exceeded expectations. Lastly Shaw and Brin and Page needed time to build their prototypes: Shaw's market was the public sector Ministry of Transport and entry into this market was accelerated due to the onset of World War II; for Brin and Page there were also step developments, such as the PageRank system, the 'BackRub' prototype and the uploading of a primitive search engine on Stanford's intranet, thus enabling them to gradually develop an understanding of the market for their product.

In all eight cases of entrepreneurship there was never any doubt about the intention to set up in business, but the aspiration to attain great wealth was not the motivator, with the exception possibly of Woodroffe. Shapero (1982), in particular, has highlighted the need for there to be a precipitating event that, as it were, kick-starts the process. Over and above the need to earn a living, Shaw and Roddick were inspired by what they perceived to be a particular social need – the former realising there was a need to invent something that would make driving on the roads at night safer, and the latter the need to produce cosmetics and lotions that ordinary women could afford. For McKechnie, the takeover of Tudor Crisps and the pressure to relocate to the London HQ was the primary reason to become self-employed and to remain in the North East where his wife had a successful medical practice. Perhaps later there was a secondary pressure: realising that there was a strong socio-economic reason in the North East for successful entrepreneurs to remain there and become role models for a further generation of entrepreneurs. In the cases of Strzelecki, Gold and Woodroffe there was a felt need to prove themselves. Strzelecki felt slighted and under-valued; he knew (intuitively) that he could produce a better product than his then employers and so he resigned and set out to prove it. Gold was born into a family of entrepreneurs (her father and uncle), but rather than being given any special favours she had to prove that she could take over and make a success of Ann Summers – originally four sex shops aimed at male customers. Woodroffe, after a divorce and some soul searching, and having been in the music industry for some years but never making it big, was actively looking for a business opportunity that would fly. Arguably, had Brin and Page not gone to Stanford and not met, there may never have been Google as we know it. But they knew there was a need for a much better quality search engine than existed at the time – the mid-1990s. Hence the socio-cultural environment created the social norms and pressures that led them inexorably towards their goal.

However, with the experiences of the business owner-managers, Marilyn, George and Frank, arguably there were recognisable precipitating events that led them either into self-employment or to take the decisions they did to grow their extant enterprise. Thus, the precipitating event does not of itself lead to entrepreneurship.

Finally, were these people born to be? Social constructionism does not assume determinism of behaviour (see Chapter 7). Socio-economic life is complex; people make decisions with the knowledge and beliefs that they hold at the time; to suggest that those decisions were determined, fated or caused would involve an infinite regress of causation. Moreover, perception and recall are selective and it is such selected images and factors that influence a person's judgement – influence in the sense that they are considered, weighed in the balance, before a decision is made. However, if an instinctive decision is made, how is anyone to know what the unconscious machinations were that influenced the judgement? Indeed it would be a retrograde step to think of the world as being mechanically determined in all its aspects, including those skills and capabilities that a person may acquire and hone and by which means they are able to make appropriate, indeed sound, decisions. In short, social constructionism holds that people are free to choose and create their own future.

Notes

1 In the case of the study with Jane Wheelock and Susan Baines (1995–1998) that focused on the socio-economic family unit of micro-enterprises in business services, both the enterprise and the family were examined from an institutional/societal perspective (Wheelock and Chell, 1996). The analysis was primarily quantitative, with some qualitative data to provide illustrative 'colour'. On the whole individual cases were not reported, with the exception of a heavily disguised 'failed' enterprise used to illustrate the Critical Incident method and reported in Symon and Cassell (1998).

2 Consistent with the view that an individual may become or cease to be entrepreneurs, as they are only entrepreneurs when they enact those behaviours that demonstrate entrepreneurship (Schumpeter, 1934; Chell *et al.*, 1991).

3 I am indebted to Professor Helga Drummond, University of Liverpool Business School, for access to this case. Marilyn is a pseudonym. We jointly interviewed her in 2002. Professor Drummond is developing her thesis of 'entrapment' as applied to market traders like Marilyn.

4 I acknowledge and thank Dr Luke Pittaway for his help in conducting this interview. I especially thank Simon Woodroffe for generously giving his time and that of his key staff to enable us to realise insights into the case.

5 From the Government Loan Guarantee Scheme.

6 http://www.yosushi.com/history.php (March 2007).

7 The case of Henri-Lloyd was first published in Chell *et al.* (1991: 107–115). In particular, I thank Dr Jean Haworth for her help in carrying out the interview and to Henri Strzelecki for giving generously of his time and his permission to publish the case. This is an abbreviated version of the original.

8 Anita Roddick died on Monday 10 September 2007, during the final stages of the preparation of this book. It is my regret that she did not see this exposition of her case.

9 Apartheid was still in operation in South Africa at this time.

10 We would argue that such a claim is contentious, although we can see how in the social milieu of the time, surrounded as Roddick often was by 'grey suits', that she might draw such a conclusion. However, if one considers that networking is a fundamental tactic for business and opportunity development the importance of developing relationships would appear to be paramount regardless of gender (Chell and Baines, 1998, 2000).

11 There are many examples emanating in nineteenth-century Britain – the Quakers apparently influenced Roddick; in addition, we might cite Cadbury and Bourneville, Titus Salt and Saltaire, and Rowntree as examples. The prevalent social

construction of Victorian philanthropy however is rather of patronising behaviour, whereas the 'Trade not Aid' campaign, arguably, gives positive, socially responsible action that is enabling rather than patronising.

12 This was founded in 1990 and is a charitable organisation called 'Children on the Edge'.

13 http://en.wikipedia.org/wiki/Anita_Roddick.

14 L'Oréal is reportedly involved in animal testing, and is part of Nestlé, which was involved in marketing baby milk powder to Third World countries.

15 I would like to acknowledge and thank Elaine Adam for her research assistance in conducting this interview and preparing the transcript.

16 Phileas Fogg is the main character in Jules Verne's novel 'Around the World in Eighty Days'.

17 An off-licence in the UK is a shop that is licensed to sell alcoholic beverages that may be consumed off the premises only.

18 A 'bookie' or bookmaker is someone who accepts bets on race horses and pays out the winnings.

19 I thank and acknowledge Dr Paul Tracey's contribution to the development of this case study and to the (then) NEBS Management for funding the research.

20 I am indebted to Dr Jean Haworth for her support on this ESRC-funded project.

21 This is a pseudonym.

22 *Hebden Bridge Times*, May 1989.

23 C&A are known to have been incurring losses from 1995 – a fact that emerged three years later to the shock of its staff. In June 2000 the company closed.

24 The creator of the World Wide Web is Sir Timothy Berners-Lee, an Oxford University graduate.

25 For example, Hewlett-Packard and Sun Microsystems.

9 The entrepreneurial personality: the state of the art

Introduction

The purposes of this chapter are to draw together some of the threads of the preceding chapters in a sensible and coherent way and to highlight areas where further work might usefully be carried out. The key question to be addressed: is there a need theoretically, methodologically and practically to assume an 'entrepreneurial personality'? What arguments and evidence has been adduced over the preceding seven chapters?

I commence this process by revisiting the issue of interdisciplinarity. In this section I present an overview and summary of the three disciplinary approaches taken in this book. I then elaborate in subsequent sections on the model of the entrepreneur and entrepreneurial process that emanates from this work through a process of integration and synthesis. This includes summarising the evidence from the case studies analysed in Chapter 8, positioning the entrepreneur in the entrepreneurial process and focusing in some detail on the 'entrepreneur–opportunity interchange'. I discuss the nature of the entrepreneurial personality raised by the social constructionist, cognitive constructivist and trait approaches and I draw some conclusions. Further, I consider: the implications of my analyses for social learning and the development of experiential knowledge, the work on entrepreneurial types and marginal groups that may be said to be enterprising; the importance of the inclusion of entrepreneurial performance in models of enterprise performance; the education and training of entrepreneurs; and the need to address entrepreneurial behaviour by taking a multiple-level analytical approach – this would usefully enable us to draw on what have hitherto been separate literatures, such as individual and firm level, and innovation and entrepreneurship. Finally, I draw five key conclusions from this work in respect of: (a) the crucial importance of the question, 'who is an entrepreneur?' in theory and research on entrepreneurship; (b) the need to include qualitative and case study methods in further theory building in entrepreneurship; (c) the enhanced role for psychology that this research has highlighted; (d) the practical and policy implications for developing entrepreneurial capability; and (e) the serious issue of 'anyone can attempt to be an entrepreneur' for virgin, would-be and nascent entrepreneurs.

Interdisciplinarity

No single discipline has a claim on entrepreneurship or the nature and function of an entrepreneur. Entrepreneurship is a social phenomenon, thus economists have tended to undertheorise entrepreneurship, sociologists have omitted the entrepreneur from the analysis and psychologists have recognised insufficiently the importance of context in influencing entrepreneur's actions. Hence, to move the discipline of entrepreneurship forward there is a real need for interdisciplinarity. I commence this by summarising the key contributions that have emerged from the preceding chapters.

Economists, on the whole, disclaimed the entrepreneur until the twentieth century, when a minority placed the entrepreneur centre stage. Classical economists were concerned to identify sources of the nation's wealth – land, labour and capital – while neo-classical economists considered questions of value, the marginal utility of goods and rational decision-making over the allocation of resources in conditions of perfect information. This left no room for the entrepreneur; indeed, it was not until after severe criticisms of the assumptions underpinning equilibrium theory were made that a role for the entrepreneur in economic decision-making was developed (Schumpeter, 1934; Hayek, 1937; Kirzner, 1973; Casson, 1982).

Economists have inferred personality characteristics from their theoretical assumptions, but evidence from empirical research is needed. Thus, entrepreneurs are said to:

- be dynamic, proactive, innovative agents of change in economies (Schumpeter, 1934);
- base their subjective judgements on imagined future possibilities (Shackle, 1972, 1979);
- be alert to opportunities in the market (Kirzner, 1982a, 1982b), however the psychological components of the concept are not developed by Kirzner;
- be specialists in judgemental decision-making and have imagination and foresight (Casson, 1982);
- combine self-knowledge and communication skills (Casson, 2000);
- have a low aversion to risk, confidence in his/her judgement and optimistic about the success of his/her project (Casson, 2005);
- be persuasive communicators, with leadership, social skills and imagination (Witt, 1998, 1999).

In contrast, a sociological approach to entrepreneurship suggests the need to focus on the entrepreneur from the perspective of the socio-economy and society. This enables the construction of context, specifically the institutional framework, culture and the competitive conditions in which decisions are taken, at multiple levels of analysis, namely, macro-, meso- and micro-. Thus, the premise taken suggests that social structures shape agentic behaviour, and that agentic behaviour, reflexively, produces and reproduces structure (Giddens, 1984):

At the macro-environmental level, Giddens' structuration theory was assumed: rules and resources drive agentic-structure engagement; rules vary in strength and flexibility, hence structure is not wholly deterministic; and the nature of the agent in this theory is underdeveloped.

At the meso-environmental level, the focus was maintained on the institutional structures of industry and firm: engagement in the socio-economy is through network linkages, especially weak ties (Granovetter, 1973); at this level firms are seen as administrative envelopes for requisite resources identified for the purposes of the pursuit of firm aims and objectives; and the more particular the resource envelope, the more likely the firm will secure a competitive advantage (Penrose, 1959). Firms with difficult to imitate resources (knowledge) will be more competitive and such resources are more likely to be intangible or socially complex and/or secret. Idiosyncratic knowledge that is difficult to imitate leads to different visions and decisions; imagination and the social skills associated with informal leadership imply that one vision would be selected over other rival concepts (Witt, 1998, 1999). In this model, knowledge and information are synthesised to create an opportunity and move the firm forward. Moreover, at the established firm level, a set of external social relationships and an internal set of cognitive capabilities are critical to the furtherance of firm-level opportunity realisation (Eisenhardt and Schoonhoven, 1996).

At the micro-level, entrepreneurs are said to be embedded in the local culture that facilitates the reproduction of the local socio-economy through the development of local knowledge and the building of firm business relationships (Jack and Anderson, 2002). Developing the entrepreneur as agent, Chiasson and Saunders (2005) suggest a socio-cognitive view of opportunity formation within structuration theory. Entrepreneurs develop scripts, which are a form of 'behavioural grammar' that enable them to take socially meaningful, legitimate and influential decisions in order to take steps in the pursuit of an opportunity. Shane and Venkataraman (2000) suggest the key to the entrepreneurial process is that of understanding the individual–opportunity nexus. However, the assumption is that opportunities exist externally to the entrepreneur rather than their being created through the synthesising capability of entrepreneurs (Endres and Woods, 2007). Sarason *et al.* (2006) develop the concept of the individual–opportunity nexus by viewing it as an interdependent duality that is idiosyncratic and path dependent. Hence, entrepreneurs create opportunities through a process of structuration that takes place over time and interactively in which they construe information as a potentially meaningful opportunity, evaluate its potential and use their power to control and transform resources in its exploitation.

Structuration theory, however, fails to theorise about the nature of the agent – the entrepreneur – and yet the cognitive and social capabilities implicit in this analysis suggest that the agent is assumed to have such characteristics. There is thus room for greater psychological inquiry.

A further, largely independent line of inquiry has been pursued by psychologists, who initially focused on three characteristics of entrepreneurs: their 'need for achievement', 'internal locus of control' and 'risk-taking propensity'. Ironically, these 'traits', as they became known, had their origins in the analysis of social context, but the research upon which they have been based in entrepreneurship has nonetheless been roundly criticised. The search for alternative traits has led to the identification of characteristics that, arguably, more closely fit the socio-economic theory of entrepreneurial behaviour. From this later research, the traits that emerge include: opportunity recognition, proactive personality, self-efficacy, social competence and intuition – such characteristics (and there are some others) relate primarily to the cognitive capability of the entrepreneur and entrepreneurial process. Implicit in opportunity recognition is synthesising capability, which enables the entrepreneur to put together public and private sources of information and knowledge in the process of the formulation of an opportunity. The role of imagination and creativity has been downplayed, whilst the 'act of innovation' has been underscored. Nevertheless, the identification and accurate psychometric measurement of such traits remains problematic.

Psychology has its own 'version' of structuration theory, namely interactionism, where the interaction between the person and situation is construed to be 'organismic' rather than mechanical (Burns and Stalker, 1961; Chell, 1985a, 1985b). Pursuit of this line of inquiry has led to the reconceptualisation of traits as 'social learning person variables' (Mischel, 1968, 1973) and the theorisation of a cognitive-affective stable structure to information processing that presents an outwardly consistent behavioural signature typical of an individual (Mischel and Shoda, 1995). These elements would explain how an entrepreneur engages with socio-economic phenomena, synthesises information and develops stable capabilities of opportunity recognition, formation and exploitation. It is in part a repertoire of learnt capabilities that are honed through experience and social interaction processes. Hence, social psychology may provide the link with the socio-economic context of entrepreneurial behaviour and to the mental processes that surround decision-making. The latter – the cognitive – has been a focus of recent entrepreneurship research.

Cognitive research in entrepreneurship recognises the importance of this element of entrepreneurial behaviour, but underplays the importance of affect. Affect is indicative of what a person feels about an idea, the importance they place on it and how they believe it is valued; it is thus a crucial aspect of a person's drive and motivation. Social, as well as economic, reasons for the pursuit of an opportunity and the serious intent to do so are motivated by what the entrepreneur feels and not simply the reasons that s/he may articulate (Kwiatkowski, 2004; Chell, 2007a).

A social constructivist approach to personality assumes the view of multiple observers in making subjective judgements and attributions to a person's behaviour. Presumably, from these different views there is sufficient agreement to enable a construction to be placed on the personality of the incumbent. The methodology for this would be complex and the procedure for resolving conflicting views is not evident (Hampson, 1988). However, a not dissimilar criticism has been levelled at trait theory (Wright and Mischel, 1987). The nub of social constructivist theory is that it identifies character as relational, and thereby it is not essentialist. Observers learn about other people through social interaction, identifying consistencies in their behaviour that enable them to make judgements about what is 'in character'. Adjectives are applied to describe behaviour and, indeed, it is such adjectival terms that are the basis of traits. The English language is rich in adjectival terms, many of which have similar meanings; it is therefore not surprising that in some instances different people will use slightly different terms to label another's behaviour. Nouns, on the other hand, are used to label different types of people. Applied to the entrepreneurial personality the question is: are there natural categories of behaviour that may be identified as prototypical of the entrepreneur? Preliminary empirical research demonstrated such characteristics: opportunity-seeking, imaginative/ideas person, proactive, restless/easily bored, adventurous, agent of change and tends to adopt a broad financial strategy (Chell *et al.*, 1991). This early example of the application of the social construction of the entrepreneurial persona has been developed further in this volume (see Chapter 8). Using case study methodology, and the behavioural dimensions distilled from the three disciplinary perspectives, a set of 20 dimensions and expert terms were applied to nine twentieth-century entrepreneurs. Using this method comparatively, it was shown that entrepreneurs (judged as such independently by society) exhibited the 20 capabilities in large measure, whereas small business owners who had failed to develop or sustain their business were shown to demonstrate the characteristics weakly.

In sum, taking the three disciplinary approaches it is possible to identify the deficiencies of each taken on their own, and the strands of similarity that enable an interdisciplinary model to be constructed. The key elements to this model would comprise: social-economic environment and agentic interaction at a number of levels; centrality of decision-making where agent–opportunity interaction occurs; and the cognitive-affective capability of the entrepreneur. The model is holistic in that it assumes that behaviour emerges from individual–opportunity interaction, where the individual is defined in terms of cognitions, affect and behaviour. To identify the individual's behaviour as that of an entrepreneur suggests that they *do* engage in particular acts that are prototypical of entrepreneurs. However, interdisciplinarity raises a number of methodological issues:

The unit of analysis is identified as individual–opportunity interaction, where the decision to pursue an idea that is believed to be an opportunity is subjective, intuitive and instinctive. There are no guarantees that the opportunity would be realised or that there would be a market; that too must be created. Alertness may be necessary, but it is not sufficient to explain entrepreneurial behaviour that has both temporal and spatial aspects. The entrepreneurial behaviours arise from the situation, but the engagement with the situation is psychological. Thus, there is a larger role to be played by psychology, but it is not to measure traits, rather it is to investigate the psychological engagement of the entrepreneur in each of three aspects – what they think, how they feel and what they intend to do – about the socio-economic opportunity as they perceive it. Psychologists, however, are not ultimately the judges of whether their subjects are entrepreneurs. There is a wider socio-economic remit whereby others will apply their constructions on whether someone is an entrepreneur. This socio-economic construction yields criteria by which those judgements are made and shifts the perception from the subjective and the private (possibly idiosyncratic) to the 'objective' (facticity) and the public arena. The criteria arise from a social construction of the role and function of entrepreneur in a capitalist economy and as such the behaviours are generic; cultural issues – some differences in institutional arrangements – would suggest particular differences in what might be thought, felt and done, but overall an entrepreneur is someone who makes a subjective judgement that his/her perceived idea represents an opportunity that s/he should develop and exploit with a view to creating socio-economic value.

Thus in the next two sections I consider further the evidence from the case studies, the criteria and their application to the entrepreneurial process.

Evidence of the entrepreneurial personality from the case studies

The eleven cases, labelled entrepreneurs and non-entrepreneurs, presented in Chapter 8 have in common that ultimately each individual was seeking an opportunity; their judgement was subjective and they each had nothing other than their hopes and personal conviction (right or wrong) that the opportunity would be realised. Hence, 'alertness' is necessary but not sufficient to explain entrepreneurial behaviour; additional decisions are required throughout the subsequent process.

To assume structuration theory (a variant of social constructionism) as part of our methodology of analysis, it is clear that all the entrepreneurs and business owner-managers featured in Chapter 8 found their behaviour constrained. Without exception, they started with an idea and then sought to develop it into a more tangible opportunity. Thus, the idea was moved from phenomenon to product/service during this process. Moreover, the idea, at some point, ceased to be a part of the agent's mental processes and took on an external reality by which process others could consider, judge and assess it. As part of this process, the idea was tested against the constraints (structures) iteratively, while the agent/entrepreneur would make a series of judgemental decisions in the face of uncertainty. In three of those cases, those judgements proved to be wrong (leading to the demise of the enterprise). Thus, engaging in the process is necessary but not sufficient to explain entrepreneurship. The initial stage in the process comprises the identification of an idea, whereas the further stages – formation and exploitation – comprise the development of that idea as an opportunity. The questions are: how good was the initial idea and how skilful, adept and so forth is the entrepreneurial decision-making within the process? Thus, anyone may engage in the process, but not necessarily in a way that would lead to sustained entrepreneurial outcomes – the creation of social and economic value.

It is facile to slip into the vocabulary that associates entrepreneurial behaviour with successful business performance. There may be a fine line to be drawn, but it is both theoretically and practically possible for an entrepreneur to exhibit the 20 characteristics in spades but not realise an opportunity. This is because in a global economy an entrepreneur may be missing some vital piece of information that affects his/her decision. They may not see, for example, that their initiative might be blocked or that a competitor might be able to manage more adeptly the institutional environment on this occasion. Thus, not to be successful in respect of realising a particular opportunity is not the same as failure, nor does it necessarily suggest that labelling the individual's behaviours as entrepreneurial is inappropriate. Failure, however, arises from serious misjudgement: for instance, Crowther (see Chapter 8 for details) produced an undifferentiated product – men's trousers – and having received one large order one season from a large highstreet retailer he gambled on repeat business to such an extent that he invested heavily by equipping another site. Without the repeat business he was plunged suddenly into financial crisis from which the business could not recover. The lack of discernment, business acumen and market awareness is clear, but also Crowther exhibited insufficient nous in managing risk. To put it colloquially, he put all his eggs in one basket, with no contingency plan in place; in effect he bet the business.

It might be argued that failure is simply the consequence of insufficient testing, having insufficient access to information that delineates the constraining features of the situation. This would imply that no further information about the nature of the agent – the entrepreneur – is required either from a theoretical or practical perspective. However, the above example and the method that was adopted in Chapter 8 contest drawing such a conclusion.

The entrepreneurs identified in Chapter 8 exhibited a set of behaviours that were not evident or were only weakly evident in the non-entrepreneurs. They demonstrated their ability to take ideas and synthesise them to produce novelty – an innovation. All gave a very strong impression of their confidence in their idea and in their judgement, often sticking to their guns against the prevailing tide of opinion. The envisioning and opportunity development process showed a set of well-honed capabilities that include imagination, alertness, accurate interpretation of a social need or market gap, resourcefulness and self-belief. In identifying and garnering the requisite resources, the entrepreneurs were able to bring under their control other human capital, equipment, premises and financial capital. To do this, they had to communicate effectively and convincingly, negotiate deals and demonstrate leadership. They often used informal methods or leastways showed that they could relate to others. Motives were less than clearcut: certainly there was a need in the majority of cases to earn a living, yet the pursuit of considerable wealth was not an apparent motive; rather, they were in part solving a social 'problem' as they saw it, finding a better solution to a social need.

In structuration theory the agent appears to be invisible but structures are powerful determinants of behaviour,[1] constraining or facilitating what is possible. Yet my analysis of entrepreneurs in practice suggests a number of elements that make up their character: the cognitive, affective and behavioural components. The cognitive is indicative of the thought processes, intelligence, skill and knowledge that they bring to the opportunity development process (e.g. creativity, alertness, veridical perception, judgement, adeptness and strategic competence – the English language is rich in co-related terms). However, on the affective side there is strong commitment and involvement, drive and energy evident in bold persistence, a sense of humour and fun and the ability to form meaningful relationships, whereas on the behavioural side the entrepreneurial way of doing includes the ability to garner resources, manage risk, shoulder responsibilities, overcome difficulties, learn the 'rules', leverage opportunities and operate strategically. The process is dynamic, engaging and goal-oriented, indeed driven; this gives the particular style and ways of doing that presents the distinctive character and culture of the enterprise. To focus on the structural and not the agentic elements is to miss seeing the entrepreneur and those factors that contribute to the success or downfall of their business enterprise.

Further, to take a single disciplinary approach is to risk producing incomplete explanations of entrepreneurial phenomena: for example, economic theories of entrepreneurship, such as Kirznerian 'alertness', place emphasis on the ability of entrepreneurs to identify gaps in the market. Indeed, this is a crucial difference with Schumpeterian theory of innovation. Thus, in radical cases of innovation, arguably the identification of market gaps would be a post hoc construction; rather, entrepreneurs often produce a novel idea for which there is no extant market or niche products that, at best, may be indicative of the potential of the market. Part of the later opportunity development and exploitation process is the testing of the *possibility* of a market, though its size cannot be known in advance (only estimated, as McKechnie and his team did, discovering to their delight that they had in fact underestimated the market). It is this element that underscores the riskiness of entrepreneurial venturing and indicates another aspect of character – the ability to handle risk. This appears to be related to their confidence in their idea, ability to hedge bets, turn problems into opportunities, reduce certain sorts of risk and, through the strength of their belief and determination, convince others (Chell *et al.*, 1991: 42–43).

Furthermore, entrepreneurs appear initially to operate instinctively; the idea seems to them to be a good one and worth pursuing, and the business analysis will come later (Allinson *et al.*, 2000). This seems true irrespective of educational achievements or intelligence. They appear to have unshakeable confidence in their idea, self-belief and sense that a market can be created. The gap in this process is turning the idea into a viable business proposition. They do this by sharing sufficient of the idea with others that ways and means can be found to develop it. This is a heuristic learning process; four of the entrepreneurs – Shaw, Roddick, George and Woodroffe – had prior experience of setting up a business, though not in the specific sector; some – McKechnie, Strzelecki and Gold – had *relevant* experience that they could draw upon. The process of knowledge and skills transfer that was apparent indicates that people may learn generic skills and know-how from the process that they can draw on in a future non-related business venture.

However, whilst the analysis has demonstrated the cognitive capabilities of the entrepreneur, the social and relational aspect of the process reveals that they are adept at doing two things to enhance this capability: (a) they convince others to join them, thus expanding the available human capital; and (b) they attract others to furnish the enterprise with complementary skills. The cognitive capability provides them with the necessary equipment to make judgemental decisions, to source and synthesise information and to weigh up the optional scenarios before them. Cognitive capability may be necessary, but social learning and relationship building are also important. To 'go it alone' in a self-centred, individualistic way is a very hard path to tread and, not only that, it underplays the role of others in providing the socio-economic context in which the entrepreneur operates. The role of 'others' is in fact quite considerable: providing social and pecuniary support, a sounding board for ideas, a conduit to valuable contacts and, in many cases, into the marketplace, a source of reputation and profile, and so forth. So, what lubricates this social process? I would suggest two key factors: humour and reliability. Humour manifests itself in a number of ways: a sense of fun, recognition of the importance of play, informality of style. Reliability is demonstrated through the ability to pull something off, to be trustworthy, responsible and not to duck tough issues. This incidentally serves to strengthen leadership capability. Further, there is a sense of mission and purpose about what our entrepreneurs set about doing and this mission is not fuelled at the outset by grandiose ideas of wealth creation – earning a living certainly, but there are mixed motives. These may include proving oneself, but there is also a level of engagement with humanity – the fundamental social motivation through one's efforts to improve another person's lot. Undoubtedly, the rewards and the accolades in many cases have followed, but as a nascent entrepreneur, when making their first judgemental decisions, they could not have known what lay in store.

The entrepreneur and entrepreneurial process

Drawing on the work of the preceding chapters and the above discussion, the entrepreneur and entrepreneurial process is elaborated and summarised in Figure 9.1. From the left side of Figure 9.1, social psychological theory of personality development indicates the importance of social learning (Bandura, 1977). Social constructivism is indicative of the formative value of early experience in both the cognitive and affective dimensions, with later experience enabling the individual to learn coping behaviours and skills – often referred to as 'recipes'. This yields the cognitive, affective and behavioural components of the persona, onto which the behaviours, skills and expert terms identified in Table 8.1 can be mapped. This is the entrepreneurial persona that engages in the individual–opportunity interchange. It is sufficiently generic that it may be applied to those individuals whom society labels as 'entrepreneurs'. Thus, an entrepreneur is judged to be someone who exhibits those capabilities that enable him or her to engage in

Agent: Entrepreneur

Cognitive Process:	Idea =>Opportunity =>Opportunity =>Opportunity => Outcome
	Recognition Formation Exploitation

Knowledge:	Insight Intuitive	Explicit	Explicit	=> Personal and
	(private/phenomenal)	and implicit	and implicit	social goods

Decision:	SJ SJ	SD	SD	

Affect:	Feelings =>empathy => social and => commitment => pride
	re idea towards interpersonal confidence
	others

Time	ti ──────────────────────────────► tn

Structure: the socio-economic and socio-cultural environment

Key

SJ = subjective judgement (private judgements made by the entrepreneur/agent)
SD = subjective decisions taken in the context of uncertainty by the principals (the entrepreneur and close partners/confidantes)
ti → tn denotes a timeline during which iterations between entrepreneur and socio-structure take place; the line indicates a progression, not a linear process, and the principals may decide not to proceed with the process at any point

Figure 9.1 The individual–opportunity interchange.

the opportunity recognition–formation–exploitation process with a view to creating socio-economic value. Turning this on its head, entrepreneurship is a form of life that people experience in different ways and that the entrepreneur actively chooses as his/her preferred modus vivendi. This means adapting, developing and learning new ways of working, new skills and attitudes that will enable him/her to operate effectively, as tested against the socio-economic structure.

The entrepreneur and entrepreneurial process as depicted also includes outcomes by which society judges whether the individual may be labelled an 'entrepreneur'. Society includes the lay person as well as experts – business angels, investors, bankers, academics, trainers, and so forth. The criteria of success constitute the achievement – the launch of the enterprise, its sustainability, its market share, profitability, and so forth. However, these criteria are different from the inputs, so if the enterprise fails to meet these criteria, then is the application of the label 'entrepreneur' deemed inappropriate? As was demonstrated in Chapter 8, there was a wide gulf between entrepreneurs and non-entrepreneurs. Entrepreneurs can get it wrong sometimes, but they must first demonstrate their entrepreneurial capability and the occasional later failure may then be judged in context. The lessons learnt from success or failure are fed back into experience as the cycle repeats itself.

This social construction of the entrepreneur and entrepreneurial process comprises a holistic theory that recognises the complexity of its various elements – the psychological, social and economic at one level, the cognitive, affective and behavioural at another, and the social learning and the developmental within a complex layering of socio-economic structure. The system is organic and dynamic and ultimately unpredictable, because the precursors of the decision to engage with an opportunity are unknowable *ex ante*.

The entrepreneur–opportunity interchange

To make (entrepreneurial) decisions the entrepreneur synthesises public and private information, which constitutes the initial recognition of an enterprise. The balance of public to private information/knowledge will determine what other kinds of actions must be taken to protect the germinal venture. The greater the private knowledge, the more idiosyncratic the cognitive structure being developed and the more difficult to imitate. This personal experience and history underpin the social learning capability of the individual and the cognitive constructs that are responsible for sense-making and understanding. These are the *inalienable* resources of the entrepreneur that give the enterprise a competitive edge.[2] They also shape expectations of the behaviour of others and guide the person's decisions, strategies and plans. The entrepreneurial process that the agent is now embarking on has commenced with the synthesis of information leading to the germ of an idea. Knowledge of the socio-economic structure enables the entrepreneur to consider the significance of the idea. Does it meet a social need? Will it engage with the desires of a particular social group? The understanding of the socio-economic structure at this level and point in the process is likely to be intuitive. A positive decision at this point would then lead to the further formation of the idea as an opportunity and its careful testing through engagement with significant others. Once the opportunity is legitimated the subsequent developmental process would constitute the gathering of resources. However, the whole process is iterative and involves flexibility and adjustment.

The person-characteristics needed to address these three steps in the process include: insight and empathetic understanding of the socio-economy or socio-culture; imagination for the envisioning of different forms of the idea and ingenuity that facilitates the development of an innovation; social and leadership abilities to convince others and glean support; identification of sources of intelligence to convert the idea into something workable and the ability to synthesise different (public and private) sources of information – often termed creativity; the ability to identify appropriate criteria for the evaluation of the idea and their appropriate application signifies sound judgement; affect or personal feelings associated with the valuing of the idea, drive and motivation. Table 9.1 provides a summary of the entrepreneur– opportunity interchange characteristics. Socio-structural behaviour is what is manifested at the different stages of development of an opportunity; the agentic characteristics are what are required at those stages, mapped one to one with the behaviours; and it is suggested that the nature of the decision changes over time from the instinctive, intuitive and implicit style of decision-taking to the explicit and analytical as opportunity development moves to formation and exploitation. The agentic characteristics map onto the skills and characteristics shown in Table 8.1. The engagement of the entrepreneur in the socio-economic process provides a source of energy and motivation through commitment-exchange as evaluation proceeds over time.

The structure that surrounds the entrepreneur comprises the operation of social institutions at various levels. Institutional rules and resources (e.g. banking, venture capitalists, business angels) will hold variable significance for the entrepreneur, as will their legitimacy within the entrepreneur's sphere of operation and their power and influence to affect his/her decisions and plans. Drawing on such *alienable resources* will help to address crucial aspects of the process, including product development, enterprise planning, financing and other aspects of management of enterprise development (Chell, 2007a: 13).

Structuration (or organismic interaction between person and situation) is the third aspect of the theory that enables us to understand the engagement of the entrepreneur with the socio-economic structure, learning what is possible, understanding what will and will not work as s/he attempts to take the enterprise forward. This enables the production of a new (albeit

Table 9.1 Entrepreneur–opportunity interchange characteristics summarised

Socio-structural behaviour	Agentic characteristics	Decision type
Opportunity recognition		
Empathetic understanding	Insight/imagination	Intuitive
Opportunity identification	Social/market awareness	Implicit
Preliminary envisioning	Imagination	Implicit
Trust in own judgement	Confidence, self-efficacy	Implicit
Recognition of potential value	Calculative, discernment	Implicit/explicit
Social and economic import	Drive, energy, impetus	Implicit
Opportunity formation		
Synthesis of public and private information	Creativity	Explicit/implicit
Evaluation of opportunity	Judgement	Implicit/intuitive
Scenario-planning	Imagination, counter-factual thinking	Explicit/implicit
Mustering support	Communication, social skill	Explicit
Identification of competition and strategic advantage	Tactical and strategic capability	Explicit/implicit
Engagement in the socio-economy	Networking, social skill, adept	Explicit/implicit
Growing awareness	Self-belief, confidence	Implicit/intuitive
	Self-efficacy	Explicit
Social recognition of innovation	Ingenuity, application, commitment	Implicit/explicit
Opportunity exploitation		
Garnering capitals	Resourceful, negotiation and leadership skills	Explicit, analytical
Gaining institutional support	Communication, self-belief	Explicit, analytical
	Patience, conviction	
Ability to cope with difficulties	Resilience, self-efficacy	Implicit
	Stamina, energy	Intuitive
	Discernment, judgement	Analytical
Identification of team and human capitals	Self- and other awareness	Intuitive
	Discernment, judgement	Explicit, analytical
Financial strategy	Flexibility, financially adept	Analytical, explicit
	Calculative risk manager	Intuitive, implicit

fragile) structure – the nascent enterprise – by gaining acceptance within the socio-economy. This acceptance will depend on it being perceived as a significant and legitimate development, whereby significant others will be enjoined to use their influence in its support. By the same token the entrepreneur will begin to build a notable reputation within the socio-economic structure, giving him/her power to influence and effect change.

People who engage effectively in this process are termed entrepreneurs.

Social constructionism, cognitive constructivism, trait theory and the entrepreneur

The term 'entrepreneurial personality' is a social construction that is drawn from different perspectives and understandings and people have hitherto only seen an aspect of entrepreneurial behaviour that has governed their personal understanding. Research, however, has enabled us to develop a better understanding of the entrepreneurial process as described in the above section, and from which it is worth considering the possible reconciliation between social constructionist, cognitive constructivist and trait theories in respect of the nature of the entrepreneur and entrepreneurial practices in a socio-economy.

Social constructionism enables us to understand agentic behaviour within society, where social institutions through socially-derived rules shape choices and ultimately behavioural possibilities. Narrowing our concept of society somewhat to focus particularly on the socio-economy, cognitive structures develop through learning about business and enterprise. Multiple observers of agentic behaviour, especially in interaction with others or themselves, make judgements about the nature of that behaviour and label it accordingly. Such behaviour is overt and a matter of perception. However, cognitive constructivism assumes the *necessary* existence of cognitive processing elements that enable the individual to: accumulate knowledge and experience about their world; learn how to deal with situations, other people and unexpected occurrences; remember past experiences and selective elements of their personal history; consider a future that is unknown and develop strategies and plans to engage in a preferred way in the future; and develop a personal value system that distinguishes personal preferences, a code of ethics and shapes attitudes and beliefs towards other people and things. This apparatus is fuelled by the affective system of feelings, motives and personal reasons for making particular choices and engaging in one activity rather than another. Whilst some personal preferences may be predictable – a liking for fast cars, adventurous sports and healthy food – others may be less so or even unlikely. For example, why and how might someone trained as a schoolteacher give all that up and become a world famous entrepreneur? How can someone with no social advantages and little formal education become a millionaire? Why and how might someone highly educated pursue a potential entrepreneurial venture that may well not have succeeded? Why are some people who are presented with an opportunity to develop an enterprise unable to make a go of it? If we knew all that, we might be closer to being able to articulate the entrepreneurial process; we appear to be a way off from being able to predict who (at the individual level) will become an entrepreneur. This is because the choice is subjective, private and inherently unpredictable.

However, the entrepreneurial process, as described above, has implications for aspects of the entrepreneurial persona. World view and lifestyle choice are influenced reflexively by the person's cognitive-affective system. But, our knowledge of the motivations that drive the nascent entrepreneur is probably insufficiently developed. Many of the cases described in Chapter 8 suggest that the motivation could vary from personal need, curiosity, a perceived challenge or need to prove oneself rather than simply the desire to amass great wealth. Further, the cognitive-affective system includes: synthesising ability – a creative process requiring creativity and imagination; social nous – a social competence that enables the entrepreneur to understand a social want or need, manage and influence other people's judgements and see off rivals; envisioning capability – develop a concept of the opportunity, show insight and future awareness; progress opportunity development flexibly, proactively and determinedly; back one's judgement – show confidence and optimism for one's enterprise; have a strong self-concept that enables the entrepreneur to see the venture through (see Tables 8.1 and 9.1).

From this analysis it is evident that social learning and experience are crucial aspects of building the entrepreneur's character. But it is only part of his/her character; how s/he engages with family and friends, on holiday or at a dinner party is not known, predictable or necessarily relevant. It is, however, not surprising that adopting the trait approach to understanding the entrepreneur has been inadequate. It is, of course, partly because researchers have sampled extant entrepreneurs and thus have not been able to distinguish between what has been learnt and what would be assumed to be deeply held characteristics over a lengthy period. Rather, trait psychologists have not engaged sufficiently with entrepreneurship theory to be able to test hypotheses rigorously about the nature of that personality. Moreover, they have sampled business founders at different stages in the opportunity development process where different skills and abilities were required of the entrepreneur. They have assumed the 'entrepreneurial personality' to be static and internal rather than fluid and emergent, as the agent deals with environmental contingencies. There is thus a need to question the theoretical assumptions being made and consider other methods for researching the engagement of the entrepreneur in the entrepreneurial process.

The implications for entrepreneurship research and practice

Social learning and tacit knowledge

Nascent entrepreneurs cannot tell all that they know:[3] they absorb socio-cultural knowledge routinely through social interaction; some knowledge and understanding within the cognitive-affective structure becomes 'taken-for-granted'; socio-cultural beliefs and attitudes in particular form part of the individual's tacit knowledge and are enacted implicitly. It then becomes difficult (indeed impossible) for the entrepreneur to articulate how they know a product concept is not simply an idea, but an opportunity worthy of development. This may be particularly evident when operating in areas where 'fashion', 'style' and 'design' are important dimensions of the product. As such, entrepreneurs and entrepreneurial managers are perceived to take intuitive decisions, acting on hunch or gut feeling (Allinson *et al.*, 2000).

The process of knowledge accumulation and behavioural learning is still underdeveloped in entrepreneurship. Entrepreneurship does depend on making the right judgements at the right time – a cognitive process – but it also depends on enactment and behaviour. Social learning theory is compatible with the heuristic way entrepreneurs appear to learn and with social cognitive constructivism:

> [B]ehaviour is in reciprocal interaction with the cognitive processes of person and the environment. The cyclical nature of this process is such that . . . a person may conceive of the consequences of their proposed behaviour, decide among alternative courses of action, behave accordingly and thus modify the environment in which they are operating. This environmental modification creates a new situation which may suggest new alternative behaviours among which the individual can again exert choice.
>
> (Chell, 1993: 68)

Social learning also occurs through observation of other people's behaviour; such vicarious learning or role modelling underscores the inherently social nature of entrepreneurship. However, there are also covert cognitive processes at work. The entrepreneur draws upon private knowledge and experience in order to make sense of current experience, including possible new enterprise ideas. This private filtering of information and categorisation process affect the way later experiences are conceptualised. From this they imagine different scenarios and act them out in their mind. However, this is not the only aspect of the experiential process; rather, entrepreneurs talk about these different possibilities to valued others, seeking further information, advice and opinion before making their judgement. This suggests that entrepreneurs have a flexibility of mind that permits leaps of imagination through counter-factual thinking and the ready absorption of novel information and possibilities.

The social constructionist analysis has highlighted the importance of the self, and reflexive mental processes through social interaction have indicated self-awareness. Entrepreneurship research has also pointed to social competences of entrepreneurial self-efficacy and self-confidence (Markman *et al.*, 2002). The application of social learning theory also includes processes of behavioural self-management. Insufficient is known about an entrepreneur's awareness of the contingencies that affect his/her behaviour. This requires self-observation, self-monitoring and self-determination. The entrepreneur can choose the situations that s/he is subjected to by methods such as avoidance and select situations to which s/he wishes to attend. Moreover, entrepreneurs have been characterised as enjoying feedback (McClelland, 1961;

Timmons *et al.*, 1985), hence they may choose to manage their behaviour through consideration of the consequences of their actions. Hence there is scope to expand our knowledge and understanding of entrepreneurs through the investigation of social learning processes.

Entrepreneurial types

The model of the entrepreneur and entrepreneurial process is generic and applicable to all types of *nascent* entrepreneurial developments from new firm formation to entrepreneurial growth and innovation within an extant enterprise. A nascent[4] entrepreneur is someone who engages in the process of opportunity recognition, formation and exploitation. They may be an employee within a small, medium or large company; alternatively, they may already own a business and be considering new ways of developing that business or floating off a new enterprise; they may be operating in any industrial sector – in the private or public sector of an economy. As an employee, the nascent entrepreneur, in engaging with institutional structure and the socio-culture, should have: (a) an understanding of how the internal institutional structure works; and/or (b) a supportive manager, who can enable the nascent entrepreneur to negotiate a path through. Conditions (a) and (b) apply whether the individual is employed in the private or public sector. Without that support the employee could leave and set up a rival enterprise – a not uncommon occurrence – denying the employer the benefit that they may well have accrued.

A small business owner who does not engage in the process of opportunity recognition, formation and exploitation is not an entrepreneur. A nascent entrepreneur who engages in the process, but at some point comes unstuck due to the exigencies of the constraining structure, may be an entrepreneur if s/he not only has the serious intention of realising an opportunity but has demonstrated the requisite capabilities of an entrepreneur. For example, in the public sector – health or, say, defence industries – the regulatory environment in some instances may present a constraining wall that even the most adept entrepreneur cannot work around. Thus, it is both theoretically and practically important to differentiate between structure and agency, to be able to make veridical attributions within this highly complex process. In the case studies outlined in Chapter 8, Marilyn is not an entrepreneur because she did not engage in the process and did not exhibit the requisite skills and behaviours. Marilyn had a dream, which gave her some kind of hope, but she did not take any of the steps needed to turn the dream into an opportunity structure. In contrast, Jacqueline Gold, Anita Roddick, Henri Strzelecki and the other entrepreneurs did so. One, whom we called Crowther, commenced the process and came unstuck; he did not exhibit the qualities required to demonstrate successful engagement in the process. The exigencies of the situation were not insurmountable by an adept entrepreneur but, even though he probably could not have foreseen that his major customer would default on him, he failed to manage the inherent risk. This underlines the crucial importance of the judgemental process involved. Crowther made a judgement based on his vision of the future. He attempted to enact that vision, but a vision is a vision until the enactment of the process is complete.

Single, serial and portfolio entrepreneurs all engage in each stage of the entrepreneurial process, exhibiting the key capabilities as described. For example, Percy Shaw, after an initial business venture making roads, had the vision that became Catseye Road Studs and this was the single venture that he pursued for the remainder of his life. Henri Strzelecki similarly had a single product idea, although the garnering resources included taking over support facilities and through careful design the product is now also sold as a 'fashion' item. Roger McKechnie, on the other hand, might be described as a serial entrepreneur; he has engaged in the process successfully on several occasions, whereas Richard Branson, who appears to engage in the entre-preneurial process regularly, is a portfolio entrepreneur holding a number of different business ventures simultaneously (Brown, 1988).

Research on typologies, such as novice, habitual and portfolio entre-preneurs, should focus on the detailed entrepreneurial behaviours that each has in common, in particular at the individual–opportunity interchange within the creation–formation–exploitation process. Idiosyncratic strategies that characterise each type are likely to be revealing of particular attitudes, skills, plans and strategies. For example, habitual and portfolio entre-preneurs engage in repeat performances that may become formulaic. They appear to resist the management of enterprise (leaving that to others) and, showing a keen self-awareness, maintain focus on what they consider they can do best and probably what they enjoy most – nascent entrepreneurship. Arguably, single enterprise entrepreneurs are more adaptable, showing abil-ity to develop managerial skills to grow their business (as was true of Shaw and Strzelecki), or they may partner a 'right hand man' who is able to complement, indeed temper, their entrepreneurialism with sound operational capabilities (Chell and Tracey, 2005).

Entrepreneurial performance and enterprise performance

To form a new enterprise through engagement in the entrepreneurial pro-cess is one thing, but the cases just described demonstrate superior entre-preneurial performance. Superior entrepreneurial performance is adjudged by socio-economic criteria such as wealth creation, capital accumulation, employment of large numbers, contribution to the economy and the ability to lead/change an industry. The entrepreneurial skill set is relevant to this. The nascent entrepreneurial process occurs throughout the duration of an enterprise. Shaw, Roddick, Strzelecki, McKechnie, Gold and Woodroffe are not simply prototypical entrepreneurs; they have exhibited superior entrepreneurial performances. For example, Shaw's product was highly innovative and met a widely felt social need; he overcame the obstacles to acceptance of an innovation and he also was able to vertically integrate the business in order to be the lead producer of the road stud. Roddick could have set up one or two shops for her product and left it there, but she franchised the operation and continued to engage in the entrepreneurial process in order to grow the business. McKechnie and his team grew Phileas Fogg, sold it and demonstrated the ability to continue to be entrepreneurial through his business angel activities and founding of further new business ventures. Superior entrepreneurial performance thus arises from the capability to repeat the entrepreneurial process successfully in establishing and developing a major enterprise or enterprises.

Superior entrepreneurial performance is adjudged to be world class, but there are differences in levels of performance that may also be assessed using the same 20 criteria. Sound entrepreneurial performance would be considered robust where entrepreneurial performances fall short of international, producing regionally or nationally based enterprises, whereas the average entrepreneurial performance does sufficient to sustain the enterprise but otherwise may be regarded as pedestrian or mediocre. Below average performances would be characterised as uninspired or poor, as the three cases demonstrated in different ways. Most would be better categorised as non-entrepreneurial, as the above analysis has demonstrated. These different levels of entrepreneurial performance affect enterprise goals and strategies, leading to positive (successful) outcomes such as business creation, growth and development. This is because superior or sound entrepreneurial performances create quality opportunities, which, within an extant enterprise, result in the application of resources and managerial capabilities for the development of that opportunity (Chandler and Hanks, 1994). Resource-based theory is thus one theoretical framework that facilitates the link between the entrepreneurial skills profile and enterprise performance outcomes. The entrepreneurial skills profile may be construed as the entrepreneurial persona of the individual entrepreneur or entrepreneurial team, as appropriate. However, it is important to distinguish the role of entrepreneur as leader within an entrepreneurially led team (Chell *et al.*, 1991; Witt, 1998, 1999).

Superior or sound entrepreneurial performance may be associated with high-growth enterprises (sometimes termed 'gazelles' or 'flyers'), whereas average or pedestrian entrepreneurial performance might be associated with enterprises that are termed 'trundlers' and the uninspired entrepreneurial performance is likely to be related to poor enterprise performance or even failure of an enterprise.

At the nascent level of analysis entrepreneurs work informally with the teams that they are developing to 'win hearts and minds' and see off rival proposals. This means that the entrepreneur engages others through both the cognitive and affective communication. Furthermore, entrepreneurs are agents of change; they disrupt the status quo through radical innovations or make incremental changes to enable the enterprise to capture a new market, for example.

These attributes appear to be related to those 'dynamic capabilities' that enable the entrepreneur and entrepreneurial team to drive enterprise development forward (Zahra *et al.*, 2006). Such attributes are the source of energy and motivation that ensure the continuous development and growth of an enterprise – new or established. Thus, at the level of the firm, the process and capabilities that were identified at the nascent level are also evident. This means that within the theory of the entrepreneurial firm outlined in Chapter 3 the entrepreneurial dimension may be added.

Hence, entrepreneurial firms comprise a bundle of difficult to imitate resources within an organising framework that give the firm a competitive edge. Further, they comprise substantive entrepreneurial capabilities, arising from a cognitive-affective base, and dynamic capabilities (including efficacy, confidence, adeptness, etc.) that are energising and the source of drive and motivation. The substantive entrepreneurial capabilities ensure an idiosyncratic knowledge base, absorptive capacity, ability to synthesise information, imagination and insight, and judgement. The dynamic capabilities include leadership (which is transformative), alertness to opportunity (which I suggest is a state of readiness), business and social skills (that reach out to the socio-economic community and abstract intelligence), attitudinal orientation (i.e. a complex dispositional set labelled variously as versatility, flexibility, resilience, optimism and confidence) and organising skills (that enable the identification and garnering of appropriate resources). These capabilities are drawn upon at different points of the entrepreneurial process: opportunity recognition (insight that is meaningful in a socio-economic sense), formation (development through various legitimation steps, including testing and reputation building) and exploitation (where influence, leadership and various dynamic capabilities are needed to exploit the opportunity successfully).

Hence, the entrepreneurial profile that I have identified at the level of the individual may be applied at team and enterprise level, resulting in product, market, financial and related enterprise performance outcomes. I highlight this as an area where further work should be carried out.

Marginal groups

Research has suggested that gender, age, work status, education, income and access to finance are all significant factors that affect a person's decision to start their own business (Arenius and Minniti, 2005; Minniti *et al.*, 2005). These human capital factors are part of the socio-economy and social culture of a locale; indeed, they form the institutional structure in which entrepreneurs and others engage. These are the factors that help to shape decision-making. However, when considered from the other side of the coin – the agent – there is nothing inherent in the demographic description of particular classes of individual that will ensure that they would engage in the entrepreneurial process. Rather, the socio-economic structure acts as a constraint (or occasionally as a facilitator). For example, statistically, a teenager is less likely than an adult in their mid-thirties to engage in the process; on the other hand, it may just be that tacit (empathetic) understanding of the teenage mentality and culture enables a teenage nascent entrepreneur to light on an idea that may be successfully developed and exploited. Women are less likely than men to engage in the process for socio-cultural reasons, but, as is evident, women can become highly successful entrepreneurs. Many of the demographic factors are double-edged, as Minniti *et al.* (2005) discuss, and complex, requiring fine-grained analysis, as shown by Edwards and Ram (2006), who identify factors in the socio-economy (in particular, institutions such as the family) that influence the enterprise behaviour of immigrant family firms. Separating out the socio-structural in the structuration model is important if we are to be able to analyse the impact of structural influences independently of the part played by the agent in the structuration process (Archer, 1988).

Education and training

On the one hand, the entrepreneurial personality is a social construction, but in order to understand the entrepreneurial process in which the entrepreneur as agent is a principal component, a cognitive-affective-behavioural structure has been identified. This structure develops through learning and experience. However, fundamental to the entrepreneurial persona is the ability to generate ideas, synthesise different sorts of information, solve problems and/or provide solutions in recognition of a perceived social need. The recognition of an opportunity, that is, the very early stage of identification and insight, would appear to be that part of the individual–opportunity structure that is difficult to develop through education and training. It is that moment of insight that has been termed the 'Eureka' moment, beyond which are the rather more lengthy formation and exploitation stages:

> He was a few miles from home, but . . . [he] had no means of calculating the curve in the road, and no idea . . . where he was.
> Suddenly, two points of light pierced the gloom. A cat sitting on a fence, saved him from almost certain death. In the moment of shock, he had a vision – just a fleeting vision – of his future road studs, like so many cat's eyes strung out along the road. His idea had begun to germinate. It was born of the combination of the real cat's eyes and the tram tracks.
> (Edwards, 1972: 20)

Then ensued many years of trial and error as Percy Shaw attempted to put together a prototype and get the Ministry of Transport to recognise his invention.

By no means all entrepreneurial ideas require an invention, however many draw on industry-specific knowledge and skills, whether that is how to produce potions based on natural ingredients that care for the body and hair, how to produce a high-quality garment that protects against foul weather or how to produce a snack food that would be up-market, cosmopolitan and highly profitable. Once the idea emerged, the other skills needed to form and exploit the opportunity developed heuristically and experientially. However, while the inspiration may occur in a flash, the formation and exploitation processes may take from months to many years, especially in the case of a patented invention:

> Genius is one per cent inspiration and ninety-nine per cent perspiration.
> (Thomas Alva Edison (1847–1931))

Nevertheless, not all ideas are generated by a 'eureka moment': some ideas are built incrementally on an existing cognitive set, where the extant knowledge base is particularly important; others are developed through group discussion and consensus; yet other ideas are recognised through search by employing a network of information sources and the outcome is a synthesis; alternative methods of idea generation occur through debating alternative models and options, using a dialectical approach to generate a novel idea; and 'assessors' take a critical approach to idea generation (Vandenbosch *et al.*, 2006). But the nature of innovation and exploitation often means that the entrepreneur works in a solitary fashion, possibly using a network of contacts to generate information without them necessarily being aware of the role they may be playing. Entrepreneurs may also act as catalysts, stimulating others to generate ideas that the entrepreneur will then synthesise into a potential 'solution'; this enables the entrepreneur to enact the 'opportunity formation stage' in such a way that there is already acceptance of the proposed solution (see, for example, the case of Don Whitehead, VSW: Chell *et al.*, 1991: 115–121).

Entrepreneurial capability is thus developed heuristically and experientially but, whilst entrepreneurs learn, can they be taught? The behavioural skills of entrepreneurs are sophisticated, higher order skills that require engagement in the process. It is difficult to see how they could be taught through traditional methods; rather, they may be developed through real projects that facilitate emersion in the entrepreneurial process through which heuristic and experiential learning may occur (McMullan and Gillin, 1998). Katz (2007) points out that much of the education and training of potential entrepreneurs and small business owners has focused on the development of business skills. However, he acknowledges that the recent work on opportunity recognition and the psychological aspects of entrepreneurship are opening up entrepreneurship education. This should take entrepreneurship beyond the training in business planning, finance and management to the heart of entrepreneurship. It should enable individuals to become more self-aware, for example, of their creative potential and desire to develop sound, if not superior, entrepreneurial capabilities.

Conclusion

In this chapter I have drawn together a number of themes that have been explored more fully in the preceding chapters in an effort to provide answers to the question: is there a need theoretically, methodologically and practically to assume an 'entrepreneurial personality'? This book addresses itself to the call for more research that addresses the question 'who is an entrepreneur?' within a well-developed interdisciplinary theoretical framework (Ucbasaran *et al.*, 2001). Economic and sociological approaches have largely addressed the process and function of the entrepreneur, whilst under-theorising his/her nature. In taking an interdisciplinary and a multi-level approach to analysis, it has been possible to develop models of complex patterns of entrepreneurial behaviour emerging from the entrepreneurial process. In focusing on this pattern through a specific disciplinary lens it has been possible to develop a theoretical approach that recognises the subjective nature of opportunity creation at the kernel of entrepreneurial behaviour and then to build up the behavioural pattern through each layer of opportunity formation, development and exploitation. Social constructionism and its paradigmatic assumptions have facilitated the recognition that the entrepreneurial personality within society is a social construction through which entrepreneurial behaviour as a form of life may be recognised. Cognitive constructivism, however, permits the integration of a cognitive-affective structure that enables the demonstration of skills, capabilities, goals, strategies, feelings, and so forth, which are developed experientially and heuristically. These are two critically important halves of the same coin – that of the entrepreneurial persona. From this base of theory and methodology, it was possible to build from detailed case study analysis. This approach also highlights the importance of qualitative research to build theory in entrepreneurship.

It is clear that there are still gaps in our knowledge, propositions that require empirical testing and many doctoral theses that could be produced in order to deepen our understanding. A clear implication of this work, however, is the need for very carefully designed methodologies to ensure further insights and further testing. Qualitative design work is essential; large samples are not really necessary at this stage of research, but multiple levels of analysis would be particularly helpful to enable us to see and position the entrepreneur in the enterprise that s/he has conceived. Case study methods such as those of Yin (1994), developing the approach taken in this book, would be particularly illuminating. Identification of nascent entrepreneurs and longitudinal analyses would help to further the understanding of the process and also the social learning that occurs to build the knowledge base and cognitive-affective structure.

The social construction of the entrepreneur and entrepreneurial persona has enabled an explanation of the entrepreneur and entrepreneurial process regardless of: (a) the heterogeneity of entrepreneurs and their enterprises; (b) the multiple perspectives of different experts, lay personnel and entrepreneurs themselves; (c) the level of knowledge and understanding; and (d) the use of different labels to describe particular behaviours. Undoubtedly, that social construction remains and will remain, however what I have argued, based on detailed reviews of extant research, is that whatever the external persona of various entrepreneurs, there is a common cognitive-affective core. Identification of the cognitive alone is not sufficient as it fails to explain the drive, the motivational core, that propels the entrepreneur and entrepreneurial process forward. This analysis also gives psychology a central role to play in the development of entrepreneurship theory.

There are some practical and policy issues that this book highlights. The assumption of the entrepreneurial personality as a social construction does not mean that 'anyone can be an entrepreneur'. Anyone can pursue an entrepreneurial career and attempt to develop the kinds of skills and motivation identified in this book, but putting these various behaviours into practice is not easy. The analysis of the cases alone should be sufficient testament to contest the claims of popular books such as that of Sahar and Bobby Hashemi (2002), *Anyone Can Do It* (i.e. become an entrepreneur).

The training implications for extant business owner-managers should be focused on their judgemental decision-making, enabling them to be more discerning about what are good or poor opportunities to be pursued or quickly dropped. Nascent entrepreneurs should focus on the early stages of the opportunity formation process, increase their self-awareness and develop those social and interpersonal skills that will enable them to interactively test and develop an opportunity within the socio-economic/business environment. Entrepreneurship should be taught through real-life project work so that students may hone their skills heuristically and experientially.

Final word

The latest safari – the hunt for the heffalump[5] – has ended. I believe that it is now possible to see all the structural parts that make up the beast. But it is not possible to understand the beast without an understanding of the context – the plains in which it roams. This safari has been most enjoyable; I wish such joy to all who continue the trek.

Notes

1 No doubt it could be argued that choice and free will are but illusions, however each entrepreneur faced with a judgemental decision in which the future is unknown and uncertain will act as if they have a real choice and they will make their decision. We cannot know (ever) what might have been had they taken the

opposite decision. Nor can we deduce from this that the individual's decision was fated or predetermined. Furthermore, individuals are able to use their memory and imagination to consider possibilities and on that basis choose between imagined futures. We therefore suggest that the agent also has power to structure situations and that it is this process of producing new structures – new opportunities – that is the essence of entrepreneurship.

2 Also included are inalienable resources of partners and members of the venture team where closely involved in the opportunity recognition, formation and/or exploitation process.

3 Inspired by Polyani's famous dictum: We can know more than we can tell (Polyani, 1966).

4 'Nascent' is defined as 'coming into being' and so aptly denotes my definition of the entrepreneurial process as being 'emergent'.

5 The 'heffalump' is a mythical beast described in A. A. Milne's *Winnie-the-Pooh*; it has been used metaphorically in research to investigate the nature of the entrepreneur (Kilby, 1971: 1; quoted in Chell *et al.*, 1991: 2).

Bibliography

Agor, W. H. (1986) 'The logic of intuition – how top executives make important decisions', *Organizational Dynamics*, 14: 5–18.

Ajzen, I. (1987) 'Attitudes, traits, and actions – dispositional prediction of behavior in personality and social-psychology', *Advances in Experimental Social Psychology*, 20: 1–63.

Ajzen, I. (1991) 'The theory of planned behavior', *Organizational Behavior and Human Decision Processes*, 50: 179–211.

Aldrich, H. (1999) *Organisations Evolving*, London: Sage.

Aldrich, H. and Whetton, D. (1981) 'Making the most of simplicity: organisation sets, action sets, and networks', in P. Nystrom and W. H. Starbuck (Eds) *Handbook of Organisational Design*, New York: Oxford University Press, pp. 385–408.

Aldrich, H. and Zimmer, C. (1986) 'Entrepreneurship through social networks', in D. L. Sexton and R. W. Smilor (Eds) *The Art and Science of Entrepreneurship*, Cambridge, MA: Ballinger, pp. 2–23.

Alexander, A. P. (1967) 'The supply of industrial entrepreneurship', *Explorations in Entrepreneurial History*, 4: 136–149.

Allinson, C. W. and Hayes, J. (1996) 'The cognitive style index: a measure of intuition-analysis for organizational research', *Journal of Management Studies*, 33: 119–135.

Allinson, C. W., Chell, E. and Hayes, J. (2000) 'Intuition and entrepreneurial behavior', *European Journal of Work and Organizational Psychology*, 9: 31–43.

Allport, G. W. (1937) *Personality: a Psychological Explanation*, New York: Holt.

Alvarez, S. A. and Barney, J. B. (2004) 'Organizing rent generation and appropriation: toward a theory of the entrepreneurial firm', *Journal of Business Venturing*, 19: 621–635.

Alvarez, S. A. and Busenitz, L. W. (2001) 'The entrepreneurship of resource-based theory', *Journal of Management*, 27: 755–775.

Amabile, T. M. (1983) *The Social Psychology of Creativity*, New York: Springer.

Amabile, T. M. (1990) 'Within you, without you: the social psychology of creativity, and beyond', in M. A. Runco and R. S. Albert (Eds) *Theories of Creativity*, Newbury Park, London: Sage, pp. 61–91.

Amit, R., Glosten, L. and Muller, E. (1993) 'Challenges to theory development in entrepreneurship research', *Journal of Management Studies*, 30: 815–834.

Angleitner, A. and Demtroder, A. I. (1988) 'Acts and dispositions: a reconsideration of the act frequency approach', *European Journal of Personality*, 2: 121–141.

Archer, M. S. (1988) *Culture and Agency; The Place of Culture in Social Theory*, Cambridge: Cambridge University Press.

Ardichvili, A., Cardozo, R. and Ray, S. (2003) 'A theory of entrepreneurial opportunity identification and development', *Journal of Business Venturing*, 18: 105–123.

Arenius, P. and Minniti, M. (2005) 'Perceptual variables and nascent entrepreneurship', *Small Business Economics*, 24: 233–247.

Argyle, M. and Little, B. (1972) 'Do personality traits apply to social behaviour?', *Journal for the Theory of Social Behaviour*, 2: 1–35.

Atkinson, R. H. and Birch, D. (1979) *Introduction to Motivation*, New Jersey: Van Nostrand.

Audretsch, D. B., Baumol, W. J. and Burke, A. E. (2001) 'Competition policy in dynamic markets', *International Journal of Industrial Organisation*, 19: 613–634.

Bandura, A. (1977) *Social Learning Theory*, Englewood Cliffs, NJ: Prentice Hall.

Bandura, A. (1986) *The Social Foundations of Thought and Action*, Englewood Cliffs, NJ: Prentice Hall.

Bandura, A. (1997) *Self-efficacy: the Exercise of Control*, New York: Freeman.

Bandura, A. (1999) 'Social cognitive theory of personality', in D. Cerzone and Y. Shoda (Eds), *The Coherence of Personality: Social Cognitive Biases in Consistency, Variability and Organization*, New York: Guilford, pp. 185–241.

Barnard, C. I. (1938) *The Functions of the Executive*, Cambridge, MA: Harvard University Press.

Baron, R. A. (1998) 'Cognitive mechanisms in entrepreneurship: Why and when entrepreneurs think differently than other people', *Journal of Business Venturing*, 13: 275–294.

Baron, R. A. (2000) 'Psychological perspectives on entrepreneurship: Cognitive and social factors in entrepreneurs' success', *Current Directions in Psychological Science*, 9: 15–18.

Baron, R. A. (2004) 'The cognitive perspective: a valuable tool for answering entrepreneurship's basic "why" questions', *Journal of Business Venturing*, 19: 221–239.

Baron, R. A. and Markman, G. D. (2003) 'Beyond social capital: the role of entrepreneurs' social competence in their financial success', *Journal of Business Venturing*, 18: 41–60.

Baron, R. A. and Ward, T. B. (2004) 'Expanding entrepreneurial cognition's toolbox: potential contributions from the field of cognitive science', *Entrepreneurship Theory and Practice*, 28: 553–574.

Barreto, H. (1989) *The Entrepreneur in Micro-economic Theory: Disappearance and Explanation*, New York: Routledge.

Barrick, M. R. and Mount, M. K. (1993) 'Autonomy as a moderator of the relationships between the Big 5 personality dimensions and job-performance', *Journal of Applied Psychology*, 78: 111–118.

Bateman, T. S. and Crant, J. M. (1993) 'The proactive component of organizational-behavior – a measure and correlates', *Journal of Organizational Behavior*, 14: 103–118.

Baum, J. R. and Locke, E. A. (2004) 'The relationship of entrepreneurial traits, skill, and motivation to subsequent venture growth', *Journal of Applied Psychology*, 89: 587–598.

Baum, J. R., Locke, E. A. and Smith, K. G. (2001) 'A multidimensional model of venture growth', *Academy of Management Journal*, 44: 292–303.

Baum, J. R., Freese, M. and Baron, R. A. (2007) *The Psychology of Entrepreneurship*, Mahwah, NJ: Lawrence Erlbaum Associates.

Baumol, W. J. (1968) 'Entrepreneurship and economic theory', *American Economic Review (Papers and Proceedings)*, 58: 64–71.

Baumol, W. J. (1990) 'Entrepreneurship: productive, unproductive, and destructive', *Journal of Political Economy*, 98: 893–921.

Becherer, R. C. and Maurer, J. G. (1999) 'The proactive personality disposition and entrepreneurial behavior among small company presidents', *Journal of Small Business Management*, 37: 28–36.

Bechhofer, F. and Elliott, B. (1981) *The Petite Bourgeoisie, Comparative Studies of the Uneasy Stratum*, London: Macmillan.

Begley, T. M. and Boyd, D. P. (1985) 'The relationship of the Jenkins Activity Survey to Type A behaviour and business executives', *Journal of Vocational Behaviour*, 27: 316–328.

Begley, T. M. and Boyd, D. P. (1986) 'Psychological characteristics associated with entrepreneurial performance', in R. Ronstadt, J. A. Hornaday, R. Peterson and K. H. Vesper (Eds) *Frontiers of Entrepreneurship Research*, Wellesley, MA: Babson College, Centre for Entrepreneurial Studies, pp. 146–165.

Belbin, M. (1981) *Management Teams: Why they Succeed or Fail*, London: Heinemann.

Bentham, J. (1787) *Defence of Usury*. University of London: T. Payne & Son.

Berger, P. and Luckmann, T. (1967) *The Social Construction of Reality*, New York: Doubleday.

Bird, B. (1988) 'Implementing entrepreneurial ideas: the case for intention', *Academy of Management Review*, 13: 442–453.

Bird, B. J. (1989) *Entrepreneurial Behavior*, Glenview, IL: Scott, Foresman & Co.

Birley, S. (1985) 'The role of networks in the entrepreneurial process', *Journal of Business Venturing*, 1: 107–117.

Birley, S. (1986) 'The role of new firms – births, deaths and job generation', *Strategic Management Journal*, 7: 361–376.

Birley, S. and Stockley, S. (2000) 'Entrepreneurial teams and venture growth', in D. Sexton and H. Landstrom (Eds) *The Blackwell Handbook of Entrepreneurship*, Oxford: Blackwell, pp. 287–307.

Birley, S. and Westhead, P. (1993) 'A comparison of new businesses established by "novice" and "habitual" founders in Great Britain', *International Small Business Journal*, 12: 38–60.

Blackburn, R. and Curran, J. (1993) 'In search of spatial differences: evidence from a study of small service sector enterprises', in J. Curran and D. Storey (Eds) *Small Firms in Urban and Rural Locations*, London: Routledge, pp. 164–193.

Bonnett, C. and Furnham, A. (1991) 'Who wants to be an entrepreneur – a study of adolescents interested in a Young Enterprise Scheme', *Journal of Economic Psychology*, 12: 465–478.

Borland, C. M. (1974) Locus of control, need for achievement and entrepreneurship. Unpublished dissertation, University of Texas.

Bouchikhi, H. (1993) 'A constructivist framework for understanding entrepreneurial performance', *Organization Studies*, 14: 551–569.

Bowen, D. D. and Hisrich, R. D. (1986) 'The female entrepreneur: a career development perspective', *Academy of Management Review*, 11: 393–407.

Bowers, K. S. (1973) 'Situationism in psychology: an analysis and a critique', *Psychological Review*, 80: 307–336.

Boyd, D. P. (1984) 'Type-A behaviour, financial performance and organizational growth in small business firms', *Journal of Occupational Psychology*, 57: 137–140.

Boyd, N. G. and Vozikis, G. S. (1994) 'The influence of self-efficacy on the development of entrepreneurial intentions and actions', *Entrepreneurship Theory and Practice*, 19: 63–77.

Brandstätter, H. (1997) 'Becoming an entrepreneur – a question of personality structure?', *Journal of Economic Psychology*, 18: 157–177.

Briggs, D. G. and Myers, I. (1993) *Introduction to Types*, Oxford: Oxford Psychologists Press.

Brigham, K. H., De Castro, J. O. and Shepard, D. A. (2007) 'A person-organization fit model of owner-managers' cognitive style and organizational demands', *Entrepreneurship Theory and Practice*, 31: 29–52.

Brittain, J. W. and Freeman, J. H. (1980) 'Organization proliferation and density dependent selection', in J. R. Kimberley and R. H. Miles (Eds) *The Organizational Life Cycle*, San Francisco: Jossey-Bass.

Brockhaus, R. H. (1980a) 'Psychological and environmental factors which distinguish the successful from the unsuccessful entrepreneur: a longitudinal study', paper presented at the Academy of Management Meeting, pp. 368–372.

Brockhaus, R. H. (1980b) 'Risk taking propensity of entrepreneurs', *Academy of Management Journal*, 23: 509–520.

Brockhaus, R. H. (1982) 'The psychology of the entrepreneur', in C. A. Kent, D. L. Sexton and K. H. Vesper (Eds) *Encyclopaedia of Entrepreneurship*, Englewood-Cliffs, NJ: Prentice-Hall, pp. 39–57.

Brockhaus, R. H. and Nord, W. R. (1979) 'An exploration of factors affecting the entrepreneurial decision: personal characteristics vs. environmental conditions', *Proceedings of the National Academy of Management*, 39: 364–368.

Brown, M. (1988) *Richard Branson The Inside Story*, London: Headline.

Brush, C. G. (1992) 'Research on women business owners: past trends, a new perspective and future directions', *Entrepreneurship Theory and Practice*, 16: 5–30.

Burke, A. E., FitzRoy, F. R. and Nolan M. A. (2000) 'When less is more: distinguishing between entrepreneurial choice and performance', *Oxford Bulletin of Economics and Statistics*, 62: 565–587.

Burns, B. and Kippenberger, A. (1988) *Entrepreneur*, London: Macmillan.

Burns, T. and Stalker, G. M. (1961) *The Management of Innovation*, London: Tavistock.

Burr, V. (1995) *An Introduction to Social Constructionism*, London: Routledge.

Burrell, G. and Morgan, G. (1979) *Sociological Paradigms and Organizational Analysis*, London: Heinemann.

Busenitz, L. W. and Barney, J. B. (1997) 'Differences between entrepreneurs and managers in large organizations: Biases and heuristics in strategic decision-making', *Journal of Business Venturing*, 12: 9–30.

Busenitz, L. W. and Lau, C. M. (1996) 'A cross-cultural model of new venture creation', *Entrepreneurship Theory and Practice*, 20: 25–38.

Buttner, E. H. (1992) 'Entrepreneurial stress: Is it hazardous to your health?', *Journal of Managerial Issues*, 4: 223–240.

Cantillon, R. (1755) *Essai sur la Nature du Commerce en General* (ed. by H. Higgs), London: Macmillan, 1931.

Cantor, N. and Mischel, W. (1979) 'Prototypes in person perception', *Advances in Experimental Social Psychology*, 12: 3–52.

Caplan, R., Cobb, S., French, J., van Harrison, R. and Pinneau, S. (1975) *Demands and Worker Health: Main Effects and Organisational Differences*, Washington, DC: US Government Printing Office.

Carland, J. W. (1982) 'Entrepreneurship in a small business setting: an exploratory study', University of Georgia, Athens.

Carland, J. W., Hoy, F., Boulton, W. R. and Carland, J. A. C. (1984) 'Differentiating entrepreneurs from small business owners: a conceptualization', *Academy of Management Review*, 9: 354–359.

Carland, J. W., Hoy, F. and Carland, J.- A. C. (1988a) ' "Who is an Entrepreneur?" is a question worth asking', *American Journal of Small Business*, 12: 33–39.

Carland, J. W., Carland, J. C., Hoy, F. and Boulton, W. R. (1988b) 'Distinctions between entrepreneurial and small business ventures', *International Journal of Management*, 5: 98–103.

Carolis, D. M. De and Saparito, P. (2006) 'Social capital, cognition, and entrepreneurial opportunities: a theoretical framework,' *Entrepreneurship Theory and Practice*, 30: 41–56.

Carroll, G. R. and Delacroix, J. (1982) 'Organization mortality in the newspaper industry of Argentina and Ireland: an ecological approach', *Administrative Science Quarterly*, 27: 169–198.

Carson, R. C. (1989) 'Personality', *Annual Review of Psychology*, 40: 227–248.

Carsrud, A. L. and Krueger, N. F. Jr (1995) 'Entrepreneurship and social psychology: behavioural technology for the new venture initiation process', in J. A. Katz and R. H. Brockhaus, Sr. (Eds), *Advances in Entrepreneurship, Firm Emergence and Growth*, Greenwich, CT: JAI Press, pp. 73–96.

Casson, M. (1982) *The Entrepreneur – An Economic Theory*, Oxford: Martin Robertson.

Casson, M. (1995) *Entrepreneurship and Business Culture – Studies in the Economics of Trust*, vol. 1, Aldershot: Edward Elgar.

Casson, M. (2000) *The Entrepreneur – An Economic Theory (2nd ed.)*, Cheltenham: Edward Elgar.

Casson, M. (2005) 'Entrepreneurship and the theory of the firm', *Journal of Economic Behavior and Organization*, 58: 327–348.

Castells, M. (1996) *The Rise of the Network Society*, Malden, MA: Blackwell.

Castells, M. and Hall, P. (1994) *Technopoles of the World: The Making of 21st Century Industrial Complexes*, London: Routledge.

Cattell, R. B. (1946) *Description and Measurement of Personality*, London: George Harrap.

Cattell, R. B. (1971) *Abilities: Their Structure, Growth and Action*, New York: Houghton Mifflin.

Cattell, R. B. and Kline, P. (1977) *The Scientific Analysis of Personality and Motivation*. New York: Academic Press.

Cattell, R. B., Eber, H. W. and Tatsuoka, M. M. (1970) *Handbook for the Sixteen Personality Factor Questionnaire*, Champaign, IL: Institute for Personality and Ability Testing.

Chandler, G. N. and Hanks, S. H. (1994) 'Founder competence, the environment, and venture performance', *Entrepreneurship Theory and Practice*, 18: 77–89.

Chell, E. (1985a) 'The entrepreneurial personality: a few ghosts laid to rest?', *International Small Business Journal*, 3: 43–54.

Chell, E. (1985b) *Participation and Organization: A Social Psychological Approach*, London: Macmillan.

Chell, E. (1986) 'The entrepreneurial personality: a review and some theoretical developments', in J. Curran, J. Stanworth and D. Watkins (Eds) *The Survival of the Small Firm, Vol.1: The Economics of Survival and Entrepreneurship*, Aldershot: Gower, pp. 102–119.

Chell, E. (1993) *The Psychology of Behaviour in Organizations* (2nd ed.), London: Macmillan.

Chell, E. (1998) 'The critical incident technique', in G. Symons and C. Cassell (Eds) *Qualitative Methods and Analysis in Organizational Research: A Practical Guide*, London: Sage, pp. 51–72.

Chell, E. (2000) 'Toward researching the "opportunistic entrepreneur"; a social constructionist approach and research agenda', *European Journal of Work and Organizational Psychology*, 29: 153–172.

Chell, E. (2004) 'The nature of enterprise in a global economy: some critical observations from a socio-historical perspective', in P. C. van der Sijde, A. Ridder and A. J. Groen (Eds) *Entrepreneurship and Innovation – Essays in Honour of Wim During*, Enschede, The Netherlands: Nikos, The Dutch Institute for Knowledge Intensive Entrepreneurship, pp. 33–51.

Chell, E. (2007a) 'Social enterprise and entrepreneurship: towards a convergent theory of the entrepreneurial process', *International Small Business Journal*, 25: 5–23.

Chell, E. (2007b) 'The training and development of managers and entrepreneurs: the role of integrative capability in the context of innovation', in M. Ozbilgin and A. Malach-Pines (Eds) *Career Choice in Entrepreneurship and Management*, London: Edward Elgar, pp. 327–348.

Chell, E. and Allman, K. (2003) 'Mapping the motivations and intentions of technology-oriented entrepreneurs', *R & D Management*, 33: 117–134.

Chell, E. and Baines, S. (1998) 'Does gender affect business "performance"? A study of micro-businesses in business service in the UK', *Entrepreneurship and Regional Development*, 10: 117–135.

Chell, E. and Baines, S. (2000) 'Networking, entrepreneurship and micro-business behaviour', *Entrepreneurship and Regional Development*, 12: 195–215.

Chell, E. and Haworth, J. M. (1987) 'Entrepreneurship and the entrepreneurial personality: a review', in H. Edwards (Ed.) *London Business School, Small Business Bibliography 1985–86*, London: London Business School, pp. 6–33.

Chell, E. and Oakey, R. (2004) 'Knowledge creation, its transfer, and the role of science enterprise education: a research agenda', *Innovation: Management, Policy and Practice*, 6: 444–457.

Chell, E. and Pittaway, L. (1998) *The Social Construction of Entrepreneurship*. Paper presented at the ISBA, Durham University, UK.

Chell, E. and Tracey, P. (2005) 'Relationship building in small firms: the development of a model'. *Human Relations*, 58: 577–616.

Chell, E., Haworth, J. M. and Brearley, S. (1991) *The Entrepreneurial Personality: Concepts, Cases and Categories*, London: Routledge.

Chen, C. C., Greene P. G. and Crick, A. (1998) 'Does entrepreneurial self-efficacy distinguish entrepreneurs from managers?', *Journal of Business Venturing*, 13: 295–316.

Chiasson, M. and Saunders, C. (2005) 'Reconciling diverse approaches to opportunity research using the structuration theory', *Journal of Business Venturing*, 20: 747–767.

Choi, Y. B. (1993) *Paradigms and Conventions: Uncertainty, Decision Making and Entrepreneurship*, Michigan: University of Michigan Press.

Ciavarella, M. A., Buchholtz, A. K., Riordan, C. M., Gatewood, R. D. and Stokes, G. S. (2004) 'The Big Five and venture survival: Is there a linkage?', *Journal of Business Venturing*, 19: 465–483.

Clark, J. B. (1907) *Essentials of Economic Theory* (reprinted in 1968), New York: Augustus M. Kelley.

Coase, R. H. (1937) 'The nature of the firm', *Economica*, 4: 386–405.

Cochran, T. C. (1965) 'The entrepreneur in economic change', *Explorations in Entrepreneurial History*, 3: 25–38.

Cochran, T. C. (1969) 'Entrepreneurship', in D. L. Sills (Ed.) *International Encyclopaedia of the Social Sciences*, vol. 5, New York: Macmillan and The Free Press, pp. 87–90.

Collins, C. J., Hanges, P. J. and Locke, E. A. (2004) 'The relationship of achievement motivation to entrepreneurial behavior: A meta-analysis', *Human Performance*, 17: 95–117.

Conn, S. R. and Rieke, M. L. (1994) *The 16 PF Fifth Edition Technical Manual*, Champaign, IL: Institute for Personality and Ability Testing.

Costa, P. T., Jr and McCrae R. R. (1992) 'Four ways five factors are basic', *Personality and Individual Differences*, 135: 653–665.

Craib, I. (1992) *Anthony Giddens*, London: Routledge.

Crandall, R. (1973) 'Measurement of self-esteem and related constructs', in J. P. Robinson and P. R. Shaver (Eds) *Measurement of Social Psychological Attitudes*, Ann Arbor: University of Michigan.

Crant, J. M. (1996) 'The proactive personality scale as a predictor of entrepreneurial intentions', *Journal of Small Business Management*, 34: 42–49.

Cromie, S. (1988) 'Motivations of aspiring male and female entrepreneurs', *Journal of Occupational Behaviour*, 8: 251–261.

Csikszentmihalyi, M. (1996) *Creativity: Flow and the Psychology of Discovery and Invention*, New York: Harper Collins.

D'Andrade, R. G. (1974) 'Meaning and the assessment of behavior', in H. M. Blalok Jr. (Ed.) *Measurement in the Social Sciences*, Chicago: Aldine-Atherton, pp. 159–186.

Davidsson, P. (2004) *Researching Entrepreneurship*, New York: Springer.

Davidsson, P. and Honig, B. (2003) 'The role of social and human capital among nascent entrepreneurs', *Journal of Business Venturing*, 18: 301–331.

Davies, B. (1998) 'Psychology's subject: a commentary on the relativism/realism debate', in I. Parker (Ed.) *Social Constructionism, Discourse and Realism*, London: Sage, pp. 133–145.

Deary, I. J. and Matthews, G. (1993) 'Personality traits are alive and well', *The Psychologist*, 6: 299–311.

Deetz, S. (1996) 'Describing differences in approaches to organization science: rethinking Burrell and Morgan and their legacy', *Organization Science*, 7: 191–207.

Delmar, F. and Davidsson, P. (2000) 'Where do they come from? Prevalence and characteristics of nascent entrepreneurs', *Entrepreneurship and Regional Development*, 12: 1–23.

De Raad, B. (2000) *The Big Five Personality Factors: The Psycholexical Approach to Personality*, Seattle, WA: Hogrefe and Huber.

Derrida, J. (1978) *Writing and Difference* (trans. by A. Bass), London: Routledge & Kegan Paul.

Descartes, R. (1637) *Discourse on Method*, New York: Dover.

Dodd, S. D. (2002) 'Metaphors and meaning – a grounded cultural model of US entrepreneurship', *Journal of Business Venturing*, 17: 519–535.

Drummond, H. (1996) *Escalation in Decision Making*, Oxford: Oxford University Press.

Dubini, P. and Aldrich, H. (1991) 'Personal and extended networks are central to the entrepreneurial process', *Journal of Business Venturing*, 6: 305–313.

Dutta, D. K. and Crossan, M. M. (2005) 'The nature of entrepreneurial opportunities: understanding the process using the 4I organizational learning framework', *Entrepreneurship Theory and Practice*, 29: 425–449.

Edwards, F. (1972) *Cats Eyes*, Oxford: Blackwell.

Edwards, P. and Ram, M. (2006) 'Surviving on the margins of the economy: working relationships in small, low wage firms', *Journal of Management Studies*, 43: 895–916.

Eisenhardt, K. M. and Schoonhoven, C. B. (1996) 'Resource-based view of strategic alliance formation: strategic and social effects in entrepreneurial firms', *Organization Science*, 7: 136–150.

Ekehammer, B. (1974) 'Interactionism in personality from a historical perspective', *Psychological Bulletin*, 81: 1026–1048.

Endler, N. (1983) 'Interactionism: a personality model, but not yet a theory', in M. M. Page (Ed.) *Nebraska Symposium on Motivation 1982: Personality – Current Theory and Research*, Lincoln, NE: University of Nebraska Press.

Endler, N. and Parker, J. (1992) 'Interactionism revisited: reflections on the continuing crisis in the personality area', *European Journal of Personality*, 6: 177–198.

Endres, A. M. and Woods, C. R. (2007) 'The case for more "subjectivist" research on how entrepreneurs create opportunities', *International Journal of Entrepreneurial Behaviour and Research*, 13: 222–234.

Engle, D. E., Mah, J. J. and Sadri, G. (1997) 'An empirical comparison of entrepreneurs and employees: implications for innovation', *Creativity Research Journal*, 10: 45–49.

Envick, B. R. and Langford, M. (2000) 'The Five-Factor model of personality: assessing entrepreneurs and managers', *Academy of Entrepreneurship Journal*, 6: 6–17.

Epstein, S. (1977) 'Traits are alive and well', in D. Magnusson and N. S. Endler (Eds) *Personality at the Crossroads*, Hillsdale, NJ: Lawrence Erlbaum Associates, Inc., pp. 83–98.

Eysenck, H. J. (1967) *The Biological Basis of Personality*, Springfield, IL: Charles C. Thomas.

Eysenck, H. J. (1997) 'Personality and experimental psychology: the unification of psychology and the possibility of a paradigm', *Journal of Personality and Social Psychology*, 73: 1224–1237.

Eysenck, H. J. and Eysenck, S. B. J. (1991) *The Eysenck Personality Questionnaire – Revised*. Sevenoaks: Hodder and Stoughton.

Fagenson, E. A. (1993) 'Personal value-systems of men and women entrepreneurs versus managers', *Journal of Business Venturing*, 8: 409–430.

Fairdough, N. (1991) 'What might we mean by "enterprise discourse"?', in R. Keat and N. Abercrombie (Eds) *Enterprise Culture*, London: Routledge, pp. 38–57.

Filion, L. J. (1991) 'Vision and relations: elements for an entrepreneurial meta-model', *International Small Business Journal*, 9: 16–40.

Fineman, S: (1977) 'The achievement motive construct and its measurement: where are we now?', *British Journal of Psychology*, 68: 1–22.

Fleishman, E. (1957) 'The Leadership Opinion Questionnaire', in R. M. Stogdill and A. E. Coons (Eds) *Leader Behavior: Its Description and Measurement*, Columbus, OH: Ohio State University, Bureau of Business Research.

Fletcher, D. E. (2006) 'Entrepreneurial processes and the social construction of opportunity', *Entrepreneurship and Regional Development*, 18: 421–440.

Follett, M. P. (1940) *Dynamic Administration*, New York: Harper.

Forbes, D. P. (2005) 'The effects of strategic decision making on entrepreneurial self-efficacy', *Entrepreneurship Theory and Practice*, 29: 599–626.

Ford, J. L. (1990) 'Shackle's theory of decision-making under uncertainty: a brief exposition and critical assessment', in S. F. Frowen (Ed.) *Unknowledge and Choice in Economics – Proceedings of a Conference in Honour of GLS Shackle*, Houndsmills: Macmillan, pp. 20–45.

Foss, N. J. (2000) 'Equilibrium vs. evolution in resource based perspective: conflicting legacies of Demsetz and Penrose', in N. J. Foss and P. L. Robertson (Eds) *Resources, Technology and Strategy Explorations in Resource-based Perspective*, London: Routledge, pp. 11–30.

Foss, N. J. and Robertson, P. L. (2000) *Resources, Technology and Strategy Explorations in Resource-based Perspective*, London: Routledge.

Foucault, M. (1979) *Discipline and Punishment*, New York: Vintage.

Foucault, M. (1984) 'The order of discourse', in M. Shapiro (Ed.) *Language and Politics*, Oxford: Basil Blackwell, pp. 108–138.

Frowen, S. F. (1990) *Unknowledge and Choice in Economics Proceedings of a conference in Honour of GLS Shackle*, Houndsmills: Macmillan.

Funder, D. C. (2001) 'Personality', *Annual Review of Psychology*, 52: 197–221.

Furnham, A. (1986) 'Economic locus of control', *Human Relations*, 39: 29–43.

Furnham, A. (1992) *Personality at Work*, London: Routledge.

Furnham, A. and Lewis, A. (1986) *The Economic Mind – The Social Psychology of Economic Behaviour*, Brighton: Wheatsheaf.

Gaglio, C. M. (1997) 'Opportunity identification: review, critique and suggested research directions', *Advances in Entrepreneurship, Firm Emergence and Growth*, 3: 139–201.

Gaglio, C. M. (2004) 'The role of mental simulations and counterfactual thinking in the opportunity identification process', *Entrepreneurship Theory and Practice*, 28: 533–552.

Gaglio, C. M. and Katz, J. A. (2001) 'The psychological basis of opportunity identification: Entrepreneurial alertness', *Small Business Economics*, 16: 95–111.

Galton, F. (1884) 'Measurement of character', *Fortnightly Review*, 36: 179–185.

Gardner, W. L. and Martinko, M. J. (1996) 'Using the Myers-Briggs type indicator to study managers: a literature review and research agenda', *Journal of Management*, 22: 45–83.

Gartner, W. B. (1989) ' "Who is an Entrepreneur?" Is the Wrong Question', *Entrepreneurship Theory and Practice*, 12: 47–68.

Gartner, W. B., Bird, B. J. and Starr, J. A. (1992) 'Acting as if: differentiating from organizational behaviour', *Entrepreneurship Theory and Practice*, 16: 13–31.

Gergen, K. J. (1999) *An Invitation to Social Constructionism*, London: Sage.

Giddens, A. (1984) *The Constitution of Society*, Cambridge: Polity Press.

Giddens, A. (1991) *Modernity and Self-identity: Self and Society in the Late Modern Age*, London: Blackwell.

Gilligan, C. (1982) *In a Different Voice*, Cambridge, MA: Harvard University Press.

Ginsberg, A. and Buchholtz, A. (1989) 'Are entrepreneurs a breed apart? a look at the evidence', *Journal of General Management*, 15: 32–40.

Gioia, D. A. and Pitre, E. (1990) 'Multi-paradigm perspectives on theory building', *Academy of Management Review*, 15: 584–602.

Gold, J. (1995) *Good Vibrations*, London: Pavilion.

Gooding, R. Z. (1989) 'Decision-making and the structure of strategic problems', *The Working Conference on Managerial Cognition*, Washington, DC (cited in Park, J. S., 2005).

Gordon, L. (1984) *Survey of Personal Values (Examiner's Manual)*, Chicago: Science Research Associates.

Gorton, M. (2000) 'Overcoming the structure – agency divide in small business research', *International Journal of Entrepreneurial Behaviour and Research*, 6: 276–292.

Granovetter, M. (1973) 'The strength of weak ties', *American Journal of Sociology*, 78: 1360–1380.

Granovetter, M. (1985) 'Economic action and social structure: the problem of embeddedness', *American Journal of Sociology*, 91: 481–510.

Granovetter, M. (1992) 'Economic institutions as social constructions: a framework for analysis', *Acta Sociologica*, 35: 3–11.

Gray, C. (1998) *Enterprise and Culture*, London: Routledge.

Guildford, J., Christensen, P., Merrifield, P. and Wilson, R. (1978), *Alternate Uses (Form B, Form C)*, Orange, CA: Sheridan Psychological Services.

Habermas, J. (1978) *Knowledge and Human Interests*, London: Heinemann.

Hacker, W. (1981) 'Perceptions of, and reactions to, work situations: some implications of an action control approach', in D. Magnusson (Ed.) *Toward a Psychology of Situations: An Interactional Perspective*, Hillsdale, NJ: Lawrence Erlbaum Associates, Inc.

Hampson, S. E. (1982) *The Construction of Personality*, London: Routledge & Kegan Paul.

Hampson, S. E. (1984) 'Personality traits: in the eye of the beholder or the personality of the perceived?', in M. Cook (Ed.) *Psychology in Progress: Issues in Person Perception*, London: Methuen, pp. 28–47.

Hampson, S. E. (1988) *The Construction of Personality* (2nd ed.), London: Routledge.

Hansemark, O. C. (2003) 'Need for achievement, locus of control and the prediction of business start-ups: A longitudinal study', *Journal of Economic Psychology*, 24: 301–319.

Harding, S. (1991) *Whose Science? Whose Knowledge?*, Ithaca, NY: Cornell University Press.

Harré, R. (1979) *Social Being*, Oxford: Blackwell.

Harré, R. (1983) *Personal Being*, Oxford: Blackwell.

Harré, R. and Gillett, G. (1994) *The Discursive Mind*, London: Sage.

Harris, J. A., Saltstone, R. and Fraboni, M. (1999) 'An evaluation of the job stress questionnaire with a sample of entrepreneurs', *Journal of Business and Psychology*, 13: 447–455.

Hart, M. M., Stevenson, H. H. and Dial, J. (1995) 'Entrepreneurship: definition revisited', in W. D. Bygrave, B. J. Bird, S. Birley (Eds) *et al. Frontiers of Entrepreneurship Research 1995*, Wellesley, MA: Babson College, Centre for Entrepreneurial Studies, pp. 75–89.

Harwood, E. (1982) 'The sociology of entrepreneurship', in C. A. Kent, L. Sexton and K. H. Vesper (Eds) *Encyclopaedia of Entrepreneurship*, Englewood-Cliffs, NJ: Prentice-Hall.

Hashemi, S. and Hashemi, B. (2002) *Anyone Can Do It – Building the Coffee Republic from our Kitchen Table*, Chichester: Capstone.

Hassard, J. (1988) 'Overcoming hermeticism in organisation theory: an alternative to paradigm incommensurability', *Human Relations*, 41: 247–259.

Haworth, J. M. (1988) 'An investigation of entrepreneurial characteristics using latent class analysis', unpublished PhD Thesis, Department of Business and Management Studies, University of Salford.

Hayek, F. A. von (1937) 'Economics and knowledge', *Economica*, 4: 33–54; reprinted in Casson, M. (Ed.) *Entrepreneurship*, Aldershot: Edward Elgar, 1995.

Hayek, F. A. von (1949) *Individualism and Economic Order*, London: Routledge & Kegan Paul.

Hayek, F. A. von (1952) *The Counter-Revolution of Science: Studies in the Abuse of Reason*, Glencoe, IL: The Free Press.

Hebb, D. O. (1949) *The Organization of Behaviour*, New York: Wiley.

Hébert, R. F. and Link, A. N. (1988) *The Entrepreneur – Mainstream Views and Radical Critiques* (2nd ed.), New York: Praeger.

Hébert, R. F. and Link, A. N. (2006) *Historical Perspectives on the Entrepreneur, Foundations and Trends in Entrepreneurship*, vol. 2, Hanover, MA: now Publishers, pp. 261–408.

Herrmann, N. (1988) *The Creative Brain*, Lake Lure, NC: Brain Books.

Higgins, E. T. (1996) 'Knowledge activation: accessibility, applicability, and salience', in E. T. Higgins and A. W. Kruglanski (Eds) *Social Psychology: Handbook of Basic Principles*, New York: Guilford, pp. 133–168.

Hofstede, G. (1980) *Culture's Consequences: International Differences in Work-Related Values*, Newbury Park, CA: Sage.

Hogan, R., Desoto, C. B. and Solano, C. (1977) 'Traits, tests, and personality-research', *American Psychologist*, 32: 255–264.

Holland, R. (1990) 'The paradigm plague: prevention, cure and inoculation', *Human Relations*, 43: 23–48.

Honey, P. and Mumford, A. (1986) *Using Your Learning Styles*, Maidenhead: Peter Honey.

Hornaday, J. A. and Aboud, J. (1971) 'Characteristics of successful entrepreneurs', *Personnel Psychology*, 24: 141–153.

Hornaday, J. A. and Bunker, C. S. (1970) 'The nature of the entrepreneur', *Personnel Psychology*, 23: 47–54.

Hornaday, R. W. (1990) 'Dropping the E-words from small business research: an alternative typology', *Journal of Small Business Management*, 28: 22–33.

Howard, P. J., Medina, P. L. and Howard, J. M. (1996) 'The Big-Five locator: a quick assessment tool for consultants and trainers', in J. W. Pfeiffer (Ed.) *The 1996 Annual: Volume 1, Training*, San Francisco, CA: Jossey-Bass.

Hoy, F. and Carland, J. W. (1983) 'Differentiating between entrepreneurs and small business owners in new venture formation', in J. A. Hornaday, J. A. Timmons and K. H. Vesper (Eds) *Frontiers of Entrepreneurship Research*, Wellesley, MA: Babson College, Centre for Entrepreneurial Studies, pp. 157–166.

Huefner, J. C., Hunt, H. K. and Robinson, P. B. (1996) 'A comparison of four scales predicting entrepreneurship', *Academy of Entrepreneurship Journal*, 1: 56–80.

Hull, D. L., Bosley, J. J. and Udell, G. G. (1980) 'Renewing the hunt for the heffalump: identifying potential entrepreneurs by personality characteristics', *Journal of Small Business*, 18: 11–18.

Hyrsky, K. (2000) 'Entrepreneurial metaphors and concepts: an exploratory study', *International Small Business Journal*, 18: 13–34.

Isenberg, D. J. (1984) 'How senior managers think', *Harvard Business Review*, November: 81–90.

Ivancevich, J. M. and Matteson, M. T. (1984) 'A type A–B person–work environment interaction model for examining occupational stress and consequences', *Human Relations*, 37: 491–513.

Jack, S. L. and Anderson, A. R. (2002) 'The effects of embeddedness on the entrepreneurial process', *Journal of Business Venturing*, 17: 467–487.

Jackson, N. and Carter, P. (1991) 'In defence of paradigm incommensurability', *Organization Studies*, 12: 109–127.

Jackson, N. and Carter, P. (1993) 'Paradigm wars: a response to Hugh Wilmott', *Organization Studies*, 14: 721–725.

James, L. R. and Sells, S. B. (1981) 'Psychological climate: theoretical perspectives and empirical research', in D. Magnusson (Ed.) *Toward a Psychology of Situations: an Interactionist Perspective*. Hillsdale, NJ: Lawrence Erlbaum Associates, pp. 275–295.

Jenkins, M. and Johnson, G. (1997) 'Entrepreneurial intentions and outcomes: a comparative causal mapping study', *Journal of Management Studies*, 34: 895–920.

Johannisson, B. (1987) 'Anarchists and organizers: entrepreneurs in a network perspective', *International Studies of Management & Organization*, 17: 49–63.

Johannisson, B. (1995) 'Entrepreneurial networking in the Scandinavian context: theoretical and empirical positioning', *Entrepreneurship and Regional Development*, 7: 189–192.

Johnson, B. R. (1990) 'Towards a multidimensional model of entrepreneurship: the case of achievement motivation and the entrepreneur', *Entrepreneurship Theory and Practice*, 14: 39–54.

Johnson, J. A. (1999) 'Persons in situations: distinguishing new wine from old wine in new bottles', *European Journal of Personality*, 13: 443–453.

Julian, J. W., Lichtman, C. M. and Ryckman, R. M. (1968) 'Internal–external control and need to control', *Journal of Social Psychology*, 76: 43–48.

Kaish, S. and Gilad, B. (1991) 'Characteristics of opportunities search of entrepreneurs versus executives – Sources, interests, general alertness', *Journal of Business Venturing*, 6: 45–61.

Kanter, R. M. (1983) *The Change Masters: Innovation and Entrepreneurship in the American Corporation*, New York: Simon & Schuster.

Kanter, R. M. (1989) *When Giants Learn to Dance: Mastering the Challenges of Strategy, Management, and Careers in the 1990s*, London: Routledge.

Kanter, R. M. (1995) *World Class: Thriving Locally in the Global Economy*, New York: Simon & Schuster.

Katz, J. A. (2007) 'Education and training in entrepreneurship', in J. R. Baum, M. Frese and R. Baron (Eds) *The Psychology of Entrepreneurship*, Mahwah, NJ: Lawrence Erlbaum Associates, Inc., pp. 209–235.

Keh, H. T., Foo, M. D. and Lim, B. C. (2002) 'Opportunity evaluation under risky conditions: the cognitive process of entrepreneurs', *Entrepreneurship Theory and Practice*, 27: 125–148.

Kelly, G. A. (1955) *The Psychology of Personal Constructs*, New York: Norton.

Kenrick, D. T. and Funder, D. C. (1988) 'Profiting from controversy: lessons from the person–situation debate', *American Psychologist*, 43: 23–34.

Kets de Vries, M. F. R. (1977) 'The entrepreneurial personality: a person at the crossroads', *Journal of Management Studies*, 14: 34–57.

Kickul, J. and Gundry, L. K. (2002) 'Prospecting for strategic advantage: the proactive entrepreneurial personality and small firm innovation', *Journal of Small Business Management*, 40: 85–97.

Kilby, P. M. (1971) *Entrepreneurship and Economic Development*, New York: Macmillan.

King, A. S. (1985) 'Self-analysis and assessment of entrepreneurial potential', *Simulation and Gaming*, 16: 399–416.

Kirton, M. J. (1976) 'Adaptors and innovators: a description and measure', *Journal of Applied Psychology*, 61: 622–629.

Kirton, M. J. (1980) 'Adaptors and innovators in organizations', *Human Relations*, 33: 213–224.

Kirzner, I. M. (1973) *Competition and Entrepreneurship*, Chicago: Chicago University Press.

Kirzner, I. M. (1979) *Perception, Opportunity and Profit*, Chicago: University of Chicago Press.

Kirzner, I. M. (1982a) 'The theory of entrepreneurship in economic growth', in C. A., Kent, D. L. Sexton and K. H. Vesper (Eds) *Encyclopaedia of Entrepreneurship*, Englewood Cliffs, NJ: Prentice Hall, pp. 273–276.

Kirzner, I. M. (1982b) 'Uncertainty, discovery and human action: a study of the entrepreneurial profile in the Misean system', in I. M. Kirzner (Ed.) *Method, Process and Austrian Economics: Essays in Honour of Ludwig von Mises*, Lexington, MA: DC Heath, pp. 139–159.

Kirzner, I. M. (1985) *Discovery and the Capitalist Process*, Chicago: University of Chicago Press.

Kirzner, I. M. (1997) *How Markets Work*, IEA Hobart Paper No. 133, London: Institute of Economic Affairs.

Knight, F. H. (1921) *Risk, Uncertainty and Profit*, New York: Houghton Mifflin.

Knights, D. and Wilmott, H. (1990) *Labour Process Theory*, London: Macmillan.

Kodithuwakku, S. S. and Rosa, P. (2002) 'The entrepreneurial process and economic success in a constrained environment', *Journal of Business Venturing*, 17: 431–465.

Korunka, C., Frank, H., Lueger, M. and Mugler, J. (2003) 'The entrepreneurial personality in the context of resources, environment, and the startup process – a configurational approach', *Entrepreneurship Theory and Practice*, 28: 23–42.

Kregel, J. A. (1990) 'Imagination, exchange and business enterprise in Smith and Shackle', in S. F. Frowen (Ed.) *Unknowledge and Choice in Economics – Proceedings of a Conference in Honour of GLS Shackle*, Houndsmills: Macmillan, pp. 81–95.

Krueger, N. F. (2000) 'The cognitive infrastructure of opportunity emergence', *Entrepreneurship: Theory and Practice*, 24: 5–23.

Krueger, N. F. and Brazeal, D. V. (1994) 'Entrepreneurial potential and potential entrepreneurs', *Entrepreneurship Theory and Practice*, 18: 91–105.

Krug, S. E. and Johns, E. F. (1986) 'A large-scale cross-validation of second-order personality structure defined by the 16 PF', *Psychological Reports*, 59: 683–693.

Kuhn, T. S. (1962) *The Structure of Scientific Revolutions*, Chicago: University of Chicago Press.

Kwiatkowski, S. (2004) 'Social and intellectual dimensions of entrepreneurship', *Higher Education in Europe*, 29: 205–220.

Lachmann, L. M. (1990) 'GLS Shackle's place in the history of subjectivist thought', in S. F. Frowen (Ed.) *Unknowledge and Choice in Economics – Proceedings of a Conference in Honour of GLS Shackle*, Houndsmills: Macmillan, pp. 4–17.

Langan-Fox, J. and Roth, S. (1995) 'Achievement-motivation and female entrepreneurs', *Journal of Occupational And Organizational Psychology*, 68: 209–218.

Leavitt, H. (1988) *Managerial Psychology: Managing Behavior in Organizations*, Chicago, IL: Dorsey Press,

Lee, D. Y. and Tsang, E. W. K. (2001) 'The effects of entrepreneurial personality, background and network activities on venture growth', *Journal of Management Studies*, 38: 583–602.

Leibenstein, H. (1966) 'Allocative efficiency vs "X-efficiency" ', *American Economic Review*, 56: 392–415.

Levenson, H. (1973) 'Multidimensional locus of control in psychiatric patients', *Journal of Consulting and Clinical Psychology*, 41: 397–404.

Littunen, H. (2000) 'Entrepreneurship and the characteristics of the entrepreneurial personality', *International Journal of Entrepreneurial Behaviour and Research*, 6: 295–306.

Livesay, H. C. (1982) 'Entrepreneurial history', in C. A. Kent, D. L. Sexton and K. H. Vesper (Eds) *Encyclopaedia of Entrepreneurship*, Englewood-Cliffs, NJ: Prentice-Hall, pp. 7–14.

Loasby, B. J. (1983) 'Knowledge, learning and enterprise', in J. Wiseman (Ed.) *Beyond Positive Economics?*, London: Macmillan, pp. 104–121.

Loasby, B. J. (1991) *Equilibrium and Evolution: An Exploration of Connecting Principles in Economics*, Manchester: Manchester University Press.

Loasby, B. (2002) 'The organizational basis of cognition and the cognitive basis of organization', in M. Augier and J. G. March (Eds) *The Economics of Choice, Change and Organization, Essays in the Honor of Richard M Cyert*, Cheltenham: Edward Elgar, pp. 147–167.

Low, M. B. and MacMillan, I. C. (1988) 'Entrepreneurship: past research and future Challenges', *Journal of Management*, 14: 139–161.

Lumpkin, G. T. and Dess, G. G (1996) 'Clarifying the entrepreneurial orientation construct and linking it to performance', *Academy of Management Review*, 21: 135–172.

March, J. G. and Simon, H. A. (1958) *Organizations*, New York: Wiley.

Markman, G. D., Balkin, D. B. and Baron, R. A. (2002) 'Inventors and new venture formation: the effects of general self-efficacy and regretful thinking', *Entrepreneurship Theory and Practice*, 27: 149–166.

Markman, G. D., Baron, R. A. and Balkin, D. B. (2005) 'Are perseverance and self-efficacy costless? Assessing entrepreneurs' regretful thinking', *Journal of Organizational Behavior*, 26: 1–19.

Marshall, A. (1920) *Principles of Economics* (8th ed.), London: Macmillan.

Martin, J. and Sugarman, J. (1996) 'Bridging social constructionism and cognitive constructivism: a psychology of human possibility and constraint', *Journal of Mind and Behaviour*, 17: 291–320.

Maslow, A. (1968) *Toward a Psychology of Being*, New York: Van Nostrand.

Matthews, G. (1999) 'Personality and skill: a cognitive-adaptive framework', in P. L. Ackerman, P. C. Kyllonen and R. D. Roberts (Eds) *The Future of Learning and Individual Differences Research: Processes, Traits and Content*, Washington, DC: American Psychological Association, pp. 251–270.

Matthews, G. and Dorn, L. (1995) 'Cognitive and attentional processes in personality and intelligence', in D. H. Saklofske and M. Zeidner (Eds) *International Handbook of Personality and Intelligence*, New York: Plenum Press, pp. 367–396.

Matthews, G. and Oddy, K. (1993) 'Recovery of major personality dimensions from trait adjective data', *Personality and Individual Differences*, 15: 419–431.

Matthews, G., Deary, I. J. and Whiteman, M. C. (2003) *Personality Traits* (2nd ed.), Cambridge: Cambridge University Press.

Mayo, E. (1933) *The Human Problems of an Industrial Civilisation*, New York: Macmillan.

McClelland, D. C. (1961) *The Achieving Society*, Princeton, NJ: Van Nostrand.

McClelland, D. C. (1965) 'Achievement motivation can be developed', *Harvard Business Review*, 43: 6–24, 178.

McClelland, D. C. (1987) 'Characteristics of successful entrepreneurs', *Journal of Creative Behavior*, 21: 219–233.

McClelland, D. C. (1996) 'Does the field of personality have a future?', *Journal of Research in Personality* 30: 429–434.

McClelland, D. C. and Winter, D. G. (1971) *Motivating Economic Achievement*, New York: Free Press.

McCrae, R. R. (2000) 'Trait psychology and the revival of personality and culture studies', *American Behavioral Scientist*, 44: 10–31.

McMullan, M. E. and Gillin, L. M. (1998) 'Industrial viewpoint – entrepreneurship education', *Technovation*, 18: 275–286.

Meredith, G. G., Nelson, R. E. and Neck, P. A. (1982) *The Practice of Entrepreneurship*, Geneva: International Labour Office.

Mick, L. A. (1940) *The Life of Amasa Walker*, PhD Dissertation, Ohio State University.

Mill, J. S. (1965) *Principles of Political Economy*, Books 1–5, London: Routledge & Kegan Paul.

Miller, D. (1983) 'The correlates of entrepreneurship in three types of firm', *Management Science*, 29: 770–791.

Miller, D. and Friesen, P. H. (1982) 'Innovation in conservative and entrepreneurial firms: two models of strategic momentum', *Strategic Management Journal*, 3: 1–25.

Miller, D. and Toulouse, J.-M. (1986) 'Chief executive personality and corporate strategy and structure in small firms', *Management Science*, 32: 1389–1409.

Miner, J. B. (1997) 'The expanded horizon for achieving entrepreneurial success', *Organizational Dynamics*, 25: 54–67.

Miner, J. B. (2000) 'Testing a psychological typology of entrepreneurship using business founders', *Journal of Applied Behavioral Science*, 36: 43–69.

Miner, J. B. and Raju, N. S. (2004) 'Risk propensity differences between managers and entrepreneurs and between low- and high-growth entrepreneurs: A reply in a more conservative vein', *Journal of Applied Psychology*, 89: 3–13.

Miner, J. B., Smith, N. R. and Bracker, J. S. (1992) 'Defining the inventor-entrepreneur, in the context of established typologies', *Journal of Business Venturing*, 7: 103–113.

Minniti, M., Bygrave, W. D. and Autio, E. (2005) *Global Entrepreneurship Monitor*, Babson Park, MA: Babson College.

Mintzberg, H. (1979) *The Structuring of Organizations: A Synthesis of the Research*, Englewood Cliffs, NJ: Prentice Hall.

Miron, D. and McClelland, D. C. (1979) 'The impact of achievement motivation training on small business performance', *California Management Review*, 21: 13–28.

Mischel, W. (1968) *Personality and Assessment*, New York: Wiley.

Mischel, W. (1973) 'Towards a cognitive social learning reconceptualisation of personality', *Psychological Review*, 80: 252–283.

Mischel, W. (1981) *Introduction to Personality* (3rd ed.), New York: Rinehart & Winston.

Mischel, W. and Shoda, Y. (1995) 'A cognitive-affective system of personality: reconceptualizing situations, dispositions, dynamics and invariance in personality structure', *Psychological Review*, 102: 246–268.

Mischel, W. and Shoda, Y. (1998) 'Reconciling processing dynamics and personality dispositions', *Annual Review of Psychology*, 49: 229–258.

Mischel, W., Shoda, Y. and Mendoza-Denton, R. (2002) 'Situation–behaviour profiles as a locus of consistency in personality', *Current Directions in Psychological Science*, 11: 50–54.

Mises, L. Von (1949) *Human Action: A Treatise on Economics*, New Haven, CT: Yale University Press.

Mitchell, J. R., Friga, P. N. and Mitchell, R. K. (2005) 'Untangling the intuition mess: intuition as a construct in entrepreneurship research', *Entrepreneurship Theory and Practice*, 29: 653–679.

Mitchell, R. K., Smith, B., Seawright, W. and Morse, E. A. (2000), 'Cross-cultural cognitions and the venture creation decision', *Academy of Management Journal*, 43: 974–993.

Mitchell, R. K., Busenitz, L., Lant, T., McDougall, P. P., Morse, E. A. and Smith, J. B. (2004) 'The distinctive and inclusive domain of entrepreneurial cognition research', *Entrepreneurship Theory and Practice*, 28: 505–518.

Moran, P. (1998) 'Personality characteristics and growth-orientation of the small business owner-manager', *International Small Business Journal*, 16: 17–38.

Morgan, G. (1996) *Images of Organisation*, London: Sage.

Mueller, S. L. and Thomas, A. S. (2000) 'Culture and entrepreneurial potential: A nine country study of locus of control and innovativeness', *Journal of Business Venturing*, 16: 51–75.

Müller, G. F. and Gappisch, C. (2005) 'Personality types of entrepreneurs', *Psychological Reports*, 96: 737–746.

Nicholls, J. G., Licht, B. G. and Pearl, R. A. (1982) 'Some dangers of using personality questionnaires to study personality', *Psychological Bulletin*, 92: 572–580.

Nicholson, L. and Anderson, A. R. (2005) 'News and nuances of the entrepreneurial myth and metaphor: Linguistic games in entrepreneurial sense-making and sense-giving', *Entrepreneurship Theory and Practice*, 29: 153–172.

Nicholson, N. (1998) 'How hard-wired is human behavior?', *Harvard Business Review*, 76: 134–147.

Nicholson, N. (2005a) 'Objections to evolutionary psychology: reflections, implications and the leadership exemplar', *Human Relations*, 58: 393–409.

Nicholson, N. (2005b) 'Personality and domain-specific risk taking', *Journal of Risk Research*, 8: 157–176.

Nonaka, I. and Takeuchi, H. (1995) *The Knowledge Creating Company: How Companies Create the Dynamics of Innovation*, Oxford: Oxford University Press.

Northwestern Mutual Life Assurance Company (1985) *What's your EQ?*, Milwaukee, WI: Northwestern Mutual Life Assurance Company.

Ogbor, J. O. (2000) 'Mythicizing and reification in entrepreneurial discourse: ideology-critique of entrepreneurial studies', *Journal of Management Studies*, 37: 605–635.

Olson, P. D. (1985) 'Entrepreneurship: process and abilities', *Entrepreneurship Theory and Practice*, 10: 25–32.

Palich, L. E. and Bagby, D. R. (1995) 'Using cognitive theory to explain entrepreneurial risk-taking – challenging conventional wisdom', *Journal of Business Venturing*, 10: 425–438.

Palmer, M. (1971) 'The application of psychological testing to entrepreneurial potential', *California Management Review*, 13: 32–38.

Parikh, J., Neubauer, F. and Lank, A. G. (1994) *Intuition: The New Frontier of Management*, Oxford, UK: Blackwell.

Park, J. S. (2005) 'Opportunity recognition and product innovation in entrepreneurial hi-tech start-ups: a new perspective and supporting case study', *Technovation*, 25: 739–752.

Parker, M. and McHugh, G. (1991) 'Five texts in search of an author: a response to John Hassard's "Multiple Paradigms and Organisation and Analysis" ', *Organization Studies*, 12: 451–456.

Penrose, E. (1959) *The Theory of the Growth of the Firm*, New York: Wiley.

Perlman, M. (1990) 'The fabric of economics and the golden threads of GLS Shackle', in S. F. Frowen (Ed.) *Unknowledge and Choice in Economics – Proceedings of a Conference in Honour of GLS Shackle*, Houndsmills: Macmillan, pp. 9–19.

Pervin, L. A. (1990) *Handbook of Personality: Theory and Research*, New York: Guilford Press.

Pittaway, L. A. (2000) *The Social Construction of Entrepreneurial Behaviour*, Doctoral Thesis, The University of Newcastle upon Tyne, Faculty of Law, Environment and Social Sciences.

Pittaway, L. A. (2005) 'Philosophies in entrepreneurship: a focus on economic theories', *International Journal of Entrepreneurial Behaviour and Research*, 11: 201–221.

Polyani, M. (1966) *The Tacit Dimension*, London: Routledge & Kegan Paul.

Porter, M. E. (1980) *Competitive Strategy: Techniques for Analyzing Industries and Competitors*, New York: The Free Press.

Porter, M. E. (1990) *The Competitive Advantage of Nations*, Houndsmills: Macmillan.

Ramachandran, K. and Ramnarayan, S. (1993) 'Entrepreneurial orientation and networking – some Indian evidence', *Journal of Business Venturing*, 8: 513–524.

Rausch, A., Frese, M., and Utsch, A. (2005) 'Effects of human capital and long term human resource development and utilization on employment growth of small scale businesses: a causal analysis', *Entrepreneurship Theory and Practice*, 29: 681–698.

Reason, P. (1981) '*Methodological approaches to social science by Ian Mitroff and Ralph Kilmann: an appreciation*', in P. Reason and J. Rowan (Eds) *Human Inquiry*, London: Wiley, pp. 43–51.

Reynierse, J. H. (1995) 'A comparative analysis of Japanese and American managerial types through organizational levels in business and industry', *Journal of Psychological Type*, 25: 11–23.

Reynierse, J. H. (1997) 'An MBTI model of entrepreneurism and bureaucracy: the psychological types of business entrepreneurs compared to business managers and executives', *Journal of Psychological Type*, 40: 3–19.

Reynolds, P. (1997) 'Who starts new firms? Preliminary explorations of firms-in-gestation', *Small Business Economics*, 9: 449–462.

Ricardo, D. (1962) *The Principles of Political Economy and Taxation*, Letchworth: Aldine Press.

Richardson, G. (1960) *Information and Investment*, Oxford: Oxford University Press.

Ricketts, M. (1987) *The Economics of Business Enterprise – New Approaches to the Firm*, Brighton: Wheatsheaf.

Ring, P. S. and Van de Ven, A. H. (1989) 'Formal and informal dimensions of transactions', in A. H. Van de Ven, H. L. Angle and M. S. Poole (Eds) *Research on the Management of Innovation*, New York: Ballinger, pp. 171–192.

Roberts, P. W. (2000) 'A processual account of innovative capabilities', in N. J. Foss and P. L. Robertson (Eds) *Resources, Technology and Strategy Explorations in Resource-based Perspective*, London: Routledge, pp. 80–99.

Robinson, P. B., Stimpson, J. C., Huefner, J. C and Hunt, H. K. (1991) 'An attitude approach to the prediction of entrepreneurship', *Entrepreneurship Theory and Practice*, 15: 41–52.

Roddick, A. (1992) *Body and Soul*, London: Vermilion.

Rosch, E. (1978) 'Principles of categorization', in E. Rosch and B. B. Lloyd (Eds) *Cognition and Categorization*, Hillsdale, NJ: Lawrence Erlbaum Associates, Inc., pp. 27–48.

Rosch, E., Mervis, C. B., Gray, W. D., Johnson, D. M. and Boyes-Bream, P. (1976) 'Basic objects in natural categories', *Cognitive Psychology*, i: 332–439.

Rothwell, R. (1975) 'Intra-corporate entrepreneurs', *Management Decision*, 13: 142–154.

Rothwell, R. and Zegfeld, W. (1982) *Innovation and the Small and Medium Sized Firms – Their Role in Employment and Economic Change*, London: Pinter.

Rotter, J. B. (1966) 'Generalised expectancies for internal versus external control of reinforcement', *Psychological Monographs, Whole No. 609*, 80: 1–28.

Ryle, G. (1949) *The Concept of Mind*, Harmondsworth: Penguin.

Sadler-Smith, E. (2004) 'Cognitive style and the management of small and medium-sized enterprises', *Organization Studies*, 25: 155–181.

Sadler-Smith, E. and Shefy, E. (2004) 'The intuitive executive: understanding and applying "gut feel" in decision-making', *Academy of Management Executive*, 18: 76–91.

Sagie, A. and Elizur, D. (1999) 'Achievement motive and entrepreneurial orientation: a structural analysis', *Journal of Organizational Behavior*, 20: 375–387.

Sarason, Y., Dean, T. and Dillard, J. F. (2006) 'Entrepreneurship as a nexus of individual and opportunity: a structuration view', *Journal of Business Venturing*, 21: 286–305.

Sarasvathy, D. K., Simon, H. A. and Lave, L. (1998) 'Perceiving and managing business risks: differences between entrepreneurs and bankers', *Journal of Economic Behavior and Organization*, 33: 207–225.

Saxenian, A. L. (1993) *Regional Networks: Industrial Adaptation in Silicon Valley and Route 128*, Cambridge, MA: Harvard University Press.

Say, J. B. (1821) *A Treatise on Political Economy: Or, The Production, Distribution and Consumption of Wealth* (trans. of 4th ed. by C. C. Biddle, 1880), New York: Augustus M. Kelley, 1964.

Schere, J. C. (1982) 'Tolerance of ambiguity as a discriminating variable between entrepreneurs and managers', *Academy of Management Proceedings*, 45: 404–408.

Schlenker, B. R. and Weigold, M. F. (1989) 'Goals and the identification process: constructing desired identities', in L. A. Pervin (Ed.) *Goal Concepts in Personality and Social Psychology*, Hillsdale, NJ: Lawrence Erlbaum Associates, pp. 243–290.

Schmitt-Rodermund, E. (2004) 'Pathways to successful entrepreneurship: Parenting, personality, early entrepreneurial competence, and interests', *Journal of Vocational Behavior*, 65: 498–518.

Schon, D. A. (1965) 'Champions for radical new inventions', *Harvard Business Review*, 41: 77–86.

Schrage, H. (1965) 'The R & D entrepreneur: profile of success', *Harvard Business Review*, 43: 56.

Schultz, T. W. (1975) 'The value of the ability to deal with disequilibria', *Journal of Economic Literature*, 13: 827–847.

Schultz, T. W. (1980) 'Investment in entrepreneurial ability', *Scandinavian Journal of Economics*, 82: 437–448.

Schumpeter, J. A. (1934) *The Theory of Economic Development*, Cambridge, MA: Harvard University Press.

Schumpeter, J. A. (1943) *Capitalism, Socialism and Democracy*, New York: Harper.

Schumpeter, J. A. (1961), *History of Economic Analysis* (ed. by E. Boody), London: George Allen & Unwin.

Schwenk, C. R. (1988) 'The cognitive perspective on strategic decision making', *Journal of Management Studies*, 25: 41–55.

Selden, R. (1991) 'The rhetoric of enterprise', in R. Keat and N. Abercrombie (Eds) *Enterprise Culture*, London: Routledge, pp. 58–71.

Sexton, D. L. and Bowman-Upton, N. B. (1984) 'Personality inventory for potential entrepreneurs: evaluation of a modified JPI/PRF-E test instrument', in J. A. Hornaday, F. Tarpley, J. A. Timmons and K. H. Vesper (Eds) *Frontiers of Entrepreneurship Research*, Wellesey, MA: Babson College, Centre for Entrepreneurial Studies, Babson College, pp. 513–528.

Sexton, D. L. and Bowman, N. B. (1985) 'The entrepreneur: A capable executive and more', *Journal of Business Venturing*, 1: 129–140.

Sexton, D. L. and Bowman, N. B. (1986), 'Validation of a personality index: comparative psychological characteristics analysis of female entrepreneurs, managers, entrepreneurial students and business students', in R. Ronstadt, J. A. Hornaday, R. Peterson, and K. H. Vesper (Eds) *Frontiers of Entrepreneurship Research*, Wellesley, MA: Babson College, Centre for Entrepreneurial Studies, pp. 40–57.

Shackle, G. L. S. (1972) *Epistemics and Economics: A Critique of Economic Doctrines*, Cambridge: Cambridge University Press.

Shackle, G. L. S. (1979) *Imagination and the Nature of Choice*, Edinburgh: Edinburgh University Press.

Shane, S. (2000) 'Prior knowledge and the discovery of entrepreneurial opportunities', *Organization Science*, 11: 448–469.

Shane, S. (2003) *A General Theory of Entrepreneurship*, Cheltenham: Edward Elgar.

Shane, S. and Venkataraman, S. (2000) 'The promise of entrepreneurship as a field of research', *Academy of Management Review*, 25: 217–226.

Shapero, A. (1975) 'The displaced, uncomfortable entrepreneur', *Psychology Today*, November: 83–89, 133.

Shapero, A. (1982) 'Social dimensions of entrepreneurship', in C. Kent, D. Sexton and K. Vesper (Eds) *The Encyclopaedia of Entrepreneurship*, Englewood Cliffs, NJ: Prentice Hall, pp. 72–90.

Shapira, Z. (1995) *Risk-taking: A Managerial Perspective*, New York: Russell Sage Foundation.

Shaver, K. G. and Scott, L. R. (1991) 'Person, process and choice: The psychology of new venture creation', *Entrepreneurship Theory and Practice*, 16: 23–45.

Shepherd, D. A. and Krueger, N. F. (2002) 'An intentions based model of entrepreneurial teams' social cognitions', *Entrepreneurship Theory and Practice*, 27: 167–186.

Shoda, Y. and Mischel, W. (1996) 'Toward a unified, intra-individual dynamic conception of personality', *Journal of Research in Personality*, 30: 414–428.

Shoda, Y. and Mischel, W. (2000) 'Reconciling contextualism with the core assumptions of personality psychology', *European Journal of Personality*, 14: 407–428.

Shook, C. L., Priem, R. L. and McGee, J. E. (2003) 'Venture creation and the enterprising individual: a review and synthesis', *Journal of Management*, 29: 379–399.

Shotter, J. (1993) *Conversational Realities*, London: Sage.

Shweder, R. A. (1975) 'How relevant is an individual difference theory of personality ratings?', *Journal of Personality and Social Psychology*, 43: 455–485.

Shweder, R. A. (1977) 'Likeness and likelihood in everyday thought: magical thinking in judgments about personality', *Current Anthropology*, 18: 637–658.

Shweder, R. A. and D'Andrade, R. G. (1979) 'Accurate reflections or systematic distortion? A reply to Block, Weiss and Thorne', *Journal of Personality and Social Psychology*, 37: 1075–1084.

Simon, H. A. (1957) *Models of Man*, New York: Wiley.

Simon, M. and Houghton, S. M. (2002) 'The relationship among biases, misperceptions and introducing pioneering products: examining differences in venture decision contexts', *Entrepreneurship Theory and Practice*, 27: 105–124.

Simon, M., Houghton, S. M. and Aquino, K. (2000) 'Cognitive, biases, risk perception and venture formation: How individuals decide to start companies', *Journal of Business Venturing*, 15: 113–134.

Smircich, L. and Calas, M. (1987) 'Organizational culture: a critical assessment', in F. Jablin, L. Putnam, K. Roberts and L. Porter (Eds) *Handbook of Organizational Communication*, Newbury Park, CA: Sage, pp. 228–263.

Smith, A. (1976) *The Wealth of Nations* (vol. 1, book I, ch VI: 42), Everyman's Library 412, London: Dent & Sons.

Smith, N. R. (1967) *The Entrepreneur and His Firm: The Relationship Between Type of Man and Type of Company*, East Lansing, MI: Michigan State University Press.

Stark, W. (1952) *Jeremy Bentham's Economic Writings*, London: Allen & Unwin.

Staw, B. M. and Ross, J. (1987) 'Behaviour in escalation situations: antecedents, prototypes and solutions', in L. L. Cummings and B. M. Staw (Eds) *Research in Organizational Behaviour*, vol. 9, London: JAI Press, pp. 39–78.

Sternberg, R. J. (2003) *Wisdom, Intelligence and Creativity Synthesized*, Cambridge: Cambridge University Press.

Sternberg, R. J. and Lubart, T. I. (1991) 'Creating creative minds', *Phi, Delta, Kappa*, 8: 608–614.

Sternberg, R. J. and Lubart, T. I. (1995) *Defying the Crowd: Cultivating Creativity in a Culture of Conformity*, New York: Free Press.

Stevenson, H. H. and Jarillo, J. C. (1990) 'A paradigm of entrepreneurship: entrepreneurial management', *Strategic Management Journal*, 11: 17–27.

Stevenson, H. H. and Sahlman, W. A. (1989) 'The entrepreneurial process', in P. Burns and J. Dewhurst (Eds) *Small Business and Entrepreneurship*, Houndsmills: Macmillan Education, pp. 94–157.

Stewart, W. H. and Roth, P. L. (2001) 'Risk propensity differences between entrepreneurs and managers: A meta-analytic review', *Journal of Applied Psychology*, 86: 145–153.

Stewart, W. H. and Roth, P. L. (2004) 'Data quality affects meta-analytic conclusions: A response to Miner and Raju (2004) concerning entrepreneurial risk propensity', *Journal of Applied Psychology*, 89: 14–21.

Stewart, W. H., Watson, W. E., Carland, J. W. and Carland, J. C. (1999) 'A proclivity for entrepreneurship: A comparison of entrepreneurs, small business owners, and corporate managers', *Journal of Business Venturing*, 14: 189–214.

Steyaert, C., Bowen, R. and Looy, van B. (1996) 'Conversational construction of new meaning configurations in organizational innovation: a generative approach', *European Journal of Work and Organizational Psychology*, 5: 67–89.

Storey, D. J. (1982) *Entrepreneurship and the New Firm*, London: Routledge.

Storey, D. J. (1993) 'Should we abandon support to start up businesses?', *Working Paper No. 11*, SME Centre, Warwick Business School.

Storey, D. J. (1994) *Understanding the Small Business Sector*, London: Routledge.

Symon, G. and Cassell, C. (1998) *Qualitative Methods and Analysis in Organizational Research*, Thousand Oaks, London: Sage.

Thornton, P. (1999) 'The sociology of entrepreneurship', *Annual Review of Sociology*, 25: 19–46.

Timmons, J. A. (1989) *The Entrepreneurial Mind*, Andover, MA: Brick House Publishing.

Timmons, J. A., Smollen, L. E. and Dingee, A. L. M. (1977) *New Venture Creation* (1st ed.), Homewood, IL: Irwin.

Timmons, J. A., Smollen, L. E. and Dingee, A. L. M. (1985) *New Venture Creation*, (2nd ed.), Homewood, IL: Irwin.

Tushman, M. L. and Anderson, P. (1986) Technological discontinuities and organisational environments, *Administrative Science Quarterly*, 31: 439–465.

Ucbasaran, D., Westhead, P. and Wright, M. (2001) 'The focus of entrepreneurial research: contextual and process issues', *Entrepreneurship Theory and Practice*, 26: 57–80.

Utsch, A. and Rauch, A. (2000) 'Innovativeness and initiative as mediators between achievement orientation and venture performance', *European Journal of Work and Organizational Psychology*, 9: 45–62.

Utsch, A., Rauch, A., Rothfuss, R. and Frese, M. (1999) 'Who becomes a small scale entrepreneur in a post-socialist environment: On the differences between entrepreneurs and managers in East Germany', *Journal of Small Business Management*, 37: 31–42.

Vandenbosch, B., Saatcioglu, A. and Fry, S. (2006) 'Idea management: a systemic view', *Journal of Management Studies*, 43: 259–288.

Vise, D. A. (2004) *The Google Story*, London: Pan.

Wärneryd, K.-E. (1988) 'The psychology of innovative entrepreneurship', in W. F. van Raaij, G. M. van Veldhoven and K.-E. Wärneryd (Eds) *Handbook of Economic Psychology*, Dordrecht: Kluwer, pp. 404–447.

Wayne, S. J., Liden, R. C., Graf, I. K. and Ferns, G. R. (1997) 'The role of upward influence tactics in human resource decisions', *Personality Psychology*, 50: 979–1006.

Weber, M. (1930) *The Protestant Ethic and the Spirit of Capitalism*, New York: Scribner.

Weick, K. (1995) *Sensemaking in Organizations*, Thousand Oaks, CA: Sage.

Weick, K. E. and Roberts, K. H. (1993) 'Collective mind in organizations: heedful interrelating on flight decks', *Administrative Science Quarterly*, 38: 357–381.

Westhead, P. and Wright, M. (1998) 'Novice, serial and portfolio founders: are they different?', *Journal of Business Venturing*, 13: 173–204.

Westhead, P. and Wright, M. (1999) 'Contributions of novice, portfolio and serial founders located in rural and urban areas', *Regional Studies*, 33: 157–173.

Westhead, P., Ucbasaran, D. and Wright, M. (2005) 'Decisions, actions and performance: do novice, serial and portfolio entrepreneurs differ?', *Journal of Small Business Management*, 43: 393–417.

Wheelock, J. and Chell, E. (1996) *The Business Owner Managed Family Unit: An Inter-regional Comparison of Behavioural Dynamics*, End-of-Award Report, No. R000234402, Swindon: Economic and Social Research Council.

Wilken, P. H. (1979) *Entrepreneurship: A Comparative and Historical Study*, Norwood, NJ: Ablex Publishing.

Wilson, G. (1973) *The Psychology of Conservatism*, London: Academic Press.

Wiseman, J. and Littlechild, S. C. (1990) 'Crusoe's kingdom: cost, choice and political economy', in S. F. Frowen (Ed.) *Unknowledge and Choice in Economics – Proceedings of a Conference in Honour of GLS Shackle*, Houndsmills: Macmillan, pp. 96–128.

Witt, U. (1998) 'Imagination and leadership – the neglected dimension of an evolutionary theory of the firm', *Journal of Economic Behavior and Organization*, 35: 161–177.

Witt, U. (1999) 'Do entrepreneurs need firms? A contribution to a missing chapter in Austrian Economics', *Review of Austrian Economics*, 11: 99–109.

Wittgenstein, L. (1953) *Philosophical Investigations* (trans. G. E. M. Anscombe), Oxford: Blackwell.

Wittgenstein, L. (1978) *Philosophical Investigations*, Oxford: Blackwell.

Woo, C. Y., Dunkelberg, W. C. and Cooper, A. C. (1988) 'Entrepreneurial typologies: definition and implications', in B. A. Kirchhoff, W. A. Long, W. E. McMullen, K. H. Vesper and W. E. Wetzel, Jr (Eds) *Frontiers of Entrepreneurship Research*, Wellesey, MA: Babson College, Centre for Entrepreneurial Studies, pp. 165–176.

Woo, C. Y., Cooper, A. C. and Dunkelberg, W. C. (1991) 'The development and interpretation of entrepreneurial typologies', *Journal of Business Venturing*, 6: 93–114.

Wortman, M. S. (1986) 'A unified framework, research typologies, and research prospectuses for the interface between entrepreneurship and small business', in D. L. Sexton and R. W. Smilor (Eds) *The Art and Science of Entrepreneurship*, Cambridge, MA: Ballinger, pp. 273–331.

Wright, J. C. and Mischel, W. (1987) 'A conditional approach to dispositional constructs: the local predictability of social behavior', *Journal of Personality and Social Psychology*, 53: 1159–1177.

Yin, R. K. (1994) *Case Study Research Design and Methods* (2nd ed.), Thousand Oaks, London: Sage.

Zahra, S. A., Sapienza, H. J. and Davidsson, P. (2006) 'Entrepreneurship and dynamic capabilities: a review, model and research agenda', *Journal of Management Studies*, 43: 917–955.

Index

Note: Page references to tables and figures are shown in **bold**.

ability 111, 118, 166, **211**
absorptive capacity 64, 132
achievement: critique of NAch theory
    90–1, 96, 104; motivation 88–90, 99,
    107; need for 88–98, 113, 117, 121,
    126
adaptability 137–8
affect 15, 91, 114, 144, 150, 163, 169,
    171, 172, 247, 251, 253, 257–8;
    diffusion 158
agency 52–5, **58**, 73, 79, 251, **256**, 257,
    260; -structure 77, 251
Aldrich, H. 9, 82, 269
alertness 46, 171, 249; ability 45; to
    opportunities 41, 63, 112, 163–4,
    171, 226
Allport, G. W. 84, 269
Alvarez, S. A. 66–8, 269
analysis (*see also* method); multi-level
    12
Anderson, A. 73, 79, 280
Ann Summers 216–7, 241
arbitrage 12 (*see also* trader)
arbitrageur 18, 42, 66
Assessment Development Centre (ADC)
    117–8
assets, intangible 64
attitude 111, 113, 155, 169, 217,
    235; Entrepreneurial Attitude
    Orientation (EAO) 113–4, 116,
    140
autonomy 78, 133–4, 144,

Barney, J. B. 66–8, 158, 272
barriers to entry 71
Baudeau, Nicolas 19, **38**, 47
Baumol, W. V. 29, 50, 271

behaviour 188–90, 195, 198, 206, 253,
    255, **256**; mindful 187, 189, 199;
    behavioural signature 142, 150–1,
    170, 247
Bentham, Jeremy 22, **38**, **47**, 271
bias 152–3, 158–9, 164, 171, 195
Brin, Sergey 234–8, 239, 240–1
bureaucracy 53; bureaucrat 121
Burrell, G. 43, 174, 179–81, 183, 209,
    272
Business: creation 148, 161; cycle
    29–30; failure 94, 221, 231–3; family
    121, 224, 225, 240, 242, 264; founder
    123, 125, 128, 133, 134, 156, 216,
    234; founding 8, 89, 93, 95, 155; heir
    123, 128, 133; life style 121; owner–
    manager 94, 102, 233, 267; plan
    219–20, 262; start up 94, 106, 127,
    135, 138, 156, 219–20, 224–5, 230,
    231, 234–6, 263; success 99, 137,
    234, 236, 263; survival 124, 125,
    232–4

Cantillon, Richard 18–19, 20, 32, 37,
    38, 45, **47**, 49, 272
capital resources: human 2–3, 81, 106,
    138, 165–6; social 3, 138, 164–5, 171
capitalist 18, 23, 26, 45, 47; market
    economy 46; societies 57; system 22,
    31, 59, 249
career 97; choice 96
Carland, J. 9, 10, 88, 92, 102, 105, 120,
    139, 273
Casson, M. 4, 5, 8, 17, 29, 35, **38**, 43–4,
    46, **47**, 48, 50, 59, 61, 69–72, 78, 80,
    212, 245, 273
category membership 196–7

Catseyes® 218
Cattell, Raymond, B. 84–5, 123, 273;
  16PF 85, 128, 273
causation 52, 174
challenge 102, 229
change 27, 32, 42, 55, 61, 63, 126, 128,
  144, 164, 217; agent of 44, 47, 49, 51,
  126, 132, 226, 229, 245; prediction of
  42
Chell, E. 3, 4, 8–9, 10, 16, 50, 52, 71,
  75, 78, 83, 86, 88, 98, 102, 106, 123,
  126, 131, 133, 137, 139, 141, 143,
  145, 147, 170, 171, 181, 190, 197,
  198, 204, 206–7, 224, 227, 231, 238,
  242, 247, 248, 252, 255, 259, 261,
  265, 268, 273–4
choice 39, 45, 46, 49, 54–5, 60, 146,
  148, 170, 267; rational 24, 33, 72
Clark, J. B. 31, **38**, 47, 275
cognitive: adaptive theory 152; affective
  personality system (CAPS) 14,
  148–52, 170, 258; affective structure
  264–5; bias 14, 158–60; construct
  131, 254; constructivism 15, 174,
  180, 185–6, **199**, 204, 206, 207, 208,
  210, 212, 244, 257–8, 266;
  development 197; factors 69, 91, 252;
  heuristics 14, 148, 152–4;
  interpretation 42; perception 42;
  process 146, 164, 188, 252, 254,
  257, 264; schema 153, 203, 207;
  social learning 144, 252, 253;
  social learning person variables 14,
  145–6, 169–70, 247; space 55
cognition 114
competences 64, 219
competition 31, 46, 59, 61–72, 106,
  250; barriers to 64; perfect 32, 62
competitive: advantage 48, 59, 61, 63–4,
  73, 136, 217, 254; position 63, 232,
  234, 236
conation 55, 114
confidence 62, 69, 103, 104, 154, 158,
  165, 226
constraints 77 (*see also* structure)
context 205; political 56; socio-
  economic 51–80, 212, 216, 217, 226,
  235 (*see also* socio-economy)
control: perceived 148, 154
cooperation 68, 71
Costa, P. T. 85, 123, 275
counterfactual thinking 14, 158, 163–4,
  171, 259
counter-intuitive 72

creative: destruction 35–6, 43, 48;
  imagination 42 (*see also* imagination);
  thinking 153
creativity 118, 119, 132, 166–9, 171,
  212, 219, 225, 240, 247, 258
culture 55–9, 60, 86, 100–01, 161–2,
  191, 231, 235, 240, 249; counter-
  56–7; national 101; socio- 186, 216,
  240, **253**

Darwin, Charles 25
Davidsson, P. 82, 113, 275, 291
decision-making 14, 29, 33, 39–40, 41,
  42, 43–4, 59, 60, 62, 105, 106,
  136–7, 139, 140, 146, 148, 152,
  158–60, 162, 223, 228–9, 234, 242,
  247, 263, 268; escalation in 159, 171;
  judgemental 15, 43, 45, 61, 69, 103,
  200, 225, 255, 267; strategic 136,
  153; subjective 40, 61, 72, 77, **253**
decision style/type 119, 127, 137, 140,
  256
deconstruction 184, 190
Delmar, F. 82, 113, 275
demand 28, 36; market 70
demographic characteristics 113, 120
Derwent Valley Foods 227–31
determinism 39, 45, 48, 52, 75, 179,
  180, 186, 241–2
discourse 192; analysis 181–4, 205
disequilibrium 20, 37, 62, 77, 163
dualism 186; duality 185, 186, 189

economic: conditions 94, 216, 247, 250;
  development 34; growth 101;
  performance 261–3 (*see also*
  performance)
Economics 5, 210, 245; American
  School 30–34, 49; Austrian School
  17, 27–30, 46, 63; British School
  21–27; Classical 24, 27, 45, 245;
  French School 18–20; German School
  26–7; Neo-classical 24, 45, 59, 74,
  245
economy 36, 249
Edison, T. A. 265
education 36–7, 82, 93, 120, 127, 130,
  166, 218, 220, 223, 224, 235, 239,
  244, 252, 264–6
Edwards Personality Preference
  Schedule (EPPS) 114, 134
effectiveness 161; personal 138
efficiency 27
Eisenhardt, K. M. 68–9, 276

emotion 15, 39, 128, 129, 149, 157, 171, 202, 212
enterprise 256; culture 56, 89, 226
entrapment 217, 242
entrepreneur 120, 207, 245, 257–8, 263; aspirant 128; characterisation of **47**, 128, 263; 'classic' 69; definition of 43, 73; demand for 36; emergent 10; female 91 (*see also* gender); founder 34 (*see also* business); function of 21, 49, 249; growth-oriented 105, 163, (*see also* growth); habitual 9 (*see also* entrepreneurial type); ideas-based 70; income-oriented 105; -inventor 196, 214, 217; leader 78; market-maker 70; nascent 9, 94, 109, 117, 118, 119, 121, 135, 138, 165, 231, 245, 260, 262, 266, 267, 268; novice 9 (*see also* entrepreneurial type); –opportunity interchange 244, **256**; organiser 70; prototypical 196, 198, 206–7, 212, 261; realised 10; risk-avoidant 105 (*see also* risk); risk-taker 27 (*see also* risk); serial 9 (*see also* entrepreneurial type); socially constructed 207, 249, 254, 258, 267; successful 97, 112, 139 (*see also* performance); supply of 36, 77, 81; technological 135, 157; unrealised 10; unsuccessful 97
entrepreneurial: ability 36–7, 79, 131, 240, 244 (*see also* ability); alertness 163 (*see also* alertness); behaviour **211**, 253, (*see also* behaviour); career 97, 126; case studies 214–31, 234–8 (*see also* method); decisions 46, 253, (*see also* decision-making); failure 98 (*see also* performance); goals 92; parent 127; performance 96, 111, 112, 127, 141, 211, 217, 223, 225, 239–40, 244, 261–3; personality 199–200, 207, 238–40, 244–68, 247–8, 251, 257, 258; portfolio 9; posture 127, 263; potential 160–61; process 6, 10, 72–6, 79, 81, 244, 250, 253–6, 261, 263, 267; profile 88, 93, 94, 96, 117, 120, 133, 136, 144, 147, 207, **211**, **215**, 238–9, 251–2, 253, 255, **256**, 258, 263, skills 71, 93, 217, 220, 223, 251, 253, 254, 262; traits 93, 111 *ff*, 132, 247; types 23, 122, 211, 226, 244, 260–1
Entrepreneurial Attitude Orientation, The (EAO) 113, 116
Entrepreneurial Orientation (EO) 111, 117, 133, 140
Entrepreneurial Potential Questionnaire (EPQ) 121, 140
Entrepreneurial Quotient (EQ) 114, 115, 116
Entrepreneurial Self Efficacy (ESE) 132, 134–7, 140
entrepreneurship: 261; definition 2–3; competitive 61–72, 99, 232, 246; cultural 57, 220, 246; dynamic 68; environment 130 (*see also* environment); institutional 53, 235, 237; macro-level 52–5, 166; measures of 96; meso-level 59–72; micro-level 72–6; process 3, 8, 16; shocks 69; socio-economic 7, 52, 58, 145–6, 153, 216, 218, 220, 223, 235, 237, 240, 246, 247, **253**; stability 99; supportive 135, 240; theory 5–6, 207, 259; turbulence of 52, 78, 99; volatility of 72
epistemology 174, 175, **177**, **199**
equilibrium theory 6, 20, 24, 28, 29, 32, 35, 37, 40, 42, 45, 48, 59, 62, 70, 74, 245
evolution, theory of 25
evolutionary theory of the firm 59, 62, 64–5, 76, 77
expectations 62, 73, 188
experience 33, 37, 49, 53, 73, 77, 93, 124, 158, 186, 190, 206, 217, 221, 222–3, 227, 230, 247, 253; prior 113, 219, 227, 232
extraversion-introversion (E-I) 114 (*see also* MBTI)
Eysenck, H. J. 84–6, 123, 276

failure 29 (*see also* performance); fear of 104, 165, 219
family resemblance 196
firm 61; founding 8, 89; level of analysis 117; performance 117, 121, 125, 127, 263 (*see also* performance); theory of 24, 59, 61–72, 246, 263
flexibility 78, 259
form of life 191, 198, 200, 207, 211, 212, 214, 217, 238, 254, 266
Foucault, M. 175, 188, 191, 277
freedom 53, 77, 148, 168; free will 39, 146, 170, 179, 186
function: economic 2, **7**, **11**; entrepreneurial 7, 12, 19, 21, 22, 23,

26, 27, 28, 31, 34–6, 40, 41–2, 43–4, 45, 46–7, **47**, 48
Furnham, Adrian 99, 108, 271, 277

Galton, Sir Francis 84
gamble 39–40, 102
Gartner, W. 8, 10, 83, 86, 88, 107
gender 94–5, 115, 116, 127, 128, 165, 184, 216, 225 (*see also* sex)
General Enterprise Tendency (GET) 118
Giddens, Anthony 12, 51–5, 61, 72, 76, 77, 78, 80, 81, 184, 246, 277
Global Enterprise Monitor (GEM) 37
globalisation 55
Gold, Jacqueline 216–7, 220, 238, 239, 240–1, 252, 260, 261, 278
Google 235–8, 240–1
Gordon Survey of Interpersonal Values 134, 278
governance 66–7
Granovetter, Mark 59, 68, 72, 75, 246, 278
growth 63, 106, 127, 136, 263; orientation 92, 105, 118, 120, 126; stages 156

Habermas, J. 57, 278
Hampson, S. 14, 142, 175, 176, 185, 192–98, 200, 206, 210, 278
Hawley, F. B. 32
Haworth, J. M. 8, 145, 242, 243, 274
Hayek, von, F. A. 4, 5, 29–30, 38, 46, 47, 185, 245
Heffalump, hunt for the 2, 267, 268
Henri-Lloyd Ltd 220, 242
Herrmann Brain Dominance Instrument (HBDI) 114, 115, 116, 279
heuristic methods 63, 171, 225
Hofstede, Geert 101, 162, 279
human action 28, 42, 146 ; capital 7, 36, 222, 263–4; capital theory 5, 81–2, 106, 111; nature **199**

imagination 39–40, 43, 46, 62, 64, 65, 78, 81, 103, 128, 133, 163, 172, 179, 186, 223, 229, 239, 245, 247, 258
imitation 64, 77, 78, 246
impression management 137, 146, **147**, 170
independence 112, 128, 133–4, 140
individual–opportunity interchange 245, 246, 249, **253**, 253–6, 261, 264 (*see also* entrepreneur–opportunity interchange)

individual–opportunity nexus 75, 76, 245, 246
industry 34, 61, 74, 238; clothing 63, 221–3, 233–4, 240; cosmetics 138, 224, 240; engineering 217–8; food 227–31, 240; hi-tech 138; hospitality 219, 224, 240; internet 233, 234–8, 240; sex 216–7; ship repair 231–3; traditional 231; venture capital 236–7, 240; Industrial Revolution 51, 57
information 53, 69, 246, 265; bias 105, 158; overload 158; perfect 24; processing 130, 150; seeking 103; synthesis 264, 265
initiative 129 (*see also* proactivity)
innovation 2, 22, 29, 34–6, 47, 57, 59, 60, 63–4, 92, 113, 128, 156, 171, 218, 236, 240, 250, 262; incremental 2, 263; innovativeness 95, 100, 103, 113, 231, 245; innovator 19, 49, 67, 227; measurement of 92, 95; radical 2, **6**, 236–7, 251, 262
institutional behaviour 72, 78, 218, 227, 237, 255; theory 82 (*see also* structuration) institutions 189; constraints by 36, 76, 189, 218, 223
intention 9, 114, 126–7, 132, 134, 154–6, 160, 163, 170
interactionism 83, 143, 146, 169, 173, **201**, 247
interdisciplinarity 3, 5–8, 16, 174, 244, 245–9
internal locus of control 94, 95–101, 102, 121 (*see also* locus of control)
interpretation 40, 146; interpretivism 132
intuition 132, 139, 155, 225, **253**, 255, 259
Intuitive-Thinking Type 120 (*see also* MBTI)
invention 218, 220, 265; inventor 19, 136, 218
investment theory 168–9

Jackson Personality Inventory (JPI/PRF-E) 92, 114
job stress 119; questionnaire 129–30
judgement 14, 33, 34, 36, 40, 45, 62, 67, 81, 152, 153, 158, 163, 168, 170, 187, 200, 219, 220, 222–3, 225, 226, 227, 230, 232, 233, 239, 242, 245, 250, 251, **253**, 255, 257, 261

Judging-Perceiving Type (J-P) 115, 120
(*see also* MBTI)
Jungian theory 114

Kanter, R. M. 72, 117, 280
Kirton, M. J. 100, 281; Adaptation-
Innovation Inventory (KAI) 100, **108**,
113, 281
Kirzner, I. 17, 30, **38**, 41–3, 46, **47**, 48,
50, 62, 132, 133, 139, 164, 170, 197,
245, 251, 281
Knight, F. H. 32–4, **38**, 40, 45, 46, **47**,
48, 62, 281
knowledge 74, 132, 172, 189, 203, 205,
213, 230, 240, 246, **253**, 254, 265;
construction 189–90; diffusion 66;
explicit 66; perfect 30, 62 (*see also*
equilibrium theory); prior 132, 240;
problem of 175; superior 133; tacit
66, 67, 78, 80, 133, 258–60
Kuder Occupational Interest Survey
(OIS) 134

language 175, 178, 186, 189, 190–92,
198
leader 78, 262; transformational 126,
263; leadership 64, 66, 68, 81, 112,
118, 125, 225, 227, 245; leadership
style 119, 127; Leadership Opinion
Questionnaire 118
learned behaviour 99, 259; learning 64,
89, 98, 121, 155, 170, 200, 217, 226,
239, 254, 264; heuristic 163, 217,
252, 259, 265; style 118
Learning Style Questionnaire 118
Loasby, Brian 30, 282
locus of control (LOC) 13, 98–101,
102–3, **108**, 110, 114, 126, 156–7;
economic LOC 99, **108**
luck 153

McCrae, R. R. 85, 123, 283
McKechnie, Roger 227–31, 238, 239,
240–1, 251, 252, 261
McClelland, D. 86, 88–90, 102, **107**,
109, 113, 131, 184, 259
Malthus, Robert 22
management 20, 35, 98, 119, 221, 240,
261
manager 27, 33, 45, 93, 96, 102, 112,
120, 124–5, 130, 135, 137, 139, 144,
156, 158; bank 58, 63, 104, **109**, 224;
corporate 92, 98, 101, 103, 126;
information- 71, 78

Mangoldt, von, H. K. F. 27, **38**, **47**
marginal utility, theory of 28
market, awareness 214, 228, 233, 240,
250; economy 20; forces 22; gap 75,
228–9, 251; information 42;
knowledge 45; niche 223, 228, 231,
233; process 41; produce for 27; share
35, 218, 229
Marshall, Alfred 24, 25–6, **38**, 45, **47**,
282
Marxism 56
means-end 28; framework 63, 163
measuring instruments 113–131, 176
Menger, Carl 27–28, **38**, **47**, 50
method 266; case study 176, 212–14,
238, 244, 249–53, 266; ideographic
176, **177**, 180, **201**, 204; nomothetic
176, **177**, 180, 184, **201**, 204;
qualitative 176, 182, 266;
quantitative 182; scientific 176, **177**,
184; methodology **177**, 180, **199**, **201**
methodological individualism 205, 210
Mill, J. S. 19, 23–4, **38**, 45, **47**, 283
Milne, A. A. 2, 268
mind 175, 185, 186, 190, 206; mind-
body interaction 186–7
Miner Sentence Completion Test 97
Mischel, W. 4, 10, 13, 142, 144,
145–52, 170, 194, 196, 204, 247
Mises, von, Ludwig **38**, 41, 46, **47**, 62
Morgan, Gareth 43, 174, 179–81, 183,
184, 209, 284
motivation 42, 167, 169, 219, 227, 230,
237, 240, 247, 251, 252, 255, 258;
achievement 88–92, 97, 98, **107**;
intrinsic 148, 166–7, 171; self interest
44, 48
Myers-Briggs Type Indicator (MBTI)
114, 116, 118–121, 122, 123, 139,
140

need for achievement 13, 88–98 (*see also*
achievement motivation and
McClelland, D.)
network 53, 61, 73, 77, 94, 219, 221,
226, 230, 235, 246, 265; networking
3, 75, 93, 137, 242
non-(anti-) positivism 177–8, 179 (*see
also* paradigms)

objectivity 174, 176, 179, 182, 187,
189, 193, 195, 213
ontology 53, 75, **177**, **199**, 209
opportunism 65, 67, 68

opportunities 42, 47, 74, 103, 117, 127, 216, 222, 230; envisage 59; pursuit of 1–2, 216, 218, 219, 221, 224

opportunity 7; cost 19, 36, 65; creation 132, 230, 236, 246, 262; development 7, 217, 219, 222, 230, 236, 246, 249, 266; discovery 24, 66–7, 72, 79, 80; emergence 160; evaluation 79, 160, 230, 255; exploitation 7, 61, 64, 78, 79, 81, 217, 219, **253**, 266, 268; formation 73–4, 78, 81, 230, 252, **253**, 266, 268; recognition 7, 73–4, 78, 81, 131–3, 140, 162–6, 205, 217, 219, 224, 230, 235–6, 249, **253**, 268

optimism 69, 71, 80

outcomes; earnings 136, 137, 230; entrepreneurial 7, 8, 102, 104, 123, 234; failure 99, 158, 163, 232; success 99, 104, 136, 158, 163, 262; survival 123–4, 232, 234 (*see also* profit)

Page, Larry 234–8, 239, 240

paradigms 179–82, 185, 187, 190, 205, 208; bridging 186 (*see also* discourse)

path-dependency 64, 80

Penrose, E. 5, 8, 59, 61, 62, 72, 80, 246, 285

perception 196, 163, 206; social 137, 193–5; veridical 112, 163

performance, business 89, 90, 92, 94, 95, 99, 123–4, 127, 137, 213, 216, 225, 230, 232–3, 236, 250, 261; business awards 217, 218, 223, 226; enterprise 5, 16, 29, 43, 135; entrepreneurial 97, 156, 211, 213–4, 226; failure 8, 19, 29–30, 89, 94, 100, 128–9, 158, 214, 234, 250; growth 60, 92, 93, 95, 98, 141, 222, 225, 226, 236–7, 262; profitability 29, 60, 127; success 8, 19, 97, 112, 128–9, 158, 213, 217, 236, 250; superior entrepreneurial 15, 82, 112, 213, 239, 261–3; outcomes 69, 95–6, 99, 100, 104, 106, 121, 127, 129, 156, 158

perseverance 135, 140, 157

person constructs 133, 196; personal construct theory 204

personality 166, **201**; and culture 87; cognitive approach to 84; 145–69, 170–3; construction 192–98; definition of 82; perception 193–5, **201**, 206; structure 82–7, 106; The Big Five theory of 85–6, 87, 106; theory 82–7, 192, **201**

pessimism 71 (*see also* optimism)

phenomenology 178, 184, 185, 206, 209, 212 (*see also* paradigms)

Phileas Fogg 228–31, 243, 262

planning 60, 92, 99

population ecology 5

positivism 75, 132, 177–8, 179–80, 182, 187, 209 (*see also* paradigms)

power 53, 56, 73–4

price theory 28, 31

Proactive Personality Scale 126–8, 140

proactivity 112, 126, 140

problem-solver 126; problem-solving 66, 126, 218, 236–7, 264; orientation 121

production 23, 27; productivity 35

Professional Personality Questionnaire 123

profit 26, 31, 33–4, 35, 69; maximisation 45

prospector 66; prospector's paradox 67

Protestant Work Ethic (PWE) 99, **108**

Psychology **6**, 86, 185, 214, 244, 249, 253, 254

Psychometrics 83, 85, 176, 195, 204, 206

rational economic behaviour 45, 48, 78; rational economic man 41, 56; rationality 24, 33, 71, 128, 139, 155

realism 72; reality 206; construction of reality 15, 188–90

red tape 53

Reflecting Roadstuds Ltd 218, 261

reflexivity 189–90

regretful thinking 135–6, 157–8, 172, 204

relationships 60, 197, 200, 207, 209, 213, 220, 221, 231, 246; socio-economic 79, 225

resource-based theory (RBT) 59, 62, 68, 72, 77, 80, 262

resources 68, 70, 71, 78, 255; allocation 37, 42, 44; organisation of 43–4, 62, 64; scarce 25, 26

responsibility 104

reward 18, 34

Ricardo, David 22, **38**, 47, 286

right hand man 50, 227, 261

risk 31, 33, 35, 40, 46, 47, 60, 69, 103, 128–9, 158, 216, 251–2, 261; aversion 119, 245; avoidance 25, 94, 103, 105; bearing 18, 36–7, 158; calculated 102, 103; financial 104;

taking 23, 28, 37, 48, 92, 94, 101–06, 156, 168, 171; insurable 32; management 48, 103–4, 105, 130, 250, 261; minimisation 103; perception 14, 160; preference 92; uninsurable 27, 32–3 (*see also* uncertainty); risk taker, calculated 33; moderate 102

risk-taking 23, 28, 37, 48, 92, 94, 101–06, 144, 156, 157, 168, 226, propensity 13, **109**, 111, 121

rivalry 64, 70

Robinson Crusoe 41

Roddick, Anita 173, 223–7, 238, 239, 240–1, 242, 252, 260, 261–2, 286

role model 217; role of bank 227; of capitalist 19; of entrepreneur 13, 17, 18–9, 20, 21, 22, 26, 27, 28, 30, 33, 34–6, 39, 41–2, 43, 45, 46–7, **48**, 48; of leader 64–5; of team 228; task-role domain 156

Rosch, E. 195–6, 286

Rotter, J. B. 84, 98, 100, 110, 114, 286

routine 55, 60, 64, 188, 190; behaviour 36, 198

rules 53–4, 71–2, 76, 77, 78, 188, 189, 200, 207, 213, 224, 226, 251; of the game 178, 190–1

Ryle, Gilbert 186–7, 198, 206, 286

Say, Jean-Baptiste 19–20, **38**, **47**, 286

schema 153, 203, 207

Schultz, T. W. 36–7, 46, 81, 287

Schumpeter, J. 4, 5, 9, 17, 20, 23, 26, 28, 32, 34–6, **38**, 43, 46, **47**, 49, 50, 72, 102, **109**, 126, 132, 133, 184, 197, 225, 242, 245, 251, 287

scientific method 175 (*see also* method)

scripts 73–5, 78, 80, 161–2, 171, 246 (*see also* schema)

self 175, 189; self-belief 158, 171, 193, 204; -confidence 114, 129, 168, 170, 224, 259; -determination 148, 259; -efficacy 154, 155–8, 170–1, 204, 205, 208, 259; -employment 8, 82, 89, 106, 111, 154; -esteem (SE) 114; fulfilment 55; image 71; -interest 21, 44, 48, 56; knowledge 203, 208; perception 192; promotion 71; -serving 158

sense making 55, 188, 259

sensing-intuitive type (S-N) 114–6, 119; sensing-judging type (S-J) 120;

sensing-thinking type (S-T) 119; (*see also* MBTI)

sex 94–5, 115 (*see also* gender); -bias 115

Shackle, G. L. S. 24, 33, 37–41, **38**, 42, 44, 45, 46, **47**, 49, 60, 65, 76, 133, 170, 245, 277, 282, 285, 287, 290

Shane, S. 6, 75, 80, 131–2, 246, 287

Shaw, Percy 217–9, 220, 238, 239, 240–1, 252, 261–2, 264

simulation, mental 163, 171

Sinclair, Sir Clive 196, 214

situation, characteristics 128; framing 153; socio-economic 7, 53

situationism 143

skills 111, 167, 172, 213, 229, 230, 232, 235, 265; management 221, (*see also* management); new resource 96; of entrepreneur 44, 49, 68, 96, 130, 235, 237, 251

small business 53; small business owner-manager 92, 101, 105, 120–1, 127, 136, 163, 214, 216, 233, 239, 241, 260, 266

Smith, Adam 19, 21–2, 45, 288

social 192, 195; capabilities 77, 150; capital 164–5; cognition 15, 200–5; competences 68, 137–9, 140, 220; constraints 77 (*see also* structure); constructionism 4, **6**, 79, 174, 186–90, 192, 195, 197, **199**, 200–5, 207, 210, 212, 214, 241–2, 249, 257–8, 266–7; constructivism 186, 192–8, 206, 248, 253; embeddedness 61, 72, 74–5, 79, 191, 220, 237, 246; enterprise 3; group 55; learning 65, 78, 98, 110, 144, 146, 149, 150, 200, 204, 206, 207, 239, 244, 247, 253, 254, 258–60, 266; need 218, 224, 226; norms 4; order 191; problem 218; relations 59, 68, 75, 164; responsibility 4; rules 4, **6** (*see also* rules); skill 65, **211**, 214; status 77; systems 4

socialisation 89

society 56, 76, 198, 226, 246–7, 254, 257

socio-cultural theory 5, 56–7, 59, 61, 258

socio-economy 56, 59, 76, 216, 246–7, 254–5, 257, 263

Sociology **6**, 245–7

solipsism 177–8

Static State Theory 31–2

Stevenson, H. H. 87, 107, 289
strategic: advantage 77; alliance 66, 68, 78; behaviour 7, 99, 103, 104, 111, 119, 127, 222, 227, 231, 234, 261; management 96
stress: (*see also* job stress) management 130
structuration theory 6, 12, 51–5, 58, 73–6, 79, 81, 246–7, 249
structure 52, 55, 73, 254–5, 255, 260; levels in socio-economy 57, 58; socio-cultural 61, 216, 235, structural: domination 57, 58, 73, 76; legitimation 57, 58, 73, 74, 76; signification 57, 58, 73, 76
Strzelecki, Henri 220–23, 238, 239, 240–1, 252, 260, 261
subjective 189; decision-maker 72; decision-making 77, 154; judgement 33, 154; preferences 42; subjectivism 28, 37–41, 49, 59, 60, 62, 76, 176, 209
success 43, 254 (*see also* performance)
Survey of Interpersonal Values (SIV) 118
Survey of Personal Values (SPV) 118

team: 117, 161, 262; leadership 227–31; role 118
technology 34, 218
Thatcher 89; government 56
The Big Five 85, 87, 122–5, 128, 140, 151, 204
The Body Shop 223–7
Thematic Apperception Test (TAT) 89, 97
theory of planned behaviour (TPB) 134, 154–5
thinking-feeling (T-F) 115 (*see also* MBTI)
Thunen, von, Johann 27, **38**, **47**
tolerance of ambiguity 112, 117, 130–1
trader 224; market 18 (*see also* arbitrageur)
training 89, 129, 135, 136, 155, 227, 264–6, 267

trait 190, 193, 197, **199**, 247; co-occurrence 193–4, 196; critique 4–5, 10, 87–8, 112, 148–9, 193–4, 198; measurement 113–131; psychology 6, 193–4, 200; specific 106; theory 5, 13, 84–87, 106, 143, 151, **199**, 200–02, 257–8
transaction costs 60, 64, 68, 77
trust 60, 73
truth 175, 176, 178–9, 182, 187, 190, 191, 208, 213
Turgot, A. R. J. 19, **38**, **47**
Type A behaviour 129
typologies 190; of entrepreneurs 8–10, 31 (*see also* entrepreneurial types)

uncertainty 18, 27, 31, 33, 36, 39, 42, 45, 46, 47, 48, 62, 77, 112, 118, 130, 153, 218
understanding 73, 178, 255, 258; tacit 65, 258

value: creation 3, 7; subjective theory of 28
venture creation 8 (*see also* business founding)

Walker, Amasa 30–1, **38**, **47**, 196
Walker, Francis, A. 30, **38**, **47**
Walras, Leon 28, **38**, **47**, 50
Wealth of Nations 21
Weber, M. 5, 290
Weick, K. E. 53, 184, 188, 290
Witt, U. 5, 8, 64–6, 78, 80, 225, 245, 262, 290
Wittgenstein, L. 175, 190–1, 196, 209, 212, 290
Woodroffe, Simon 219–20, 238, 239, 240–1, 252, 261
world: class 213–4; physical 54; social 54

Yo! Sushi 219–20